Creating
iOS 5 Apps
DEVELOP AND DESIGN

Richard Warren

Peachpit
Press

Creating iOS 5 Apps: Develop and Design

Richard Warren

Peachpit Press

1249 Eighth Street
Berkeley, CA 94710
510/524-2178
510/524-2221 (fax)

Find us on the Web at www.peachpit.com
To report errors, please send a note to errata@peachpit.com
Peachpit Press is a division of Pearson Education
Copyright © 2012 by Richard Warren

Executive Editor: Cliff Colby
Project Editor: Dan Foster
Production Editor: Katerina Malone
Technical Editor: Shaun Austin
Copy Editor: Scout Festa
Cover design: Aren Straiger
Interior design: Mimi Heft
Compositor: Danielle Foster
Indexer: Rebecca Plunkett

ISBN-13 978-0-321-76960-2
ISBN-10   0-321-76960-0

9 8 7 6 5 4 3 2 1

Printed and bound in the United States of America

To my wife, Mika; my daughter, Haruko; and my son, Kai.
Thank you for your understanding and patience.
I owe each of you more than I could possibly express.
I would not have finished this book without your constant support.

ACKNOWLEDGMENTS

I would like to thank all the developers and Apple engineers on the Apple Developer Forums who shared information and insights leading up to the release of iOS 5. When working with brand new technologies, we don't have an established set of best practices to fall back on, so it was great to have such an active group with whom I could discuss the ins and outs of all the new features of iOS 5. By pooling our experiences, we pieced together a number of tips, tricks, hints, and clues—many of which found their way into this book.

Additionally, this book would not have been possible without a lot of hard work from many extremely talented people. Many thanks to Scout Festa for the copyediting and for otherwise bringing out the real meaning behind my words. To Shaun Austin for all the technical editing and advice. To the production team—Katerina Malone, Danielle Foster, and Rebecca Plunkett—and everyone else at Peachpit Press, who performed minor miracles of magic with the layout and design, as well as a hundred other tasks that I can barely imagine or even understand.

Finally, a big thanks to my editors, Dan Foster and Clifford Colby, for riding herd over all of us. It has been a long and often twisty road. I am glad we stuck with it and saw it to the end.

CONTENTS

i

INTRODUCTION

WELCOME TO CREATING iOS 5 APPS

This book serves two goals: introducing new developers to iOS development, and educating experienced developers about the tools and technologies available in iOS 5. We will examine a wide range of subjects—some new and some old—covering everything from building an initial iOS project to submitting your app to the iTunes App Store. Throughout this book, we focus on a few key points, providing a firm beachhead for launching your own explorations. For more information on this book, including bonus chapters, sample code, and FAQs, check out www.freelancemadscience.com/book.

iOS 5 TECHNOLOGIES AND TOOLS

Over the course of this book, we will discuss the key technologies and development tools you will need to create high-quality iOS applications. Let's take a look at the most important of these.

AUTOMATIC REFERENCE COUNTING

Automatic Reference Counting (ARC) simplifies memory management for Objective-C objects. ARC automatically tracks the object's lifetime, automatically retaining and releasing our objects as needed. This both streamlines our code and reduces the chances of memory-related bugs. And ARC, unlike garbage collection, manages our object's memory at compile time. This means that ARC-based code runs as fast as, if not faster than, manually managed memory.

STORYBOARDS

For years, Interface Builder allowed us to graphically design our user interfaces, drawing connections between our controls and our actions. With storyboards, we can extend this even further, drawing the relationships and segues between the different scenes in our application. This lets us sketch out and edit our entire application's workflow, greatly simplifying the creation of new applications.

iCLOUD STORAGE

Without a doubt, iCloud is the most important new feature in iOS 5. The iCloud storage API allows us to sync our application's data across all of the user's devices. From their iPhones and iPads to their Macs or PCs, our users can now have ubiquitous, always-up-to-date access to all their information. iCloud storage is rapidly becoming a must-have feature for all serious applications.

XCODE

Xcode provides an integrated development environment, giving us a wide range of tools to both create and manage our projects. It handles everything from running and debugging our code to designing our UI and data models. As iOS developers, we will spend most of our time in Xcode. Having a well-grounded understanding of its features is essential to our success.

iOS SIMULATOR

The iOS Simulator application lets us run, debug, test, and profile our code directly on a Mac. While the simulator will never replace testing on an actual device, it has a number of advantages. For example, developers can begin using the simulator before they join the iOS Developer Program. It's also easier and faster to run quick tests in the simulator, letting us perform rapid develop/test/iterate cycles as we add new features to our applications.

INSTRUMENTS

Apple's premier profiling tool, Instruments lets us dynamically trace and analyze code running either in the simulator or directly on an iOS device. It lets us track and record everything from object allocations and timer-based samples to file access and energy use. It also provides the tools necessary for sifting through and analyzing the data that it generates. In experienced hands, Instruments can help us to fix bugs and polish our code.

1

HELLO iPHONE

Before you can master any skill, you must first become comfortable with the tools. In this chapter, we will learn how to use Xcode, the primary development tool for iOS applications. We will start by using Xcode to create a new project from the Utility Application project template. We will then examine the files produced by this template, studying how the different pieces of a typical iOS application fit together. Once we are familiar with the template, we will expand it, using Xcode's graphical interface editor to add controls and to draw connections between these controls and their actions. This exercise will provide a solid foundation for working on the more complex projects in later chapters.

AN **INTRODUCTION** TO **iOS**

If this is your first exposure to iOS development, welcome to an exciting new world. The iOS lineup provides several great devices for you to explore. The iPhone, in particular, brings together a wide range of exciting technologies, including always-on Internet, location awareness, motion sensing, and a camera. In the not so distant past, developers had to either build custom hardware or pay tens of thousands of dollars just to experiment with these technologies. Now you can fit the entire package in your pocket and carry it with you wherever you go.

The iPhone's hardware opens up previously unimaginable opportunities. Revolutionary new social networking applications lead the charge, and location-aware apps have become a growing part of our digital lifestyle. Even augmented reality, once little more than a gimmick, is maturing into a useful tool (or at least an amusing source of entertainment). Most importantly, there's no sign that this flurry of innovation will slow down any time soon. We have just begun to scratch the surface of what these devices can do; the best ideas are yet to come.

Meanwhile, Apple has created a rich and vibrant marketplace for our applications. At the 2011 World Wide Developer's Conference, Steve Jobs announced that Apple had sold over 200 million iOS devices, with over 225 million registered iTunes customers, each only one click away. These customers have downloaded over 14 billion apps so far, resulting in over $2.5 billion paid to iOS developers over the last three years.

This provides exciting opportunities for large and small development teams alike. For larger corporations, it opens a specialized, focused channel for interacting with your customers. A well-built, tightly focused application not only enhances your customers' experiences, it becomes a powerful public relations tool. Your app will help build brand loyalty with existing customers, while improving brand awareness among potential customers.

On the other end of the spectrum, the App Store makes it much easier for one- or two-person development teams to get their products in front of millions of potential customers. You don't have to build and maintain your own online store. You don't need to collect money or process credit card transactions. Apple handles all of those details for you. You can focus on the part you love—building great applications.

While the App Store is the 800-pound gorilla in the room, don't let it distract you. It's not all about producing commercial software. A growing number of developers use iOS devices as platforms for any number of personal or educational projects. You can find iOS-based experiments in everything from middle school science fairs to robotics labs.

Finally, Apple has given us a set of high-quality development tools. Xcode 4 represents a significant improvement over previous versions. It is a full-featured integrated development environment with a wide range of utilities for testing, analyzing, and debugging your code. In particular, the Instruments utility can monitor and analyze CPU usage, memory allocation, network and file access, and much more.

Apple also provides a top-notch programming language with an excellent set of frameworks. I know, I know...a lot of new iOS programmers balk at learning Objective-C, and I admit that the learning curve can feel quite steep, especially when you're struggling to get started. Still, once you begin to get comfortable with the language, you will quickly grow to love it. Besides, it's always good to learn a new programming language. It will make you a better developer, even if you never use it for production code.

Objective-C is a dynamic, incredibly flexible programming language. It provides a number of features that will (if used properly) help you overcome many difficult programming challenges. Likewise, the iOS software development kit (SDK) provides a wide range of excellent frameworks to help us build our apps.

Frameworks are one of the most difficult pieces of software to design. Ideally, they should make it simple for developers to perform common tasks while still giving us enough freedom to strike out into uncharted territory. By those metrics, the Cocoa Touch frameworks are some of the best that I've ever worked with. Indeed, if you feel like you have to write a lot of code just to do a common task, you are almost certainly doing something wrong.

I hope that this book will provide a gentle introduction to the world of iOS development. While it's not possible to cover every aspect or explore every framework, this book should give you a strong foundation to build on, and the tools and skills to continue on your own.

Additionally, while most of the book focuses on developing for the iPhone, the concepts and techniques generally apply to any iOS device: iPod touch, iPad, and iWhateverMayCome. Specific differences will be noted as they occur. The iPad, in particular, has a few unique user interface elements, and iPad-specific development issues will be covered in depth in Bonus Chapter A at the book's website (www.freelancemadscience.com/book).

For now, let's jump right in to our first project. Let's begin by building an iPhone utility application that will display a simple, one-line message. Don't worry if you don't understand the code the first time through. We will cover the Objective-C programming language in more depth in Chapter 2, "Objective-C." For now, use this as an opportunity to familiarize yourself with the development environment.

Ask any craftsman—if you want to succeed, you must have the right tools for the job. For iOS development, this means having a Macintosh running OS X 10.7 or later and a copy of Xcode 4.2. If you want to run your programs on an actual iOS device, you will also need a compatible device (iPhone, iPod touch, or iPad) and the appropriate developer/provisioning profiles. We'll talk more about provisioning profiles in Chapter 3, "Productivity Application Architecture." For now, begin by downloading the latest version of Xcode from the Mac App Store. This is a free download for anyone running OS X Lion and is by far the easiest way to keep all your development tools up to date.

You will eventually need to join the iOS Developer Program to test your application on iOS devices or submit them to the iTunes App Store. For now, we can use Xcode to build and test our applications in the simulator. This is a great way to get started.

Xcode is an integrated development environment (IDE) specifically designed for programming both Mac OS X and iOS. As the name suggests, an IDE is more than just a text editor. It is an interconnected suite of tools that helps you organize, edit, debug, and otherwise manage all the resources that will go into your final program. Through Xcode you can visually lay out the user interface, test run your program in an iOS simulator, step through your code one command at a time, analyze your application's performance, and more.

NOTE: The projects in this book were developed using Xcode 4.2 and iOS SDK 5.0. Later versions will undoubtedly vary somewhat from what is shown. Menu options and project templates may change. More rarely, updates to the SDK can affect how your projects compile and run. If you are using a newer version of either Xcode or the SDK, everything should still work, but be prepared to do a little digging and exploration on your own.

Once you have downloaded and installed Xcode (at almost 4 GB, this will require a bit of patience), launch it and let's get started.

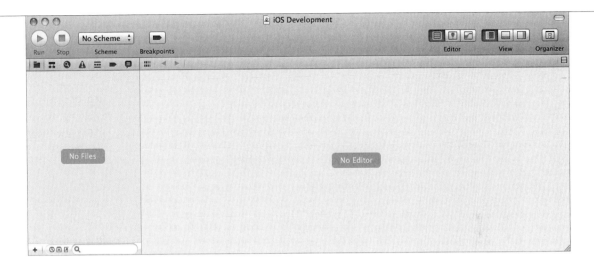

CREATING THE WORKSPACE

FIGURE 1.1 Our empty workspace

We will start by creating a new workspace. In Xcode 4, a workspace is a virtual box for organizing related projects. The workspace contains schemes for building and launching those projects, along with other related data. Xcode will allow you to search through all files in the workspace, and it will support workspace-wide indexing of those files. This allows features such as code completion, Jump to Definition, and refactoring to work smoothly across the entire workspace.

Workspaces simply let us organize our projects. They do not define where or how the individual projects are stored. Each workspace can have any number of projects, and each project can exist in any number of workspaces. This gives developers a lot of flexibility in organizing their work. You can even create specialized workspaces that focus on one particular task. For example, you may create one workspace for unit tests, another for debugging, and yet another for performance testing.

You don't need to create a workspace; you could simply start with a freestanding project. Nevertheless, it's a nice way to keep everything tidy. Let's build a workspace that will contain all the projects in this book. In Xcode, select File > New > New Workspace. Name the workspace **iOS Development**, choose a location for it, and click Save. Xcode will then open a window that shows your empty workspace: no files, no editor, and no scheme (**Figure 1.1**).

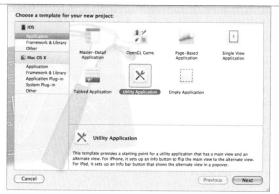

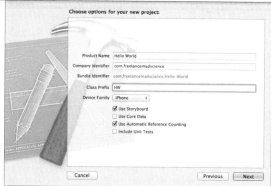

FIGURE 1.2 Selecting the iOS Utility Application template

FIGURE 1.3 Selecting the project options

CREATING THE PROJECT

With the workspace open, create a new project. In Xcode, select File > New > New Project. This will open the project template sheet (**Figure 1.2**). Xcode provides a wide range of templates for new projects. In the left-hand column, select iOS > Application. Then, select the icon for Utility Application and click Next.

We're now ready to choose the options for our project (**Figure 1.3**). Enter **Hello World** in the Product Name field. The company identifier should be a unique string that identifies your company. In most cases, we will use the company's domain name, with the levels reversed. Start with the top-level domain and work toward the second- and third-level domains. For example, I would use the reversed domain name from my blog: com.freelancemadscience.

Next, we have the class prefix. This prefix is automatically added to all the class names generated by the template. You can use any prefix you like. Just try to make it unique (e.g., avoid NS or UI since they are already used by Apple's frameworks). Typically, I select an abbreviation based on the project's name. In this case, enter HW.

NOTE: If you are writing a framework or library, you should prefix all your classes. This lets other developers use your code without worrying about possible naming conflicts. It also makes it easier to identify where a class comes from. For example, all classes starting with "RGS" come from my ReallyGreatStuff framework. If, however, you are simply writing an application, prefixes are not necessary, and I find that they often make the code harder to read. Still, I often let Xcode prefix the auto-generated files, just to make them easy to distinguish from our hand-crafted classes.

FIGURE 1.4 Selecting the project's location

Make sure that iPhone is selected in the Device Family pop-up menu and that the Use Storyboard checkbox is selected. The Use Core Data checkbox should be unselected. Next, make sure the Use Automatic Reference Counting option is selected. We will discuss Automatic Reference Counting in the section "Introducing ARC" in Chapter 2. For now, just understand that it makes it easier to write code. We will almost always want to use Automatic Reference Counting in new projects.

Finally, we typically want to include unit tests with our project. We will discuss unit tests in Bonus Chapter B (also at www.freelancemadscience.com/book), but for now just leave the Include Unit Tests checkbox unselected as well. Click the Next button. We need to select a location for our app (**Figure 1.4**). Select whatever location works best. I usually put it in the same folder as the primary workspace. By default, Xcode will create a new folder using the project's name.

You can also create a git repository for this project. Like unit tests, source control is a very good idea and should be included in all your projects. We will begin using source control in Chapter 3, and we will cover its use in more detail in the section "Managing Source Code" in Bonus Chapter B. However, for now, leave the "Create local git repository for this project" checkbox unselected.

That's it. Click Create and Xcode will set up our project.

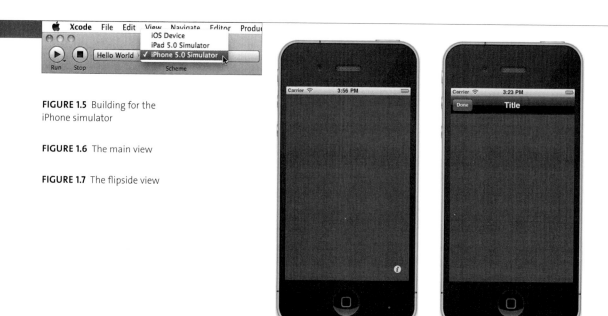

FIGURE 1.5 Building for the iPhone simulator

FIGURE 1.6 The main view

FIGURE 1.7 The flipside view

Utility applications should provide easy access to a single screen of information, with a backside view for modifying the preferences. The iPhone's Weather app is a representative example. The main screen shows simple weather forecasts for the next week (though you can page through multiple cities). The flipside view allows you to edit the list of cities, as well as change between Fahrenheit and Celsius.

The Utility Application template creates the basic skeleton for this type of application. The template is, by itself, a fully functional app—it will build and run. Of course, it won't do anything interesting, but we will fix that in a bit. For now, let's look at what we get for free.

RUNNING THE APPLICATION

First, we need to tell Xcode to use the simulator. Click the Scheme button in the Xcode toolbar and select iPhone 5.0 Simulator (**Figure 1.5**). Then click the Run button. Xcode will build the application and launch it in the simulator.

As you can see, the application has a gray main view with an info button in the lower-right corner (**Figure 1.6**). If you touch the info button, the screen flips over to show the flipside view with a title bar and a blue Done button (**Figure 1.7**). Touch the Done button and you flip back to the main view.

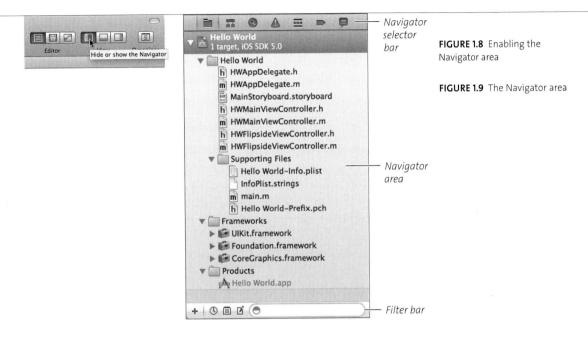

FIGURE 1.8 Enabling the Navigator area

FIGURE 1.9 The Navigator area

Navigator selector bar

Navigator area

Filter bar

EXAMINING THE FILES

Now let's look at the files that the template created for us. The Navigator area should be visible by default. If not, make sure the Navigator's View button is depressed (**Figure 1.8**).

The Navigator area will appear on the left side of Xcode's main window. It is bound on the top by the navigator selector bar, and along the bottom by the filter bar (**Figure 1.9**).

We will use the navigator to sift through and organize a wide range of information, including files, classes, compilation errors, debugging information, breakpoints, and the log. You can change the navigator type by selecting icons from the navigator selector bar. The Project navigator should be selected by default. If not, select the icon that looks like a manila folder (leftmost icon in the navigator selector bar).

The Project navigator will show several groups of resources. The Hello World group contains the header (.h) and implementation (.m) files for all our Objective-C classes. This is where we will do most of our actual coding. It also contains the MainStoryBoard.storyboard resource file. This defines the different scenes in our application and the segues between them.

The Supporting Files subgroup contains a variety of secondary files. Initially, this group contains the application's Hello World-Info.plist, InfoPlist.strings, main.m, and Prefix.pch files.

The Hello World-Info.plist file contains a number of key-value pairs used to configure our application. The InfoPlist.strings file contains localized versions of the Hello World-Info.plist file's keys. This can be useful when localizing your application, though the file is initially empty. The main.m file contains the main() function, the initial function that is executed when your application launches. The Prefix.pch file is the application's precompiled header.

To help large projects compile faster, Xcode allows us to create a precompiled prefix header file containing a number of #import, #include, and #define directives common across much of our code. For example, in a typical iOS project, most classes need to access the UIKit and Foundation frameworks. By including the #import statements for these frameworks in our prefix header, Xcode knows to preprocess those files and include the results in all of our source files. This prevents the compiler from processing common files multiple times during each build.

This may not make a lot of sense right now, and that's OK. We will not be touching the Prefix.pch file in this project. For more information, check out Apple's documentation: Xcode Build System Guidelines; Reducing Build Times; and Using a Precompiled Prefix Header.

Finally, the Frameworks group contains any iOS frameworks used by this project, while the Products group contains the end results—in this case, our compiled application. Again, we won't be touching any of these in this project.

NOTE: Much like Xcode's workspaces, the navigator's groups represent a virtual organization—they exist only within Xcode. These groups do not necessarily have any relationship with how or where the actual resources are stored, or even with what type of files they contain. You are free to place any resource in any group and to add or remove groups or sub-groups as needed.

WALKING THROUGH THE PROJECT

When I first started writing Cocoa applications, I did not really understand how all the pieces of my applications fit together. Sure, I understood the individual parts. I had a view and a view controller. They worked together to manage the user interface. Still, many of these objects seemed to magically appear at runtime. I had no idea where they came from.

Let me reassure you that there is nothing supernatural going on here. I've checked. Still, it's worth taking a few minutes to walk through all the connections, just to see what is happening. Don't worry about memorizing all the details. Instead, focus on how we trace the connections from one object to the next. That way, you will be able to trace through your own applications later on.

Let's start exactly where our application starts. Click main.m in the navigator (you may need to expand the Supporting Files group if the file isn't already visible). This file is actually very short. It imports the UIKit and our application delegate, and it then defines the main() function.

```
#import <UIKit/UIKit.h>
#import "HWAppDelegate.h"
int main(int argc, char *argv[])
{
    @autoreleasepool {
        return UIApplicationMain(argc, argv, nil,
            NSStringFromClass([HWAppDelegate class]));
    }
}
```

Basically, this creates an autorelease block. Inside the block, we launch our Objective-C application. We will discuss autorelease blocks in the "Memory Management" section of Chapter 2.

The real work happens in the UIApplicationMain() function. This function takes four arguments. The first two handle our application's command line arguments: argc gives the number of arguments, while argv contains the actual arguments themselves as an array of C-style strings. These arguments are largely a holdover from Unix command-line applications. In iOS, our apps typically have only a single argument, the name of our application's executable file. We almost never use these arguments directly.

The next two arguments define our application and our application delegate, respectively. Each takes a string that corresponds to the desired class name. If the third argument is nil, we will use the default UIApplication class. If the fourth argument is nil, we will load our UIApplicationDelegate from our main nib file.

However, as of iOS 5.0, applications will generally use storyboards instead of nibs. This means we need to manually set our application delegate's name. We want to use our custom HWAppDelegate class. Unfortunately, we cannot use it directly. Instead, we call HWAppDelegate's class method to get the class object for our delegate. Then we pass that object into the NSStringFromClass() function. This produces the correct string for our class.

Most applications will follow this pattern. Instead of subclassing the UIApplication, we typically use a standard UIApplication object but provide a custom application delegate.

NOTE: You will rarely change anything in this file. In fact, unless you are doing something very unusual, you should never touch it. Even if you're convinced that you really need to make a change or two, please take a step back and think things through one more time. There is almost always a better solution.

EXAMINING THE STORYBOARD

So far so good. The main() function calls UIApplicationMain(). This function instantiates the application and our custom HWAppDelegate class. Then it sets up the main event loop and begins processing events. If the application's info.plist file defines a main storyboard, it then loads the initial view controller and view from the storyboard.

But, what is a storyboard?

Storyboards allow us to graphically design our scenes and draw the segues that connect them. This represents the latest step in Xcode's interface development technologies.

Previous versions of Xcode used Interface Builder to graphically design our user interface. Interface Builder saved our designs as nib files. Xcode could then include the nibs in our application, loading them at runtime.

In Xcode 4, Interface Builder was incorporated into Xcode itself. This allows us to edit the interface and any related code side by side. With iOS 5, storyboards allow us to encapsulate a number of nibs, which lets us not only define a single scene's worth of information, but also draw the transitions between scenes.

As you will see throughout the rest of this chapter, our storyboards contain a lot more than just views and controls. They also contain controller objects, as well as the connections between the various controls, views, and controllers. We will get some experience drawing these connections as we expand our Hello World app in the "Modifying the Template" section, later this chapter. Additionally, we will discuss nibs, the underlying technology behind storyboards, in more detail in the Chapter 3 sidebar "The Secret Life of Nibs."

FIGURE 1.10 Enabling the Utilities area

NOTE: Originally, Interface Builder saved nib archives as binary files, with a .nib extension. As of Xcode 3.0, Interface Builder allowed storing the nib files in an intermediate XML format with a .xib extension. This allowed greater compatibility with source control and other development tools. The .xib files are then compiled into binary .nib files when the application is built. For simplicity's sake, both versions are typically referred to as "nib files." In Xcode 4.2, storyboards are also stored as XML files with a .storyboard extension. These files are automatically compiled into one or more nib files. The system then loads these nibs as needed at runtime.

How does UIApplicationMain() know which storyboard file to open? As we saw earlier, the name of the main storyboard is stored in our configuration file. Click Hello World-Info.plist in the Supporting Files group. You should see a list of key-value pairs. Look for the Main storyboard file base name key. It should be set to MainStoryboard. This means UIApplicationMain() will automatically load the MainStoryboard.storyboard file.

Let's open this file. Click MainStoryboard.storyboard in the Project navigator. This will open the storyboard file in Xcode's Editor area. You will probably want to close the Navigator area to give the editor as much space as possible. You will also want to make sure the Utilities area is open along the right-hand side of the screen. Make sure the Utilities area View button is depressed (**Figure 1.10**).

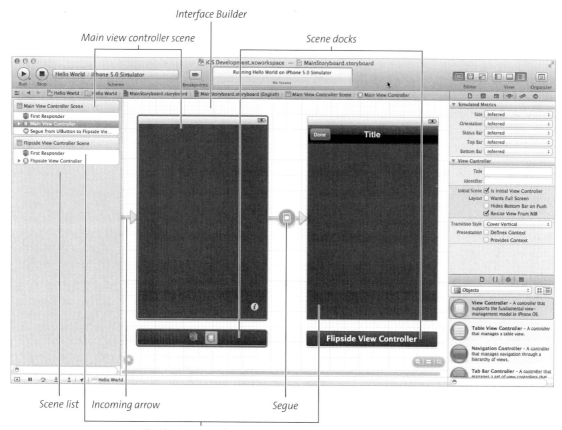

Interface Builder

Main view controller scene

Scene docks

Scene list | Incoming arrow

Segue

Flipside view controller scene

FIGURE 1.11 The Storyboard editor

The Storyboard editor consists of two separate regions. On the left, we have our scene list. This shows us all the scenes in our storyboard, as well as every object within each scene. On the right, we have the Interface Builder. This lets us view and design the actual user interface for our scenes, as well as the flow of control among the scenes (**Figure 1.11**).

Our project starts out with two scenes. If you look at the scene list, you will see that each scene has at least two top-level objects: the first responder and the scene's view controller. Let's start with the first responder. This is, in many ways, a very unusual object. Or rather, it's not an object at all—it's a proxy. The system never creates an instance of the first responder. Instead, it sets the first responder at runtime.

The first responder represents the first object in our application's responder chain. It can act as a target for any actions that must be sent to the responder chain. For example, a copy action should target the currently selected text, regardless of which control that text may be in. We don't want to hard-wire the action to a single control—instead, we want to route the action to the currently active control. By targeting the first responder, our message is automatically passed to the correct control at runtime.

Having said that, we rarely need to interact with the first responder directly in iOS.

Next, look at the view controller. Each scene has its own view controller—an instance of `UIViewController` or (more likely) one of its subclasses. We will talk about controllers in more depth when we discuss the Model-View-Controller pattern in Chapter 2. For now, just think of the controller as the link between the scene and the rest of our code.

Each view controller contains a view. This view may, in turn, contain any number of subviews and controls (which may contain their own subviews and controls). We often refer to the entire graph of views and subviews as the view hierarchy. Xcode lets us easily examine and manipulate both the view hierarchy and the view's actual appearance. The scene list shows us the hierarchy, while the Interface Builder shows us its visual layout.

Our scenes may also have other top-level objects. For example, the main view controller scene has a segue—the transition between the main view and the flipside view. Scenes may also include gesture recognizers, views, or even data objects as top-level objects.

All of these top-level objects (except the segues) also appear in the scene's dock in the Interface Builder area. This makes it easier to draw connections between the scene's interface elements and these top-level objects, especially when the list of scenes begins to grow. Segues, on the other hand, appear between the views they connect. Like the dock, this helps keep them nearby. Even more importantly, it graphically displays the flow of control through our application, giving us a feel for how everything connects.

Each storyboard designates a single scene as its initial scene. This scene's view controller is returned when you instantiate the initial scene from the storyboard. In our case, it is the scene that `UIApplicationMain()` loads when the application first launches.

The initial scene appears in the Interface Builder area with an incoming arrow pointing at it. Unlike segues and other relationships, this arrow doesn't have a scene on the other end. By default, the incoming arrow starts at the left edge of Interface Builder. The initial scene is the first scene, with additional scenes branching out as we move to the right.

We can change the initial scene by selecting a different view controller and selecting its "is Initial View Controller" attribute. Only one view controller at a time can have this attribute enabled. If you enable it in a new view controller, Interface Builder will automatically disable it for the old controller.

In our case, the main view controller scene is our initial scene. This is exactly what we want. Make sure we are zoomed in on the main scene. Double-clicking the background will toggle the zoom between an overview of the entire storyboard and the actual-size view.

Let's start by clicking each object in the main scene and examining its class. In the inspector selector bar, make sure the Identity inspector is selected (third icon from the left at the top of the Utilities area). Then click on the main view controller. Not surprisingly, it is an instance of the HWMainViewController class (**Figure 1.12**).

As we check the rest of the objects, you should see that our view is a generic UIView. Inside that, we have a UIButton (the info button at the lower-right corner). Finally, the segue doesn't display any information in the Identity inspector.

Moving on to the flipside view controller scene, we have a HWFlipsideView Controller. Inside this, we have another UIView; however, at the top of this view we have a UINavigation bar, with a UINavigationItem. Inside that, we have our Done button—a UIBarButtonItem.

Now switch to the Connection inspector (far right icon at the top of the Utilities area). This lets us view and edit the connections between objects. While it can appear somewhat complex, this inspector only shows five connection types: outlets, actions, events, segues, and relationships.

The first three are used to define connections within a single scene. Outlets are variables that can store a pointer to an object. They define the relationships between objects in our graph. Actions, on the other hand, are methods that we can connect to events. When an event occurs, the system automatically calls its corresponding action. Controls define a set of common events that occur when the user interacts with the control.

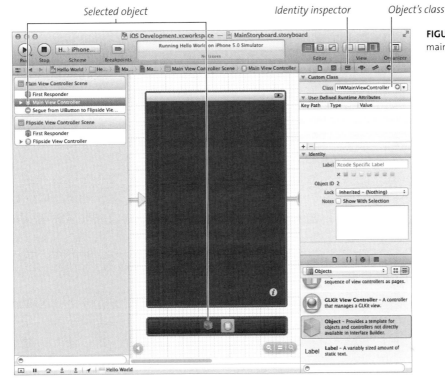

Selected object   Identity inspector   Object's class

FIGURE 1.12 Inspecting the main view controller's class

Next, segues and relationships define the connections between scenes. Segues act as transitions. When the application triggers a segue, it transitions to the next scene using the specified animation. Relationships look a lot like segues, but they are used to show ownership. Container controllers (like tab view controllers) will use relationships to connect to the views they manage.

If we look at the main view controller, we can see that it has a view outlet pointing to the contained view object. This means we can refer to this view object in our controller's code. We also have a referencing outlet from the flipside view controller. This simply means that the flipside view controller has an outlet pointing back to our main view controller—we will see this in a second (**Figure 1.13**). There's only one other connection in this scene. Click the info button; as you can see, it has a modal storyboard segue connecting its performSegueWithIdentifier:sender: method to the flipside view controller. The system will call this method automatically whenever our info button is pressed, triggering the segue to our flipside view.

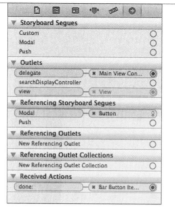

FIGURE 1.13 The main view controller's connections

FIGURE 1.14 The flipside view controller's connections

FIGURE 1.15 Inspecting the segue's attributes

Now let's look at the flipside view controller (**Figure 1.14**). As we saw earlier, we have a delegate outlet that points back to our main view controller. This allows our flipside view controller to call methods on the main view controller. Specifically, since the main view controller is the flipside view controller's delegate, the flipside view will expect the main view to implement specific methods to modify or control the flipside view's behavior. The flipside view controller also has a second outlet connecting it to its view. As you can probably guess, this is a general pattern. All view controllers have an outlet connecting to their view.

The flipside view controller also has two incoming connections. One is the info button's segue that we saw previously. Another represents an incoming action from the Done button. We will see this in a second.

There are only two other connections in this scene. The navigator item refers to the Done button in its leftBarButtonItem outlet. This positions the bar button correctly in the navigation bar. Additionally, we see the action connection from our Done button to the flipside view controller's done: method. This method will be called when the Done button is pressed.

Finally, select the Attributes inspector (third icon from the right), and select the segue. This shows our segue's details (**Figure 1.15**). The Identifier field lets us identify this segue in our code. The Style pop-up menu allows us to define how the new view will be displayed, while the Transition pop-up menu allows us to define the animation sequence used to move from one view to the next. In our case, the segue is named showAlternate. We will present our new scene as a modal view, flipping our old view over horizontally to reveal the new view on its back.

In most graphical user interfaces, a modal view is a view that must be dismissed (usually by clicking an OK or Cancel button) before the user can perform any other actions in the application. This forces the user to focus on whatever is inside the modal view—they must finish dealing with it before they can move on. On desktop applications, we generally use modal view to display things like Save or Print dialogs. On the iPhone, modal views cover the entire screen (though the iPad has a few additional options).

So, what does this all mean? Well, we're tracing through how the objects in our application get created. The UIApplicationMain() method creates an instance of the UIApplication and of our HWAppDelegate class.

Next, UIApplicationMain() looks up the main storyboard in our application's info.plist file. It then loads the storyboard's initial scene, displaying our main view controller's view in our application's window. Our application is then ready for user input.

If the user touches the info button, our segue launches. This loads the flipside view controller and displays it as a modal view. When the user presses the Done button, it calls flipside view controller's done: action. We know this dismisses the flipside view, but we don't yet know how this works. To see that, we have to examine the application's code.

EXAMINING THE CODE

While the storyboard gives us a good overview of our application, to really understand it we will need to dig into the code. Don't worry if it doesn't all make sense yet, we will go over Objective-C in more detail in Chapter 2. For now, we just want to get a feel for where things are and what they do.

Let's start with HWAppDelegate.h. This declares the interface for the HWApp Delegate class. You won't find anything terribly surprising here. HWAppDelegate implements the UIApplicationDelegate protocol—which allows it to act as an application delegate.

A delegate is an object that acts on behalf of, or in coordination with, another object. The delegate typically acts as an assistant to the main, delegating object. The main object will call predefined methods on the delegate in response to specified events. The delegate then uses those methods to monitor and control the delegating object. This allows us to alter the delegating object's behavior without changing the object itself.

We also declare the `window` property. As our application loads our storyboard, it instantiates a window object and assigns it to this property. Usually, iOS applications have a single window that fills the entire screen. This window acts as the root for our view hierarchy. It both creates a space where other views can be displayed and distributes events to the proper views or subviews.

```
#import <UIKit/UIKit.h>
@interface HWAppDelegate : UIResponder <UIApplicationDelegate>
@property (strong, nonatomic) UIWindow *window;
@end
```

The `UIApplicationDelegate` protocol defines a wide range of optional methods that we can implement to modify our application's behavior. These include methods that respond to changes to the application's state, as well as local, remote, and system notifications. You can find a complete list of these methods in the developer documentation.

Clicking the word UIApplicationDelegate in the editor will bring up a brief description of the protocol in the Quick Help inspector (the top half of the Utilities area). This technique lets us get a quick description of any classes, methods, or functions. Additionally, the Quick Help inspector contains hyperlinks to additional resources. Click the hyperlink version of the protocol's name, and Xcode will open a full description from the developer's documentation. Scroll down to the Tasks section to see a full list of methods.

If you open the `HWAppDelegate.m` file, you can see that we defined several of these methods—but none of them do anything. Right now, they are simply method stubs—holding spaces, waiting for us to fill in the details.

```
#import "HWAppDelegate.h"
@implementation HWAppDelegate
@synthesize window = _window;
- (BOOL)application:(UIApplication *)application
didFinishLaunchingWithOptions:(NSDictionary *)launchOptions
{
    // Override point for customization after application launch.
```

```
        return YES;
}


- (void)applicationWillResignActive:(UIApplication *)application
{
    /*
        Sent when the application is about to move from active to
        inactive state. This can occur for certain types of
        temporary interruptions (such as an incoming phone call or
        SMS message) or when the user quits the application and it
        begins the transition to the background state.
        Use this method to pause ongoing tasks, disable timers, and
        throttle down OpenGL ES frame rates. Games should use this
        method to pause the game.
    */

}
- (void)applicationDidEnterBackground:(UIApplication *)application
{
    /*
        Use this method to release shared resources, save user data,
        invalidate timers, and store enough application state
        information to restore your application to its current state
        in case it is terminated later.
        If your application supports background execution, this method
        is called instead of applicationWillTerminate: when the
        user quits.
    */

}
```

```objc
- (void)applicationWillEnterForeground:(UIApplication *)application
{
    /*
    Called as part of the transition from the background to the
    inactive state; here you can undo many of the changes made
    on entering the background.
    */
}
- (void)applicationDidBecomeActive:(UIApplication *)application
{
    /*
    Restart any tasks that were paused (or not yet started) while
    the application was inactive. If the application was
    previously in the background, optionally refresh the user
    interface.
    */
}
- (void)applicationWillTerminate:(UIApplication *)application
{
    /*
    Called when the application is about to terminate.
    Save data if appropriate.
    See also applicationDidEnterBackground:.
    */
}
@end
```

These methods respond to changes in our application's state. They are called when our application first loads, becomes active or inactive, goes into or out of the background, or prepares to terminate. We will discuss these (and other) methods in more detail in the Chapter 3 sidebar "Tasks Every Application Should Perform." For now, read the comments in these method stubs. They should give you a good overview of their intended use.

Next, look at HWMainViewController.h. This is even simpler than the app delegate's interface declaration. We define our class as a subclass of UIViewController. It also adopts a custom protocol, HWFlipsideViewControllerDelegate. That's it.

```
#import "HWFlipsideViewController.h"

@interface HWMainViewController : UIViewController

<HWFlipsideViewControllerDelegate>

@end
```

Look at the implementation by selecting HWMainViewController.m. Much like the app delegate, the UIViewController class has a number of methods that we can override to monitor our view. In particular, this includes any method with will or did in its name. The will methods are called just before the event takes place. The did methods are called just after.

Look up UIViewController in the developer documentation to see the complete list (click it to open the Quick Help inspector, and then click the name link to open the full description). If you scan through this file, you will see that it includes a number of these as method stubs. Most have default implementations that don't do anything; they just call the superclass's implementation.

There are only three methods containing functional code: shouldAutorotateTo InterfaceOrientation:, flipsideViewControllerDidFinish:, and prepareFor Segue:sender:.

```
- (BOOL)shouldAutorotateToInterfaceOrientation:
    (UIInterfaceOrientation)interfaceOrientation
{
    // Return YES for supported orientations.
    return (interfaceOrientation !=
        UIInterfaceOrientationPortraitUpsideDown);
```

```
}

#pragma mark - Flipside View

- (void)flipsideViewControllerDidFinish:
    (HWFlipsideViewController *)controller
{

    [self dismissModalViewControllerAnimated:YES];

}

- (void)prepareForSegue:(UIStoryboardSegue *)segue sender:(id)sender
{

    if ([[segue identifier] isEqualToString:@"showAlternate"]) {
        [[segue destinationViewController] setDelegate:self];
    }

}
```

Let's take these in order. The shouldAutorotateToInterfaceOrientation:
method is called whenever the user rotates the device to a new orientation. If it
returns YES, the view will automatically rotate to match that orientation. Otherwise, the view will remain in its current orientation. The current implementation
allows our main view to rotate into any orientation except the portrait upside-down
orientation (landscape left, landscape right, and portrait are all OK).

The flipsideViewControllerDidFinish: method is a delegate method for
our flipside view controller. As you might guess from the name, the flipside view
controller will call this method when it is finished. Our current implementation
simply dismisses the current modal view. Remember that when we examined
the segue, we saw that it displayed our flipside view controller as a modal view.
Therefore, this method simply removes our flipside view, using the same transition
(horizontal flipping) to return to the main view.

Finally, prepareForSegue:sender: is called whenever a segue is triggered from
the current scene. Although the implementation looks a little complex, it simply
checks to make sure our segue's id matches the expected value, showAlternate. If
it does, we assign our main view controller as the destination's delegate.

It's always a good idea to check the segue's identifier before doing anything
in the prepareForSegue:sender: method. Right now it's not strictly necessary.

We only have one segue, so we know the identifier will always match. However, checking the identifier helps future-proof our code. We won't suddenly have odd bugs just because we added a new segue.

Also, if you remember, the showAlternate segue connects our main view controller scene with our flipside view controller scene. This means the destination ViewController will be our HWFlipsideViewController.

So, the user presses the info button, triggering our segue. The system instantiates a copy of our HWFlipsideViewController, then calls the HWMainViewController's prepareForSegue:sender:. Here, HWMainViewController assigns itself as HWFlipside ViewController's delegate. The transition occurs, and our view flips over horizontally, revealing the flipside view. When the flipside view is finished (which we will see in a minute), the flipside view controller calls flipsideViewControllerDidFinish: on its delegate, HWMainViewController. HWMainViewController then dismisses the flipside view controller and our views flip back over, revealing the main view again.

It's important to realize that this pattern demonstrates the preferred technique for passing data from scene to scene across a segue. When passing data from the originating view controller to the destination view controller, we override the originating view controller's prepareForSegue:sender: method and pass the data along. To pass the data back, we make the originating view a delegate of the destination view and then call the appropriate delegate methods. Of course, these methods need to be declared in the delegate's protocol. We'll see the HWFlipsideView ControllerDelegate's protocol next.

Open HWFlipsideViewController.h. Here, we start by declaring our HWFlipside ViewControllerDelegate protocol. This only has a single method, which we have already seen, flipsideViewControllerDidFinish:. Next, we declare the HWFlipside ViewController class itself. This is also simple, containing only two items: the delegate outlet property and the done: action.

We've seen both of these before. We just discussed the delegate property in relationship to our HWMainViewController, and we saw the done: action back when we were exploring our storyboard. It is connected to the Done button in the navigation bar. Pressing that button will trigger this method.

```
#import <UIKit/UIKit.h>

@class HWFlipsideViewController;

@protocol HWFlipsideViewControllerDelegate
```

```
- (void)flipsideViewControllerDidFinish:
    (HWFlipsideViewController *)controller;
@end
@interface HWFlipsideViewController : UIViewController
@property (weak, nonatomic) IBOutlet id
<HWFlipsideViewControllerDelegate>
    delegate;
- (IBAction)done:(id)sender;
@end
```

NOTE: Observant readers may remember that the `delegate` outlet was also connected to the `HWMainViewController` in the storyboard. This means it has been connected twice—once in code and once in Interface Builder. Turns out, the connection in Interface Builder doesn't actually do anything. Deleting it won't affect the app—you won't even be allowed to draw it again. However, commenting out our `prepareForSegue:sender:` method breaks the connection, and the `HWFlipsideViewController`'s delegate property is never set. You will still transition to the flipside view when the info button is pressed, but pressing the Done button no longer flips us back.

Now open `HWFlipsideViewController.m`. Much like `HWMainViewController.m`, this largely contains method stubs. However, at the bottom we have the implementation for our done: action.

```
- (IBAction)done:(id)sender
{
    [self.delegate flipsideViewControllerDidFinish:self];
}
```

This simply calls the delegate's `flipsideViewControllerDidFinish:` method. Which brings us around full circle. When the user presses the Done button, the event triggers the done: action. This then calls `HWMainViewController`'s `flipsideViewControllerDidFinish:`, which dismisses the flipside view controller scene. Everything is now connected.

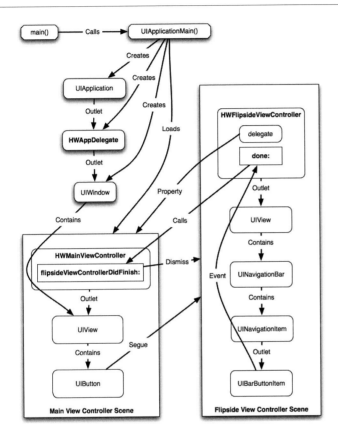

FIGURE 1.16 The full object graph

Again, there is nothing supernatural going on here. If you ever feel lost in a new project, start with the main storyboard file (as defined in the project's info.plist file) and walk your way through. You should be able to trace a series of connections from the UIApplication object to any object in your project. Some may be defined in code and some in the storyboard, but with a little patience, you will be able to track everything down.

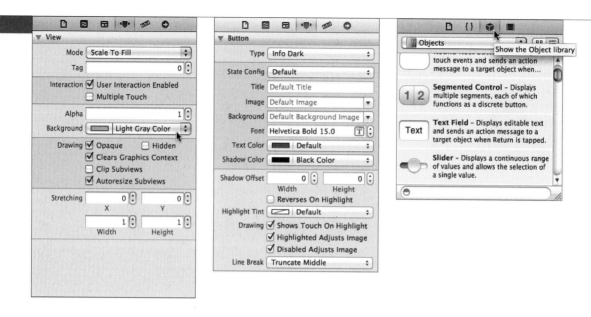

FIGURE 1.17 Setting the Background attribute

FIGURE 1.18 Setting the Type attribute

FIGURE 1.19 Selecting the Object library

OK, enough chatter. Let's start building something new. We're going to add a label to the main view that will display a short message. We will also add a text box to the flipside view, letting the user change this message. So, let's get started.

MODIFYING THE MAIN VIEW

Open MainStoryboard.storyboard again, and zoom in on the main view controller scene. The background is a little too dark for my taste. Select the View object, and then switch to the Attributes inspector. Change the Background attribute to Light Gray Color (**Figure 1.17**). Next, select the info button and change its Type setting to Info Dark (**Figure 1.18**).

Now we need to add a label. Xcode makes it easy to add user interface objects. Just drag the desired object from the Library pane (the bottom half of the Utilities area) and drop it onto the scene. Make sure the Object library is displayed (cube icon second from the right in the library selector bar) (**Figure 1.19**), and scroll so the Label object is visible. Click the Label object and drag it from the Library pane to the main view controller scene's view.

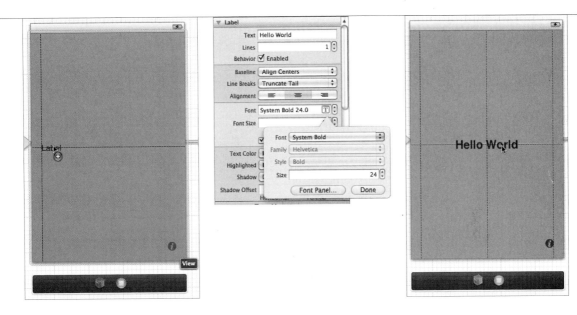

Xcode will help you correctly place the control. As you drag the label across the Editor area, it highlights and labels the current view. It also adds blue guidelines to help properly position your objects. Drag the label until it is centered vertically and aligned with the view's left margin, as shown in **Figure 1.20**.

When you release the label, it will appear surrounded by eight blue dots. You can click and drag these anchor points to resize the label. Grab the right side and stretch it until you hit the right-margin guide. Next, make it about half as tall as the enclosing view. Now, with the label still selected, let's change its appearance.

Open the Attributes inspector. In the Alignment attribute, click the button for centered text. Then click the T icon at the far right side of the Font attribute's text field. This will open a pop-up window. Change the Font setting to System Bold and the Size setting to 24 (**Figure 1.21**). Now let's change the text itself. You can either modify the label's Text attribute, or you can double-click the label and modify it directly. Replace "Label" with **Hello World**.

Finally, click and drag the label until it is centered both horizontally and vertically (if you cannot move the label, try clicking the view to clear the selection, then click and drag the label again). If you've done everything correctly, the left and right margin guidelines should appear as well (**Figure 1.22**).

Run the application. Our changes should appear on the main view.

FIGURE 1.20 Aligning the label with the view's left margin

FIGURE 1.21 Setting the label's font

FIGURE 1.22 Centering the label

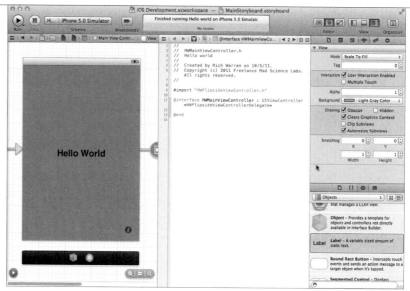

FIGURE 1.23 The Assistant Editor button

FIGURE 1.24 Side-by-side editing of the storyboard and the header file

ADDING AN OUTLET

If we want to change the label's text during runtime, we need a way to access it in our code. The easiest way is to add an outlet to the view's controller. In the pre-Xcode 4.0 days, this meant jumping back and forth between Xcode and Interface Builder as we modified our code by hand. Now there's a much simpler way.

First, we should probably collapse the scene list. Click the round, gray disclosure button in the lower-left corner of the Editor area. Next, click the Assistant Editor button (**Figure 1.23**).

This will display two Editor areas side by side. The leftmost area contains the selected file, while the rightmost contains a closely related file. For example, if you select the HWMainViewController.h header file, the right editor should display the HWMainViewController.m implementation file. In our case, the left editor shows the storyboard, while the right editor shows the controller's header file (**Figure 1.24**).

Control-click the label and drag it to the header file. You will see a blue line stretching from the label to your cursor. Place the cursor just above the @end directive, as shown in **Figure 1.25**, and then release the mouse.

A pop-up dialog will now allow you to configure the outlet. Make sure the Connection setting is set to Outlet. In the Name field, enter **label**. The Type should be UILabel, and the Storage should be Strong (**Figure 1.26**). Click Connect to continue.

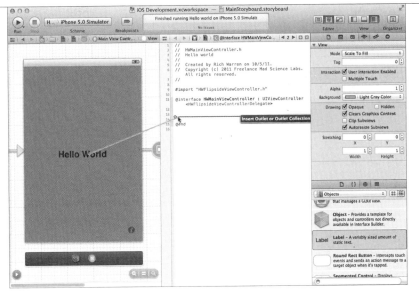

FIGURE 1.25 Creating an outlet

FIGURE 1.26 Configuring the outlet

NOTE: Although Xcode generally does a great job auto-selecting the correct companion file, there may be times when it does not work properly or when you want to select a different file instead. You can do this in the jump bar. Selecting the leaf item will let you choose an alternate file based on the same general selection rules. Selecting the root item will allow you to choose different selection rules. Xcode provides a number of different, context-specific selection rules. You can also choose to manually select the companion file, if necessary.

Xcode will make several changes to HWMainViewController.h, HWMainView Controller.m, and MainStoryboard.storyboard. In the header file, it declares our label's property.

```
#import "HWFlipsideViewController.h"
@interface HWMainViewController : UIViewController
<HWFlipsideViewControllerDelegate>
@property (strong, nonatomic) IBOutlet UILabel *label;
@end
```

FIGURE 1.27 Main View Controller's connections

In the implementation file, Xcode synthesizes our property and sets it to `nil` when the view is unloaded. This helps free up unneeded memory.

```
#import "HWMainViewController.h"

@implementation HWMainViewController

@synthesize label;

....

- (void)viewDidUnload
{
    [self setLabel:nil];
    [super viewDidUnload];
    // Release any retained subviews of the main view.
    // For example, self.myOutlet = nil;.
}
```

In the storyboard file, Xcode connects the label and the newly created outlet. You can view this using the Connection inspector. Alternatively, Control-click the Main View Controller icon to bring up a Connections dialog (**Figure 1.27**).

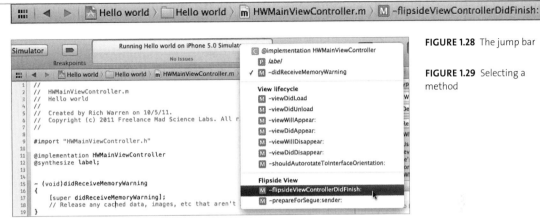

FIGURE 1.28 The jump bar

FIGURE 1.29 Selecting a method

ADDING THE TEXT FIELD

The first few steps almost exactly repeat what we did for the main view, only we use a Text Field control, not a Label object. Make sure MainStoryboard.storyboard is open and zoom in on the flipside view controller. Now, drag a Text Field control from the Library pane. Resize it so that it fills the view from margin to margin.

This time we don't need to change the height or the attributes. Just create an outlet for the text field by Control-dragging it to a point just above the delegate property. Name the outlet **labelText**. Finally, position it in the top half of the flipside view; otherwise, it may be covered by the keyboard.

Whenever we want to change the label's text, we just need to get the text value from our labelText outlet and copy it into our label outlet. The simplest solution is to change the label only when the user dismisses the flipside view. Open HWMainViewController.m and find the flipsideViewControllerDidFinish: method.

Currently our files are not very long. You can probably find the method by just scanning through the file. Still, it is often easier to use the editor's jump bar (**Figure 1.28**).

The bar across the top of the Editor area shows you the item that you are editing. Click the rightmost item and select the flipsideViewControllerDidFinish: method (**Figure 1.29**). The editor will select the method and scroll so it is visible.

Now, modify the `flipsideViewControllerDidFinish:` method as shown here.

```
- (void)flipsideViewControllerDidFinish:
(HWFlipsideViewController *)controller
{
    self.label.text = controller.labelText.text;
    [self dismissModalViewControllerAnimated:YES];
}
```

As we discussed earlier, this line simply copies the text value from the flipside view's text field to the main view's label using our outlets and properties.

That's it. Run the application again. It should display the default Hello World message when it launches. Click the info button, and type new text into the text field. Click the Done button. The label should now show your new text.

REFINING THE INTERFACE

Functionally, everything's OK, but it's not the most polished (or, for that matter, useful) app in the world. Let's make it a little bit better. When the flipside view appears, let's fill the text field with the label's current value. Additionally, let's go ahead and dismiss the flipside view when the user taps the Return key.

Let's start by passing the text from our main view's label to our flipside view. Ideally, we would like to set this value in our `prepareForSegue:sender:` method. This should be the reverse of the code in `flipsideViewControllerDidFinish:`; we copy the value from our main view's label directly to our flipside view's text field. Unfortunately, because of the way views are loaded, the text field may not exist yet. There are a couple of ways around this. Let's add a property to our `HWFlipside ViewController` class and use that to hold our text until we're sure the view is ready to go.

Open `HWFlipsideViewController.h` and add the following line just after the other properties:

```
@property (nonatomic, strong) NSString* startingText;
```

In `HWFlipsideViewController.m`, we need to synthesize this property (see the "Properties" section of Chapter 2 for more information). Add the following line at the beginning of the `@implementation` block:

```
@synthesize startingText = _startingText;
```

Now, scroll down to the `viewWillLoad:` method and modify it as shown below:

```
- (void)viewWillAppear:(BOOL)animated
{
    self.labelText.text = self.startingText;
    [super viewWillAppear:animated];
}
```

This method is called every time the flipside view appears. Here, we're just assigning the value stored in our `startingText` property to the text field. Next, open `HWMainViewController.m` again. Modify `prepareForSegue:sender:` as shown:

```
- (void)prepareForSegue:(UIStoryboardSegue *)segue sender:(id)sender
{
    if ([[segue identifier] isEqualToString:@"showAlternate"])
    {
        id flipsideViewController =
        [segue destinationViewController];
        [flipsideViewController setDelegate:self];
        [flipsideViewController setStartingText:self.label.text];
    }
}
```

Since we're setting multiple properties, we start by getting a generic reference to our `HWFlipsideViewController`. We then use that reference to set the delegate, just as we did before. Finally, we grab the string from our main view's label and save it in our `startingText` property.

SAFELY ACCESSING A VIEW CONTROLLER'S OUTLETS

In this example, we could not modify the text field's contents until after the system fully loaded the view. We will discuss this in more depth in Chapters 3 and 4. However, the simple explanation is that UIKit does not immediately load the views when it creates our view controllers. Instead, it waits until the view is actually needed (usually, just before the system displays it on the screen). While UIKit does this for performance reasons, it can cause very confusing bugs if you are not careful.

Typically, these bugs occur when you make in-code changes to a view controller's outlet—especially an outlet assigned using Interface Builder. When you run the application, the code is triggered, but the changes don't appear to take effect.

Whenever this happens, double-check to make sure the outlet actually exists. It should have a non-nil value. If it doesn't, you'll need to delay your configuration code, much as we did here.

One improvement down, one more to go. Open the assistant editor again, with the storyboard on the left and HWFlipsideViewController.h on the right. We want to connect the text field's Did End On Exit event with the controller's done: method. There are several ways to draw connections. For example, we could Control-click and drag from the text field to the done: method. Unfortunately, this does not allow us to select the event, and it will connect the Editing Did End event, not the Did End On Exit event.

Instead, Control-click the text field to bring up the Connections dialog. Click and drag from the circle that is to the right of the Did End On Exit event to the done: method, as shown in **Figure 1.30**.

There are several other equally valid alternatives. You can Control-click the HWFlipsideViewController icon in the scene's dock, and then drag from the done: action to the text field. Xcode will then prompt you for the correct event. You can also use the Connection inspector in the Utilities area, instead of using the pop-up dialogs. Most of these approaches are equivalent. Feel free to experiment with the different approaches and see which one works best for you.

NOTE: Each event can be connected to only one action, but a single action can connect to multiple events. In this case, we have both the text field and the Done button connected to the done: action.

While we're at it, let's change the appearance of the keyboard's Return key. Select the text field and open the Attributes inspector. Set the Return Key attribute to Done. While this doesn't change the keyboard's functionality, it helps communicate our intent.

You may also want to set the Clear Button attribute to "Appears while editing." After all, using the backspace to delete large amounts of text gets tedious very quickly.

That's it. Run the application. It should appear as shown in **Figures 1.31** and **1.32**.

FIGURE 1.31 The complete
main view

FIGURE 1.32 The complete
flipside view

WRAPPING **UP**

And that's it for our Hello World app. In this chapter, we've examined how iOS applications are pieced together. We've built and modified our own (albeit incredibly simple) application, and we've gotten some hands-on experience using the development tools. This should give you a good jump-off point for the rest of the book.

In Chapter 2, we will dig into Objective-C. We will look at the different building blocks used in the language, as well as some of the common design patterns found throughout Cocoa Touch. Then, in Chapter 3, we will take everything we've learned so far and start building a more complex, real-world application.

2

OBJECTIVE-C

If you want to develop native iOS applications, you must learn Objective-C. For many, this is an intimidating task with a steep learning curve. Objective-C mixes a wide range of C-language constructs with a layer of object-oriented design. In addition, iOS applications leverage a wide range of design patterns. While these patterns provide both flexibility and power, they can often confuse beginners.

This chapter presents a thorough overview of the Objective-C features needed to successfully develop iOS applications, as well as an explanation of new technologies that tame Objective-C's more complex aspects. This will help reduce the learning curve to a gentle speed bump.

THE **OBJECTIVE-C LANGUAGE**

Objective-C is a small, elegant, object-oriented extension to the C language. Strictly speaking, it is a superset of C. You can use any valid C code in an Objective-C project. This gives us access to numerous third-party libraries, in addition to the Objective-C and C frameworks. Objective-C borrows much of its object syntax from Smalltalk. Smalltalk, one of the earliest object-oriented languages, was designed to be simple—both easy to implement and easy to learn. Despite its age, Smalltalk remains one of the most innovative program languages on the market. Many modern languages are just now rediscovering techniques originally developed in Smalltalk. And Objective-C gains a lot from this heritage: a highly dynamic, very expressive foundation upon which everything else is built.

As a dynamic language, Objective-C binds methods and arguments at runtime instead of compile time. You don't need to know the object's class. You can send any object any message. This often greatly simplifies your code; however, if you send an object a message that it doesn't understand, you will crash your program at runtime.

Fortunately, Xcode warns you about undeclared messages. Furthermore, you can declare static types for your objects, which increases the compiler's ability to analyze the code and produce warnings. Objective-C is also a highly reflective language—it can observe and modify itself. We can examine any class at runtime, getting access to its methods, instance variables, and more. We can modify classes, adding our own methods using categories or extension, or even dynamically redefining methods at runtime.

Finally, Objective-C—and in particular the Cocoa and Cocoa Touch frameworks—utilize a number of design patterns to reduce the binding between the different sections of our code. Loosely bound code is easier to modify and maintain. Changes to one part of the program do not affect any other parts of your code. However, if you are not familiar with these patterns, they can make the code hard to follow.

These patterns include using a Model-View-Controller (MVC) framework for our programs, using delegates instead of subclassing, enabling key-value coding (KVC) for highly dynamic access to an object's instance variables, using key-value observing (KVO) to monitor any changes to those variables, and providing our applications with an extensive notifications framework.

As you master Objective-C, you will find that you can often solve complex problems with considerably less code than you would need in more traditional programming languages, like C++ or Java. We can more carefully tailor our solution to fit the problem, rather than trying to hammer a square peg into a round hole.

Apple has made good use of this flexibility when designing both the Cocoa Touch frameworks and Xcode's developer tools. These tools make common tasks easy to accomplish without a lot of repetitive boilerplate, while still making it possible to work outside the box when necessary.

The rest of this chapter describes the Objective-C programming language. It is not meant to be all-inclusive; you could easily write an entire book on Objective-C. In fact, several people have. You might want to check them out. Or read The Objective-C Programming Language in Apple's documentation. The guide provides all the details you will ever need. Instead, this chapter is the "vital parts" version. It provides enough information to get started, while pointing out many of the key features and common mistakes.

While previous experience with objective-oriented programming is not necessary, I assume you have a basic understanding of other C-like programming languages (e.g., C, C++, or Java). If the following example leaves you completely baffled, you may want to brush up your C skills before proceeding. If you can correctly predict the output[1], you should be fine.

```c
#include <stdio.h>
int main (int argc, const char * argv[]) {
    int total = 0;
    int count = 0;
    for (int y = 0; y < 10; y++) {
        count++;
        total += y;
    }
    printf("Total = %d, Count = %d, Average = %1.1f",
            total,
            count,
            (float)total / (float)count);
    return 0;
}
```

---

1 The correct answer is "Total = 45, Count = 10, Average = 4.5." Bonus points if you can actually compile and run the program.

NINE **FUNDAMENTAL** BUILDING **BLOCKS**

I won't kid you. Previous versions of Objective-C had a steep learning curve. Some aspects, like memory management, were only practicable by robotically follow- ing a strict set of rules. Even then, you could easily slip up and get things wrong, leading to bugs, errors, and crashes. Fortunately, Apple continues to improve the Objective-C language and reduce its complexity. As a result, we spend less time shepherding the programming language and more time solving real problems.

Still, if you haven't done any object-oriented programming before, it can be a bit much to wrap your head around. There are many new concepts to master: classes, objects, subclasses, superclasses, overriding methods, and more.

On the other hand, experience with other object-oriented programs might not help as much as you expect. Objective-C handles objects somewhat differently than languages like Java and C++. Leaning too heavily on your previous experience may lead you astray.

With all that said, there are really only nine key elements that you need to understand. These are the foundation upon which everything else is built: standard C data types, structures, enums, functions, operators, objects, methods, protocols, and categories/extensions. Once you understand these (and—most importantly— the differences between them), you are 90 percent home.

In general, these elements can be divided into two categories: data and pro- cedures. Data (C types, structures, enums, and objects) represent the information that we are processing. If you compare Objective-C code to an English sentence, the data is the nouns. Procedures (C operators, functions, and methods), on the other hand, are processes that manipulate or transform the data. They are our verbs. Our programs are basically a list of steps that define data and then manipulate it.

C DATA TYPES

Objective-C is built upon the C programming language. As a result, the C data types are some of the most primitive building blocks available. All other data structures are just advanced techniques for combining C types in increasingly complex ways.

All C data types are, at their root, fixed-length strings of 1s and 0s either 8, 16, 32, or 64 bits long. The different data types simply define how we interpret those bits. To begin with, we can divide the data types into two main categories: integer values and floating-point values (**Table 2.1**).

Integer values are used for storing discrete information. This most often means positive and negative whole numbers, but could represent other symbolic infor- mation (e.g., BOOLs are used to represent YES and NO values, while chars are used to represent ASCII characters). The integer types include BOOL, char, short, int, long, and long long data types. The main difference between them is the number of bits used to represent each value. The more bits, the wider the range of possible values—however, the data also takes up more space. Discrete values also come in signed and unsigned variants. This determines how the numbers are interpreted. Signed data types can be both positive and negative numbers, while unsigned data types are always zero or greater.

> **NOTE:** The exact size of the data type can vary depending on both the compiler that you are using and the target platform. For example, int values could be either 32 or 64 bits long. As a result, your program shouldn't make assumptions about either the number of bits or the minimum and maximum values of each data type. Instead, use the sizeof() function and the macros defined in limits.h and float.h to determine these values at runtime.

Floating-point values (float and double) are used to approximate continuous numbers—basically, any number with a decimal point. I won't go too deep into the theory and practice of floating-point numbers here—you can find all the eye-bleeding detail in any introductory computer science book. Suffice it to say, floating-point numbers are only approximations. Two mathematical formulas that are identical on paper may produce very different results. However, unless you are doing scientific calculations, you will probably only run into problems when comparing values. For example, you may be expecting 3.274 but your expression returns 3.2739999999999999. While the values aren't equal, they are usually close enough. Any difference you see is probably the result of rounding errors. Because of this, you will often want to check to see if your value falls within a given range ($3.2739 < x < 3.2741$) rather than looking for strict equality.

C has two types of floating-point values: float and double. As the name suggests, a double is twice as big as a float. The additional size improves both the range and the precision of its values. For this reason, it is tempting to always use doubles instead of floats. In some programming languages, this is idiomatically correct. I could probably count the number of times I used floats in Java on one hand. In Objective-C, however, floats are much more common.

In fact, despite the wide range of available C data types, we will typically only use BOOL, int, and floats. However, it often feels like we are using a much broader range of data types, since the core framework frequently uses typedef to create alternative names for int and float (and occasionally other data types). Sometimes this is done to provide consistency and to increase portability across multiple platforms. For example, CGFloat and NSInteger are both defined so that their size matches the target processor's integer size (either 32 or 64 bits). All else being equal, these values should be the most efficient data type for that particular processor. Other types are defined to better communicate their intent, like NSTimeInterval.

You can use the documentation to see how these types are defined. For example, in Xcode, open the documentation by selecting Documentation and API Reference from the Help menu. You might have to search around a bit, but you will find NSTimeInterval described under Reference > Foundation Data Type Reference > NSTimeInterval. The actual definition is shown as:

```
typedef double NSTimeInterval;
```

As you can see, NSTimeInterval is just an alias for double.

TABLE 2.1 Common C Data Types for iOS

INTEGER DATA TYPE	BIT LENGTH	SIGNED RANGE		UNSIGNED RANGE
BOOL	8 bits	N/A		YES or NO
char	8 bits	-128 to 127		0 to 255
short	16 bits	-32768 to 3276		0 to 65535
int	32 bits	-2147483648 to 2147483647		0 to 4294967295
long	32 bits	-2147483648 to 2147483647		0 to 4294967295
long long	64 bits	approx -1E19 to 1E19		0 to approx 2E19
NSInteger	32 bits	-2147483648 to 2147483647		0 to 4294967295
FLOAT DATA TYPE	**BIT LENGTH**	**MIN**	**MAX**	**EPSILON**
float	32 bits	1.175494E-38	3.402823E+38	1.192093E-07
double	64 bits	2.225074E-308	1.797693E+308	2.220446E-16
CGFloat	32 bits	1.175494E-38	3.402823E+38	1.192093E-07

C DATA STRUCTURES

Simple data types are all fine and good, but we often need to organize our data into more complex structures. These structures fall into three main categories: pointers, arrays, and structs.

POINTERS

The pointer is the simplest structure—at least in concept. Basically, it is a variable that points to the memory address of another value. This allows indirect access and modification of those values.

You declare a pointer by placing an asterisk between the type declaration and the variable name. You also use the asterisk before the variable name to dereference the pointer (to set or read the value at that address space). Likewise, placing an ampersand before a normal variable will give you that variable's address. You can even do crazy things like creating pointers to pointers, for an additional layer of indirection.

```
int a = 10;     // Creates the variable a.
int* b = &a;    // Creates the pointer, b, that points to the
                // address of a.
*b = 15;        // Changes the value of variable a to 15.
int** c;        // Creates a pointer to a pointer to an int.
```

> **NOTE:** When you declare a pointer, the compiler does not request memory space for the underlying values. It requests only enough space to store the memory address. You must either use the pointer to refer to an existing variable (as we did in the example above) or manually manage its memory on the heap. We will explore this issue in more depth when we discuss memory management later in this chapter.

By themselves, pointers are not very interesting; however, they form the backbone of many more-complex data structures. Additionally, while pointers are conceptually quite simple, they are difficult to master. Pointers remain a common source of bugs in programs, and these bugs are often very hard to find and fix. A full description of pointers is beyond the scope of this chapter. Fortunately, we will normally use pointers only when referencing Objective-C objects, and these objects largely have their own syntax.

ARRAYS

Arrays allow us to define a fixed-length series of values. All of these values must be of the same type. For example, if we want a list of ten integers, we would simply define it as shown here:

```
int integerList[10];     // Declares an array to hold ten integers.
```

We can then access the individual members of the list by placing the desired index in the brackets. Note, however, that arrays are zero-indexed. The first item is 0, not 1.

```
integerList[0] = 150;      // Sets the first item in the array.
integerList[9] = -23;      // Sets the last item in the array.
int a = integerList[0];    // Sets a to 150.
```

We can also use the C literal array syntax to declare short arrays with a static set of initial values. We write literal arrays as a pair of curly braces surrounding a comma-separated list of values.

```
int intList2[] = {15, 42, 9};    // Implicitly declares an array
                                 // to hold three integers,
                                 // then sets their values
                                 // using the literal array.
```

As this example shows, we do not even need to define the length of intList2. Instead, its size is automatically set equal to the literal array. Alternatively, you could explicitly set intList2's size, but it must be equal to or longer than the literal array.

Arrays are also used to represent C-style strings. For example, if you want to store someone's name in C, you usually store it as an array of chars.

```
char firstName[255];
```

Since they are based on arrays, C-style strings have a fixed size. This leads to a very common source of bugs. Yes, 254 characters should be enough to store most people's first name, but eventually you will run into a client that needs 255 characters (not to mention international character sets).

As this example implies, the string does not need to use up the entire array, but it must fit within the allocated memory space. Actually, the array's size must equal or exceed the number of characters in the string + 1. C-style strings always end with a null character.

String values can be assigned using literal strings—anything within double quotes. C will append the null value automatically. In this example, s1 and s2 are identical.

```
char s1[5] = "test";
char s2[5] = {'t', 'e', 's', 't', '\0'};
```

> **NOTE:** 'A' and "A" are completely different data types. In C, single quotes are used to represent char values. Therefore, 'A' is a char with the value of 65 (the ASCII value for the uppercase letter A). On the other hand, "A" is an array of chars with the values {'A', '\0'}.

Like pointers, arrays can become quite complex—particularly when passing them into or returning them from functions, and we haven't even begun talking about advanced topics like multidimensional arrays and dynamic arrays. Fortunately, unless you are calling a C library, we will almost never use arrays in Objective-C. Instead, we will use one of Objective-C's collection classes (NSArray, NSSet, or NSDictionary). For strings, we will use NSString.

STRUCTS

Structs are the most flexible C data type. While arrays allow us to declare an indexed list of identical types, the struct lets us combine different types of data and lets us access that data using named fields. Also, unlike C-style arrays, Cocoa Touch makes heavy use of C structures. In particular, many of the core frameworks are written in pure C, allowing them to be used in both Cocoa (Objective-C) and Carbon (pure C) projects (Carbon is an older technology that is sometimes still used for applications on the Mac OS X desktop).

To see a typical struct, look up CGPoint in Xcode's documentation. You will see that it is declared as shown here:

```
struct CGPoint {
    CGFloat x;
    CGFloat y;
};
typedef struct CGPoint CGPoint;
```

First, the framework creates a structure called CGPoint. This structure has two fields, x and y. In this case, both fields happen to be the same data type (CGFloat).

Next, we use typedef to define a type named CGPoint. This is an alias for the CGPoint struct. That may seem odd, but it is actually quite helpful. If we didn't have the typedef, we would constantly have to refer to this entity as "struct CGPoint" in our code. Now, however, we can drop the struct keyword and treat it like any other data type.

You access the fields as shown:

```
CGPoint pixelA;      // Creates the CGPoint variable.
pixelA.x = 23.5;     // Sets the x field.
pixelA.y = 32.6;     // Sets the y field.
int x = pixelA.x;    // Reads the value from the x field.
```

Apple's frameworks often provide both the data structures and a number of functions to manipulate them. The documentation tries to group related structures and methods together wherever possible. For any struct type, Apple provides a convenience method for creating the struct, a method for comparing structs, and methods to perform common operations with the struct. For CGPoint, these include CGPointMake(), CGPointEqualToPoint(), and CGRectContainsPoint().

These methods become more important as the structures grow increasingly complex. Take, for example, the CGRect struct. This also has just two fields: origin and size; however, these fields are each structs in their own right. Origin is a CGPoint, while size is a CGSize.

The following code shows three different approaches to creating a `CGRect`. All three approaches are equivalent.

```
CGRect r1;
r1.origin.x = 5;
r1.origin.y = 10;
r1.size.width = 10;
r1.size.height = 20;
CGRect r2 = CGRectMake(5, 10, 10, 20);
CGRect r3 = {{5, 10}, {10, 20}};
```

In particular, notice how we created r3 using a struct literal. Conceptually, these are simple. Each pair of curly braces represents a struct (just like the curly braces that represented literal arrays earlier). The enclosed comma-separated list represents the fields in the order they were declared.

So, the outer braces represent the CGRect structure. The first inner pair of braces is the `origin` and the second is the `size`. Finally we have the actual fields inside the two inner structures. A CGRect still isn't too complicated, but as our structures get more complex, the literal struct construction becomes harder and harder to understand. In general, I only use literal structs for simple data structures and arrays. Instead, I use the helper function (as shown for r2) to quickly make structures, and I use direct assignment (as shown for r1) when I need additional flexibility. Still, you will undoubtedly run into third-party code that uses struct literals, so you should be able to recognize them.

NOTE: If you are compiling an application with Automated Reference Counting (ARC)—and we will use ARC for all applications in this book—you cannot store Objective-C objects inside a struct. Instead, you need to use an Objective-C class to manage the data. This is one of the few rules we must follow to enable automatic memory management. We will discuss this in more detail in the "Memory Management" section later this chapter.

ENUMERATIONS

Let's say we want to represent the days of the week in our code. We could use strings and spell out the words. While this approach works, it has several problems. First, it requires extra memory and computational effort just to store and compare days. Furthermore, string comparison is tricky. Do Saturday, saturday, and SATURDAY all represent the same day? What if you misspell the name of a day? What if you enter a string that doesn't correspond to any valid day? One alternative is to manually assign an unsigned char value for each day. In this example, the const keyword tells the compiler that these values cannot be changed after they have been initialized.

```
const unsigned char SUNDAY = 0;
const unsigned char MONDAY = 1;
const unsigned char TUESDAY = 2;
const unsigned char WEDNESDAY = 3;
const unsigned char THURSDAY = 4;
const unsigned char FRIDAY = 5;
const unsigned char SATURDAY = 6;
const unsigned char HUMPDAY = WEDNESDAY;
```

This works, but there's no way to refer to the set of days as a group. For example, you cannot specify that a function's argument needs to be a day of the week. That brings us to enumerations. Enumerations provide a concise, elegant method for defining a discrete set of values. For example, our days of the week could be:

```
typedef enum {
    SUNDAY,
    MONDAY,
    TUESDAY,
    WEDNESDAY,
    THURSDAY,
    FRIDAY,
    SATURDAY
```

```
} DAY;
const DAY HUMPDAY = WEDNESDAY;
```

Just as in the earlier struct example, we use a `typedef` to declare a type for our enum. In this example, we nest the enum declaration inside the `typdef`. Both styles are perfectly valid C code. Additionally, we could give the enum a name (e.g., `typedef enum DAY { ... } DAY;`), but since we will always access it through the type's name, that seems redundant.

Now, this isn't exactly the same as the `unsigned char` example. The enums take up a little more memory. However, they sure save on typing. More importantly, the enum better communicates our intent. When we define HUMPDAY as a `const unsigned char`, we are implicitly saying that it should have a value between 0 and 255. In the enum example, we are explicitly stating that HUMPDAY should only be set equal to one of our DAY constants. Of course, nothing will stop you from setting an invalid value.

```
const DAY HUMPDAY = 143;     // While this will compile fine,
                             // it is just wrong.
```

Stylistically, it is best to always use the named constants when assigning values to enum types. And while the compiler won't catch assignment errors, it can help in other areas—especially when combining enums and `switch` statements.

By default, the enum assigns 0 to the first constant, and the values increase by 1 as we step down the list. Alternatively, you can assign explicit values to one or more of the named constants. You can even assign multiple constants to the same value—making them aliases of each other.

```
typedef enum {
    BOLD = 1;
    ITALIC = 2;
    UNDERLINE = 4;
    ALL_CAPS = 8;
    SUBSCRIPT = 16;
    STRONG = BOLD
} STYLE;
```

Cocoa Touch makes extensive use of enumerations. As you look through the iOS SDK, you will find two common usage patterns. First, it uses enums for mutually exclusive options. Here, you must select one and only one option from a limited set of choices. Our DAY enum is set up this way. Any DAY variable or argument can take one and only one DAY value.

Other times, the enums represent flags that you can combine to form more-complex values. Our STYLE enum works this way. The constant's values were chosen so that each value represents a single, unique bit. You can combine the constants using the bitwise OR operator. You can likewise pull them apart using the bitwise AND operator. This allows you to store any combination of styles in a single variable.

```
STYLE header = BOLD | ITALIC | ALL_CAPS;    // Sets the style to bold,
                                            // italic, and all caps.
if ((header & BOLD) == BOLD) {              // Checks to see if the
    // Process bold text here                 // BOLD bit is set.
}
```

OPERATORS

Operators are a predefined set of procedural units in C. You use operators to build expressions—sets of commands that the computer will execute. For example, the expression a = 5 uses the assignment operator to set the value of a variable equal to the literal value 5. In this example, = is the operator, while a and 5 are the operands (the things that get operated upon).

Operators perform a wide variety of tasks; however, most operators can be grouped into a few broad categories: assignment (=, +=, -=, *=, etc.), arithmetic (+, -, *, /, %, etc.), comparison (==, <, >, !=, etc.), logical (&&, ||, !), bitwise (&, |, ^), and membership ([ ], *, &).

You can also categorize operators by the number of operands they take. Unitary operators take a single operand. The operator can be placed either before or after the operand—depending on the operator.

```
a++    // Increment the value of variable a by 1.

-b     // The opposite of b. If b equals 5, -b equals -5.

!c     // Boolean NOT. If c is true, !c is false.
```

Binary operators take two operands and are usually placed between the operands.

```
a + b      // Adds the two values together.
a <= b     // Returns true if a is less than or equal to b.
a[b]       // Access the value at index b in array a.
```

Finally, C has only one ternary operator, the ternary conditional operator.

```
a ? b : c    // If a is true, return b. Otherwise return c.
```

> **NOTE:** In several cases, two different operators use the same symbol. For example, the multiply and indirection operators both use a single asterisk. The compiler will select the correct operator based on the number of operands. In the example *a = b * c, the first asterisk is the indirection operator (unitary operator), allowing us to set the value at the memory location pointed to by a. The second asterisk is multiplication (binary operator).

ORDER OF PRECEDENCE

Each operator has an order of precedence determining its priority relative to the other operators. Operators with a high precedence are executed before those with a lower precedence. This should be familiar to most people from elementary math classes. Multiplication and division have a higher order of precedence than addition and subtraction.

Whenever an expression has more than one operator (and most expressions have more than one operator), you must take into account the order of precedence. Take a simple expression like a = b + c. The addition (+) occurs first, and then the sum is assigned (=) to the variable a.

For the most part, the order of precedence makes logical sense; however, there are a lot of rules, and some of them can be quite surprising. You can force the expression to execute in any arbitrary order by using parentheses. Anything inside the parentheses is automatically executed first. Therefore, when in doubt use parentheses.

When an expression is evaluated, the computer takes the operand with the highest precedence and determines its value. It then replaces the operator and its operands with that value, forming a new expression. This is then evaluated until we reduce the expression to a single value.

```
5 + 6 / 3 * (2 + 5)  // Initial expression.
5 + 6 / 3 * 7        // Operand in parentheses evaluated first.
5 + 2 * 7            // When two operators have the same precedence,
                     // evaluate from left to right.
5 + 14              // Perform multiplication before addition.
19                  // Final value.
```

Here are a couple of rules of thumb: Any expressions inside a function's or method's arguments are evaluated before the function call or method call is performed. Similarly, any expression inside an array's subscript is performed before looking up the value. Function calls, method calls, and array indexing all occur before most other operators. Assignment occurs after most (but not all) other operators. Some examples are given here:

```
a = 2 * max(2 + 5, 3);  // max() returns the largest value among its
                        //arguments. Variable a is set to 14.
a[2 + 3] = (6 + 3) * (10 - 7); // The value at index 5 is set to 27.
a = ((1 + 2) * (3 + 4)) > ((5 + 6) * (7 + 8));  // Variable a is set
                                                // to false.
```

FUNCTIONS

Functions are the primary procedural workhorse for the C programming language. A C program largely consists of defining data structures and then writing functions to manipulate those structures.

We will typically use functions in conjunction with structs, especially when dealing with the lower-level frameworks. However, you will find some functions that are explicitly designed to work with Objective-C objects. In fact, we saw a function like this in Chapter 1: UIApplicationMain().

Unlike operators, functions can be defined by the programmer. This allows us to encapsulate a series of procedural steps so that those steps can be easily repeated.

Functions are defined in an implementation file (filename ending in .m). It starts with the function signature. This defines the function's name, the return value, and the function's arguments. Arguments will appear as a comma-separated list surrounded by parentheses. Inside the list, each argument declares a data type and a name.

A pair of curly brackets follows the function signature. We can place any number of expressions inside these brackets. When the function is called, these expressions are executed in the order in which they appear.

```
CGFloat calculateDistance(CGPoint p1, CGPoint p2) {
    CGFloat xDist = p1.x - p2.x;
    CGFloat yDist = p1.y - p2.y;


    // Calculate the distance using the Pythagorean theorem.
    return sqrt(xDist * xDist + yDist * yDist);
}
```

In the above example, reading left to right, `CGFloat` is the return value, `calculateDistance` is the function name, and `CGPoint p1` and `CGPoint p2` are the function's two arguments.

Inside the function, we first create two local variables. These variables are stored on the stack and will be automatically deleted when the method returns. We assign the difference between our point's x- and y-coordinates to these variables.

The next line is blank. Whitespace is ignored by the compiler and should be used to organize your code, making it easier to follow and understand. Then we have a comment. The compiler will ignore anything after // until the end of the line. It will also ignore anything between /* and */, allowing us to create comments spanning several lines.

Finally, we reach the `return` keyword. This evaluates the expression to its right and then exits the function, returning the expression's value (if any) to the caller. The `calculateDistance()` function calculates the distance between two points using the Pythagorean theorem. Here we square the x and y distances using the multiply operator. We add them together. Then we pass that value to the C math library's `sqrt()` function and return the result.

You would call the function by using its name followed by parentheses containing a comma-separated list of values. These can be literal values, variables, or even other expressions. However, the value's type must match its corresponding argument. C can convert some of the basic data types. For example, you can pass an int to a function that requires a double. If the function returns a value, we will usually assign the return value to a variable or otherwise use it in an expression.

Not all functions return values. Some functions create side effects (they create some sort of lasting change in the application—either outputting data to the screen or altering some aspect of our data structures). For example, the printf() function can be used to print a message to the console.

```
CGPoint a = {1, 3};
CGPoint b = {-3, 7};
CGFloat distance = calculateDistance(a, b);
printf("The distance between (%2.1f, %2.1f) and (%2.1f, %2.1f)
→  is %5.4f\n",
            a.x, a.y,
            b.x, b.y,
            distance);
```

In this sample, we first create our two point structs. Then we call our calculate Distance() function, passing in a for argument p1 and b for argument p2. We then assign the return value to the distance variable. Finally, we call the printf() function, passing in a format string and our data.

The printf() function constructs its message from a variable-length list of arguments. The first argument is a format string, followed by a comma-separated list of values. The printf() function will scan through the string, looking for any placeholders (a percentage symbol followed by one or more characters). In this example, we use the %2.1f conversion specifier. This tells printf() to insert a floating-point value at least two digits long with exactly one digit after the decimal point. The %5.4f conversion specifier indicates a five-digit number with four of these digits after the decimal point. Then, printf() replaces the conversion specifiers using the list of values in order.

If you run this code, it prints the following message to the console: "The distance between (1.0, 3.0) and (-3.0, 7.0) is 5.6569".

Finally, in C you must define the function before it is used. Most of the time we simply place a function declaration in a corresponding header file (filename ending in .h). The function declaration is just the function signature followed by a semicolon.

```
CGFloat calculateDistance(CGPoint p1, CGPoint p2);
```

We can then import the header file before using the function anywhere else in our application.

PASS BY VALUE

In C, all functions pass their arguments by value. This means the compiler makes local copies of the arguments. Those copies are used within the function and are removed from memory when the function returns. In general, this means you can do whatever you want to the local copy, and the original value will remain unchanged. That is a very good thing. Check out the following examples.

```
void inner(int innerValue) {
    printf("innerValue = %d\n", innerValue);
    innerValue += 20;
    printf("innerValue = %d\n", innerValue);
}
void outer() {
    int outerValue = 10;
    printf("outerValue = %d\n", outerValue);
    inner(outerValue);
    printf("outerValue = %d\n", outerValue);
}
```

Here, printf() will replace the %d specifiers with an int value. Calling outer() prints the following series of messages to the console:

```
outerValue = 10
innerValue = 10
innerValue = 30
outerValue = 10
```

As you can see, the value of outerValue does not change when we modify innerValue. However, this is only half of the story. Consider the following code:

```
void inner(int* innerPointer) {
    printf("innerValue = %d\n", *innerPointer);
    *innerPointer += 20;
    printf("innerValue = %d\n", *innerPointer);
}
void outer() {
    int buffer = 10;
    int* outerPointer = &buffer;
    printf("outerValue = %d\n", *outerPointer);
    inner(outerPointer);
    printf("outerValue = %d\n", *outerPointer);
}
```

Superficially, this looks very similar to the earlier code. However, there are some important differences. First, we create a buffer variable and set its value to 10. We then create a pointer to this buffer and pass that pointer into the inner() function. Then, inner() modifies the value pointed at by its innerPointer argument. This time, we get the following output:

```
outerValue = 10
innerValue = 10
innerValue = 30
outerValue = 30
```

Here, both the innerValue and the outerValue change. We're still passing our argument by value. However, this time the value is the address of the buffer variable. The inner() function receives a copy of this address—but the address still points to the same piece of data in memory. When we dereference the pointer (either to modify it or to print out its value), we are actually accessing the buffer's value.

DANGLING **POINTERS**

Even though the `buffer` variable is deleted when the `getPointer()` method ends, the actual value stored at that memory location may not change immediately. At some point, the application will reuse that memory space, writing over the current value. However, for the time being, the pointer may continue to function as if nothing were wrong.

This is the worst kind of bug, the kind that crashes your application at some random time in the future. The error might even occur in a completely unrelated section of code. These errors can be very hard to track down and fix.

Bottom line, functions can modify the values pointed to by pointer arguments. This is important since both Objective-C objects and C-style arrays are passed as pointers. Whenever you are using these data types, you must avoid accidentally modifying the underlying data.

Return values are also passed by value, but this has an additional complication, since the original value is deleted when the function returns. Consider the following method:

```
int* getPointer() {
    int buffer = 100;
    int* pointer = &buffer;
    return pointer;
}
```

When it is called, we create a local variable named `buffer` and then create a pointer to our `buffer`. Our function then returns the pointer. As we discussed earlier, the pointer is copied, but that simply makes a copy of `buffer`'s address. The new pointer still points at `buffer`. However, when the function ends, buffer is deleted. This leaves us with a pointer that now points to an undefined piece of memory.

OBJECTS

All the language features we've discussed so far come from C. However, with the introduction of objects, we leave C behind and enter the world of Objective-C.

Superficially, an object combines the data management of structs with a set of related functions (though in this case we call them methods). Under the hood, that's exactly how they are implemented; however, objects give us several advantages over generic C code.

ENCAPSULATION

Encapsulation is one of the main advantages of object-oriented code. Objects should hide away much of their complexity, only exposing those functions and values that a developer needs to use them effectively.

To put it another way, objects function as black boxes. They have a public interface, which describes all the methods and values that can be accessed from the outside. The actual implementation of the object may include any number of private instance variables and methods; however, you shouldn't need to know anything about these details in order to use the object in your code.

Since Objective-C is a highly dynamic, reflexive programming language, the public interface is more of a suggestion than a strict rule of law. You can always gain access to hidden instance variables and methods, but doing so breaks encapsulation. This is bad. Sure, it may make things easier in the short term, but you're probably setting yourself up for long-term pain.

In an ideal world, an object's interface should remain static and unchanging. You can add new methods over time, but you shouldn't remove or alter any existing methods. The interior details, however, are fair game. The object's developer may completely redesign the implementation from one build to the next, and as long as the rest of your code only interacts with the object through its interface, everything will continue to function properly.

Of course, we live in the real world, and we often need to alter an object's interface, especially during early development. This isn't a big deal if you're the only one using the object—but if other people depend on your classes, you will need some way of coordinating these changes with them.

Apple, for example, will occasionally mark methods as deprecated. These methods will continue to operate as normal; however, developers should stop using them, because they will disappear in some future release. This gives developers an opportunity to redesign their applications before these changes take effect.

INHERITANCE

Inheritance is the second main benefit of object-oriented code. One class can inherit the instance variables and methods of another—and can then modify those methods or add new methods and instance variables to further specialize the new class. Most importantly, we can still use the subclasses wherever we could have used the superclasses.

Say, for example, we have a class called Vehicle. This contains all the common features of a vehicle: methods to allow you to set or retrieve the driver, passengers, cargo, current location, destination, and so on. You might even have some methods to query the vehicle's capabilities: canOperateOnLand, canOperateOnWater, canFly, cruiseSpeed, and so on.

We could then create subclasses that all inherit from Vehicle—Boat, Airplane, and Car. The Boat subclass would override the canOperateOnWater method to return YES. Airplane would similarly override canFly.

Finally, we might make Maserati and Yugo subclasses of Car. Maserati's cruise speed would return 150 MPH, while Yugo's would return 15 MPH (or something close to that, I'm sure).

FIGURE 2.1 Part of the `UIView` class hierarchy

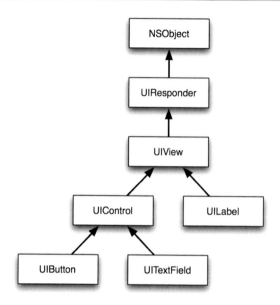

Then let's say we have a function that consumes vehicles: `canVehicleReach LocationInTime(Vehicle* vehicle, Location* location, Time* deadline)`. We could pass any instance of `Boat`, `Airplane`, `Car`, `Maserati`, or `Yugo` to this function. Similarly, we could pass any `Car`, `Maserati`, or `Yugo` object to the `estimatedTime ToFinishIndy500(Car* sampleCar)` function.

We will frequently run into inheritance and class hierarchies when we interact with Cocoa Touch view objects (**Figure 2.1**). `UIView` inherits from `UIResponder`, which inherits from `NSObject`. `NSObject` is a root class—almost all other objects inherit from it. There are a few exceptions (e.g., `NSProxy`) but these are unusual corner cases.

The `NSObject` root class ensures that all objects have a basic set of methods (memory management, testing for equality, testing for class membership, and the like). Next, `UIResponder` adds an interface for objects that respond to motion and touch events, allowing them to participate in the responder chain. Finally, `UIView` adds support for managing and displaying rectangular regions on the screen.

Figure 2.1 also shows a few subclasses of `UIView`. As you can see, some screen elements (like `UILabel`) inherit directly from `UIView`. Others (`UIButton` and `UIText Field`) inherit from `UIControl`, which adds support for registering targets for events, and for dispatching action messages when the events occur.

ABSTRACT **CLASSES**

In our sample class hierarchy, Vehicle, Boat, Airplane, and Car may be implemented as abstract classes. An abstract class is a class that cannot be instantiated into an object (or, at least, one that is not typically instantiated). Often it leaves one or more methods undefined. To use the abstract class, you first create a subclass that fully defines all the required methods. You can then create instances of that subclass.

Objective-C does not provide explicit support for abstract classes. However, we can create informal abstract classes by throwing exceptions in the undefined methods. Check out the documentation for NSCoder to see an abstract class in action.

Let's look at a concrete example. UIView has a method called addSubview:. This lets you add another UIVew to be displayed inside the current view. Since UILabel, UIButton, and UITextField all inherit from UIView (either directly or indirectly), they can all be added using the addSubview: method. In addition, they also inherit addSubview:. In theory, you could add a subview to your button or text field (though it's hard to imagine a situation where this would be useful). More practically, the subclasses also inherit the UIView's frame property. This allows you to set its size and position within the superview's coordinate system. Everything that inherits from UIView (either directly or indirectly) has a frame.

BROWSING THE **SUPERCLASS'S METHODS**

If you look at UIButton's class reference, you will not find any information about the frame property. That's because the class reference only shows the new methods declared for that particular class. So, how do you find all the inherited methods?

At the very top of the class reference, you see a line labeled "Inherits from." This lists the complete chain of superclasses going all the way back to NSObject. By slowly walking back along the inheritance chain, you can look through all available methods and properties.

INSTANTIATING AN OBJECT

Objective-C uses two-step creation of objects. First you allocate memory on the heap. Next, you initialize that memory region with the object's initial values. The first step is done with the alloc class method. The second is done with init or one of its siblings.

For example, the following line will create an empty NSString object:

```
NSString* myString = [[NSString alloc] init];
```

There are a few key points worth noting here. First, we declare our NSString variable as a pointer. It will point to the memory address where the object's data is stored on the heap.

As we will see shortly, Objective-C methods are called using square brackets. Here, we are nesting the alloc method inside the init method. This is important, since many classes are implemented using class clusters. Here the API describes a single class, but the actual implementation uses two or more variations on the class. Different versions are created and used under different circumstances, often to improve performance. However, all that complexity is hidden from the developer.

Since init (and friends) may return a new object, it is vitally important that you save the value returned by init, not the value returned by alloc. Nesting the init and alloc methods ensures that you will save the proper object.

It turns out that NSString is actually a class cluster. We can see this by breaking up the steps as shown:

```
// Create an empty string
NSString* allocString = [NSString alloc];
NSLog(@"allocString: pointer = %p, class = %@",
      allocString, allocString.class);
NSString* initString = [allocString init];
NSLog(@"initString: pointer = %p, class = %@",
      initString, initString.class);
```

NSLog() works very similarly to printf(). The first argument is a literal NSString. As we saw earlier, double quotes create C-style strings. By adding the @ before the first double quote, we tell the compiler to generate an NSString instead.

Next, NSLog scans through that string looking for placeholders. For the most part, these placeholders are identical to those used by printf(). There are some small changes, however. For example, %@ is used to display objects.

Basically, this code prints the value of the class's pointer and the class name to the console after both alloc and init. If you run this code, it will produce the following output (note that the actual pointer values will undoubtedly change):

```
allocString: pointer = 0x4e032a0, class = NSPlaceholderString
initString: pointer = 0x1cb334, class = NSCFString
```

As you can see, both the pointer and the class change after init is called. Furthermore, our NSString is actually a member of the NSCFString subclass.

MULTIPLE INITIALIZATION METHODS

An object may have more than one initialization method. NSString has several: init, initWithString:, initWithFormat:, initWithContentsOfFile:encoding:error:, and more. Each of these provides alternate ways for setting the string's initial value. The complete list can be found in the NSString class reference.

In addition, NSString has a number of convenience methods—class methods that typically start with the word string: string, stringWithString:, stringWith Format:, stringWithContentsOfFile:encoding:error:, and others. They combine the allocation and initialization steps into a single method.

While [NSString string] and [[NSString alloc] init] may seem similar, there is a subtle but significant difference in how the system manages the resulting object's memory. In the past, we had to carefully use each method correctly. Fortunately, if you are compiling your applications with ARC, these differences disappear and you can freely use whichever method best fits your application and programming style.

DEFINING A CLASS

We define a class in two steps: the interface and the implementation. The interface is ordinarily declared in the class's header file (filename ending in .h). This allows us to easily import our class declaration into any other part of our project. The interface should define all the information needed to effectively use the class—this includes the public methods (methods that can be called from outside the class) as well as the class's superclass and possibly its instance variables.

This may seem a bit odd. After all, one of the main uses of objects is encapsulation. Shouldn't the instance variables be hidden inside the implementation?

Well, yes. In an ideal world they would be. However, earlier versions of the compiler needed this information to lay out the memory of any subclasses. With Objective-C 2.0, we can use properties to help get around this limitation. When you're developing for iOS or 64-bit applications for Mac OS X 10.5 and later, you can automatically synthesize the instance variables for your properties. We will discuss properties in more depth in the next section. Just be aware that the instance variables declared in the interface may not tell the whole story.

The interface starts with an @interface keyword and ends with @end. The format is shown here:

```
@interface ClassName : SuperClassName {

    // Declare instance variables here.

    // These are optional in iOS if properties are used.

}

// Declare public methods and properties here.

@end
```

Every class in your application needs a unique class name. If you're building a library that will be used in other projects, you will want to prefix your class names to ensure that they won't conflict with other libraries and frameworks. Apple's frameworks follow this advice, typically beginning their class names with either NS or UI.

Each class also has one and only one superclass. You will usually use NSObject, unless you are explicitly subclassing another class. The instance variables are defined within the curly brackets, and the instance methods are defined after the brackets.

The actual code is stored in the implementation file (filename ending in .m). Like the interface, the implementation begins with an @implementation keyword and ends with @end. It will contain only the method and property definitions.

```
@implementation ClassName

// Define methods and properties here.

@end
```

We will discuss methods and properties in more detail in the next section.

METHODS

Once all the bells and whistles are stripped away, an Objective-C method is simply a C function. Therefore, everything we learned about functions applies equally to methods. There is one important difference, however. When we call a C function, the function and its arguments are connected at compile time (static binding). In contrast, in Objective-C we are not actually calling the method; we are sending a message to the object, asking it to call the method. The object then uses the method name to select the actual function. This connection of selector, function, and arguments is done at runtime (dynamic binding).

This has a number of practical implications. First and foremost, you can send any method to any object. After all, we may dynamically add the method's implementation at runtime, or we may forward the method to another object altogether.

More commonly, we use this feature along with the object identifier type id, which can refer to any object (including Class objects). Notice that we do not use an asterisk when declaring id variables. The id type is already defined as a pointer to an object.

```
id myString = @"This is a string";      // This is an NSString.
id myStringClass = [myString class];    // This is a class object.
```

The one-two punch of id types and dynamic binding lets us avoid a lot of the complex, verbose constructions that statically bound languages ordinarily require, but it's not just about running around naked and free; as developers, we typically know more about our application than the compiler does.

For example, if we put only NSString objects into an array, we know that all the objects in that array will respond to the length message. In C++ or Java, we would need to convince the compiler to let us make that call (usually by casting the object). Objective-C (for the most part) trusts that we know what we're doing.

Still, it's not all Wild West shooting from the hip. Xcode's compiler and static analyzer do an excellent job of analyzing our code and finding common errors (like misspelled method names), even when writing highly dynamic code.

SENDING MESSAGES TO NIL

In Objective-C it is perfectly legal to send messages to nil. This often comes as a shock to people from a Java background. In Java, if you call a method on null (null and nil are identical, a pointer with a value of 0—basically a pointer that points to nothing), your application will crash. In Objective-C, the method simply returns 0 or nil (depending on the return type).

Newcomers to Objective-C often argue that this hides errors. By crashing immediately, Java prevents the program from continuing in a bad state and possibly producing faulty output or crashing inexplicably at some later point in the application. There is a grain of truth to this. However, once you accept the fact that you can send messages to nil, you can use it to produce simple, elegant algorithms.

Let's look at one of the more common design patterns. Imagine an RSS reader that must download a hundred different feeds. First you call a method to download the XML file. Then you parse the XML. Due to potential networking problems, the first method is likely to be highly unreliable. In Java, we would need to check and make sure that we received a valid result.

```
XML xml = RSS.getXMLforURL(myURL);
// Make sure we have a valid xml object.
if (xml != null) {
    xml. parse();

    ...
}
```

In Objective-C, those checks are unnecessary. If the XML is nil, the method call simply does nothing.

```
XML* xml = [RSS getXMLforURL:myURL];
[xml parse];

...
```

Also, let's face it, null pointers are a common source of bugs in Java applications. Java's null pointer violates the language's otherwise strict static typing. If you can assign it to an object variable, you should be able to treat it just like any other object. That includes calling instance methods and receiving reasonable results.

CALLING METHODS

Objective-C methods are called using square brackets. Inside the brackets, we have the receiver and the message. The receiver can be any variable that evaluates to an object (including `self`), the `super` keyword, or a class name (for class methods). The message is the name of the method and any arguments.

```
[receiver message]
```

In C, the method's arguments are all grouped together in parentheses after the function's name. Objective-C handles them somewhat differently. If the method doesn't take any arguments, the method name is simply a single word (usually a camel-case word with a lowercase first letter).

```
[myObject myFunctionWithNoArguments];
```

If the method takes a single argument, the name ends in a colon (:) and the argument immediately follows it.

```
[myObject myFunctionWithOneArgument:myArgument];
```

Multiple arguments are spread throughout the method name. Usually, the method name will give a clue about the type of argument expected in each position.

```
[myObject myFunctionWithFirstArgument:first
                 secondArgument:second
                  thirdArgument:third];
```

When referring to the method, we typically concatenate all the parts of its name without spaces or arguments. For example, the above method is named `myFuncti onWithFirstArgument:secondArgument:thirdArgument:`.

While this style may seem awkward at first, it can be a great aid when coding. It's almost impossible to accidentally place the arguments in the wrong order (something I do all the time in C-like languages). Interleaving the method name and arguments also encourages the use of longer, more expressive method names, and—for my money—that's always a good thing.

Methods are normally declared in the class's `@interface` block and defined in the `@implementation` block. Like C functions, the declaration is simply the method signature followed by a semicolon. The definition is the method signature followed by a block of code within curly brackets.

Method signatures start with either a + or – character. The – is used for instance methods, while the + is used for class methods. Next we have the return type in parentheses, and then the method name. Arguments are defined in place within the name. Simply follow the colon with the argument type in parentheses and the argument's name.

```
- (void)simple;                    // No arguments, no return
                                   // value.

- (int)count;                      // No arguments, returns an
                                   // integer.

- (NSString*) nameForID:(int)id;   // Takes an integer argument.
                                   // Returns a string object.
                                   // Class method with multiple
                                   // arguments.
+ (NSString*) fullNameGivenFirstName:(NSString*)first
                          middleName:(NSString*)middle
                            lastName:(NSString*)last;
```

Objective-C methods always have two hidden arguments: self and _cmd. The self argument refers to the method's receiver and can be used to access properties or call other instance methods. The _cmd argument is the method's selector.

The selector is a unique identifier of type SEL that is used to look up methods at runtime. You can create a SEL from a method's name using @selector(). You can also get the string representation of a SEL using NSStringFromSelector().

The connection between C functions and Objective-C methods really becomes clear when you start dynamically adding methods to an object, as shown:

```
// Defined before the @implementation block.
void myFunction(id self, SEL _cmd) {
    NSLog(@"Executing my method %@ on %@",
        NSStringFromSelector(_cmd),
        self);
}
// Defined inside the @implementation block.
+ (void)addMethod {
    SEL selector = @selector(myMethod);
    class_addMethod(self, selector, (IMP)myFunction, "v@:");
}
```

Running the class method addMethod will add myMethod to the current class at runtime. You can then call [myObject myMethod], and it will call the function myFunction(myObject, @selector(myMethod)).

INITIALIZERS

We've already discussed an object's two-step instantiation. Now let's look at the initializer methods themselves. These are just methods like any other method we may write; however, there are a few conventions we need to follow to get everything right.

First, there's the name. All the initializers traditionally start with init. Do yourself (and anyone who might maintain your code in the future) a huge favor and always follow this naming convention.

Next, there are two methods that require special attention: the class's designated initializer and the superclass's designated initializer.

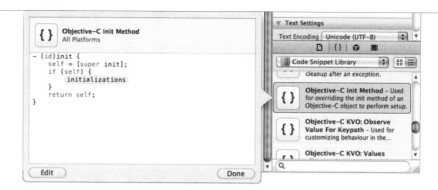

FIGURE 2.2 The init method code snippet

Each class should have a designated initializer, a single method responsible for performing all of the object's setup and initialization. Typically, this is the initializer with the largest number of arguments. All the other initializers should call the designated initializer—letting it do all the heavy lifting.

Similarly, your designated initializer needs to call your superclass's designated initializer. By chaining our class hierarchy together, designated initializer to designated initializer, we guarantee that the object gets initialized properly all the way up the class hierarchy.

Finally, your class should always override its superclass's designated initializer. This will re-route any calls to any of the superclass's initializers (or any initializer anywhere in the class hierarchy) back through your designated initializer and then up the class hierarchy.

Let's take a concrete example. Imagine we are making an Employee class. This will be a subclass of NSObject. NSObject has only one initializer, init. This is (by default) its designated initializer. Our Employee class, on the other hand, will have three instance variables: _firstName, _lastName, and _id. Its designated initializer will set all three values.

Let's start by pulling a blank init method from the Code Snippet library. At the bottom of the Utilities area, click the Code Snippet tab (it looks like a pair of curly braces) and then scroll down until you find the Objective-C init method (**Figure 2.2**). You can click and drag this out into your implementation block.

Modify the template as shown here. You will also need to copy the method's signature into the Employee class's interface block.

```objc
// Designated initializer.
- (id)initWithFirstName:(NSString *)firstName
               lastName:(NSString *)lastName
                     id:(int)id {
    self = [super init];
    if (self) {
            _firstName = [firstName retain];
        _lastName = [lastName retain];
        _id = id;
    }
    return self;
}
```

Usually, when we call a method on an object, the object first searches for a matching method defined in the object's class. If it cannot find a match, it moves to the superclass and continues searching up the class hierarchy. The super keyword allows us to explicitly start searching for methods defined in self's superclass. Often when you override an existing method, you still want to call the original implementation. The super keyword lets you access that version of the method.

So, this method starts by assigning the return value of [super init] to the self variable. This method call will ignore the current implementation of init and begin searching up the class hierarchy for an older implementation.

Assigning the return value to self may seem odd, but it is really just a variation on an issue we've seen before. Remember that when we discussed initializing objects, we always nested the init and alloc calls, because init might return a different object than alloc. This code deals with the same basic problem. The self argument contains the value returned by alloc. However, [super init] may return a different value. We need to make sure our code initializes and returns the value returned by [super init].

New Objective-C programmers often feel uncomfortable assigning new values to self, but remember, it is one of our method's hidden arguments. This means it is just a local variable. There's nothing magical about it—we can assign new values to it, just like we would any other variable.

Next, the `if` statement checks to see if [`super init`] returned `nil`. As long as we have a valid object, we perform our initialization—assigning the method's arguments to the object's instance variables. Finally, our initializer returns `self`.

So far, so good. We have a designated initializer that calls our superclass's designated initializer. Now we just need to override our superclass's designated initializer.

```
// Override superclass's designated initializer.

- (id) init {

    // This must go through our designated initializer.

    return [self initWithFirstName:@"John" lastName:@"Doe" id:-1];
}
```

This method must call our object's designated initializer. Here, we simply pass in reasonable default values. If we make any other initializers, they must also follow this pattern and call `initWithfirstName:lastName:id:` to actually set our instance variables.

NOTE: At the risk of repeating myself, let me just emphasize that you should only set instance variables in the default initializer. All other initializers should go through the default initializer. They should not set any variables or do any other initialization themselves.

CONVENIENCE METHODS

Many classes have convenience methods that instantiate objects with a single method call. Most often, these methods mirror the initializer methods.

For example, our `Employee` class may have a method `employeeWithFirstName:lastName:id`. This acts as a thin wrapper around our designated initializer. Other convenience methods may involve more-complex computations, either before or after calling the designated initializer—but the basic ideas remain the same.

```
+ (id) employeeWithFirstName:(NSString *)firstName
                     lastName:(NSString *)lastName
                           id:(int)id {
    return [[self alloc] initWithFirstName:firstName
```

```
                                lastName:lastName
                                        id:id];
}
```

There is an important convention in this sample code: We use `[self alloc]` and not `[Employee alloc]` in this method. Remember, `self` refers to the message's receiver. Since this is a class method, `self` should be set to the `Employee` class. However, let's say we create a subclass called `PartTimeEmployee`. We could call `employeeWithFirstName:lastName:id` on `PartTimeEmployee` and everything will still work as expected. By calling `[self alloc]`, our implementation correctly allocates and initializes a `PartTimeEmployee` object. If, however, we had hard-coded the class, it would always return `Employee` objects.

```
// Returns an Employee object.
id firstPerson = [Employee employeeWithFirstName:@"Mary"
                                        lastName:@"Smith"
                                              id:10];

// Returns a PartTimeEmployee object.
id secondPerson = [PartTimeEmployee employeeWithFirstName:@"John"
                                                 lastName:@"Jones"
                                                       id:11];
```

PROPERTIES

By default, an object's instance variables are not accessible outside the object's implementation block. You could declare these variables as @public, but that is not recommended. Instead, if you want to let outside code access these values, you should write accessor methods.

Historically, accessor methods were largely boring boilerplate code that just passed values into and out of your class. Thanks to manual memory management, they were often tedious to write and maintain. Fortunately, with Objective-C 2.0, Apple has provided a tool for automating the creation of accessors: properties.

We declare a property in the class's interface, as shown:

```
@property (attributes) variableType propertyName;
```

The attributes determine how our accessors are implemented. The most common attributes are described in the Common Property Attributes table (**Table 2.2**). For a full list, see The Objective-C Programming Language, Declared Properties, in Apple's documentation.

TABLE 2.2 Common Property Attributes

nonatomic	Synthesizes accessors that are not thread safe.
readwrite	Synthesizes both a getter and a setter for the property.
readonly	Only synthesizes a getter for the property.
copy	The setter stores a copy of the assigned value.
weak	The setter stores a zeroing weak reference to the assigned value (see "Memory Management").
strong	The setter stores a strong reference to the assigned value (see "Memory Management").
assign	The setter stores the assigned value but does not perform any memory management. This should only be used for storing non-object data (e.g., floats, ints, structs, etc.). Objective-C objects should use strong or weak attributes instead.

Properties are assign and readwrite by default. Also, for whatever reason, there is no explicit atomic attribute. Any attribute that does not have the nonatomic attribute will be constructed using synchronized, thread-safe getters and setters. Of course, this synchronization comes with a slight performance cost.

NOTE: Before iOS 5.0, properties often used retain attributes to handle manual memory management. However, retain attributes are no longer valid when compiling under ARC. See the "Memory Management" section, later in this chapter, for more information.

The @property declaration automatically defines the accessor methods, as shown here:

```
// This property
@property (nonatomic, copy) NSString* firstName;
// declares these methods
- (NSString*)firstName;
- (void)setFirstName:(NSString*)firstName;
```

The getter simply uses the property's name and returns the instance variable's current value. The setter adds set to the front of the property name and will assign the argument (or a copy of the argument) to the instance variable.

Now, we need to tell the compiler to implement these methods. Typically, we will add a @synthesize directive in the class's @implementation block.

```
@synthesize firstName;
```

This generates the requested methods (if they are not already implemented—you can still choose to create manual versions if you wish). By default, the accessor methods will get and set the value stored in the class's firstName instance variable. If you have already declared this variable in the @interface block, the accessors will use it. Otherwise, @synthesize will create the instance variable for you.

Alternatively, we can specify a different name for our instance variables. The following code will use _firstName instead of firstName.

```
@synthesize firstName = _firstName;
```

I always rename my instance variables as shown above. The underscore, by convention, labels the instance variable as a private value that should not be accessed directly. This is exactly what we want. In general, you should access your instance variables through their properties—even within the class's @implementation block. If you use the default instance variable name, it's too easy to forget and directly access the variable by mistake.

@synthesize VS. @dynamic

The @synthesize directive is not, strictly speaking, required. You won't need it if you implement all the accessors yourself. Alternatively, you could use the @dynamic directive. This basically tells the compiler, "Hey, trust me. These methods will be there."

You use @dynamic when you plan to provide the method at runtime (using techniques like dynamic loading or dynamic method resolution) or— more likely—when you are redeclaring a property from the class's super-class. In both cases, @dynamic suppresses any warnings about the missing accessor methods.

You can use properties either by calling the generated methods directly or by using the dot notation, as shown:

```
// These are identical
NSString* name = [myClass firstName];
NSString* name = myClass.firstName;
// These are also identical
[myClass setFirstName:@"Bob"];
myClass.firstName = @"Bob";
```

You can also access the property from within the class's instance method definitions, using the self variable.

```
// These are identical
NSString* name = [self firstName];
NSString* name = self.firstName;
// These are also identical
[self setFirstName:@"Bob"];
self.firstName = @"Bob";
```

Using the properties helps produce clean, consistent code. More importantly, it ensures that techniques like key-value observing work properly. There is, however, one place where you should access the instance variables directly: inside your class's designated initializer.

> **NOTE:** Many old-school Objective-C programmers seem to hate the dot notation with a fury usually reserved for telemarketers. They think it is unnecessary and confusing. Personally, I like the fact that it mirrors the way we get and set values in C-style structs. This makes a clear distinction between accessors and other methods. However, your mileage may vary, and you should use whichever notation feels the most comfortable.

In general, your initializers should avoid doing anything that might generate errors, call external methods, or otherwise eat up computational time. Admittedly, your properties should be relatively straightforward assignments without any unexpected side effects, so using the properties probably won't kill you. Still, there's always the chance that someone will eventually add a custom setter to one of the properties, inadvertently making your initialization method unstable. So direct assignment's not a bad idea.

PROTOCOLS

Some object-oriented languages (most notably C++ and Python) allow multiple inheritance, where a class can inherit behaviors from more than one superclass. This can create problems, especially when both parents define identical methods. This may sound like a rare corner case—but it accidentally happens all the time. If the classes share a common ancestor (and all classes share a root ancestor), both superclasses will have copies of the common ancestor's methods. If you override one of these methods anywhere in either of the superclasses' hierarchies, your subclass will inherit multiple implementations for that method.

Other languages (like Java and Objective-C) do not allow multiple inheritance, largely because of these added complexities. However, there are times when you still want to capture common behaviors across a number of otherwise unrelated classes. This is particularly true in static, strongly typed languages like Java.

Let's say you want to have an array of objects, and you want to iterate over each object, calling its makeNoise() method. One approach would be to make a NoisyObject superclass and have all the objects in your array inherit from that class. While this sounds good in theory, it is not always possible. Sometimes your objects must inherit from another, existing class hierarchy. In C++, no problem. Your class could inherit from both. In Java, we can simulate multiple inheritances using a Noisy interface. Any class implementing this interface must also implement the makeNoise() method.

In Objective-C, this is somewhat less of a concern. We don't have Java's strict static typing (and all the extra convolutions that come with it). After all, we can already send any message to any object. So, this is really a matter of communicating our intent. You could just make sure all the objects in the array implement the makeNoise method and you're good to go. However, we often want to explicitly capture these requirements. In this case, protocols fill a similar role to Java's interfaces—but they have other uses as well.

A protocol declares a number of methods. By default, these methods are required. Any class adopting the protocol must implement all of the required methods. However, we can also declare methods as optional. The adopting class may implement optional methods, but they are not required.

At first glance, optional methods may seem a bit odd. After all, any object can implement any method; we don't need the protocol's permission. However, it's important to remember that Objective-C's protocols are really about communicating developer intent. Developers most often use optional methods when developing protocols for delegates. Here they document the methods that the delegate could override to monitor or modify the delegating class's behavior. We will examine this topic in more depth when we discuss delegates later in this chapter.

ADOPTING PROTOCOLS

To adopt a protocol, simply add a comma-separated list of protocols inside angled brackets after the superclass declaration in your class's @interface block.

```
@interface ClassName : SuperClassName
<list, of, protocols, to, adopt> {
    ...
@end
```

You must also implement any required methods that have not already been implemented. Notice that you do not need to declare these methods in the @interface block. The protocol takes care of that for you.

DECLARING PROTOCOLS

Protocol declarations look a lot like class declarations, only without the block for instance variables. Like the class's @interface block, protocol declarations are normally placed in a header file—either their own header file or the header file of a closely related class (e.g., delegate protocols are often declared in the delegating class's header).

```
@protocol ProtocolName

    // Declare required methods here.

    // Protocol methods are required by default.

    @optional

    // Declare optional methods here.

    // All methods declared after the @optional keyword are

    // optional.

    @required

    // Declare additional required methods here.

    // All methods declared after the @required keyword are required

    // again.

@end
```

As you can see, you can use the @optional and @required keywords to partition your methods as you see fit. All methods after an @optional keyword (until the next @required keyword) are optional. All methods after a @required keyword (until the next @optional keyword) are required. Methods are required by default.

One protocol can also incorporate other protocols. You simply list these in angled brackets after the protocol name. Any class that adopts a protocol also adopts all the protocols it incorporates.

```
@protocol ProtocolName <additional, protocols, to, incorporate>

    ...

@end
```

CATEGORIES AND EXTENSIONS

Categories allow you to add new methods to existing classes—even classes from libraries or frameworks whose source code you otherwise cannot access. There are a number of uses for categories. First, we can extend a class's behavior without resorting to rampant subclassing. This is often useful when you just want to add one or two helper functions to an existing class—for example, adding `push:` and `pop` methods to an `NSMutableArray`.

You can also add methods to classes farther up the class hierarchy. These methods are then inherited down the class hierarchy just like any other methods. You can even modify `NSObject` or other root classes—adding behaviors to every object in your application. In general, however, you should avoid making such broad changes to the language. They may have unintended consequences. At the very least, they will undoubtedly make the code somewhat confusing to anyone else who has to work with it.

Lastly, you can use categories to break large, complex classes into more manageable chunks, where each category contains a set of related methods. The Cocoa Touch frameworks often do this, declaring specialized helper methods in their own categories.

CREATING CATEGORIES

We create categories much like we create new classes. The `@interface` block looks almost identical to its class counterpart. There are only two differences. First, instead of declaring a superclass, we provide the category name in parentheses. This can, optionally, be followed by a list of new protocols adopted by the category. Second, there is no block for declaring instance variables. You cannot add instance variables with a category. If you need additional instance variables, you must make a subclass instead.

```
@interface ClassName (CategoryName) <new protocols>

// Declare methods here.

@end
```

The @implementation block is even closer to the class version. The only change is the addition of the category name in parentheses.

```
@implementation ClassName (CategoryName)
// Implement the extensions methods here.
}
```

Here is a simple Stack category on the NSMutableArray class.

```
// In Stack.h
#import <Foundation/Foundation.h>
@interface NSMutableArray (Stack)
- (void)push:(id)object;
- (id)pop;
@end
// In Stack.m
#import "Stack.h"
@implementation NSMutableArray (Stack)
- (void)push:(id)object {
    [self addObject:object];
}
- (id)pop {
    // Return nil if the stack is empty.
    if (self.count == 0) return nil;
    // Remove the last object from the array and return it.
    id object = [self lastObject];
    [self removeLastObject];
    return object;
}
@end
```

An extension is very similar to a category, with two significant differences. First, it does not have a name. Second, the methods declared in the extension must be implemented in the class's main @implementation block. Extensions are most often used to declare private methods. They are placed in the class's main implementation file above the @implementation block.

```
@interface ClassName ()
// Declare private methods here.
@end
```

Since the extension is declared before the @synthesize call, you can declare new properties in an extension. As with other properties, we do not need to declare the instance variable in the header—the @synthesize call will create it for us. This allows us to hide private instance variables from the public interface.

You can even declare a property as readonly in the public interface, and redeclare it as readwrite in the extension. This will generate public getter and private setter methods.

NOTE: When redeclaring properties, you can only change the readwrite/readonly attributes. All other attributes must match exactly. This sometimes leads to somewhat strange attribute combinations. For example, `@property (readonly, copy) NSString* id`.

MEMORY **MANAGEMENT**

I'm not going to lie to you. Before iOS 5.0, memory management was undoubtedly the most difficult part of iOS development. Here's the problem in a nutshell. Whenever you create a variable, you set aside some space in memory. For local variables, you typically use memory on the stack. This memory is managed automatically. When a function returns, any local variables defined within that function are automatically removed from memory.

This sounds great, but the stack has two important limitations. First, it has a very limited amount of space, and if you run out of memory your application will crash. Second, it is hard to share these variables. Remember, functions pass their arguments and returns by value. That means everything going into or out of a function gets copied. This isn't too bad if you are just tossing around a few ints or doubles. But what happens when you start moving around large, complex data structures? Pass an argument from function to function, and you find yourself copying the copy of a copy. This can quickly waste a lot of time and memory.

Alternatively, we can declare variables on the heap and use a pointer to refer to the memory space. This has several advantages. We have considerably more space available on the heap, and we can pass pointers around freely; only the pointer gets copied, not the entire data structure.

However, whenever we use the heap we must manually manage its memory. When we want a new variable, we must request enough space on the heap. Then, when we're done, we must free up that space, allowing it to be reused. This leads to two common memory-related bugs.

First off, you may free the memory but accidentally continue using it. This is called a dangling pointer. These bugs can be difficult to find. Freeing a variable does not necessarily change the actual value stored on the stack. It simply tells the OS that the memory can be used again. This means that pointers to freed memory can appear to work fine. You only get into trouble when the system finally reuses the memory, writing over the old values.

This can cause very strange errors in completely unrelated sections of code. Imagine this: You free Object A's memory from the heap but accidentally continue to use its pointer. Meanwhile, an entirely unrelated section of code requests a new object, Object B, on the heap. It is given a section of memory that partially overwrites Object A. Now you change a value on Object A. This saves new data somewhere inside Object B—putting B into an invalid state. The next time you try to read from Object B, you get errors (or possibly very, very strange results).

The second common memory error occurs when you forget to free up memory. This is called a memory leak, and it can cause your application to grab more and more memory as it continues to run.

On the one hand, this isn't necessarily all that bad. All the memory will be freed when the application exits. I've even heard of server software that deliberately leaks all its memory. After all, if you're running thousands of copies of the server anyway, it may be easier to periodically kill and respawn individual copies than to risk crashes from dangling pointers.

However, on the iOS we do not have that luxury. All iOS devices have extremely limited memory. Use too much and your app will shut down. Correct and effective memory management is therefore a vital skill.

For us, our main concern is objects. All objects are created on the heap. Yes, you can create variables for C data types or structs on the heap as well, but this is very rare (consult a good book on C programming for more details). For the most part, iOS memory management means managing the lifecycle of our objects.

OBJECTS AND RETAIN COUNTS

One of the biggest problems is simply determining which portion of the code should have responsibility for freeing up an object's memory. In simple examples, the solution always appears trivial. However, once you start passing objects around, saving them in other objects' instance variables or placing them in collections, things get murky fast.

To get around this problem, Objective-C programmers traditionally used reference counting. When we created an object, it started with a reference count of 1. We could increase the reference count by calling `retain` on the object. Similarly, we could decrease the reference count by calling `release`. When the reference count hit 0, the system deleted the object from memory.

This made it possible to pass objects around without worrying about ownership. If you wanted to hold onto an object, you retained it. When you were done, you released it. As long as you got all the retains and releases correct (not to mention autoreleases and autorelease pools), you could avoid both dangling pointers and memory leaks.

Of course, getting it right was never as simple as it seemed. Objective-C's memory management conventions had a lot of rules and odd corner cases. Furthermore, as developers, we had to get it right 100 percent of the time. So we often resorted to following a robotic set of steps every time we created a new variable. This was tedious. It created a lot of boilerplate code, much of which wasn't strictly necessary, but if we didn't follow every step every single time, we ran the risk of forgetting something when it was really important.

Of course, Apple tried to help. Instruments has a number of tools to track allocations and deallocations and to search for memory leaks. In recent versions of Xcode, the static analyzer has gotten better and better at analyzing our code and finding memory management errors.

Which raises the question: If the static analyzer could find these errors, why couldn't it just fix them? After all, memory management is a tedious, detail-oriented task that follows a strict set of rules—exactly the sort of task that compilers excel at. Apple took their compiler and analyzer technologies and applied them to this task. The result is a brand new technology for managing memory: Automatic Reference Counting (ARC).

INTRODUCING ARC

ARC is a compiler feature that provides automated memory management for Objective-C objects. Conceptually, ARC follows the retain and release memory management conventions (see Apple's Memory Management Programming Guide for more information). As your project compiles, ARC analyzes the code and automatically adds the necessary retain, release, and autorelease method calls.

For developers, this is very good news. We no longer need to worry about managing the memory ourselves. Instead, we can focus our time and attention on the truly interesting parts of our application, like implementing new features, streamlining the user interface, or improving stability and performance.

In addition, Apple has worked to improve the performance of memory management under ARC. For example, ARC's automated retain and release calls are 2.5 times faster than their manual memory management equivalents. The new @autoreleasepool blocks are 6 times faster than the old NSAutoReleasePool objects, and even objc_msgSend() is 33 percent faster. This last is particularly important, since objc_msgSend() is used to dispatch every single Objective-C method call in your application.

All in all, ARC makes Objective-C easier to learn, more productive, simpler to maintain, safer, more stable, and faster. That's what I call a win-win-win-win-win-win situation. For the most part, we don't need to even think about memory management. We just write our code, creating and using our objects. ARC handles all the messy details for us.

ARC VS. GARBAGE COLLECTION

ARC is not garbage collection. They share a goal—both technologies automate memory management, making it easier to develop our applications. However, they use very different means. Garbage collection tracks objects at runtime. When it determines that an object is no longer in use, it deletes the object from memory.

Unfortunately, this creates several potential performance problems. The infrastructure needed to monitor and delete objects adds overhead to your application. We also have very little control over when a garbage collector initiates its scan. While modern garbage collectors try to minimize their impact on an application's performance, they are inherently non-deterministic. This means the garbage collector may cause your application to slow down or pause randomly during the application's execution.

ARC, on the other hand, handles all the memory management at compile time. There is no additional overhead at runtime—in fact, due to numerous optimizations, ARC code runs faster than manually managed memory. In addition, the memory management system is completely deterministic— meaning there will be no unexpected surprises.

FINDING AND PREVENTING MEMORY CYCLES

While ARC represents a huge step forward in memory management, it doesn't completely free developers from thinking about memory issues. It's still possible to create memory leaks under ARC—ARC is still susceptible to retain cycles.

To understand this problem, we have to peek a bit under the hood. By default, all variables in ARC use strong references. When you assign an object to a strong reference, the system automatically retains the object. When you remove the object from the reference (by assigning a new object to the variable or by assigning a nil value to the variable), the system releases the object.

A retain cycle occurs when two objects directly or indirectly refer to each other using strong references. This often happens in parent/child hierarchies, when the child object holds a reference back to the parent.

Imagine I have a person object defined as shown here:

```
@interface Person : NSObject
@property (nonatomic, strong) Person* parent;
@property (nonatomic, strong) Person* child;
+ (void)myMethod;
@end
```

And myMethod is implemented as shown:

```
+ (void)myMethod {
    Person* parent = [[Person alloc] init];
    Person* child = [[Person alloc] init];
        parent.child = child;
    // Do something useful with the parent and child.
}
```

In this example, when we call myMethod, two Person objects are created. Each of them starts with a retain count of 1. We then assign the child object to the parent's child property. This increases the child's retain count to 2.

ARC automatically inserts release calls at the end of our method. These drop the parent's retain count to 0 and the child's retain count to 1. Since the parent's retain count now equals 0, it is deallocated. Again, ARC automatically releases all of parent's properties. So, the child object's retain count also drops to 0 and it is deallocated as well. By the end of the method, all our memory is released, just as we expected.

Now, let's add a retain cycle. Change myMethod as shown here:

```
+ (void)myMethod {
    Person* parent = [[Person alloc] init];
    Person* child = [[Person alloc] init];
        parent.child = child;
    child.parent = parent;
    // Do something useful with the parent and child.
}
```

As before, we create our parent and child objects, each with a reference count of 1. This time, the parent gets a reference to the child, and the child gets a reference to the parent, increasing both reference counts to 2. At the end of our method, ARC automatically releases our objects, dropping both reference counts back to 1. Since neither reference count has been reduced to 0, neither object gets deallocated, and our retain cycle creates a memory leak.

Fortunately, ARC has a solution for us. We simply need to redefine the parent property so that it uses a zeroing weak reference. Basically, this means changing the property attribute from strong to weak.

```
@interface Person : NSObject
@property (nonatomic, weak) Person* parent;
@property (nonatomic, strong) Person* child;
+ (void)myMethod;
@end
```

Zeroing weak references provide two key advantages. First, they do not increment the object's retain count—therefore they do not extend the lifetime of the object. Second, the system automatically sets them back to nil whenever the objects they point to are deallocated. This prevents dangling pointers.

Applications typically have object graphs that branch out from a single root object. We will usually use zeroing weak references when referring to objects back up the graph (anything closer to the graph's root). Additionally, we should use zeroing weak references for all our delegates and data sources (see the "Delegates" section later in this chapter). This is a standard convention in Objective-C, since it helps prevent inadvertent retain cycles.

So far, the cycles we have seen have all been somewhat obvious, but this is not always the case. A retain cycle can include any number of objects—as long as it eventually loops back on itself. Once you get beyond three or four levels of references, tracking possible cycles becomes nearly impossible. Fortunately, our developer tools come to the rescue again.

With Xcode 4.2, Instruments now has the ability to search for retain cycles, and it will even display the retain cycle graphically.

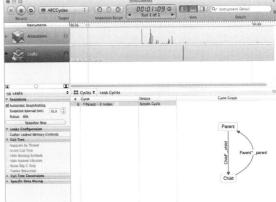

Simply profile your application. Select Product > Profile from the main menu. Select the Leaks template in Instrument's pop-up window and click Profile (**Figure 2.3**). This will launch both Instruments and your app.

Instruments will start up with two diagnostic tools. Allocations tracks memory allocations and deallocations, while Leaks looks for leaked memory. Leaks will appear as red bars in the Leaks instrument. Select the Leaks instrument row, and the details will appear below. In the jump bar, change the detail view from Leaks to Cycles, and Instruments will display your retain cycles (**Figure 2.4**). You can now double-click the offending reference, and Xcode will automatically navigate to it. Fix it (either by changing it to a zeroing weak reference, or by restructuring the flow of our application), and test again. We will discuss Instruments in more detail in Bonus Chapter B (www.freelancemadscience.com/book).

FIGURE 2.3 Selecting the Leaks profile

FIGURE 2.4 Finding and displaying retain cycles

RULES OF THE ROAD

It's incredibly easy to use ARC. Most of the time, we don't need to do anything. All of Xcode 4.2's project templates use ARC by default—though we can enable manual memory management on a per-file basis, if necessary. This lets us freely mix ARC and non-ARC code. ARC can be used on any projects targeting iOS 4.0 and above (with some limitations). And Xcode even has tools for converting non-ARC applications (choose Edit > Refactor > Convert to Objective-C ARC).

For ARC to work properly, the compiler must be able to correctly interpret our intent. This requires a few additional rules to help remove any ambiguity. Don't worry if you don't understand what many of these rules refer to—most rarely occur during day-to-day coding. The important thing is that the compiler will enforce all of these rules, and breaking them will generate errors. This makes the problems easy to find and fix.

All the rules are listed here.

- Don't use object pointers in C structs. Instead, create an Objective-C class to hold the data.

- Don't create a property with a name that begins with "new."

- Don't call the dealloc, retain, release, retainCount, or autorelease methods.

- Don't implement your own retain, release, retainCount, or autorelease methods. You can implement dealloc, but it's usually not necessary.

- When implementing dealloc in ARC, don't call [super dealloc]. The compiler handles this automatically.

- Don't use NSAutoreleasePool objects. Use the new @autoreleasepool{} blocks instead.

- In general, don't cast between id and void*. You must use augmented casts or macros when moving data between Objective-C objects and Core Foundation types (see the next section).

- Don't use NSAllocateObject or NSDeallocateObject.

- Don't use memory zones or NSZone.

ARC AND TOLL-FREE BRIDGING

First, it's important to realize that ARC applies only to Objective-C objects. If you are allocating memory for any C data structures on the heap, you must still manage that memory yourself.

Real problems start to crop up when using Core Foundation data types. Core Foundation is a low-level C API that provides a number of basic data management and OS services. There is also a similar Objective-C framework named Foundation (are you confused yet?). Not surprisingly, Foundation and Core Foundation are closely related. In fact, Foundation provides Objective-C interfaces for many Core Foundation services and data types.

Now here's the cool part. Many Foundation and Core Foundation data types are actually interchangeable. Under the skin, NSString and CFString are identical. We can freely pass a CFString reference to an Objective-C method expecting an NSString—or pass an NSString to a Core Foundation function expecting a CFString. This interoperability is referred to as toll-free bridging (see Apple's Cocoa Fundamentals Guide > Cocoa Objects > Toll-Free Bridging for more information).

Unfortunately, when casting back and forth, memory management quickly becomes confusing. Who is responsible for managing which data? Will we manually manage the memory using CFRetain() and CFRelease(), or will we let ARC take care of it?

There are three basic scenarios we need to be aware of: Core Foundation data returned by Objective-C methods, code that uses Core Foundation memory management functions, and code that transfers data to and from Core Foundation without using any memory management functions.

The first case is easy. If we get access to a Core Foundation object by calling an Objective-C method, we don't need to do anything at all. We can freely cast the data, and the compiler won't generate any errors.

This works because Objective-C methods all follow Objective-C memory management conventions (see Apple's Memory Management Programming Guide for more information). ARC understands these conventions, correctly interprets the data's ownership, and does the right thing.

```
UIImage* myImage = [UIImage imageNamed:@"myPhoto"];

id myCGImage = (id)[myImage CGImage];

[photoArray addObject:myCGImage];
```

In this sample, we call UIImage's CGImage property. This returns a CGImageRef. Then we cast the C data to an Objective-C id and place it in an array. Because we used an Objective-C method to access the C data, the compiler allows the simple cast, and ARC handles the rest.

Next, if we call any Core Foundation memory management functions, we need to let ARC know about it. These functions include CFRetain(), CFRelease(), and any function that has the words Create or Copy embedded in its name (see Apple's Memory Management Programming Guide for Core Foundation for more information).

If the Core Foundation function retains the data (CFRetain, Create, or Copy), then we need to cast it using the __bridge_transfer annotation. If Core Foundation releases the data (CFRelease), then we use the __bridge_retain annotation. Examples of both are shown here.

```
// The Core Foundation function retains the data.
// We need to tell ARC to release it when we're done.
NSString* myString =
    (__bridge_transfer NSString*)CFStringCreateMutableCopy(NULL, 0,
                                                    myCFString);
...now do something useful with myString
// This time, our Core Foundation code will release the object.
// We need to tell ARC to retain it.
CFStringRef myCFString = (__bridge_retain NSString*)[myString copy];
...now do something useful with myCFString
CFRelease(myCFString);
```

Finally, if we get the Core Foundation data in some other way (not a Create or Copy function and not an Objective-C method), and we don't call either CFRetain() or CFRelease() on it, we simply need to add the __bridge annotation to the cast, as shown here. ARC will then manage the memory for us, as normal.

```
// From Objective-C to Core Foundation
CFStringRef myCFString = (__bridge CFStringRef) myString;
CFShow(myCFString);

...

// From Core Foundation to Objective-C
myLabel.text = (__bridge NSString*)myCFString;
```

GETTING TO KNOW THE DOCUMENTATION

It's worth spending a little time to get familiar with Xcode's documentation. It's an excellent resource when first learning Objective-C, and it will continue to function as an indispensable reference manual throughout your iOS developing career.

Let's get a little practice. Open the documentation and search for UIWindow, and then select UIWindow Class Reference from the results. The class reference is divided into several sections. It starts with a brief description of the class, including the class hierarchy it inherits from, the protocols it implements, and any sample code that uses the class.

Below this, we have an overview of the class. This section describes its basic usage, including any important implementation or usage details.

Next we have a list of tasks. This groups the class's properties and methods by their intended use (for UIWindow, these are Configuring Windows, Making Windows Key, Converting Coordinates, and Sending Events). Each item on the list has a hyperlink to a more detailed description later in the documentation.

Then we have sections describing the class's properties, class methods, instance methods, constants, and notifications. (Not all classes have all of these categories. UIWindow, for example, does not have any class methods.) Each section includes all the relevant public items defined for the class. For items declared in the superclass (or farther up the class hierarchy), you will need to search for the relevant class's reference.

The detailed entry for each item shows how the item is declared, describes its use, and provides information about its availability. For example, the UIWindow's rootViewController property provides access to the UIViewController that manages the window's contents. Its default value is nil, and it is only available in iOS 4.0 and later.

By comparison, search for CGPoint. Unlike the UIWindow class, CGPoint does not have its own reference. It is described in the CGGeometry reference. Like the class reference, this starts with a short header and an overview. Then it lists the geometry functions, grouped by task. Finally the reference lists all relevant data types and constants.

The CGPoint entry includes the struct's declaration and a description of all its fields and its availability.

As we work our way through the book, periodically take some time to look up any new classes or structures in the documentation. I will try to show good examples of the class's typical usage, but most classes contain too many methods and features to describe in detail. Besides, looking through the documentation may give you ideas for alternative usages that would work better in your own applications.

IMPORTANT DESIGN PATTERNS

We've covered most of the basic features of Objective-C, but there are a number of common design patterns that are often used throughout the iOS SDK. It's worth taking a little bit of time to go over these patterns so you will understand them when you see them.

MODEL-VIEW-CONTROLLER

Model-View-Controller (MVC) is a common architectural pattern for building applications with a graphical user interface (GUI). This pattern divides the application into three sections. The model maintains the application's state. This typically includes both managing the state during runtime and saving and loading the state (archiving objects to file, persisting the data to an SQL database, or using frameworks like Core Data).

As the name suggests, the view is responsible for displaying application information, possibly in an interactive manner. Most of the time this means displaying the information using a GUI. However, it could include printing documents and generating other logs and reports.

The controller sits between the two. It responds to events (usually from the view) and then sends commands to the model (to change its state). It must also update the view whenever the model changes. An application's business logic may be implemented in either the controller or the model, depending on the needs of the application. However, you should really pick one approach and stick with it throughout the entire application.

The ideal MVC components should be very loosely bound. For example, any number of views could observe the controller, triggering controller events and responding to any change notifications. One might display information in the GUI. One might save data to a log file. The controller doesn't know or care about the details. On the other end, the model and the controller should be similarly loosely bound.

In practice, the different layers are often more tightly bound than this, sacrificing a bit of idealism for pragmatics. Cocoa Touch is no exception. Typically, the views are more tightly bound to their controllers. Each scene has a custom controller tailored toward managing that scene (see the "Examining the Storyboard" section in Chapter 1 for more information on the relationship between scenes and view controllers). On the model side, there's a lot more wiggle room. In the simplest applications, the model might be implemented directly in the controllers. For the most part, though, we want to keep these areas as cleanly separated as possible.

Cocoa Touch uses `UIView` subclasses for the view, and `UIViewController` subclasses for the controller. Communication between the model and the view generally uses target/action connections.

On the model side, we can implement our models using a number of different techniques: custom classes, SQLite, or Core Data. In many cases, models and controllers communicate directly with each other—though we can create more-loosely bound connections using notifications and delegates (see the data sources discussion in the next section for more information).

DELEGATES

Delegates allow you to extend or modify an object's behavior without having to subclass the object. You can even change the object's behavior at runtime by swapping delegates—though in practice, this is somewhat rare.

We have already seen delegates in action. For example, instead of subclassing the `UIApplication` class within each project, we use a generic `UIApplication` and implement a custom `UIApplicationDelegate`. The application delegate protocol defines more than 20 optional methods that we can override to both monitor and alter the application's behavior.

Any class that uses a delegate usually has a property named (not surprisingly) `delegate`. By convention, delegate properties should always use weak references. This helps avoid retain loops. However, we need to make sure we have a strong reference to our delegate object somewhere else in our application—otherwise ARC will deallocate it.

```
@property (nonatomic, weak) IBOutlet id<DelegateProtocol> delegate;
```

As this example shows, we typically declare a protocol that our delegate must implement. This defines the interface between the delegating class and our delegate. Note that the delegating class is the active partner in this relationship. It calls these methods on the delegate. Some of them pass information to the delegate; others query the delegate. In this way, we pass information back and forth between the two objects.

A delegate's methods usually have a somewhat formulaic name. By convention, the names start with an identifier that describes the delegating object. For example, all the UIApplicationDelegate methods start with the word application.

In many cases, the method passes a reference to the delegating object back as its first argument. UITableViewDelegate does this. This means that you could use a single UITableViewDelegate to manage multiple UITableViews (though this is rarely done). More importantly, you can avoid saving the delegating class in an instance variable, since the delegate can always access its delegating class through this argument.

Additionally, the delegate's methods often have will, did, or should in their names. In all three cases, the system calls these methods in response to some change. Will methods are called before the change occurs. Did methods are called after the change. Should methods, like will methods, are called before the change, but they are expected to return a YES or NO value. If they return YES, the change should proceed as normal. If they return NO, the change should be canceled.

Finally, delegate methods are almost always optional. As a result, the delegating class must first check to make sure the delegate has implemented the method before calling it. This code shows a typical hypothetical implementation:

```
- (void) doSomething {
    BOOL shouldDoSomething = YES;
    // Ask if we should do it.
    if ([self.delegate
            respondsToSelector:
            @selector(someObjectShouldDoSomething:)]) {
        shouldDoSomething =
            [self.delegate someObjectShouldDoSomething:self];
    }
    // Abort this method if the delegate returns NO.
    if (!shouldDoSomething) return;
    // Tell the delegate that we will do it.
    if ([self.delegate
```

```
        respondsToSelector:
        @selector(someObjectWillDoSomething:)]) {
    [self.delegate someObjectWillDoSomething:self];
  }
  // Just do it.
  [self.model doSomething];
  // Tell the delegate that we did it.
  if ([self.delegate
        respondsToSelector:
        @selector(someObjectDidDoSomething:)]) {
    [self.delegate someObjectDidDoSomething:self];
  }
}
```

Delegates are easy to implement. Simply create a new class and have it adopt the protocol. Then implement all the required methods (if any), as well as any optional methods that interest you. Then in your code, create an instance of your delegate class and assign it to the main object's delegate property. Many of UIAppKit's view subclasses can take delegates. This means you will often connect views and delegates using Interface Builder (hence the IBOutlet tag in our @property declaration).

> **NOTE:** Optional protocol methods were introduced with Objective-C 2.0. Before this, most delegates were implemented using informal protocols. This convention involved declaring categories on the NSObject class; however, the methods were left undefined. While this worked, the IDE and compiler could not provide much support. Over time, Apple has slowly replaced most of the informal protocols with actual protocols; however, you may still run into them on occasion.

Some view subclasses also require data sources. Data sources are closely related to delegates. However, delegates are used to monitor and change an object's behavior, while data sources are specifically geared toward providing data for the object. Other differences flow from this distinction. For example, delegates are usually optional; the delegating object should function perfectly without one. Data sources, on the other hand, are often required for the main class to function properly. As a result, data sources often have one or more required methods declared in their protocol.

Otherwise, data sources act just like delegates. The naming convention is similar, and just like the delegate, the main class should have a weak reference to its data source.

NOTIFICATIONS

Notifications allow objects to communicate without tightly coupling them. In iOS, notifications are managed using a notification center. Objects that wish to receive notifications must register with the notification center. Meanwhile, objects that wish to broadcast notifications simply post them to the center. The notification center will then filter notifications by both the sending object and the notification name—forwarding each notification to the proper receivers.

Notifications are easy to implement. Usually you will start by creating an NSString constant for your notification's name in a common header file. Both the sending and receiving objects need access to this constant.

```
static NSString* const MyNotification = @"My Notification";
```

Next, objects can register to receive notifications. You can specify the sender and the notification names that you are interested in. In addition, you can pass nil for either of these values. If you pass nil for the name, you will receive all the notifications sent by the specified object. If you pass nil for the sender, you will receive all notifications that match the notification name. If you pass nil for both, you will receive all notifications sent to that notification center.

```
NSNotificationCenter* center = [NSNotificationCenter defaultCenter];
[center addObserver:self
        selector:@selector(receiveNotification:)
          name:MyNotification
        object:nil];
```

Here we get a reference to the default notification center and then add ourselves as an observer. We register to receive all notifications from any objects whose name matches the MyNotification constant. We also specify the selector that the notification center will call when a matching notification is found.

Next, we need to implement the method for our selector. This method should accept a single NSNotification object as an argument.

```
- (void)receiveNotification:(NSNotification*)notification {
    NSLog(@"Notification Received");
    // Now do something useful in response.
}
```

Finally, it's important to remove the observer before it (or any object mentioned in addObserver:selector:name:object:) is deallocated. Otherwise, the notification center will contain dangling pointers. Often this should be done in the observing object's dealloc method.

```
- (void)dealloc {
    NSNotificationCenter* center =
    [NSNotificationCenter defaultCenter];
    // Remove all entries for the given observer.
    [center removeObserver:self];
}
```

Sending a notification is even simpler. Our sending object just needs to get a pointer to the default notification center and then post the desired method.

```
NSNotificationCenter* center = [NSNotificationCenter defaultCenter];
[center postNotificationName:MyNotification object:self];
```

Notifications are posted synchronously. This means that the call to post NotificationName will not return until after the notification center has finished calling all the specified selectors for all matching observers. This could take a considerable amount of time, especially if there are a large number of observers or the responding methods are slow.

Alternatively, we can send asynchronous notifications using NSNotification Queue. Notification queues basically delay a notification until the current event loop ends (or possibly until the event loop is completely idle). The queue can also coalesce duplicate messages into a single notification.

The following sample code delays the notification until the run loop is idle:

```
NSNotification* notification =
    [NSNotification notificationWithName:MyNotification
                                 object:self];
NSNotificationQueue* queue = [NSNotificationQueue defaultQueue];
[queue enqueueNotification:notification
            postingStyle:NSPostWhenIdle];
```

KEY-VALUE CODING

Key-value coding is a technique for getting and setting an object's instance variables indirectly using strings. The NSKeyValueCoding protocol defines a number of methods for accessing or setting these values. The simplest examples are valueForKey: and setValue:forKey:.

```
NSString* oldName = [emp valueForKey:@"firstName"];
[emp setValue:@"Bob" forKey:@"firstName"];
```

For this to work, your objects must be KVC compliant. Basically, the valueFor Key: method will look for an accessor named <key> or is<key>. If it cannot find a valid accessor, it will look for an instance variable named <key> or _<key>. On the other hand, setValue:forKey: looks for a set<key>: method and then looks for the instance variables.

Fortunately, any properties you define for your instance variables are automatically KVC compliant.

KVC methods can also use key paths. These are dot-separated lists of keys. Basically, the getter or setter will work its way down the list of keys. The first key is applied to the receiving object. Each subsequent key is then used on the value returned from the previous key. This allows you to dig down through the object graph to get to the value you want.

```
// Will return the company name, assuming all intermediate values
// are KVC compliant.
NSString* companyName =
[emp valueforKey:@"department.company.name"];
```

While KVC can be used to produce highly dynamic, very loosely bound code, it is a somewhat specialized technique. You may never end up using KVC code directly. However, it enables a number of interesting technologies (for example, key-value observing).

KEY-VALUE OBSERVING

Key-value observing allows one object to observe any changes to another object's instance variables. While this superficially resembles notifications, there are some important differences. First, there is no centralized control layer for KVO. One object directly observes another. Second, the object being observed generally does not need to do anything to send these notifications. As long as their instance variables are KVC compliant, notifications are automatically sent whenever your application uses either the instance variable's setter or KVC to change the instance variable's value.

Unfortunately, if you are changing the value of an instance variable directly, the observed object must manually call `willChangeValueForKey:` before the change and `didChangeValueForKey:` after the change. This is yet another argument for always accessing instance values through a property.

To register as an observer, call `addObserver:forKeyPath:options:context:`. The observer is the object that will receive the KVO notification. Key path is the dot-separated list of keys used to identify the value that will be observed. The options argument determines what information is returned in the notification, and the context lets you pass arbitrary data that will be added to the notification.

```
// You will receive notifications whenever this employee's
// last name changes.
[emp addObserver:self
    forKeyPath:@"lastName"
      options:NSKeyValueObservingOptionNew |
              NSKeyValueObservingOptionOld
      context:nil];
```

As with notification centers, it's important to remove an observer before it is deallocated. While the NSNotificationCenter had a convenience method that would remove all the notifications for a given observer, in KVO you must release each addObserver call separately.

```
[emp removeObserver:self forKeyPath:@"lastName"];
```

Next, to receive the notification, you must override the observeValueForKey Path:ofObject:change:context: method. The object argument will identify the object you were observing. The keyPath argument indicates the particular property that changed. The change argument holds a dictionary containing the values requested when registering as an observer. Finally, the context argument simply contains the context data provided when registering as an observer.

```
- (void)observeValueForKeyPath:(NSString *)keyPath
                      ofObject:(id)object
                        change:(NSDictionary *)change
                       context:(void *)context {
    if ([keyPath isEqualToString:@"lastName"]) {
        NSString* oldName =
        [change objectForKey:NSKeyValueChangeOldKey];
        NSString* newName =
        [change objectForKey:NSKeyValueChangeNewKey];
        NSLog(@"%@'s last name changed from %@ to %@",
            object, oldName, newName];
    }
}
```

SINGLETONS

In its most basic concept, a singleton is a class that will only ever have a single object instantiated from it. Whenever you request a new object of that class, you gain a pointer back to the original.

Singletons are typically used to represent objects where only a single version exists. The UIApplication class is a good example. Each application has one and only one application object. Furthermore, you can access that application anywhere through the [UIApplication sharedApplication] method.

Of course, singletons are a constant source of Internet debates. Some argue that they are the spawn of all that is evil and that they should be avoided like the plague. If you use singletons, the terrorists win. Or, somewhat more rationally, a singleton is nothing more than an over-engineered global variable with good PR.

There is some truth to these complaints. When developers first encounter the singleton pattern, they often overdo it. Too many singletons can make your code very hard to follow. Singletons are also deceptively hard to write correctly (and there are different ideas about what "correctly" means). However, they can be incredibly useful when used appropriately. Most importantly, Cocoa Touch uses a number of singleton classes—so you should at least understand the basics, even if you never write your own.

The following is a typical, relatively safe implementation. In the class's header file, declare a class method to access your shared instance:

```
+ (SampleSingleton*)sharedSampleSingleton;
```

Then open the implementation file and add an extension to your class. This extension will declare a private designated initializer.

```
@interface SampleSingleton()
- (id)initSharedInstance;
@end
```

Remember, we can call any method on any object—declaring the initializer as private only communicates our intent. Developers should only call methods that are declared in the header file—in this case, the developers should only access the shared object through the sharedSampleSingleton method.

Finally, in the @implementation block, implement the following methods:

```objectivec
+ (SampleSingleton*)sharedSampleSingleton {
    static SampleSingleton* sharedSingleton;
    static dispatch_once_t onceToken;
    dispatch_once(&onceToken, ^{
            sharedSingleton = [[SampleSingleton alloc]
                                initSharedInstance];
    });
    return sharedSingleton;
}
// Private Designated Initializer.
- (id)initSharedInstance {
    self = [super init];
    if (self) {
            // Do initialization here.
    }
    return self;
}
// Override the superclass's designated initializer to prevent
// its use.
// Calling this method will throw an exception.
- (id)init {
    [self doesNotRecognizeSelector:_cmd];
    return nil;
}
```

This code uses lazy initialization to create our shared instance (we don't actually allocate the instance until sharedSampleSingleton is called). Within sharedSample Singleton, we use a dispatch_once block to protect our shared instance. The dispatch_once block is a thread-safe way to ensure that a block of code is only executed once during an application's lifetime.

> **NOTE:** Before ARC, many singleton implementations would override a number of additional methods: allocWithZone:, copyWithZone:, mutableCopyWithZone:, and release were all common candidates. Locking these down helped prevent developers from accidentally creating additional copies of the singleton. However, these methods either cannot be overridden when compiling under ARC or are simply unnecessary. Apple currently recommends using a simpler singleton and relying on convention and communication to prevent duplicates.

We also override the superclass's designated initializer, causing it to throw an exception if called. Hiding our designated initializer, and disabling the superclass's designated initializer, prevents developers from accidentally creating copies (e.g., by calling [[SampleSingleton alloc] init]).

Note that copy and mutableCopy are also disabled by default. Since we did not implement copyWithZone: or mutableCopyWithZone:, these methods will automatically throw exceptions.

This implementation doesn't deal with the tricky issue of loading or saving your singleton from disk. How you implement the archiving code depends a lot on what loading and saving the singleton means in your application. Do you load the singleton once from disk when it is first created? Or does loading the singleton simply change the value stored in the singleton? For example, your application may have a GameState singleton. You will only ever have the one GameState object—but the state values may change as the user loads and saves games.

For an even more advanced twist, some of Cocoa Touch's singletons let you specify the singleton's class in the application's info.plist file. This allows you to create a subclass of the singleton class yet still ensure the proper version is loaded at runtime. If you need this sort of support, modify your code as shown here:

```
+ (SampleSingleton*)sharedSampleSingleton {
    static SampleSingleton* sharedSingleton;
    static dispatch_once_t onceToken;
    dispatch_once(&onceToken, ^{
            NSBundle* main = [NSBundle mainBundle];
        NSDictionary* info = [main infoDictionary];
        NSString* className =
        [info objectForKey:@"SampleSingleton"];
            Class singletonClass = NSClassFromString(className);
            if (!singletonClass) {
            singletonClass = self;
        }
            sharedSingleton =
            [[singletonClass alloc] initSharedInstance];
    });
    return sharedSingleton;
}
```

This code accesses the info.plist file and looks for a key named SampleSingleton. If it finds one, it interprets the corresponding value as a class name and attempts to look up the corresponding class object. If that succeeds, it uses that class to create the singleton object. Otherwise, it just uses the default singleton class.

BLOCKS

Blocks are, hands down, my favorite addition to Objective-C 2.0. They are only available for iOS 4.0 or later. However, unless you are targeting really old devices, blocks can greatly simplify many algorithms.

For example, the UIView class has a number of methods for animating views using blocks. These methods provide a much more concise, much more elegant solution than the older animation API.

Blocks are somewhat similar to methods and functions in that they are a way of bundling up a number of expressions for later execution. Blocks, however, can be stored as variables and passed as arguments. We can create block variables as shown:

```
returnType (^blockName)(argument, types);
```

For example, let's declare a block variable named sum that returns an integer and takes two integer arguments:

```
int (^sum)(int, int);
```

You can define a literal block starting with the caret (^) and then declaring the arguments in parentheses and the actual code in curly brackets.

```
sum = ^(int a, int b){return a + b;};
```

Once a block variable is assigned, you can call it just like any other function.

```
NSLog(@"The sum of %d and %d is %d", 5, 6, sum(5, 6));
```

It's important to note that blocks can capture any data that is in scope when the block is defined. For example, in this sample, addToOffset will take a single argument and add the offset variable to it.

```
int offset = 5;
int (^addToOffset)(int) = ^(int value){return offset + value;};
```

> **NOTE:** When a block captures a local variable stored on the stack, it treats this variable as a const value. You can read the value but not modify it. If you need to mutate a local variable, you must declare it using the __block storage type modifier. Generally, this only applies to local C types and structs. You can already mutate objects, instance variables, and anything else allocated on the heap.

Usually, however, we don't create or call block variables. Instead, we pass literal blocks to methods and functions as arguments. For example, NSArray has a method, enumerateObjectsUsingBlock:, that takes a single block. This method will iterate through all the objects in the array. For each object, it calls the block, passing in the object, the object's index, and a reference to a stop value.

The stop value is only used as output from the block. Setting it to YES halts enumerateObjectsUsingBlock:. Here is a simple example using this method:

```
NSArray* array = [NSArray arrayWithObjects:@"Bill", @"Anne",
                     @"Jim", nil];
[array enumerateObjectsUsingBlock:
 ^(id obj, NSUInteger idx, BOOL *stop) {
    NSLog(@"Person %d: %@", idx, obj);
}];
```

This returns the following output to the console:

```
Person 0: Bill
Person 1: Anne
Person 2: Jim
```

Notice that we could duplicate the functionality of enumerateObjectsUsing Block: by passing in a selector and having our enumeration method call the selector for each item in the array. We start by creating a category on NSArray.

```
@implementation NSArray (EnumerateWithSelector)
- (void)enumerateObjectsUsingTarget:(id)target
                          selector:(SEL)selector {
    for (int i = 0; i < [self count]; i++) {
        [target performSelector:selector
                withObject:[self objectAtIndex:i]
                withObject:[NSNumber numberWithInt:i]];
    }
}
```

Then, to use this enumerator, we need to implement our callback method:

```
- (void)printName:(NSString*)name index:(NSNumber*)index {
    NSLog(@"Person %d: %@", [index intValue], name);
}
```

Then we can call our method, passing in the selector:

```
[array enumerateObjectsUsingTarget:self
    selector:@selector(printName:index:)];
```

That's arguably a little chunkier than our block example—but it's not too bad. Still, that's not the point. What happens if we want to change the enumerator's behavior? Say we want to add a stop value—when the value is reached, we stop enumerating.

Well, we could add a stop parameter both to our enumerateObjectsUsingTarget:Selector: method and to our printName:index: method. Sure, that's not a ton of work, but the changes get scattered around our project. Worse yet, if we have to do it more than once—well, the complexity adds up fast. We may soon find ourselves juggling multiple enumeration methods, each handling slightly different cases.

Alternatively, we could create an instance variable to hold the stop name and just access it in the printName:index: method. That avoids changing the enumeration method, but it's somewhat sloppy. The stop name really shouldn't be part of our class—we're just adding it as a sneaky way to avoid extra parameters. And what happens if we need several different behaviors? How many instance variables are we willing to add?

Fortunately, blocks don't have any of these problems. We can modify the enumerateObjectsUsingBlock: method's behavior locally.

```
NSString* stopName = @"Anne";

[array enumerateObjectsUsingBlock:
 ^(id obj, NSUInteger idx, BOOL *stop) {
        NSLog(@"Person %d: %@", idx, obj);
    *stop = [obj isEqualToString:stopName];
    }];
```

Notice that we did not need to alter the implementation of enumerateObjects UsingBlock: at all. We also didn't need any instance variables. Most importantly, everything is kept nicely in one place.

Best of all, the solution is scalable. If we want different behaviors somewhere else—no problem. We write a new block, capture all the local variables we need, and then call our generic enumeration method. A single generic method handles all our needs.

NOTE: Before ARC, we had to be a little careful with blocks. By default, blocks were built on the stack, and they were destroyed once they went out of scope. To store a block in an instance variable for later execution, we had to copy the block to the heap. Then we had to release it once we were done. Fortunately, ARC has simplified things yet again. We can create blocks, store them, use them, and even return them. We don't need to worry about whether they're on the heap or on the stack. ARC handles all the copying and memory management details for us.

WRAPPING **UP**

Whew. This chapter has covered a lot of ground. Don't worry if you didn't catch it all on the first pass. We will get a lot of practice using Objective-C in future chapters. And, unfortunately, this chapter really only scratches the surface. Many of these topics are quite deep. If you have any questions, be sure to check out Apple's documentation. In particular, I recommend the following: The Objective-C Programming Language, Programming with ARC Release Notes, Key-Value Observing Programming Guide, and Block Programming Topics.

Next up, let's start applying what we've learned and build a productivity application from scratch.

3

PRODUCTIVITY APPLICATION **ARCHITECTURE**

Throughout the rest of this book, we will focus on developing a single application. Chapter by chapter, we will cover every step required to build and test this application, from creating the initial project to prepping it for sale.

In this chapter, we will focus on our application's overall architecture. We will define the user's flow through the application, connecting our basic views and the transitions between them. We will also build our application's model and link it to our view controllers. Finally, we will touch on a number of smaller topics: enabling compiler warnings to produce cleaner code, implementing the methods that control vital aspects of our app, running our application on iOS devices, and even exploring the inner workings of nib files.

UNDERSTANDING
PRODUCTIVITY **APPS**

The original iPhone Human Interface Guidelines (HIG) organized applications into three general categories: utility, productivity, and immersive applications. Utility applications provide a single view of the data with little or no interaction. Productivity applications manage and organize complex data. Immersive applications use custom views and controls, taking over the entire screen to provide a rich, interactive user experience.

Apple has since dropped these categories from the iOS HIG, and that makes a certain amount of sense. As the platform continues to mature, developers naturally push against these boundaries. Few modern applications fit cleanly into one of these categories. Even back when the iPhone first came out, many applications used a hybrid approach. Look at the iPod app. Its Cover Flow interface injects an immersive element into an otherwise straightforward productivity app.

However, there seems to be some benefit to at least thinking about these categories, especially when you are designing a new application. They can help you identify your application's core features and then focus your design to maximize those features.

We looked at a simple utility application in Chapter 1. Honestly, there's not a lot to say about them. Utility apps provide a quick way to access relatively simple information. One screen, a few settings—if you're thinking of anything more complicated than that, you should probably consider a different approach.

Over the next few chapters, we will look at productivity applications. These apps manage and organize complex data. While you may provide some custom user interfaces, you should focus heavily on usability. Work to create a clean, streamlined solution that helps the user to move through the data in an unobtrusive and intuitive manner.

Productivity applications typically use three tools to organize and interact with your data: `UITabBarController`, `UINavigationController`, and `UITableView`. You may not need all three, but these are the primary built-in tools for sifting through data.

The `UITabBarController` lets the user easily switch between different tasks or different groups of data. For example, the Clock application lets the user choose between the different time-related tasks: World Clock, Alarm, Stopwatch, and Timer. The iPod app, on the other hand, allows the user to select different views of their data: Albums, Artists, Genres, Songs, Playlists, Videos, and so on. The App Store mixes both approaches, displaying three data groups (Features, Categories, and Top 25) and two tasks (Search and Updates).

The tab bar can support any number of tab items. However, it can only show five tabs at a time. UITabBarController automatically manages any extra tab items by providing a More button and letting the user customize the items that appear on the tab bar. Note that if you have more than five tabs, the tab bar will display only four of them, since the More button takes up one of the spaces.

Next, the UINavigationController lets users move from general to more specific views. This controller maintains a stack of views. When a new view is added to the top of the stack, that view slides in from the right while the old view slides off to the left. When the top view is popped from the top of the stack, the animation is reversed. This provides a very intuitive interface for moving through a hierarchy of views.

While both UITabBarController and UINavigationController manage navigation between views, UITableView handles the actual display of data. Tables are often used to present lists. For example, the list of email accounts, the list of mailboxes within a single account, or even the list of messages within a single mailbox. UITableView displays a single column of cells. Individually, each cell can be quite complex, combining images, icons, and formatted text. In general, a single cell type is used throughout the table. Each cell represents a different entry from a list of similar items.

However, UITableView has a secondary use as well. We can create a static table to organize a fixed set of heterogeneous pieces of data. In this case, the entire table is used to represent a single entry. Each row has its own unique formatting, displaying some aspect of this entry. As we change entries, the number and type of rows remain the same, only the data changes. We often use static tables to display detailed information about a selected leaf object in our data hierarchy.

TAB BARS VS. NAVIGATION CONTROLLERS

An application may have multiple UINavigationControllers or UITableViews; however, they should have only a single UITabBarController. Additionally, the UITabBarController should always be the root controller for your application. You can add a UINavigationController to a UITabBarController, but you should never add a UITabBarController to a UINavigationController.

If you really need to, you can add tab bars to a view managed by a navigation controller, but you must create your own tab bar controller class. Generally, this should be a subclass of UIViewController and should adopt the UITabBarDelegate protocol. It's not hard, but you will need to write custom code for managing the list of subviews, swapping them in and out as the user selects new tabs.

Apple's documentation strongly recommends having a single tab bar, making it your application's root view, and having it visible and accessible in every scene. If this does not fit your application's needs, then perhaps you should rethink your user interface. For example, a table view might better fit your needs.

A productivity application combines some or all of these tools into a user interface that naturally matches the application's data. In general, UITabBarController provides the coarsest organization, defining our broadest groups. Within each group, UINavigationController lets the user move from general to specific, while UITableView displays the information available at each level of detail.

If you're like me, you spend much of your day sitting in front of a computer. This has led to an ongoing battle to lose weight. To help in this fight, let's build an application that will let users track their weight over time.

Health Beat will have three main tasks: Users can enter new weights, they can view a graph showing how their weight changes over time, and they can bring up the complete history showing all their weight entries. We will use a tab view to navigate between these tasks. In addition, we will use a table view/navigation controller combination to manage our history view.

This chapter will focus on the overall architecture of the application, on building a storyboard that connects our tab bar, table view, and navigation controllers, and on building and attaching our application's model. We will flesh out this design and cover additional topics, such as saving and loading the data and drawing custom views, in later chapters.

CREATING THE PROJECT

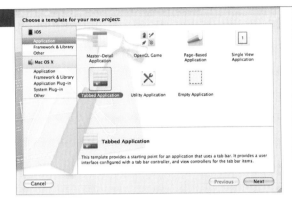

Open the iOS Development workspace we created in Chapter 1. It should contain our Hello World project. Add a new project by selecting File > New > New Project from the menu. Then select iOS > Application > Tabbed Application and click the Next button (**Figure 3.1**).

In the "Choose options" panel, name the project Health Beat, and set the Class Prefix to **HB**. Make sure that the Device Family pop-up menu is set to iPhone and that the Use Storyboard, Use Automatic Reference Counting, and Include Unit Tests checkboxes are all selected. Then click Next (**Figure 3.2**).

In the final panel, select the location for the project. Make sure the "Create local git repository for this project" checkbox is selected, and that the Group drop-down is set to our iOS Development workgroup. Then click Create (**Figure 3.3**).

This creates a basic tabbed application. In Xcode's toolbar, change the scheme to Health Beat > iPhone 5.0 Simulator (**Figure 3.4**) and run the application.

As you can see, the application template gives us a simple two-tab application (**Figure 3.5**). You can press the tab buttons to switch between the first and second views.

Looking at the code, our template created an app delegate (HBAppDelegate), two view controllers (HBFirstViewController and HBSecondViewController), the storyboard (MainStoryboard.storyboard), our tab-bar icons (first.png, first@2x.png, second.png, second@2x.png), and our supporting files. We also have a new group for our unit tests.

FIGURE 3.1 Select the Tabbed Application template

FIGURE 3.2 Naming the product

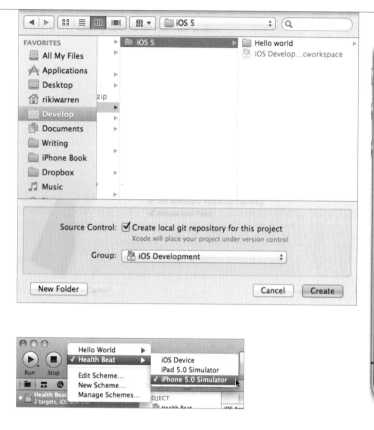

FIGURE 3.3 Selecting the project's location

FIGURE 3.4 Setting the scheme

FIGURE 3.5 Running the template

INITIAL HOUSECLEANING

Before we start building our application, let's tidy things up. First, while we could modify the existing controllers and storyboard elements, it will be easier to just create our own from scratch. So, let's delete them. Delete HBFirstViewController.h, HBFirstViewController.m, HBSecondViewController.h, HBSecondViewController.m, and all four .png files. This should leave just HBAppDelegate, MainStoryboard.storyboard, and the support files in our Health Beat group.

Now, open the storyboard and delete the first view controller and the second view controller. This should remove both of their scenes, leaving us with just the tab view.

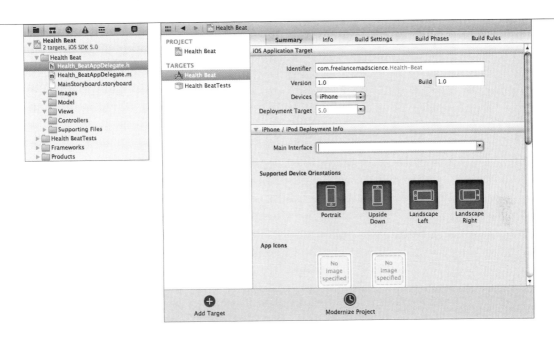

Next, let's add some organization. We want to add four groups to our Project Navigator: Images, Model, Views, and Controllers. right-click the Health Beat group, select New Group, and then give it an appropriate name. When you're done, move the groups around so they match **Figure 3.6**.

Now, click the Health Beat project icon (blue icon at the top). This allows us to edit numerous project and target settings. Make sure the Health Beat target and the Summary tab are selected. This lets us edit the version number, device type, and other settings. Right now, our primary concern is the Supported Device Orientations setting. We want our app to rotate freely into any orientation, so make sure all four buttons are selected (**Figure 3.7**).

FIGURE 3.6 Arrange the groups

FIGURE 3.7 Setting the supported device orientations

NOTE: The Supported Device Orientations setting determines the allowable orientations. This setting (in combination with the application's current orientation) will determine the initial orientation when your application launches. However, we still need to modify the individual view controllers to enable autorotations at runtime.

FIGURE 3.8 Enabling the static analyzer

SETTING ADDITIONAL WARNINGS

Xcode can perform sophisticated analysis and provide quite a bit of feedback on your code, helping to avoid a great number of common programming errors. Unfortunately, many of these settings are turned off by default. Let's fix that.

With the Health Beat project icon still selected, click the Build Settings tab in the Editor area. Make sure the All and Combined buttons are pressed, and then type **analyzer** in the search bar. This will bring up the Run Static Analyzer setting. Change this value to Yes. This will force the compiler to run the static analyzer every time you build your application (**Figure 3.8**).

Running the static analyzer on every build provides a great sanity check; however, it can significantly slow down compile time. You may find that you need to turn it off when working on very large projects or when developing on slower computers. In my experience, however, it can take such a long time to upload a new copy of the application onto the device (or even onto the simulator) that a little extra compile time is hardly noticeable. Still, your mileage may vary.

Next, clear the search bar, and scroll down until you find the section labeled Apple LLVM compiler 3.0 – Warnings (it should be near the bottom). These settings let us configure the warnings that the compiler generates. Xcode already has a number of useful warnings enabled; however, I highly recommend turning on all of the following:

1. Check Switch Statements (on by default)

2. Hidden Local Variables

3. Implicit Conversion to 32 Bit Type

4. Incomplete Objective-C Protocols (on by default)

5. Initializer Not Fully Bracketed

6. Mismatched Return Type (on by default)

7. Missing Braces and Parentheses (on by default)

8. Missing Fields in Structure Initializers

9. Missing Function Prototypes

10. Missing Newline At End Of File

11. Overriding Deprecated Objective-C Methods

12. Pointer Sign Comparison (on by default)

13. Sign Comparison

14. Strict Selector Matching

15. Suspicious Implicit Conversions

16. Treat Warnings as Errors

17. Typecheck Calls to printf/scanf (on by default)

18. Undeclared Selector

19. Unused Functions

20. Unused Labels

21. Unused Values (on by default)

22. Unused Variables (on by default)

23. Warn About Deprecated Functions (on by default)

24. Warn About Undefined Use of offsetof Macro (on by default)

Now, I'm not going to lie to you. In the short run, turning these warnings on may force you to do some extra typing—sometimes a lot of extra typing. You will occasionally have to add unnecessary steps to your methods just to keep the compiler happy. Some developers prefer to turn these warnings off when focusing on rapid build-test-modify cycles; then they turn them back on when polishing up the code. Of course, there's a risk that you might never have time to come back and fix things. I recommend leaving them on as much as possible. One of these days they will save you from an embarrassing bug and you will thank me.

Of all these warnings, the most important is undoubtedly Treat Warnings as Errors. This forces you to clean up your code and get rid of all your warnings. This is a very good habit to get into. As frustrating as it may be, you really want to clear out all warnings. Otherwise, you may overlook something truly important one day.

Trust me, nothing's worse than compiling someone else's code and watching a steady stream of warnings scroll by. You get that sinking feeling in the pit of your stomach. Are these serious issues that need to be resolved, or are they trivial matters that you can simply ignore? Do everyone a favor and fix your warnings.

This brings up another point. Not all developers will follow this advice. You will find that some third-party libraries may trigger hundreds of warnings. As always, it's better to be pragmatic and finish a project than to be dogmatic and proud of yourself. If you have to turn off one of the warnings to move forward, then turn off the warning.

ADDING IMAGES

We will need icons for our tab buttons. These are a little odd. They need to be 30 by 30 PNG files (60 by 60 @2x.png files for phones with the Retina display). The actual color of the image does not matter; the tab-bar icons just use their alpha level. For this reason, I find it easiest to draw the icons in black on a transparent background. If I want shading, I change the opacity of the black ink. That way, the image I see in my graphics application will at least be close to what I get when I load the icon.

Feel free to create your own icons. Alternatively, you can just download the source code from www.freelancemadscience.com/source and copy over the artwork. Right-click the Images group, and select Add Files to "Health Beat." Make sure the "Copy items into destination group's folder (if necessary)" checkbox is selected. Then select graph.png, graph@2x.png, plus.png, and plus@2x.png from the downloaded code. Click Add.

The plus icon will be used on our tab for entering new weights. The graph tab will be used for our graph view (surprise, surprise). We will use a built-in icon for the history view, so it doesn't need any additional artwork.

RUNNING AND TESTING ON iOS DEVICES

If you are using Mac OS X Lion, you can download Xcode from the app store for free ($4.99 for Snow Leopard users). This gives you full access to the iOS SDK and the simulator. However, if you want to build and run your applications on actual iOS devices, then you need to join the iOS Developer Program. You can register as either an individual or a company team for $99 a year.

There are also a few less-common options. The iOS Developer University Program is free for qualifying academic institutes, allowing universities to offer iOS development classes as part of their curriculum. At the higher end, the iOS Developer Enterprise Program allows larger companies to produce and deploy proprietary, in-house applications. Still, most of us will probably either purchase an individual membership or find ourselves added to an existing company team.

Once you have an iOS Developer membership, you must set up the proper developer certificates and provisioning profiles before you can build and test on your devices. Originally, this was a tedious and somewhat error-prone process. The iOS provisioning portal has detailed information covering all the necessary steps (https://developer.apple.com/ios/manage/overview/index.action).

However, there is good news. Apple has worked hard to automate and simplify these procedures over the years. If you just need a generic provisioning profile, Xcode can manage most of the setup automatically. Simply follow the steps below.

1. Open the Organizer and select the Devices tab. Connect your device to your Mac. Once it has finished synchronizing, select it from the list and press the Use for Development button.

2. The Organizer will prompt you for your iPhone provisioning portal login information. Fill in the username and password for your developer account, and press Login.

3. You may get a message prompting you to submit a developer certificate. Press the Submit Request button to continue.

4. Select Library, Provisioning Profiles in the left-hand column. Make sure Automatic Device Provisioning is selected. Click Refresh if there are no profiles shown on the list.

5. You may be prompted to wait and refresh while the certificate is generated. If the provisioning profile appears in the Organizer but it is still not working, try quitting and restarting Xcode.

6. If you still cannot get a functioning provisioning portal, try using the Web-based assistant on the provisioning portal.

7. Once your profile appears, change your scheme to the iOS device and run the application. It should upload and run on your device.

The iOS SDK has a handful of methods that are commonly used to perform vital application tasks. You don't necessarily need to implement each of these in every application; however, you should give them some thought. In addition, most of these methods have a corresponding notification that could be used to monitor these events in other parts of your code.

App Opening

These methods are called when the application first launches or when it returns from the background state (for iOS 4.0 or later). You will often use these methods to load the application's state and to perform other one-time configuration activities.

`application:didFinishLaunchingWithOptions:`

UIKit calls this `UIApplicationDelegate` method when the application first launches. We will often use it to perform one-time configuration tasks. Note, however, that the application will not appear onscreen until after this method returns. Therefore, we should avoid doing any potentially time-consuming activities during this method.

In particular, try to avoid tasks like accessing remote servers. These may work fine in testing but fail when deployed to actual users (especially when using the phone in areas with poor reception). This could cause the application to freeze until the network connection times out, creating an unacceptably long delay when launching.

While this may seem like a rare corner case, many third-party frameworks (e.g., analytic toolkits, social gaming frameworks, or ad networks) will perform network calls when initialized.

`applicationWillEnterForeground:`

UIKit calls this `UIApplicationDelegate` method in iOS 4.0 and later when the application returns from the background state. This may be called multiple times as the user closes and opens the app.

`applicationDidBecomeActive:`

This `UIApplicationDelegate` method is called both when the application launches and whenever it returns from the background state.

`viewDidLoad`

UIKit calls this `UIViewController` method once the controller's view has fully loaded. This method is called regardless of how the view was created—it could be loaded from a nib or programmatically built using the `loadView` method.

We will implement this method to perform additional setup or configuration. Since views can be loaded and unloaded automatically as part of regular memory management, this method may be called more than once. Additionally, any resources created during the viewDidLoad method should be released in the viewDidUnload method.

App Closing

These methods are called when the application is closing or when it is moving to the background (for iOS 4.0 and later). You will often use these methods to save the application's state or to perform any cleanup activities before the application closes. In general, applicationWillTerminate: is used only by pre-iOS 4.0 devices, while applicationDidEnterBackground: is used by everything from iOS 4.0 and on. If you are supporting both devices, the methods are often duplicates of each other.

applicationWillTerminate:

UIKit calls this UIApplicationDelegate method just before an application terminates on devices before iOS 4.0. It may be called on iOS 4.0 and later, but that is somewhat rare. The application must be executing in the background when it needs to terminate suddenly (e.g., in response to a low memory warning). More typically, when the user taps the home button, your application will move first to the background and will then become suspended. Then when suspended applications are terminated, they die silently without any additional notifications.

This method has approximately 5 seconds to perform any cleanup activities and return. If it takes longer than 5 seconds, the application will be killed.

applicationDidEnterBackground:

In iOS 4.0 and later, this UIApplicationDelegate method is called before the application is sent to the background. You should perform any cleanup activities here, since your application may be terminated while in the background. As mentioned earlier, applicationWillTerminate: is not called when your application is suspended, so you may not receive any additional notifications.

Like applicationWillTerminate:, you have approximately 5 seconds to complete any actions. However, you can request additional time by calling beginBackgroundTaskWithExpirationHandler:.

continues on next page

Low Memory Warnings

These methods are called whenever your application receives a low memory warning. You should implement these methods to free up any unneeded memory. If the low memory condition persists, your app may crash, and memory shortages are the most common source of iOS application crashes.

applicationDidReceiveMemoryWarning:

This UIApplicationDelegate method is called when the application receives a low memory warning. You can use it to free up any unneeded memory (for example, any cache memory your app may be holding onto).

didReceiveMemoryWarning

This UIViewController method is called when the application receives a low memory warning. By default, if the controller's view does not have a superview (so it is not currently being displayed), and if it can be rebuilt either by calling loadView or by loading it from a nib, then the view is unloaded.

Most of the time, the default implementation is sufficient. You can override this method and perform any additional actions to free up memory here, but be sure to call the super method when you are done.

viewDidUnload

This UIViewController method is called whenever the view is unloaded as part of a low memory warning. The viewDidUnload method is often the inverse of viewDidLoad. Anything you created in viewDidLoad should be released in viewDidUnload.

In addition, if you have any outlets or instance variables that contain references to user interface elements (such as buttons, text fields, or subviews), you should release them here. These will be rebuilt when the view is reloaded.

Additionally, you should not refer to self.view (or similar variants, such as self.tableview) in this method. This will force the view to reload, and since you are experiencing a memory shortage, it could cause the app to crash.

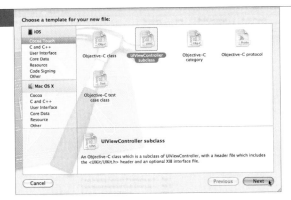

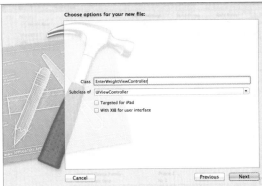

Now that our house is in order, let's start building the app. We will begin with the tab bar. To do that, we need the controllers for our three main views: `EnterWeightViewController`, `HistoryViewController`, and `GraphViewController`.

Right-click the Controllers group and select New File from the pop-up menu. In the panel, select iOS > Cocoa Touch > UIViewController subclass and click the Next button (**Figure 3.9**).

In the "Choose options" panel, type **EnterWeightViewController** in the class field. The "Subclass of" setting should be set to `UIViewController`. The "Targeted for iPad" and "With XIB for user interface" checkboxes should be unselected. Once you verify the settings, click Next (**Figure 3.10**).

The last panel lets us set the save location. Here, the default settings should be fine. We want to save it in the Health Beat directory. It should be part of the Controllers group, and we want to add it to the Health Beat target (**Figure 3.11**). Click Create.

Repeat this procedure for the `GraphViewController`. When you create the `HistoryViewController`, there is one slight change. In the "Choose options" panel, change "Subclass of" to `UITableViewController` (**Figure 3.12**).

While we're here, let's make a second `UITableViewController`, but name this one `DetailViewController`. We will use this to display a detailed view of any items selected from our history view. Our Controllers group should now contain eight files—a header file and an implementation file for each of our four view controllers. Let's start linking them together.

Open the `MainStoryboard.storyboard` file, and zoom out a bit. We want to add new scenes for our four new controllers. First, drag a view controller from the Object library and place it next to our tab bar controller (**Figure 3.13**). In the Identity inspector, change its class to `EnterWeightViewController`.

FIGURE 3.9 Creating a new UIViewController subclass

FIGURE 3.10 Configuring the UIViewController subclass

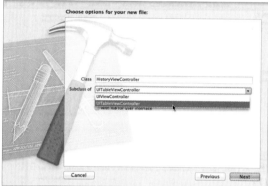

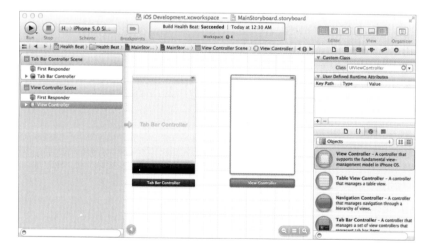

FIGURE 3.11 Saving the
`EnterWeightViewController`

FIGURE 3.12 Selecting the
`UITableViewController`
subclass

FIGURE 3.13 Adding a new
scene

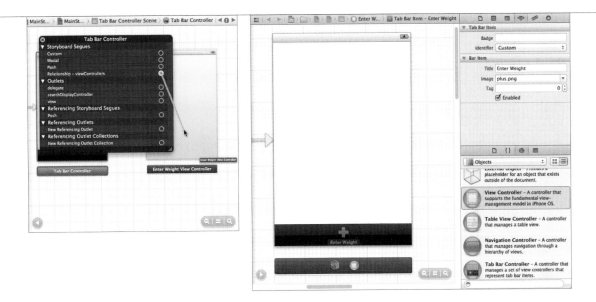

Now, Control-click the tab bar controller to bring up its connections pop-up. Drag a connection from the `Relationship - viewControllers` storyboard segue to the new view controller. This will add that scene to the tab bar (**Figure 3.14**).

Zoom in on our new view and select its tab bar item. In the Attributes inspector, set the Title attribute to **Enter Weight** and the Image attribute to `plus.png`. These set the tab's label and icon, respectively (**Figure 3.15**).

FIGURE 3.14 Adding our scene to the tab bar

FIGURE 3.15 Setting the tab's icon and title

> **NOTE:** When we add a view controller to the tab bar's `viewControllers` storyboard segue, Interface Builder draws a segue-like connection between our two view controllers. However, this connection is technically a relationship—not a segue. We cannot change its attributes, and it does not trigger the `prepareForSegue:sender:` method.

Next, add the graph view. Just repeat the previous steps. Drag out a view controller. Set its class to `GraphViewController`. Connect it to the tab bar's `viewControllers` storyboard segue; we can connect `viewControllers` to as many view controllers as we need. Then set the tab bar item's Title attribute to **Graph** and its Image attribute to `graph.png`.

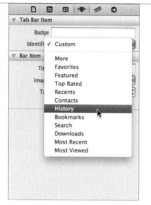

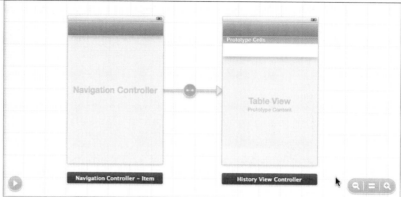

FIGURE 3.16 Embedding the history view controller in a navigation controller

FIGURE 3.17 Setting a preset tab bar item

Lastly, we need to add our history view; however, we want this view to be embedded in a navigation controller. Start by dragging out a table view controller and set its class to `HistoryViewController`. Now, select the controller and choose Editor > Embed In > Navigation Controller. This will add a navigation controller to our view and connect our `HistoryViewController` to it (**Figure 3.16**).

Now we just connect the tab bar controller's `viewControllers` segue to our new navigation controller. Be sure to connect it to the navigation controller—not to our history view controller. Also, instead of setting the tab bar item's Title and Image attributes, we will use one of Xcode's preset tabs. Simply change its Identifier attribute from Custom to History (**Figure 3.17**). This will automatically set the icon and label text.

As you can see, Xcode provides a number of preset tab bar items. You should use these whenever possible. This helps provide consistency across applications. When the user sees these tab bar items, they will recognize them and instantly understand their intended use.

We still need to link in our `DetailViewController`. Drag out another table view controller and place it next to our history view controller. Set its class to `Detail ViewController`. Our history view will display a running list of weight entries sorted by date. We want to open a detailed view for an entry whenever the user selects it from the list, but how do we link it up in our storyboard?

Zoom in on our two table views. As you can see, each view controller contains a single prototype table-view cell. We can use these prototype cells to lay out custom rows for our table views. We can also draw connections to and from these cells.

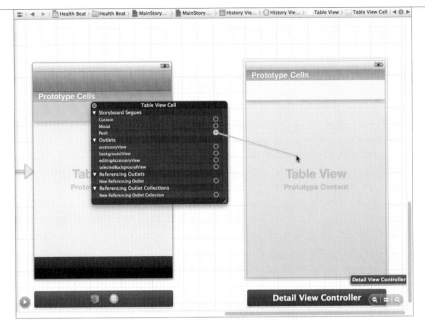

FIGURE 3.18 Connecting a segue from the cell prototype

Right-click our history view controller's prototype cell. Draw a connection from its Push storyboard segue to our detail view controller (**Figure 3.18**). That's it. As long as we create all our history view's table cells using that prototype, they will automatically launch the detail view when selected.

You may also notice that interface builder automatically adds the navigation bar to all the views linked to our navigation controller. However, these bars look a little bit plain. Let's add custom titles to them. In our history view controller scene, double-click the navigation bar and set its title to **History** (alternatively, select the navigation bar and set the Title attribute). Do the same for the detail view controller, but set the title to **Weight Entry**.

That's it. Take a few seconds to zoom out and organize your storyboard. When you're done, it should look like **Figure 3.19**.

Let's take our new user interface out for a spin. Unfortunately, there are a few loose threads we need to tie off before it will compile. Zoom in on our history view controller again, and select its prototype cell. We need to set the cell's reuse identifier. We'll discuss reuse identifiers in detail in the "Showing Weight History" section of Chapter 4. For now, open the Attributes inspector, and set the Identity attribute to History Cell.

FIGURE 3.19 The completed
storyboard

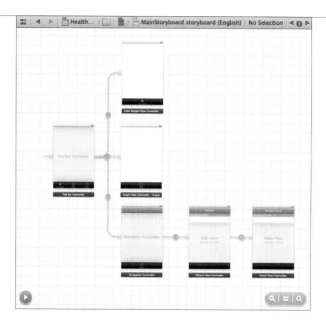

Do the same thing for the detail view controller, but set its cell identifier to
Detail Cell.

Next, open `HistoryViewController.m` and navigate to the `numberOfSections
InTableView:` method. We need to get rid of the #warning directive before our code
will compile. Also, if we want to be able to open the detail view, we need to have
at least one section and one row. To do this, modify the method as shown here:

```
- (NSInteger)numberOfSectionsInTableView:(UITableView *)tableView
{
    // TODO temporary code to get the interface to run
    // Return the number of sections.
    return 1;
}
```

We need to do something similar in `tableView:numberOfRowsInSection:`. This
method should return the number of rows for a given section. Let's give ourselves
a single row, so we can test out our connections.

```
- (NSInteger)tableView:(UITableView *)tableView
 numberOfRowsInSection:(NSInteger)section
{
    // TODO temporary code to get the interface to run
    // Return the number of rows in the section.
    return 1;
}
```

Finally, we need to tell our controller to use our reuse identifier. Navigate to
tableView:cellForRowAtIndexPath:. This method returns the cell for a given
row—reusing cells where possible, creating new ones when necessary. Again, we
will discuss this in more detail in Chapter 4. For now, just change the cell identifier to History Cell.

```
- (UITableViewCell *)tableView:(UITableView *)tableView
        cellForRowAtIndexPath:(NSIndexPath *)indexPath
{
    static NSString *CellIdentifier = @"History Cell";
    UITableViewCell *cell =
    [tableView dequeueReusableCellWithIdentifier:CellIdentifier];
    if (cell == nil) {
        cell = [[UITableViewCell alloc]
                initWithStyle:UITableViewCellStyleDefault
                reuseIdentifier:CellIdentifier];
    }
    // Configure the cell...
    return cell;
}
```

Finally, switch to DetailViewController.m. We need to make the same changes,
but this time we set the cell identifier to Detail Cell.

FIGURE 3.20 Our skeletal user interface

Run the application. The tab bar will appear with our three tabs (**Figure 3.20**). You can tap the tabs to switch between views. Also, if you tap the top row in the history view, you will navigate to the detail view. Tapping the History button takes us back to the history view. Notice how our navigation controller automatically sets the back button's name using the titles from our previous views.

It's a little boring, what with all the views and table cells being empty. Also, since nothing's labeled, it can be a bit hard to tell what's going on. Still, it works—and that's all that matters at this point. We'll fill in all the details later.

We have the skeleton for our application. Now we need to add some meat. Let's sketch out the model layer for our application and then wire it in to our view controllers.

BUILDING THE MODEL

As we discussed in Chapter 2, most iOS applications can be divided into three main sections: the model, the view, and the controller. So far, we've been laying out and linking our controllers and views. However, we still need the model—the repository that will manage and store our data.

For this project, our model will consist of two separate classes. A WeightEntry object will represent a single entry, while the WeightHistory class will manage the entire set of entries.

WEIGHTENTRY CLASS

The data for Health Beat is relatively simple. We will have a number of entries. Each entry will have a date and a weight. Let's start by building an object to represent a single entry. Right-click the Model group, and select New File. Select an iOS > Cocoa Touch > Objective-C class, and make it a subclass of NSObject. Name the class WeightEntry, and save it.

We need to add two properties to this class, one for the weight and one for the date. For simple data-storage classes like these, I like to make my classes immutable—once you set the value, you cannot change it. This helps keep the code simple and clean.

Open WeightEntry.h, and declare our properties as shown here:

```
@interface WeightEntry : NSObject
@property (nonatomic, assign, readonly) CGFloat weightInLbs;
@property (nonatomic, strong, readonly) NSDate* date;
@end
```

Here, I've chosen to store the weight as a simple float value, and the date (and time) using the NSDate object. As the property name suggests, we will store the weight in pounds. Also, even though these are readonly properties, we still need to give an ownership attribute to the date property. I've also added the assign attribute to the weightInLbs property. It's not strictly necessary, since properties use assign ownership by default, but I like to make it clear.

Switch to the WeightEntry.m implementation file and add the lines to synthesize these properties inside the @implementation block:

```
@implementation WeightEntry
@synthesize weightInLbs = _weightInLbs;
@synthesize date = _date;
```

Weights, currency, date formats—all these simple-seeming concepts tend to get overly complicated whenever you want to support multiple countries or cultures. For the purpose of this project, we will want to support both pounds and kilograms. To keep the code as streamlined as possible, we will use pounds as the canonical weight internally. We will then add helper functions to convert from pounds to kilograms and from kilograms to pounds as needed.

Let's start by defining an enumeration of our weight units. Switch back to the header file and add the following code right before the @interface declaration:

```
#import <Foundation/Foundation.h>
typedef enum {
    LBS,
    KG
} WeightUnit;
@interface WeightEntry : NSObject {
```

Now, declare our designated initializer right after the @property declarations:

```
@property (nonatomic, assign, readonly) CGFloat weightInLbs;
@property (nonatomic, strong, readonly) NSDate* date;
- (id) initWithWeight:(CGFloat)weight
        usingUnits:(WeightUnit)unit
           forDate:(NSDate*)date;
@end
```

This will take a weight, the unit type for our weight, and a date and initialize our WeightEntry object. Switch back to the implementation file. We need to implement both our designated initializer and our superclass's designated initializer.

```objc
// Designated initializer.
- (id) initWithWeight:(CGFloat)weight
         usingUnits:(WeightUnit)unit
            forDate:(NSDate*)date {
    self = [super init];
    if (self) {
        if (unit == LBS) {
            _weightInLbs = weight;
        }
        else {
            _weightInLbs = [WeightEntry convertKgToLbs:weight];
        }
        _date = date;
    }
    return self;
}
// Must override the superclass's designated initializer.
- (id)init {
    NSDate* referenceDate =
    [NSDate dateWithTimeIntervalSince1970:0.0f];
    return [self initWithWeight:0.0f
                    usingUnits:LBS
                       forDate:referenceDate];
}
```

If our weight value is already in pounds, we simply assign it to the _weightInLbs variable. If not, we convert it to pounds first and then assign it. Finally, we assign our date object. The init method is included for completeness. Here, we create an object with no weight and with a zero-valued time stamp. This won't be particularly useful, but we should always override the superclass's designated initializer, even if we just throw an exception.

ADDING HELPER METHODS

You may have noticed that there is a problem with our designated initializer. The class method [WeightEntry convertKgToLbs:weight] does not actually exist. Let's fix that. Switch back to the header file and declare the following two class methods:

```
@interface WeightEntry : NSObject {

}
@property (nonatomic, assign, readonly) CGFloat weightInLbs;
@property (nonatomic, strong, readonly) NSDate* date;
+ (CGFloat)convertLbsToKg:(CGFloat)lbs;
+ (CGFloat)convertKgToLbs:(CGFloat)kg;
- (id) initWithWeight:(CGFloat)weight
        usingUnits:(WeightUnit)unit
          forDate:(NSDate*)date;
@end
```

Go back to the implementation file. Just before the @implementation block, add the following static variables. LBS_PER_KG will be used to convert from pounds to kilograms and back, while formatter will be used to provide a standard format for all weight values, using the proper number formatting for your current locale. Yes, number formatting changes from country to country as well.

```
static const CGFloat LBS_PER_KG = 2.20462262f;
static NSNumberFormatter* formatter;
```

Now, in the @implementation block, add our class methods:

```
+ (CGFloat)convertLbsToKg:(CGFloat)lbs {
    return lbs / LBS_PER_KG;
}
+ (CGFloat)convertKgToLbs:(CGFloat)kg {
    return kg * LBS_PER_KG;
}
```

Converting the float values is fine, but we will also want to standardize how our weights are displayed. Let's add some helper methods to create standardized strings from our weights. Back in the header file, declare the following class methods:

```
+ (NSString*)stringForUnit:(WeightUnit)unit;
+ (NSString*)stringForWeight:(CGFloat)weight
                      ofUnit:(WeightUnit)unit;
+ (NSString*)stringForWeightInLbs:(CGFloat)weight
                          inUnit:(WeightUnit)unit;
```

Now switch back to WeightEntry.m and add the implementations:

```
+ (void)initialize {
    formatter = [[NSNumberFormatter alloc] init];
    [formatter setNumberStyle:NSNumberFormatterDecimalStyle];
    [formatter setMinimum:[NSNumber numberWithFloat:0.0f]];
    [formatter setMaximumFractionDigits:2];
}
+ (NSString*)stringForUnit:(WeightUnit)unit {
    switch (unit) {
        case LBS:
            return @"lbs";
        case KG:
            return @"kg";
        default:
            [NSException raise:NSInvalidArgumentException
                format:@"The value %d is not a valid WeightUnit",
                unit];
    }
    // This will never be executed.
    return @"";
}
```

```
+ (NSString*)stringForWeight:(CGFloat)weight
                    ofUnit:(WeightUnit)unit {
    NSString* weightString =
        [formatter stringFromNumber:
        [NSNumber numberWithFloat:weight]];
    NSString* unitString = [WeightEntry stringForUnit:unit];
    return [NSString stringWithFormat:@"%@ %@",
            weightString,
            unitString];
}
+ (NSString*)stringForWeightInLbs:(CGFloat)weight
                        inUnit:(WeightUnit)unit {
    CGFloat convertedWeight;
    switch (unit) {
        case LBS:
            convertedWeight = weight;
            break;
        case KG:
            convertedWeight = [WeightEntry convertLbsToKg:weight];
            break;
        default:
            [NSException raise:NSInvalidArgumentException
                    format:@"%d is not a valid WeightUnit",
                    unit];
    }
    return [WeightEntry stringForWeight:convertedWeight
                            ofUnit:unit];
}
```

The `initialize` method is a special method that the Objective-C runtime calls once when the class is first loaded. You can implement it to perform class-level configurations. Here we use it to format our static `format` variable. This one variable will be used for all our number formatting needs. It will format decimal-styled numbers with up to two digits after the decimal place (rounding weights to the closest hundredth).

We are also limiting it to positive numbers. By default, the `NSNumberFormatter` uses our current locale to determine how decimal numbers should be formatted. For example, here in the United States I use a period for the decimal point. However, in some parts of Europe you would use a comma instead. `NSNumberFormatter` transparently manages those details, letting us automatically localize our application.

Next, the `stringForUnit:` method uses a switch statement to evaluate the value of the `unit` argument. If `unit` equals `LBS`, it returns `@"lbs"`. If `unit` equals `KG`, it returns `@"kg"`. For anything else, it throws an exception.

Exceptions should be familiar to anyone with a Java background. They are raised when something has gone wrong in your application. If the exception is left uncaught, the application will crash, printing an appropriate message to the console. However, there is a significant difference in philosophy between Java and Objective-C.

In Java, exceptions are caught and processed as a regular part of executing the program. They are often used to manage the flow of control whenever relatively common errors occur (for example, trying to open a file that doesn't exist).

In Objective-C, exceptions are reserved for things that are truly exceptional. Or to put it another way, they are reserved for problems that should never occur during the regular operation of our application. As a result, exceptions are usually caused by developer errors (in our example here, by passing in an invalid `WeightUnit` value). As a result, we rarely write code to catch exceptions in Objective-C. Instead, when we see a raised exception during testing, we look for the error in our code and fix it.

The `stringForWeight:ofUnit:` method takes a weight value and a unit value and combines them into a single string. We start by creating a string from our number. We wrap the float-valued weight in an `NSNumber` object and then pass that to the formatter's `stringFromNumber:` method. This will produce a correctly formatted, localized decimal string. Next, we get the unit string. We then combine the two with a space in between.

Finally, `stringForWeightInLbs:inUnit:` takes a weight value in pounds and converts it to the proper unit (if necessary). Then it builds a properly formatted string. Notice that each of these methods build upon the previous ones: `stringForWeightInLbs:inUnits:` calls `stringForWeight:ofUnit:` to format the weight string, while `stringForWeight:ofUnit:` calls `stringForUnit:` to get the proper unit string.

Now, let's add a couple of instance methods that will leverage these class methods. Remember, class methods are called using the class name. They don't have any access to an individual instance's internal values. They often deal with class-level details (like providing convenience methods for allocating and initializing objects). In this case, we are simply using the class as a convenient location for storing a set of related helper methods.

Instance methods, on the other hand, will be called on objects directly. They will have access to the object's internal values. Switch back to the header file, and declare the following methods:

```
- (CGFloat)weightInUnit:(WeightUnit)unit;

- (NSString*)stringForWeightInUnit:(WeightUnit)unit;
```

The `weightInUnit:` method will return the weight value for the given Weight Entry object in the specified unit. The `stringForWeightInUnit:` method will return a string containing the weight value (rounded to the nearest hundredth) followed by the unit label for the specified unit. Let's look at the implementation:

```
- (CGFloat)weightInUnit:(WeightUnit)unit {
    switch (unit) {
        case LBS:
            return self.weightInLbs;
        case KG:
            return [WeightEntry convertLbsToKg:self.weightInLbs];
        default:
            [NSException raise:NSInvalidArgumentException
                format:@"The value %d is not a valid WeightUnit",
                unit];
```

```
    }
    // This will never be executed.
    return 0.0f;
}
- (NSString*)stringForWeightInUnit:(WeightUnit)unit {
    return [WeightEntry stringForWeight:[self weightInUnit:unit]
                                ofUnit:unit];
}
```

The weightInUnit: method simply uses a switch statement to evaluate the unit argument, just as we saw before. If the unit is LBS, it returns the object's weight in pounds. For KG units, it converts the object's weight before returning it. For anything else, it throws an exception.

REFACTORING

We have seen the switch statement used in almost identical ways three different times. In general, this is a sign that the code may need to be refactored to remove these repetitive structures. Imagine if we wanted to add another weight unit—for example, stones. We would need to go through our code and change all the switch statements individually.

One approach to refactoring this code would be to convert WeightEntry to an abstract class and then implement a subclass for each unit type. We can then have each subclass's weight and description methods just return the appropriate values in the proper units. We would probably need additional methods to convert from one subclass to the other, but it wouldn't be hard to get rid of all the switch statements. And, if we ever needed to add another unit type, we could just create a new WeightEntry subclass.

However, in this case, the repeated code is short enough and the class is small enough that it's probably not worth the effort. Still, you should always keep an eye out for places where you can remove repetitive code.

The `stringForWeightInUnit:` method simply gets the object's current weight value in the specified unit and calls the `stringForWeight:ofUnit:` class method to generate the properly formatted string.

THE WEIGHTHISTORY CLASS

Now we need a class to manage all of our `WeightEntries`. Internally we will use an `NSMutableArray` to manage the list of entries; however, we don't want anything outside the model to modify it. Instead, let's wrap it up a bit, giving us more control over its use.

Create a new class inside the Model group. This should be a subclass of `NSObject`. Name the class `WeightHistory`. Now open `WeightHistory.h`. The first thing we want to do is import our `WeightEntry` class. While we're at it, let's add a few string constant keys. Our controllers will use these later to observe changes within the `WeightHistory` class. Add the highlighted code as shown:

```
#import <Foundation/Foundation.h>
#import "WeightEntry.h"
static NSString* const WeightHistoryChangedDefaultUnitsNotification =
    @"WeightHistory changed the default units";
static NSString* const KVOWeightChangeKey = @"weightHistory";
@interface WeightHistory : NSObject {
}
```

Normally, I prefer to avoid putting `#import` directives in my header files. You can often use forward declarations for any unknown object pointers and then import the actual header file in your implementation files. This reduces the number of dependencies between headers and can greatly reduce the amount of time it takes to compile large projects.

Here, however, we will need access to the `WeightUnit` type in our `WeightHistory.h` header. Remember, `WeightUnit` is an enum, not an object, so we cannot use forward declarations. If we wanted to be really anal, we could move `WeightUnit` to its own header file and just import that, but importing `WeightEntry.h` works well enough.

Now let's add our properties to the @interface block:

```
@interface WeightHistory : NSObject {

}
// This is a virtual property.
@property (nonatomic, readonly) NSArray* weights;

@property (nonatomic, assign, readwrite) WeightUnit defaultUnits;

@end
```

As the comment indicates, the weights array is a virtual property. Unlike most properties, weights will not simply provide accessors to an instance variable. Instead, the value returned by weights will be dynamically generated during runtime. As we will see, this requires some extra work on our part.

Now let's add two instance methods to this class. Place these below the @property declarations.

```
- (void)addWeight:(WeightEntry*)weight;
- (void)removeWeightAtIndex:(NSUInteger)index;
```

This declares a method to add a new WeightEntry and a method to remove any specified WeightEntry. That's it, the interface is done, at least for now. We'll come back and add a few more methods in Chapter 6, when we start saving and loading the model.

Now let's switch to the implementation file (`WeightHistory.m`). We will start by using an extension to declare a private property. This property should only be accessed inside `WeightHistory`'s implementation. Add the following code right before the `@implementation` block:

```
@interface WeightHistory()
@property (nonatomic, strong) NSMutableArray* weightHistory;
@end
```

Next, let's synthesize our properties. Since `weights` is a virtual property, we don't need to synthesize it. We will implement its getter manually. This also means our compiler won't create an instance variable for us—which is exactly what we want. Both `defaultUnits` and `weightHistory` should be synthesized.

```
@implementation WeightHistory
@synthesize weightHistory = _weightHistory;
@synthesize defaultUnits = _defaultUnits;
@end
```

Now let's add support for the `weights` virtual property. We need to do two things. First, we need a getter that returns our `weightHistory` property cast as an immutable `NSArray`. Second, we need to ensure that key-value observing (KVO) will work properly—anyone observing our virtual property needs to be alerted whenever the underlying data changes.

NOTE: The rest of this section includes a discussion of advanced topics. Don't worry if you do not follow all of it the first time. Go ahead and type in the code as written, then come back and review it once the project is complete. It should make more sense once you see it in action. You can also find more information in Apple's Key-Value Coding Programming Guide and Key-Value Observing Programming Guide.

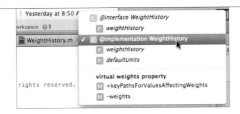

FIGURE 3.21 Using the #pragma mark directive to organize your code

To get started, add the highlighted code shown here:

```
@implementation WeightHistory
@synthesize weightHistory = _weightHistory;
@synthesize defaultUnits = _defaultUnits;
#pragma mark - virtual weights property
// This ensures key-value observing works for weights.
+ (NSSet *)keyPathsForValuesAffectingWeights {
    return [NSSet setWithObjects:@"weightHistory", nil];
}
// Virtual property implementation.
- (NSArray*) weights {
    return self.weightHistory;
}
@end
```

First things first, the #pragma mark directive is a convenient technique for organizing your code. The compiler ignores it completely; however, Xcode will use the #pragma mark directives to add labels and dividing lines when displaying your class's details in the jump bar. For example, after entering the code, click the @implementation WeightHistory item in the editor's jump bar (or whatever the last item in the jump bar happens to be). It will now have a line and header separating our new methods from the rest of the class (**Figure 3.21**).

Next, we have a method named keyPathsForValuesAffectingWeights. Whenever KVO is used to observe a value, the runtime looks for a method named keyPaths ForValuesAffecting<key>, where <key> is the name of the value being observed. This method, if it exists, should return an NSSet containing all the keys that the observed value depends upon. Anyone observing <key> will be notified whenever any of the listed values are changed. In our case, anyone using KVO to monitor the weights property should receive notifications whenever weightHistory changes.

Then we have the accessor itself. Here we just return a reference to our weight History object. This isn't the most bulletproof approach. We could create an immutable copy and return that, or we could remove the weights property entirely, creating additional indexed accessors as needed. However, this approach is fast, and it does communicate our intent. The weightHistory array should never be modified outside the WeightHistory class. Given Objective-C's dynamic nature, a determined developer can always find ways to break encapsulation and monkey with our internal data, so this is probably good enough.

We still need to initialize our object. Simply override the init method, as shown:

```
#pragma mark - initialization

- (id)init
{
    self = [super init];
    if (self) {
        // Set initial defaults.
        _defaultUnits = LBS;
        _weightHistory = [[NSMutableArray alloc] init];
    }
    return self;
}
```

Here we simply set up reasonable initial defaults—creating an empty history list and setting the default units to pounds.

OK, let's look at our accessor methods. The @synthesize directive automatically creates a default implementation for setDefaultUnits:, but we want to do some additional custom processing. Let's implement our own version.

```
#pragma mark - accessor methods
- (void)setDefaultUnits:(WeightUnit)units {
    // If we are setting the current value, do nothing.
    if (_defaultUnits == units) return;
    _defaultUnits = units;
    // Send a notification.
    [[NSNotificationCenter defaultCenter]
    postNotificationName:
     → WeightHistoryChangedDefaultUnitsNotification
    object:self];
}
```

The setDefaultUnits: method is straightforward. First, we check to see if the unit argument is the same as our current default units. If they are different, we set the default units and post a notification to the notification center.

This raises an interesting question. Why would we use notifications instead of key-value observing? Well, the simplest answer is that I wanted to show you both approaches. However, KVO and notifications both have unique strengths and weaknesses.

As long as we are observing KVO-compliant values, KVO doesn't require any actions on the part of the observed object. All the notifications are posted automatically. However, on the receiving side, everything is routed through the observeValueForKeyPath:ofObject:change:context: method. As you can imagine, if you start observing a large number of values, this method can quickly become long and hard to read.

The notification framework, on the other hand, gives us more flexibility. Any object registering to receive notifications can specify a selector that is called whenever the notification is received. Yes, we have to manually post our notifications, but that also gives us the freedom to design exactly when and why our notifications are posted.

Next, look at our implementation of addWeight: and removeWeightAtIndex:.

```
- (void)addWeight:(WeightEntry*)weight {
    // Manually send KVO messages.
    [self willChange:NSKeyValueChangeInsertion
     valuesAtIndexes:[NSIndexSet indexSetWithIndex:0]
              forKey:KVOWeightChangeKey];
    // Add to the front of the list.
    [self.weightHistory insertObject:weight atIndex:0];
    // Manually send KVO messages.
    [self didChange:NSKeyValueChangeInsertion
     valuesAtIndexes:[NSIndexSet indexSetWithIndex:0]
              forKey:KVOWeightChangeKey];
}
// This will be auto KVO'ed.
- (void)removeWeightAtIndex:(NSUInteger)weightIndex;{
    // Manually send KVO messages.
    [self willChange:NSKeyValueChangeRemoval
     valuesAtIndexes:[NSIndexSet indexSetWithIndex:weightIndex]
              forKey:KVOWeightChangeKey];
    // Add to the front of the list.
    [self.weightHistory removeObjectAtIndex:weightIndex];
    // Manually send KVO messages.
    [self didChange:NSKeyValueChangeRemoval
     valuesAtIndexes:[NSIndexSet indexSetWithIndex:weightIndex]
              forKey:KVOWeightChangeKey];
}
```

These should be relatively straightforward wrappers, letting us add objects to and remove objects from the private `weightHistory` array. However, we also need to make these methods key-value observing compliant.

Key-value observing's automatic notification only works if you modify variables using KVO-compliant accessor methods. Most of the time, this is automatic. When we define a property, the synthesized accessors are (by default) KVO compliant.

However, collections are a little trickier. First of all, collection notifications not only alert you to changes but also pass on information about what has changed, such as whether you added, removed, or replaced a value, as well as the index of the change. To support these, you must have the proper indexed accessor methods: `insertObject:in<Key>AtIndex:`, `replaceObjectIn<Key>AtIndex:`, and (optionally) `removeObjectFrom<Key>AtIndex:`.

This means that if we replace `addWeight:` and `removeWeightAtIndex:` with `insertObject:inWeightHistoryAtIndex:` and `removeObjectFromWeightHistory AtIndex:`, we would gain automatic KVO compliance. However, the KVO-compliant methods don't quite do what we want.

We want our weight entries to appear in reverse chronological order, so the most recent entry is always the first in the list. We can enforce this by always adding `WeightEntry` objects to the front of the `weightHistory` array.

We could use a KVO-compliant method for just the removals, but that doesn't help either. We must implement both the insert-indexed and the remove-indexed accessors to generate automatic notifications. Implementing `removeObjectFrom WeightHistoryAtIndex:` by itself does nothing.

So, instead, I have chosen to use slightly more informative method names (in my opinion, at least) and to manually send out KVO messages. We do this by calling `willChange:valuesAtIndexes:forKey:` before the change is made and then calling `didChange:valuesAtIndexes:ForKey:` afterwards.

For more information on key-value observing, I highly recommend reading through both the Key-Value Coding Programming Guide and the Key-Value Observing Programming Guide in Apple's documentation.

CONNECTING THE MODEL

Now we need to connect our model objects to our controllers. This often causes some confusion—after all, the controllers are created by our storyboard. How do we get our data objects into them?

In theory, we could add our model objects to the storyboard and let it create them as well. This isn't a bad approach; however, we lose some control over our objects. Any objects in the storyboard will be created when the scene is loaded. If our data object is loaded as part of our initial scene, it could cause a delay when launching our application—especially when loading a particularly large file or loading resources from the network.

More importantly, we cannot connect the outlets in one scene to objects in another. If we could add our model to our initial scene and then connect it to outlets in all our other scenes, I would be strongly tempted to add objects to storyboards. As it is, there are probably better solutions.

Another common approach involves creating a singleton class for our model or storing our model in the app delegate (which effectively does the same thing). Personally, I find the app delegate approach a little sloppy, and I try to avoid the dark temptation of singleton classes whenever possible.

Instead, let's use lazy initialization to create our model in our initial scene's controller, and then pass the data to our new scenes when they are loaded.

Let's start by creating a custom UITabBarController subclass. Right-click the Controllers group and select New File > UIViewController subclass. In the options panel, UITabBarController is not one of the options in the "Subclass of" dropdown menu. Instead, we have to type it directly into the field. Then name the controller TabBarController and create it.

Now open TabBarController.h. We also need to add a property to hold our WeightHistory object. Modify the header as shown here:

```
@class WeightHistory;

@interface TabBarController : UITabBarController

@property (nonatomic, strong) WeightHistory* weightHistory;

@end
```

Most of this should be self-explanatory. The only real trick is the first line—@class WeightHistory; is a forward declaration for the WeightHistory class. As mentioned earlier, forward declarations let us avoid importing other classes in our header files. It tells the compiler that we have a class named WeightHistory but that the compiler doesn't need to know the details right away.

Now, switch to the implementation file. Let's start by importing WeightHistory.h and synthesizing our weightHistory property.

```
#import "TabBarController.h"
#import "WeightHistory.h"
@implementation TabBarController
@synthesize weightHistory = _weightHistory;
```

Now, navigate down to the viewDidLoad method stub. It is currently commented out. Uncomment it and add the following:

```
- (void)viewDidLoad
{
    [super viewDidLoad];
    self.weightHistory = [[WeightHistory alloc] init];
    // Create a stack and load it with the view controllers from
    // our tabs.
    NSMutableArray* stack =
        [NSMutableArray arrayWithArray:self.viewControllers];
    // While we still have items on our stack
    while ([stack count] > 0) {
        // pop the last item off the stack.
        id controller = [stack lastObject];
        [stack removeLastObject];
        // If it is a container object, add its controllers to
        // the stack.
        if ([controller respondsToSelector:
            @selector(viewControllers)]) {
```

```
        [stack addObjectsFromArray:
            [controller viewControllers]];
    }
    // If it responds to setWeightHistory, set the weight
    // history.
    if ([controller respondsToSelector:
            @selector(setWeightHistory:)]) {
        [controller setWeightHistory:self.weightHistory];
    }
}}
```

We start by creating a new WeightHistory object and assigning it to our weight
History property. Then things get interesting. We create a mutable array and fill
it with the controllers for our tabs. We then use this array as a stack, taking each
controller off the stack and processing it in turn.

If the controller acts as a container for other controllers (i.e., navigation controller, tab bar controller, split view controller, or page view controller), we add its
controllers to our stack. Finally, if the controller has a setWeightHistory: method,
we call it, passing in our newly created WeightHistory object.

For our current project, we will assign the weight history directly to our Enter
WeightViewController and GraphViewController objects. However, when we get
the navigation controller, we grab the HistoryViewController from our navigation controller and add it to our stack. Then when the HistoryViewController is
popped off the stack, we assign our weight history to it as well.

We could have simply hard-coded paths to our three main controllers and
passed the data objects directly, but this approach gives us additional flexibility for
future enhancements. We can easily add new view controllers, and our system will
handle them appropriately. We can even handle most view controller containers
without any modification to this code.

This is also an excellent example of how Objective-C's dynamic nature can
greatly simplify our code. We pull an object from the viewControllers array. We
don't need to know its class—or really anything about it. If it responds to the
methods we're interested in, we call those methods. If not, we simply move on to
the next object in our stack.

We still need to tell our application to use this class. Open up the storyboard and zoom in on the tab bar controller. Change its class to our new TabBarController class. Good. Now we just need to add the weightHistory property to our view controllers. Let's start by opening EnterWeightController.h. Modify the interface as shown here:

```
@class WeightHistory;

@interface EnterWeightViewController : UIViewController

@property (nonatomic, strong) WeightHistory* weightHistory;

@end
```

This should look familiar. It's almost exactly what we did to the TabView Controller. Again, we simply create a forward declaration for our WeightHistory class and then declare a weightHistory property. Now, switch to the implementation file. As before, we need to import the WeightHistory class and then synthesize our weightHistory property.

```
#import "EnterWeightViewController.h"

#import "WeightHistory.h"

@implementation EnterWeightViewController

@synthesize weightHistory = _weightHistory;
```

That's it. That's all we have to do. Repeat these steps for our GraphView Controller and HistoryViewController classes.

That just leaves the DetailViewController class. This class is different for two reasons. First, it's not connected directly to our tab bar controller. Instead, our detail view controller scene is loaded when the user selects a row in our history view controller. Second, we want to pass both the WeightHistory and the index of the currently selected row.

Open DetailViewController.h and modify it as shown here:

```
@class WeightHistory;

@interface DetailViewController : UITableViewController

@property (nonatomic, strong) WeightHistory* weightHistory;

@property (nonatomic, assign) NSUInteger selectedIndex;
```

Now, switch to the implementation file, import our `WeightHistory`, and synthesize both properties.

```
#import "DetailViewController.h"
#import "WeightHistory.h"
@implementation DetailViewController
@synthesize weightHistory = _weightHistory;
@synthesize selectedIndex = _selectedIndex;
```

Next, we need to assign values to these properties. To start with, we need to give our segue an identifier so we can recognize it in our code. Open `MainStoryboard` `.storyboard`. Select the segue connecting the history view controller and the detail view controller. Set its Identifier attribute to Push Detail View.

Now open `HistoryViewController.m`. Import our `DetailViewController` class and add a string constant containing our segue identifier.

```
#import "HistoryViewController.h"
#import "WeightHistory.h"
#import "DetailViewController.h"
static NSString* const DetailViewSegueIdentifier =
@"Push Detail View";
@implementation HistoryViewController
@synthesize weightHistory = _weightHistory;
```

Then add the following method:

```
- (void)prepareForSegue:(UIStoryboardSegue *)segue
                sender:(id)sender {
    if ([segue.identifier isEqualToString:
        DetailViewSegueIdentifier]) {
        NSIndexPath* path =
        [self.tableView indexPathForSelectedRow];
        DetailViewController* controller =
        segue.destinationViewController;
```

```
        controller.weightHistory = self.weightHistory;
        controller.selectedIndex = path.row;
    }
}
```

Here, we simply verify that we have a segue opening a detail view, and then we get the index path to the selected row and a reference to our destination view controller. We then assign both the weightHistory and selectedIndex properties for our new DetailViewController.

That's it. We can verify that our data is making it all the way to our detail view by opening DetailViewController.m and navigating to the viewDidApepar: method. Modify this method as shown:

```
- (void)viewDidAppear:(BOOL)animated
{
    [super viewDidAppear:animated];
    NSLog(@"Weight History = %@", self.weightHistory);
    NSLog(@"Selected Index = %d", self.selectedIndex);
}
```

Now run the application. Navigate to the history view, and tap the top row. The following message should appear in the console (of course, the WeightHistory's memory address will probably change).

```
2011-07-21 00:58:39.059 Health Beat[760:207] Weight History =
 →  <WeightHistory: 0x6a1e690>
2011-07-21 00:58:39.061 Health Beat[760:207] Selected Index = 0
```

You can remove the NSLog() calls once you've verified that everything works.

THE **SECRET LIFE** OF **NIBS**

Nibs are the underlying technology behind storyboards. The compiler will break the storyboard into a number of nib files, loading them as necessary. Therefore, to understand what happens when a storyboard loads a scene, we really need to understand the lifecycle of the underlying nibs. I give a brief summary here, but for the full blow-by-blow details, check out Apple's Resource Programming Guide: Nib Files.

When a nib loads, memory is set aside for all the objects and resources inside the nib, and then the entire object graph is instantiated. Objects that conform to the NSCoding protocol will be instantiated by calling initWithCoder:. All other objects are instantiated by calling init.

All outlets are then connected using the setValue:forKey: method. All actions are connected using addTarget :action:forControlEvents:. Once the entire object graph is created, UIKit calls awakeFromNib on each of the objects created by the nib. You can implement an object's awakeFromNib method to perform any additional configuration steps after all the outlets and actions are properly configured.

Note: UIViewController subclasses should do their additional configuration in viewDidLoad instead. The controllers may be created in a different nib than their views. As a result, the awakenFromNib method may be called before the view has loaded, and any outlets connecting to user interface elements in the view's nib may not be properly set up yet.

After the nib has finished loading, any objects that are not stored in a strong reference somewhere will be deallocated. Most of the time, we won't need to worry about this. Unless we're programmatically loading the scene ourselves, the system will automatically store the view controller in our view controller hierarchy (e.g., in the navigation stack or as a modal view controller). The main view is stored in the view controller, and any other user interface elements and gesture recognizers are automatically stored in their containing view.

However, if we add any new top-level objects (data objects or views not yet placed into the view hierarchy), we will need to store a reference to them somewhere. Typically, this means creating an outlet in our view controller and connecting the object to that outlet.

There are a few key points here that are worth emphasizing:

1. Many of the details of how nibs are loaded are different on Mac OS X and iOS. If you are moving back and forth between desktop and mobile development, be sure to double-check the documentation.

2. Any object that conforms to NSCoding will be loaded using initWithCoder:. Unlike other init methods, this does not end up calling your designated initializer. If you are loading custom objects (including UIViewController subclasses) in your nibs, be sure to perform all additional initialization steps in the awakeFromNib method (or viewDidLoad for UIViewController subclasses).

3. If you add a top-level object, be sure to add an outlet for it in your view controller. We need a strong reference to the top-level object, otherwise it will disappear after the nib loads.

4. `UIViewController` subclasses will automatically unload and reload their nibs as part of regular memory management. You cannot assume that a nib will only be loaded once. Similarly, you cannot assume that the controller's `viewDidLoad` method will only be called once.

5. Any outlets set by the nib should be cleared in `viewDidUnload`. Similarly, anything you do in `viewDidLoad` should be undone in `viewDidUnload`. For example, if you assign an object to a property in `viewDidLoad`, be sure to set the property to `nil` in `viewDidUnload`. If the view loads again, we'll reset the property anyway. There's no sense in holding onto memory that we're not currently using.

WRAPPING **UP**

Our app builds and launches. We can switch between the three tabs. Yes, it's just a skeleton—but the next few chapters will put some meat on these bones. In Chapter 4, we will flesh out the `EnterWeightView` and `HistoryView`. In Chapter 5, we will look at drawing custom views with the `GraphView`, and in Chapter 6, we will save both the application data and the user defaults. Finally, in Chapter 7, we will replace Health Beat's current model using Core Data.

One last step before we go. Let's commit our changes to the git repository. It's best to get into the habit of committing changes early and often. That way we can compare our current files with any of the previously committed versions, and if we have to roll back our changes, we can minimize the amount of work we're undoing. It's always better to have a large number of small, incremental steps than to have a few giant strides. Besides, the more commits you have, the more useful version control becomes.

To commit all our changes, go to File > Source Control > Commit. Enter **Chapter 3** as the commit message, and click Commit. That's it. Xcode should take care of the rest.

4

DEVELOPING **VIEWS** AND **VIEW** **CONTROLLERS**

In this chapter, we will flesh out the enter weight and history views for our Health Beat application. As we proceed, we will gain more experience graphically laying out views and linking user interface elements to their view controllers. We will also learn how to populate, monitor, and control a table view; how to set up static table views; and the differences between using a navigation controller and simply presenting modal views.

This chapter also includes a discussion of advanced techniques. We use Core Animation to modify a view's appearance, which lets us create rounded buttons with custom background colors.

FIGURE 4.1 Centering the label

FIGURE 4.2 Stretching a label to fill the view

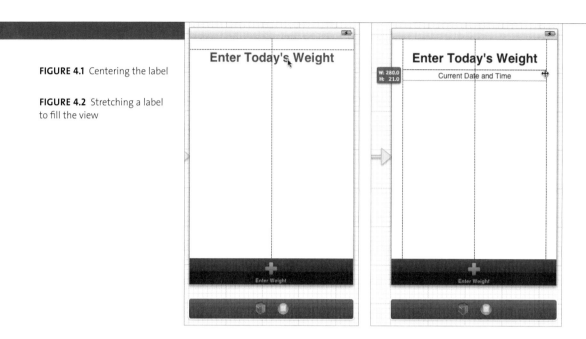

FIGURE 4.1 Centering the label

FIGURE 4.2 Stretching a label to fill the view

Let's start by modifying our enter weight view. Open the `MainStoryboard.storyboard` file, and zoom in on the enter weight scene.

Drag a label from the library and drop it anywhere in the view. Double-click the label, and change the text to **Enter Today's Weight**. In the Attributes inspector, change the font to System Bold 24.0. You can tap the [T] icon to bring up the Fonts window. Next, choose Editor > Size to Fit Content from the menu bar. Finally, center the label along the top of the view using the guidelines (**Figure 4.1**).

Drag out a second label and position it below the first. Change its text to **Current Date and Time**. Don't worry, that's just a placeholder. We will replace this text at runtime. Of course, we don't know exactly how long the date and time string will be, but we still want it centered under our title. The easiest way to do this is to set the label's Alignment attribute to Centered, and then stretch the label so that it fills the view from margin to margin (**Figure 4.2**).

Next, place a text field under the Current Date label. Stretch it so that it also fills the view from margin to margin. Set the attributes as shown in **Table 4.1**.

TABLE 4.1 Text Field Attributes

ATTRIBUTE NAME	VALUE
Alignment	Centered
Capitalization	None
Correction	No
Keyboard	Numbers and Punctuation
Return Key	Done
Auto-enable Return Key	On

FIGURE 4.3 Completed enter weight view controller scene

Whew, that's a lot of settings. Let's step through them one at a time. We want to restrict the input to valid decimal numbers. Also, since we're only allowing numbers, it doesn't make sense to enable autocorrection and capitalization. We may as well turn them off. The Numbers and Punctuation keyboard gives us all the keys we need (all the numbers, a Return key, and—for US English—a period). It actually allows too many characters, so we'll need to filter our input. We'll cover that in a bit.

The last two settings will help us create a more streamlined user interface. Essentially, we want to automatically create a new WeightEntry object and switch to the graph view as soon as the user presses the Return key. This reduces the total number of taps needed to enter a new weight. To help support this, we change the Return key's label to Done to better communicate our intent. More importantly, auto-enabling the Return key means it will be disabled as long as the text field is empty. The system automatically enables the Return key once the user has entered some text. This—when paired with our input filtering—will guarantee that we have a valid weight entry whenever the Return key is pressed.

The interface should now match **Figure 4.3**. The basics are in place, but we're going to spice it up a bit.

As of iOS 4.1 there is a new keyboard type, the UIKeyboardTypeDecimalPad. This keyboard has only numbers, a decimal point, and a backspace. At first glance, this appears perfect for this project. However, it does not have a Return key—and we really want to allow the user to submit the weight value directly from the keyboard.

We could add a Return key (possibly in a custom input accessory view; see the Text, Web, and Editing Programming Guide for iOS), but that creates a more complex user interface.

iOS 5.0 adds another keyboard type, the UIKeyboardTypeTwitter. While not particularly useful for this project, the Twitter keyboard is optimized for writing tweets. It displays all the letters plus the @ and # keys.

Unfortunately, neither of these options appears in Interface Builder—at least, not in the current version of Xcode. Instead, you must set the text field's keyboardType property in code. This isn't hard. In the viewDidLoad method, just add self.weightTextField.keyboardType = UIKeyboardTypeDecimalPad; or self.weightTextField.keyboardType = UIKeyboardTypeTwitter;.

SET AUTOROTATING AND AUTOSIZING

We will want our view to rotate into any orientation. There are two steps to this. First, we must modify the controller to allow autorotation.

Open EnterWeightViewController.m and navigate to the shouldAutorotateTo InterfaceOrientation: method. This method should return YES if the controller's view can rotate to the given interfaceOrientation. In the default implementation, it allows rotation only into the right-side-up portrait orientation.

To allow the app to rotate into any orientation, simply have the method return YES, as shown here:

```
- (BOOL)shouldAutorotateToInterfaceOrientation:
    (UIInterfaceOrientation)interfaceOrientation {
    return YES;
}
```

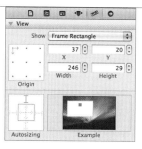

FIGURE 4.4 Autorotation works, but autosizing does not.

FIGURE 4.5 Locking the control to the top of the view

However, if you run the app you may notice that autorotation still isn't working. No matter how you twist the device, the interface remains locked in the portrait orientation.

That's because there's a trick. By default, tab views only allow autorotation if all of the contained view controllers support autorotation. Make the same change to the HistoryViewController and the GraphViewController, and then run the app again.

And...it's still not working. OK, I lied. There were two tricks. When we created a custom tab view, it turns out that we inadvertently overrode the tab bar's default shouldAutorotateToInterfaceOrientation: implementation. Open TabBarController.m, and delete the shouldAutorotateToInterfaceOrientation: method. This will restore the default behavior. Run it one last time. It should finally rotate as expected. Unfortunately, we have another problem (**Figure 4.4**). The UI elements are not properly resizing or repositioning themselves in the new, wider view.

To fix this, open MainStoryboard.storyboard again. Select the Enter Today's Weight label, and open the Size inspector. The Autosizing control allows us to lock the object's position relative to the top, bottom, left, or right sides. It also allows us to automatically stretch and shrink our control horizontally or vertically.

By default, the view is locked to the left and top. We want it locked to the top—but we want it to remain centered in the view. Click the red I-bar on the left side of the Autosizing control to turn it off. After you make changes in the Autosizing control, check the Example preview to make sure the control will behave as you expect. In this case, it should remain centered at the top of the view as the size changes (**Figure 4.5**).

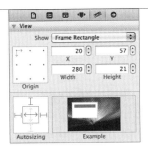

FIGURE 4.6 Stretching the control to fill the view horizontally

FIGURE 4.7 Correct autorotation and autosizing

We want the Current Date and Time label to stretch so it fills the view from margin to margin. Select the label and then lock it to the top, left, and right sides. Also, turn on the horizontal resizing as shown in **Figure 4.6**. Use the same settings for the text field as well.

Run the app again. Now when it rotates into landscape mode, the app should position and resize the controls appropriately (**Figure 4.7**).

MAKING ROOM FOR THE KEYBOARD

Tapping the text field will automatically display the specified keyboard. The system slides the keyboard up from the bottom, covering the lower portion of your content. This will not trigger any autosizing behaviors (the view's size remains unchanged, the bottom portion is simply covered up). You need to make sure your users can see the selected text field and reach your controls. This can create problems, especially in landscape orientation, since the keyboard will cover most of the screen.

In our EnterWeightView, we deliberately positioned all the controls so that they are still visible even in landscape orientation. However, this has two limitations: It makes the view appear somewhat top-heavy, and it's only possible for the simplest views.

Most of the time, you will need to manually reposition or resize the controls (typically using a scroll view) so that the selected control is visible. The keyboard sends out a number of notifications that you can use to make these modifications: UIKeyboardWillShowNotification, UIKeyboardDidShowNotification, UIKeyboard WillHideNotification, and UIKeyboarddidHideNotification.

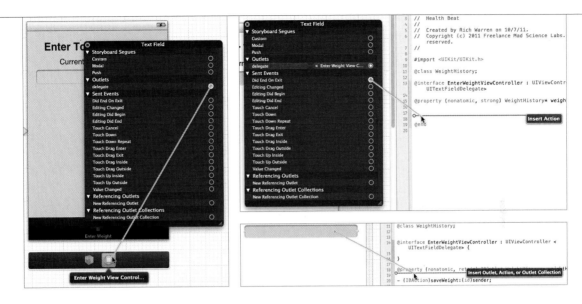

ADDING OUTLETS AND ACTIONS

Let's start by opening EnterWeightViewController.h. We want our controller to conform to the UITextFieldDelegate protocol. This will let us respond to changes in our text field. Modify the header as shown here:

```
@interface EnterWeightViewController : UIViewController
    <UITextFieldDelegate> {

}
```

Switch back to MainStoryboard.storyboard and open the Assistant editor. Make sure EnterWeightViewController.h is shown in the second panel. Then right-click the text field, and drag a connection from the delegate to the view controller icon in the scene's dock (**Figure 4.8**).

Next, drag the Did End On Exit event to the header file and create a new action (**Figure 4.9**). Name the action saveWeight.

Dismiss the connections pop-up window, and Control-drag the text field to the header file (**Figure 4.10**). Create a new strong outlet named weightTextField.

Finally, Control-drag from the Current Date and Time label and create a strong outlet named dateLabel.

FIGURE 4.8 Connecting the text field's delegate

FIGURE 4.9 Creating a new action

FIGURE 4.10 Creating a new outlet

The header file should now appear as shown here:

```
#import <UIKit/UIKit.h>

@class WeightHistory;

@interface EnterWeightViewController : UIViewController
<UITextFieldDelegate>

@property (nonatomic, strong) WeightHistory* weightHistory;

@property (strong, nonatomic) IBOutlet UITextField *weightTextField;

@property (strong, nonatomic) IBOutlet UILabel *dateLabel;

- (IBAction)saveWeight:(id)sender;

@end
```

CREATING THE UNIT BUTTON

Now we want to add a unit button inside the text field. This will allow us to both display the current unit type and change units.

Our unit button is somewhat odd. We won't be adding it directly to our view hierarchy. Instead, we will programmatically assign it to our text field's rightView property. This is not something we can do in Interface Builder.

Of course, we could still create the button in Interface Builder and assign it as a new top-level object. We could then use Interface Builder to configure its settings. Unfortunately, this doesn't really help us, since we won't be able to visually inspect it as we edit it. All things considered, it's probably easiest to just create the button in code.

Open EnterWeightViewController.h and add the following property and action:

```
@property (nonatomic, strong) WeightHistory* weightHistory;

@property (strong, nonatomic) IBOutlet UITextField *weightTextField;

@property (strong, nonatomic) IBOutlet UILabel *dateLabel;

@property (strong, nonatomic) UIButton* unitsButton;

- (IBAction)saveWeight:(id)sender;

- (IBAction)changeUnits:(id)sender;
```

Next, switch to the implementation file and synthesize the property.

```
@synthesize unitsButton=_unitsButton;
```

Now, scroll down to the viewDidLoad method. Modify it as shown:

```
- (void)viewDidLoad
{
    [super viewDidLoad];
    self.unitsButton = [UIButton buttonWithType:UIButtonTypeCustom];
    self.unitsButton.frame = CGRectMake(0.0f, 0.0f, 25.0f, 17.0f);
    self.unitsButton.backgroundColor = [UIColor lightGrayColor];
    self.unitsButton.titleLabel.font =
    [UIFont boldSystemFontOfSize:12.0f];
    self.unitsButton.titleLabel.textAlignment =
    UITextAlignmentCenter;
    [self.unitsButton setTitle:@"lbs"
                    forState:UIControlStateNormal];
    [self.unitsButton setTitleColor:[UIColor darkGrayColor]
```

```
                        forState:UIControlStateNormal];
    [self.unitsButton setTitleColor:[UIColor blueColor]
                        forState:UIControlStateHighlighted];
    [self.unitsButton addTarget:self
                        action:@selector(changeUnits:)
                forControlEvents:UIControlEventTouchUpInside];
    self.weightTextField.rightView = self.unitsButton;
    self.weightTextField.rightViewMode = UITextFieldViewModeAlways;}
```

We start by creating a custom button. Then we configure it. It's 17 points tall and 25 points wide, with a light gray background. We also configure its title. It uses a 12-point bold system font and is center aligned. It's important to center the title; as the user changes units, we will switch the button's label between "lbs" and "kg." Centering the label gives the button a nice, consistent appearance, even when the label's size changes.

Next, we set the default title to "lbs" and then assign text colors for the different control states. Normally the text is dark gray, but when the button is highlighted, the text turns blue.

We also assign the changeUnits: action to our button's UIControlEventTouchUp Inside event. This is identical to drawing a connection between a button's Touch UpInside event and the desired action in Interface Builder. When the unitsButton is touched, the system will call changeUnits:.

Finally, we assign the unit button to the text field's rightView property. This will cause it to appear inside the text field along the right side. We then set the view mode so that our button is always visible.

As always, since we assigned the button in viewDidLoad, we should clear it in viewDidUnload. Navigate down to viewDidUnload and add the following line:

```
self.unitsButton = nil;
```

Finally, add a method stub for our changeUnits: action. We will flesh out this method after adding the change units view to our storyboard.

```
- (IBAction)changeUnits:(id)sender {
    // method stub
}
```

IMPLEMENTING ACTIONS AND CALLBACK METHODS

Now switch to EnterWeightViewController.m. Before we start tackling the action and delegate methods, let's add an extension with a couple of private properties.

```
@interface EnterWeightViewController()
@property (nonatomic, strong) NSDate* currentDate;
@property (nonatomic, strong) NSNumberFormatter* numberFormatter;
@end
```

We're adding two properties: currentDate will hold the current date (based on the date and time when the view appeared), and we will use the numberFormatter to process our user's input.

Next, synthesize these properties.

```
@synthesize currentDate = _currentDate;
@synthesize numberFormatter = _numberFormatter;
```

Then, navigate to the viewDidLoad method. Add the following code to instantiate and configure our number formatter:

```
- (void)viewDidLoad
{
    [super viewDidLoad];
    self.numberFormatter = [[NSNumberFormatter alloc] init];
    [self.numberFormatter
     setNumberStyle:NSNumberFormatterDecimalStyle];
    [self.numberFormatter
     setMinimum:[NSNumber numberWithFloat:0.0f]];
    self.unitsButton = [UIButton buttonWithType:UIButtonTypeCustom];
    self.unitsButton.frame = CGRectMake(0.0f, 0.0f, 25.0f, 17.0f);
    self.unitsButton.backgroundColor = [UIColor lightGrayColor];
    ...
}
```

UICONTROLS AND STATE

Both setTitle:forState: and setTitleColor:forState: refer to the button's state. Every control has a state: normal, highlighted, selected, or disabled. Different actions can change the control's state (see Table 4.2). Our button uses only two. It is highlighted when touched; otherwise, it is normal.

When setting per-state attributes, if you don't explicitly assign a value to a given state, that state will default back to the UIControlStateNormal setting. For example, in our code we only had to set the title once. Unless we say otherwise, every other state will use this value as well.

This brings up a point that is often confused. If you look up UIControlState in the developer documentation, the enum is designed as a bitmask. This means we should be able to combine multiple states using the bit-wise OR operator (|). As a result, you might be tempted to explicitly set the title for all the states using code like this:

```
UIControlState all = UIControlStateNormal |
                     UIControlStateSelected |
                     UIControlStateHighlighted |
                     UIControlStateDisabled;
[self.button setText:@"default text" forState:all]
```

Unfortunately, this does not work. Instead of setting the title for all states, you are actually setting the title for a single state: specifically, the state in which the control is selected, highlighted, and disabled—all at the same time (in this case, UIControlStateNormal is ignored).

This can be handy when creating things like custom two-state buttons. These buttons have an ON and an OFF state, and each of these states can be displayed either normally or highlighted. This means we need to define four different appearances for these four different states.

We can use the button's selected property to indicate its ON/OFF state. Our appearances are then defined as follows: UIControlStateNormal means the button is OFF; UIControlStateHighlighted means the button is OFF and touched; UIControlStateSelected means the button is ON; and UIControlStateHighlighted | UIControlStateSelected means the button is both ON and touched (**Figure 4.11**). Note that UIControlState Disabled is not used here.

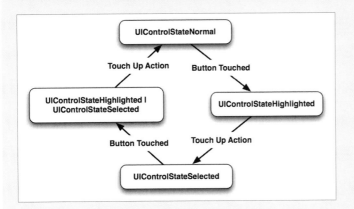

FIGURE 4.11
UIControlState changes
for a two-state button

However, if you're simply trying to set a default appearance across all the states, just use
UIControlStateNormal and let the others default back to it.

TABLE 4.2 Control States

STATE	TRIGGER
UIControlStateNormal	Default control state.
UIControlStateHighlighted	The highlighted state is often used to alter the control's appearance when it is touched. This state is automatically set and cleared as touches enter and leave the control. Our application can also access this state through the highlighted property.
UIControlStateSelected	Often, this state has no effect on the control's appearance; however, controls like the UISwitchControl will use it when toggling between the ON and OFF states. This state can also be accessed through the control's selected property.
UIControlStateDisabled	This state is typically set using the control's enabled property. When disabled, the control does not respond to touch events. Many controls also change their appearance when disabled.

In the last chapter, we used number formatters to create number strings that would format properly regardless of the device's language and country settings. In this chapter, we will see the other side. We will use the NSNumberFormatter to verify and filter the user's input. Here, we set it to accept only positive decimal numbers. We will also use the formatter to parse the user input, converting it from a string into a float value.

Again, anything we set up in viewDidLoad needs to be torn down in viewDid Unload. Add the following line:

```
- (void)viewDidUnload
{
    [self setWeightTextField:nil];
    [self setDateLabel:nil];
    self.unitsButton = nil;
    self.numberFormatter = nil;
    [super viewDidUnload];
}
```

We still need to reset the screen each time it appears. Remember, a view might be created only once but appear many times. Actually, it's even more complicated than this. A view may be loaded and unloaded multiple times (usually due to memory shortages). Each time it is loaded, it may appear onscreen more than once. Therefore, it's important to think things through. Which configuration items need to be performed once and only once? These are typically performed in the application delegate's application:didFinishLaunchingWithOptions: method. Which configuration items should be performed each time a view loads? These should be performed in the view controller's viewDidLoad method. Finally, which ones should be performed every time the view appears onscreen? These are done in the viewWillAppear: or viewDidAppear: method.

viewWillAppear: AND viewDidAppear:

The viewWillAppear: and viewDidAppear: methods can be somewhat confusing. For the most part, the system calls these methods whenever a view controller is used to display another view controller. This includes displaying modal views, adding new views to a navigation controller, or switching between views on a tab bar. The system will even call these notification methods when a view reappears. For example, when returning from a modal view or when a covering view is popped off the navigation stack.

However, manually adding a view using the addSubview: method does not trigger these notifications. Nor does changing a view's hidden or alpha properties to hide or show a view. And, just to make things even more confusing, adding a view to the application's window using addSubview: will trigger the notifications (though in iOS 4.0 and later, you should assign the view controller to the window's rootViewController property instead).

While these rules and exceptions may seem confusing, they do point to a common design problem. If your view appears onscreen but your view controller's viewWillAppear: and viewDidAppear: methods are not called, you may have an inconsistent view hierarchy. This occurs when you add a view to the view hierarchy without properly adding its view controller to the view controller hierarchy.

There are a number of ways to fix this. Most simply, you could get rid of the view controller and add the view directly to its superview's controller. After all, view controllers often manage more than one view at a time. We're doing this anytime we create an outlet for one of our controls.

Alternatively, in iOS 5.0 we could create a custom container view controller and use it to present our subview's controller. As the name suggests, a container view controller manages one or more other view controllers. Examples in UIKit include UINavigationController, UITabViewController, and UIPageViewController. iOS 5 has extended the UIViewController class, giving us methods to add (addChildViewController:) or remove (removeFromParentViewController) controllers from the controller hierarchy. This allows us to create a controller hierarchy that mirrors our views. As a result, the system can correctly forward important messages along both hierarchies.

For more information, check out the UIViewController documentation. In particular, look at the automaticallyForwardAppearanceAndRotationMethodsToChildViewControllers property. This contains a list of all the messages that need to be forwarded along the view controller hierarchy. We will also create our own custom container view controller in the "Creating a UIViewController Container" section of Chapter 8.

In our case, we want to update the current date and make sure our text field is ready to receive new information. Implement the viewWillAppear: method as shown:

```
- (void)viewWillAppear:(BOOL)animated {
    // Sets the current time and date.
    self.currentDate = [NSDate date];
    self.dateLabel.text =
        [NSDateFormatter localizedStringFromDate:self.currentDate
            dateStyle:NSDateFormatterLongStyle
            timeStyle:NSDateFormatterShortStyle];
    // Clear the text field.
    self.weightTextField.text = @"";
    [self.weightTextField becomeFirstResponder];
    [super viewWillAppear:animated];
}
```

Here we create a new NSDate object set to the current date and time. We then use the NSDateFormatter class method localizedStringFromDate:dateStyle: timeStyle: to produce a properly localized string representation. As you might expect, the formatting of dates and times also varies greatly from country to country and language to language. The NSDateFormatter lets us easily create date strings based on the device's language and region settings.

NOTE: Both NSNumberFormatter and NSDateFormatter are subclasses of the NSFormatter abstract class. NSFormatter is designed to act as a base class for objects that format, validate, or parse strings. For more information on using formatters or even creating your own, see the Data Formatting Guide in Apple's documentation.

Next, we clear the text field and make it the first responder. Making a text field the first responder will automatically display the keyboard. Now, we've already linked the text field's Did End On Exit event to the saveWeight: method. This method will be called whenever the keyboard's Done button is pressed.

FIGURE 4.12 Adding a swipe gesture recognizer

As we described earlier, this provides a very streamlined system for entering the weights. When the user opens this view, the text field is automatically selected and the keyboard is ready and waiting. The user just types in the weight value and presses Done. They don't need to select the text box or press a Save button. Everything is simple, automatic, and clean.

However, it does create one small problem. The keyboard covers our tab bar. This prevents our users from navigating away from this screen without entering a new weight.

Obviously, this is not ideal. We need to provide a way (preferably something intuitive and non-intrusive) to dismiss the keyboard, giving us access to the tab bar again. Let's add a gesture recognizer that responds to a simple down swipe.

Open `MainStoryboard.storyboard` again. Drag a swipe gesture recognizer from the library and drop it onto the enter weight view controller scene's main view (**Figure 4.12**).

The gesture recognizer will appear in the scene's dock. Select it and open the Attributes inspector. Set the Swipe attribute to Down. Leave the Touches attribute at 1. This will now trigger on a single-finger, downward swipe.

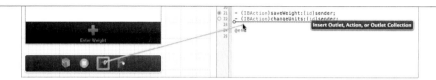

FIGURE 4.13 Connecting a gesture recognizer

If we're going to recognize downward swipes, we should recognize upward swipes as well. So, let's add a second recognizer. Drag out another swipe gesture recognizer and add it to the view. Set its Swipe attribute to Up. Leave the Touches attribute at 1.

Now open the Assistant editor, and make sure the EnterWeightViewController.h file is showing. Right-click and drag from the down swipe gesture recognizer to just below the declaration of our changeUnits: method (**Figure 4.13**). Change the Connection to Action, and name it handleDownwardSwipe. Then do the same for the up gesture recognizer. Name its action handleUpwardSwipe.

Then create an outlet for each gesture recognizer. Control-drag from the recognizer to the header file. Name the first outlet downSwipeRecognizer. Name the second upSwipeRecognizer.

Now switch to EnterWeightViewController.m and implement the actions:

```
- (IBAction)handleDownwardSwipe:(id)sender {
    // Get rid of the keyboard.
    [self.weightTextField resignFirstResponder];
}
- (IBAction)handleUpwardSwipe:(id)sender {
    // display keyboard
    [self.weightTextField becomeFirstResponder];
}
```

The handleDownwardSwipe method simply has the text field resign as first responder. Just as before, the keyboard is automatically linked to the first responder. When the text field resigns, the keyboard disappears. The handleUpwardSwipe method is just the inverse of that. It assigns the text field as the first responder, causing the keyboard to appear again. Of course, the user could do the same thing by simply tapping the text field, but many users will automatically try to undo a downward swipe with an upward swipe. Adding the inverse operation makes the interface feel more complete.

While this is an elegant solution, it brings up a common problem with iOS development. We can easily build complicated touch-, gesture-, and motion-based controls (see Chapter 8 for more examples), but how do we make sure the user knows they exist? iOS applications usually don't have help screens, and—in my experience—few users actually read the help information that does exist.

For example, you might create a great three-finger swipe that radically simplifies your application's workflow. However, unless your users stumble upon it by accident, most will never know it exists. That's not to say that you should avoid using unusual gestures. On the contrary, many applications use novel gestures to great effect. The Twitter app is an excellent example: You scroll through the table view of incoming tweets. When you get to the top, you just pull down to check for new messages.

This is a brilliant gesture. Users will almost certainly stumble upon it as they accidentally try to scroll past the end of their tweets. More importantly, once you find it, the gesture is so natural that it quickly becomes part of your regular workflow.

The bottom line is that successfully communicating how your app operates can be one of the biggest challenges in iOS development. Typically, this involves extensive usability testing to make sure your interface is as intuitive and natural as possible.

OK, let's switch gears and tackle the saveWeight: action.

```
#pragma mark - Action Methods
- (IBAction)saveWeight:(id)sender {
    // Save the weight to the model.
    NSNumber* weight = [self.numberFormatter
                        numberFromString:self.weightTextField.text];
    WeightEntry* entry = [[WeightEntry alloc]
                            initWithWeight:[weight floatValue]
                            usingUnits:self.weightHistory.defaultUnits
                            forDate:self.currentDate];
    [self.weightHistory addWeight:entry];
    // Automatically move to the second tab.
    // Should be the graph view.
    self.tabBarController.selectedIndex = 1;
}
```

First, we parse the text field to extract the weight's floating point value. Normally you want to check numberFromString:'s return value. If the number does not match the specified format, this method will return nil. However, in this case we know that the text field can only have valid values. The saveWeight: action is only triggered when the keyboard's Done button is pressed, and the Done button only becomes active when our text field contains text. Since we will be filtering the user input, this text can only contain a valid decimal number.

Next, we instantiate a new WeightEntry object using this weight value, our defaultUnits, and the currentDate property (if you remember, currentDate was set when the enter weight view appeared onscreen). We add this entry to our model.

Finally, we change the tab bar's selected controller. This will automatically move us to the second tab—currently set to the graph view. Again, we are trying to make entering new weights as streamlined as possible. For the most part, this means removing unnecessary touches. Users will typically enter only one weight at a time. Therefore, we should streamline their interaction and automatically bring up the weight trends graph after each new value.

We're going to skip the changeUnits: method for now. We'll get back to it in the "Changing Weight Units" section. Instead, let's begin filtering the user's input.

FILTERING KEYBOARD INPUT

The UITextFieldDelegate protocol has a number of optional methods that we can use to monitor and control our text field. In particular, we will implement textField:shouldChangeCharactersInRange:replacementString: to filter the user input. Implement the method as shown:

```
#pragma mark - Delegate Methods
- (BOOL)textField:(UITextField *)textField
shouldChangeCharactersInRange:(NSRange)range
replacementString:(NSString *)string {
    // It's OK to hit return.
    if ([string isEqualToString:@"\n"]) return YES;
    NSString* changedString =
    [textField.text stringByReplacingCharactersInRange:range
                                    withString:string];
```

```
    // It's OK to delete everything.
    if ([changedString isEqualToString:@""]) return YES;
    NSNumber* number =
    [self.numberFormatter numberFromString:changedString];
    // Filter out invalid number formats.
    if (number == nil) {
        // We might want to add an alert sound here.
        return NO;
    }
    return YES;
}
```

This method is called whenever the user presses a button on the keyboard (including the backspace button). If we return YES, the change is made. If we return NO, the change is canceled.

We start by checking to see if the user hit the Return key. Since this is the trigger for our saveWeight: action, we need to accept it.

Next, we create a new string by applying the proposed change to textField's current contents. If the resulting string represents a valid decimal number, we accept the change. Otherwise, we reject it.

Of course, it's not quite that simple. First, we have to deal with another corner case. If the resulting string is empty, we allow the change. Technically, an empty string is not a valid decimal number; however, we really want to let the users delete all the characters, just in case they made a typing mistake and want to start over.

If the string is not empty, we use our numberFormatter to parse our string. Again, we use the numberFromString: method. If the string does not match the expected format, this method returns nil. We simply check the return value and return YES or NO as appropriate.

Technically, we could simplify the code and just return the result from parsing the string as shown here:

```
return [self.numberFormatter numberFromString:changedString];
```

FIGURE 4.14 The completed enter weight view

However, we may want to add an alert sound or other feedback to the user. Using the more verbose version of the code will make those additions easier.

Run the application. The text field should appear with the embedded unit button. Check to make sure the input filtering works correctly. When you press the Done button, the view should switch to the graph view. Nothing shows up yet (of course), but the transition should work. Go back to the enter weight view. The system should automatically clear and select the text field. The keyboard should be visible. Swipe down to dismiss the keyboard. Swipe up to re-enable it. You can even tap the units button, but it won't do anything yet. We'll fix that next (**Figure 4.14**).

CHANGING WEIGHT UNITS

When the user presses the units button, we need to open a new view and let them change the default units. To do this, we will use a modal view. Modal views are perfect for presenting focused, short-term tasks that the user must either complete or explicitly cancel.

Let's start by adding another `UIViewController` subclass. Name it `UnitSelector ViewController` and place it in the Controllers group (if you need help, follow the step-by-step instructions in "Configuring the Tab Bar" in Chapter 3).

Now open `MainStoryboard.storyboard`. Drag out a new `UIViewController` object and place it next to our enter weight view controller scene. Switch to the Identity inspector, and change its Class setting so that it uses our new `UnitSelector ViewController` class.

Ideally, we want a segue from our `changeUnits:` action to the unit selector view. Unfortunately, we cannot draw segues from actions directly. Instead, let's create a segue that we can manually call from our code.

Control-drag from the enter weight view controller icon to our new scene. In the pop-up window, select `modal`. This creates a generic modal storyboard segue. This sets the segue between the two scenes. Select the segue and switch to the Attributes inspector. Set the Identifier attribute to Unit Selector Segue, and the Transition attribute to Flip Horizontal. Now we just need to trigger this segue from our `changeUnits:` action.

Switch back to `EnterWeightViewController.m`. Let's start by defining a string constant for our segue's identifier. Add the following line before the `@implementation` block:

```
static NSString* const UNIT_SELECTOR_SEGUE = @"Unit Selector Segue";
```

Now navigate down to the `changeUnits:` action. We just need to call our controller's `performSegueWithIdentifier:sender:` method.

```
- (IBAction)changeUnits:(id)sender {
    [self performSegueWithIdentifier:
    UNIT_SELECTOR_SEGUE sender:self];
}
```

This will trigger our segue. Our enter weight view will flip over and reveal the new unit selector view.

So, let's design that view. Open the storyboard again, and zoom in on our unit selector scene. Select the view and change its Background attribute to View Flipside Background Color. Next, drag a picker view from the Object library and place it at the top of the view. In the Size inspector, make sure it is locked to the left, right, and top and that it scales horizontally.

Next, drag out a button and place it at the bottom of the view. Stretch it so that it fills the view from margin to margin. Its autosizing settings should lock it to the left, bottom, and right, with horizontal scaling enabled. Finally, set its Title attribute to Done.

We ideally want a colored button. The iOS 5 SDK gives us a number of functions for customizing the appearance of our controls. Unfortunately, this doesn't include setting a button's background color. There are a number of ways to work around this. For example, many developers create stretchable background images for their buttons. However, this does not give us very much control at runtime. We could create a UIButton subclass and provide custom drawing code—but that's a lot of work. Instead, we'll modify the button's appearance using Core Animation (while also looking at some of the problems with this approach).

Change the button's Type attribute to Custom, and set the Background attribute to a dark green. I selected Clover from the crayon box color selector. Click the Background attribute. When the pop-up menu appears, select Other. Make sure the crayon box tab is selected, and then choose the Clover crayon (third from the left on the top row).

Finally, set the Text Color attribute to Light Text Color.

The interface should now match **Figure 4.15**. Everything looks OK—except for the square corners on our Done button. We'll fix that shortly. In the meantime, let's set up our outlets and actions.

First, open UnitSelectorViewController.h. This class needs to adopt both the UIPickerViewDelegate and the UIPickerViewDataSource protocols.

```
@interface UnitSelectorViewController : UIViewController

    <UIPickerViewDelegate, UIPickerViewDataSource> {

}
@end
```

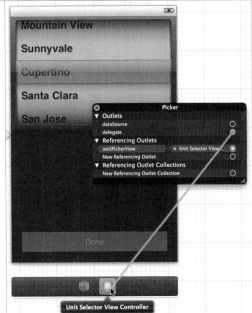

Then switch back to the storyboard file, and open the Assistant editor. Make sure UnitSelectorViewController.h is showing. Control-drag the picker view to the header file, and create a strong outlet named unitPickerView. Next, Control-drag the button twice. First, create a strong outlet named doneButton. Then create an action named done. Make sure its Event is set to Touch Up Inside.

Now we need to link the picker view to its delegate and data source. Right-click the picker view, and then drag from the pop-up window's delegate outlet to the view controller icon in the scene's dock (**Figure 4.16**). Next, drag the pop-up's dataSource outlet to the view controller as well.

FIGURE 4.15 The unit selector view

FIGURE 4.16 Connecting the delegate

DEFINING THE VIEW DELEGATE

Switch back to the Standard editor and the UnitSelectorViewController.h file. It should now appear as shown here:

```
#import <UIKit/UIKit.h>

@interface UnitSelectorViewController : UIViewController

<UIPickerViewDelegate, UIPickerViewDataSource>
```

```
@property (strong, nonatomic) IBOutlet UIPickerView *unitPickerView;
@property (strong, nonatomic) IBOutlet UIButton *doneButton;
- (IBAction)done:(id)sender;
@end
```

We still need to make a few additional changes. Start by importing our WeightEntry class, and add a forward declaration for the UnitSelectorViewControllerDelegate protocol before its @interface block.

```
#import <UIKit/UIKit.h>
#import "WeightEntry.h"
@protocol UnitSelectorViewControllerDelegate;
@interface UnitSelectorViewController :
UIViewController <UIPickerViewDelegate, UIPickerViewDataSource> {
    ...
```

Now let's declare two additional properties: one for our delegate, the other for our default unit.

```
@property (strong, nonatomic) IBOutlet UIButton *doneButton;
@property (weak, nonatomic) id<UnitSelectorViewControllerDelegate>
    delegate;
@property (assign, nonatomic) WeightUnit defaultUnit;
- (IBAction)done:(id)sender;
```

Finally, we need to define our protocol. Add the following, after the @interface block:

```
@protocol UnitSelectorViewControllerDelegate <NSObject>
- (void)unitSelectorDone:(UnitSelectorViewController*)controller;
- (void)unitSelector:(UnitSelectorViewController*)controller
        changedUnits:(WeightUnit)unit;
@end
```

That's it. We're done with the interface. Now we need to implement these methods.

IMPLEMENTING THE CONTROLLER

Open `UnitSelectorViewController.m` and synthesize the `delegate` and the `defaultUnit`.

```
@synthesize delegate = _delegate;
@synthesize defaultUnit = _defaultUnit;
```

Now we want to automatically select the current default unit when our view loads. To do this, uncomment `viewDidLoad` and make the following changes:

```
#pragma mark - View lifecycle

- (void)viewDidLoad
{
    [super viewDidLoad];
    // Set the default units.
    [self.unitPickerView selectRow:self.defaultUnit
                       inComponent:0
                          animated:NO];}
```

Remember, our `WeightUnit` enum values are assigned sequentially starting with 0. Our picker view is also zero-indexed, with exactly one row for each `WeightUnit` value. This means we can use `WeightUnits` and row indexes interchangeably. Each row index maps to a corresponding `WeightUnit`. Here, we simply select the row that corresponds with the default unit value.

Next, we need to enable autorotation to any orientation. As before, simply have the `shouldAutorotateToInterfaceOrientation:` method return YES.

```
- (BOOL)shouldAutorotateToInterfaceOrientation:
    (UIInterfaceOrientation)interfaceOrientation {
    return YES;
}
```

Now let's implement the done: action. We just call the delegate's unitSelector
Done: method, as shown here:

```
- (IBAction)done:(id)sender {
    [self.delegate unitSelectorDone:self];
}
```

OK, we're almost done with this controller. We still need to implement the
UIPickerViewDataSource methods:

```
#pragma mark - UIPickerViewDataSource Methods
- (NSInteger)numberOfComponentsInPickerView:
(UIPickerView *)pickerView {
    return 1;
}
- (NSInteger)pickerView:(UIPickerView *)pickerView
    numberOfRowsInComponent:(NSInteger)component {
    return 2;
}
```

The numberOfComponentsInPickerView: method simply returns the number of
components that our picker view will use. Each component represents a separate
settable field. For example, a date picker has three components: month, day, and
year. In our case, we only need a single component.

The pickerView:numberOfRowsInComponent: method returns the number of
rows (or possible values) for the given component. We know that our picker view
only has a single component, so we don't need to check the component argument.
Since we only have two possible values, pounds and kilograms, we can just return 2.

Now let's look at the delegate methods:

```
#pragma mark - UIPickerViewDelegate Methods
- (NSString *)pickerView:(UIPickerView *)pickerView
             titleForRow:(NSInteger)row
            forComponent:(NSInteger)component {
```

```
    return [WeightEntry stringForUnit:row];
}
- (void)pickerView:(UIPickerView *)pickerView
    didSelectRow:(NSInteger)row
    inComponent:(NSInteger)component {
  [self.delegate unitSelector:self changedUnits:row];
}
```

The pickerView:titleForRow:forComponent: method should return the title that will be displayed for the given row and component. In our case, we can map the rows directly to the WeightUnit enum values and simply call stringForUnit: to generate the correct string (@"lbs" or @"kg").

Meanwhile, the pickerView:didSelectRow:inComponent: method is called whenever the user changes the current selection. Here, we simply call the delegate's unitSelector:changedUnits: method, passing in the row value. Again, our row values correspond directly to the appropriate WeightUnit values.

PASSING DATA BACK AND FORTH

We still need to pass data into and out of our modal view. Start by opening EntryWeightViewController.h. We need to import UnitSelectorViewController.h and declare that EnterWeightViewController will adopt the UnitSelectorView ControllerDelegate protocol.

```
#import <UIKit/UIKit.h>
#import "UnitSelectorViewController.h"
@class WeightHistory;
@interface EnterWeightViewController : UIViewController
<UITextFieldDelegate, UnitSelectorViewControllerDelegate> {
```

Now switch to the implementation file. We trigger the modal segue in our changeUnits: method—but we cannot set the default unit value there. Our destination view controller may not exist yet. Instead, we wait for the prepareForSegue:sender: method—just as we did in Chapter 3.

```
- (void)prepareForSegue:(UIStoryboardSegue *)segue
                sender:(id)sender {
    if ([segue.identifier isEqualToString:UNIT_SELECTOR_SEGUE]) {
        UnitSelectorViewController* unitSelectorController =
            segue.destinationViewController;
        unitSelectorController.delegate = self;
        unitSelectorController.defaultUnit =
            self.weightHistory.defaultUnits;
    }
}
```

Here, we check the segue's identifier, just to make sure we have the correct segue. Then we grab a reference to our UnitSelectorViewController, and we set both the delegate and the default unit value.

To get data from our modal view, we simply implement the UnitSeletorView ControllerDelegate methods. Let's start with unitSelector:changedUnits:.

```
-(void)unitSelector:(UnitSelectorViewController*) sender
        changedUnits:(WeightUnit)unit {
    self.weightHistory.defaultUnits = unit;
    [self.unitsButton setTitle: [WeightEntry stringForUnit:unit]
                    forState:UIControlStateNormal];}
```

This method is called whenever the user changes the units in the Unit SelectorViewController. Here, we tell the model to change its default units and then update the title in our unit button. Again, we only update the title for the UIControlStateNormal. All other control states will default back to this setting.

Now let's look at unitSelectorDone:.

```
-(void)unitSelectorDone:(UnitSelectorViewController*) sender {
    [self dismissModalViewControllerAnimated:YES];
}
```

This method is called when the user presses the UnitSelectorViewController's Done button. Note that we could have dismissed the modal view within UnitSelector ViewController's done: method by calling [self.parentViewController dismiss ModalViewControllerAnimated:YES]. However, the pattern we're using here is generally best.

Passing control back to the parent view through a delegate method and then letting the parent view dismiss the modal view may take a bit more code, but it also gives us additional flexibility. For example, our parent controller might want to access the delegate view's properties before dismissing it. Or we may want to perform some postprocessing after dismissing the modal view. We can easily add these features in our delegate method. Additionally, it just feels cleaner. If a class presents a modal view, then it should also dismiss that view. Splitting the presentation and dismissal code into different classes makes everything just a little harder to follow.

And this isn't an entirely academic argument. As our code is currently written, we will change our default unit value whenever the user changes the value in the picker view. However, this is not necessarily the best approach. We may want to wait until the user presses the Done button, and then set the default unit value based on their final selection. With the delegate methods in place, we can easily change our implementation based on actual performance testing. More importantly, we can change this behavior in our EnterWeightViewController class; we don't need to touch our modal view at all.

> **NOTE:** Most delegate methods will follow the format shown for the UnitSelectorViewControllerDelegate. The method name begins with a description of the delegating class (e.g., tableView, pickerView, unitSelector), and the first argument is a reference back to the delegating class. While you may not use the reference, having it can greatly simplify your delegate methods. For example, for modal view delegates you don't need to assign your modal view to an instance method—you can access it through the delegating reference instead.

Run the application. You should be able to press the unit button and bring up the unit selector view. Change the units to kilograms and press Done. The button's title should change from "lbs" to "kg." There's only one problem remaining: Our Done button still looks chunky. Let's fix that.

FIGURE 4.17 Adding a new framework

ROUNDING CORNERS WITH CORE ANIMATION

NOTE: Manipulating views with Core Animation is an advanced topic. While this represents a useful technique for modifying the appearance of controls without having to subclass them, it can get a bit complicated. However, since it doesn't add any critical features to the application, you can safely skip this section. Your application will still function normally.

Most of the time when you talk about Core Animation, you're talking about smoothly moving user interface elements around the screen, having them fade in and out, or flipping them over. Here, however, we will hijack some of the more obscure features of Core Animation to round off our button's corners, add a border, and layer over a glossy sheen.

As you might guess, Core Animation is a deep and complex subject. We will look at techniques for animating view properties in "Managing Pop-Up Views" in Chapter 8. However, even that only scratches the surface. If you want to get all the gory details, I recommend reading the Core Animation Programming Guide in Apple's documentation.

First things first, we need to add the QuartzCore framework to our project. Click the blue Health Beat icon to bring up the project settings. Make sure the Health Beat target is selected, and click the Build Phases tab. Next, expand the Link Binary With Libraries build phase, and click the plus button to add another framework. Scroll through the list and add QuartzCore.framework (**Figure 4.17**).

Next, open UnitSelectorViewController.m. We need to import the Quartz-Core header.

```
#import <QuartzCore/QuartzCore.h>
```

Then navigate to the viewDidLoad method. Modify it as shown:

```
- (void)viewDidLoad
{
```

```objc
[super viewDidLoad];
// Set the default units.
[self.unitPickerView selectRow:self.defaultUnit
                    inComponent:0
                       animated:NO];
//Build our gradient overlays.
CAGradientLayer* topGradient = [[CAGradientLayer alloc] init];
topGradient.name = @"Top Gradient";
// Make it half the height.
CGRect frame = self.doneButton.layer.bounds;
frame.size.height /= 2.0f;
topGradient.frame = frame;
UIColor* topColor = [UIColor colorWithWhite:1.0f alpha:0.75f];
UIColor* bottomColor = [UIColor colorWithWhite:1.0f alpha:0.0f];
topGradient.colors = [NSArray arrayWithObjects:
                        (__bridge id)topColor.CGColor,
                        (__bridge id)bottomColor.CGColor, nil];
CAGradientLayer* bottomGradient =
[[CAGradientLayer alloc] init];
bottomGradient.name = @"Bottom Gradient";
// Make it half the size.
frame = self.doneButton.layer.bounds;
frame.size.height /= 2.0f;
// And move it to the bottom.
frame.origin.y = frame.size.height;
bottomGradient.frame = frame;
topColor = [UIColor colorWithWhite:0.0f alpha:0.20f];
bottomColor = [UIColor colorWithWhite:0.0f alpha:0.0f];
```

```
bottomGradient.colors = [NSArray arrayWithObjects:
                        (__bridge id)topColor.CGColor,
                        (__bridge id)bottomColor.CGColor, nil];
// Round the corners.
[self.doneButton.layer setCornerRadius:8.0f];
// Clip sublayers.
[self.doneButton.layer setMasksToBounds:YES];
// Add a border.
[self.doneButton.layer setBorderWidth:2.0f];
[self.doneButton.layer
 setBorderColor:[[UIColor lightTextColor] CGColor]];
// Add the gradient layers.
[self.doneButton.layer addSublayer:topGradient];
[self.doneButton.layer addSublayer:bottomGradient];
}
```

There's a lot going on here, so let's step through it slowly. This code modifies our button's Core Animation layer. The CALayer is a lightweight object that encapsulates the timing, geometry, and visual properties of a view. In UIKit, a CALayer backs each UIView (and therefore, anything that inherits from UIView). Because of the tight coupling between layers and views, we can easily access and change the visual properties contained in our button's layer.

We start by creating a CAGradientLayer and giving the layer a name. We will use this name to identify our gradient layer in later methods. Next, we calculate the frame for this layer. We start with the button layer's bounds, but we divide the height in half. Remember, the frame is the object's coordinates and size in the containing view or layer's coordinate system. The bounds represent the object's coordinates and size in its own coordinate system. In other words, the origin is almost always set to {0.0f, 0.0f} (there are situations where you might use a non-zero origin as an offset, for example when clipping part of an image, but these cases are rare). Using the superlayer's bounds for the sublayer's frame means the sublayer will fill the superlayer completely. By dividing the height in half, we end up with a sublayer that will cover just the top half of the main layer.

CAGradientLayers accept an NSArray filled with CGColorRefs. By default, it creates a linear, evenly spaced gradient that transitions from one color to the next. We will just pass in two colors, which will represent the two end points.

Note that an NSArray technically only accepts pointers to Objective-C objects. A CGColorRef is simply a pointer to a CGColor structure—definitely not an Objective-C object. However, we can cast them into id objects to get around the compiler warnings. It's a bit wacky, but we do what we have to do.

For the curious, this works because NSArray is toll-free bridged with the Foundation CFArray class (under the surface, they are the same objects). While NSArrays are only used to store Objective-C objects, CFArrays can be used to store any arbitrary pointer-sized data. In fact, the CFArrayCreate() method includes parameters that define how the objects are (or are not) retained when placed in the array. When we create an NSArray, we are really creating a CFArray that uses ARC for memory management, which is good. Our CGColors came from an Objective-C method call—so ARC is already managing their memory (see "ARC and Toll-Free Bridging" in Chapter 2 for more information).

As a result, this trick requires considerably less typing than creating a CFArray directly. We do need to use the __bridge annotation to tell ARC that we're not transferring the references' ownership, but other than that, memory management works as expected.

In our code, we create two colors. One is white with a 75 percent alpha. The other is completely transparent. We place these into an array and pass the array to the gradient. The CAGradientLayer then makes a smooth, linear transition that slowly fades out as you move down the screen. This adds a highlight to the top of our button.

We do the same thing for the bottomGradient. The only difference is that we increase its origin's *y* value to position it on the bottom half of the button. We also use black colors whose alpha values will transition between 20 percent and completely clear. These will slightly darken the bottom half of our control.

Next, we set the corner radius, thus rounding the corners. We then clip our drawing to the area bounded by our rounded corners. This will clip our gradient sublevels as well.

Then we give our button a 2-pixel border, whose color matches the button's title color. Notice, however, that whereas the button used a UIColor object, the CALayer uses CGColor structures. Again, we can request a CGColor reference from our UIColor object.

FIGURE 4.18 Done button with rounded corners

Run the application again. Now when you press the unit button, our modal view's Done button looks all fancy (**Figure 4.18**).

This works fine in portrait mode, but if you rotate the view, you'll notice that our gradients don't stretch to fill the button. The problem is, we cannot automatically resize these layers. Instead, we need to manually resize them whenever the system lays out our views. To do this, implement the view controller's viewDid LayoutSubviews method.

```
- (void)viewDidLayoutSubviews {
    CALayer* layer = self.doneButton.layer;
    CGFloat width = layer.bounds.size.width;
    for (CALayer* sublayer in layer.sublayers) {
        if ([sublayer.name hasSuffix:@"Gradient"]) {
            CGRect frame = sublayer.frame;
            frame.size.width = width;
            sublayer.frame = frame;
        }
    }
}
```

This method is called right after the system lays out all our subviews. Here, we just grab a reference to our doneButton's layer and the layer's width. We then iterate over all the sublayers. If the sublayer has a name that ends with "Gradient," we resize it to match the button's width. This way our custom layers will be resized, but we won't alter any of the button's other layers.

Try it out. Switch back and forth between the enter weight and unit select views. Rotate the interface to all the different orientations. If everything is working, commit all our changes. Next stop, the history view.

CORE ANIMATION AND PERFORMANCE

While we used the CALayer to give our button rounded corners, you could use the same technique for any UIView. One obvious example would be to create UIImageView objects with rounded corners and possibly even a glassy sheen. However, you may find it useful for any number of UIView objects: text views, Web views, scroll views, map views, or any of the custom views you may build.

While this approach is convenient, it can become computationally expensive. Performing these types of Core Animation manipulations require our views to be drawn to an offscreen buffer before being drawn onto the main view. This occurs on each and every frame both for our altered view and for any of its subviews.

This is particularly important in any view that expects smooth animation (for example, scroll views or table views). Having a number of objects performing offscreen rendering will quickly turn a smoothly scrolling interface into a jerking, stuttery mess.

We can use Instruments to detect views that are using offscreen rendering (see Bonus Chapter B for more information on Instruments). Connect your test iOS device, and set the scheme to run on it. Then select Product > Profile from the main menu. This will launch Instruments. When prompted, start the Core Animation template. Select the Core Animation track, and make sure the Color Offscreen-Rendered Yellow option is selected (**Figure 4.19**). This will highlight any views that are rendered offscreen in yellow, making them easy to spot.

As you can see, when you touch the units button, the entire screen is rendered offscreen as it flips. However, once the transition animation finishes, the rest can be rendered directly. Only our custom button continues to render offscreen (**Figure 4.20**).

If Core Animation becomes a performance issue, the easiest fix is to set the CALayer's shouldRasterize property to YES. This tells Core Animation that the layer will require offscreen rendering and will force it to cache the offscreen image and reuse it whenever possible. In some cases, this can dramatically improve Core Animation's performance.

However, shouldRasterize isn't a magic "run faster" flag. It should only be used under very specific circumstances. Obviously, if our view's appearance is changing, then caching doesn't make sense. Core Animation will need to throw out the cache and re-render the view for each new frame. Worse yet, if the view wouldn't have required an offscreen pass, setting shouldRasterize will force it to be rendered offscreen. This will actually reduce the app's performance.

In Health Beat, shouldRasterize doesn't help us at all. Our button's final image is only rendered once, so we would never reuse the cache. Creating it only wastes memory. However, if we had placed our button in a scroll view, setting shouldRasterize might make a big difference.

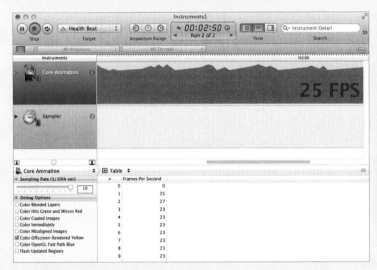

If we cannot use shouldRasterize to solve our performance problems, we may need to revert back to custom drawing. In our case, we could create a subclass of UIButton and override the drawRect: method, manually drawing our curved rectangle and gradient fills. Typically, the drawing code is only called once, when the object is first placed onscreen. It is then cached in the view's CALayer and can be scrolled, resized, or otherwise animated without requiring additional drawing. Of course, the initial drawing may be slightly slower than the Core Animation method calls, but we're converting a per-frame cost into a one-time cost. In many cases, this produces significant performance improvements.

We'll cover custom drawing in more depth in Chapter 5, "Drawing Custom Views."

FIGURE 4.19 Highlighting offscreen-rendered views using Instruments

FIGURE 4.20 All offscreen-rendered views are highlighted in yellow

Now let's shift over to our history view. Here, we display a list of all the entries in our WeightHistory. We will use a UITableView to present these entries, showing one entry per row. Let's start by designing a custom cell for these rows.

Right-click the Views group and select New File > Objective-C Class. Make sure it is a subclass of UITableViewCell, and name it HistoryCell. Now open HistoryCell.h. Modify the header file as shown:

```
#import <UIKit/UIKit.h>
#import "WeightEntry.h"
@interface HistoryCell : UITableViewCell
@property (nonatomic, strong) IBOutlet UILabel* weightLabel;
@property (nonatomic, strong) IBOutlet UILabel* dateLabel;
- (void)configureWithWeightEntry:(WeightEntry*)entry
                     defaultUnits:(WeightUnit)unit;
@end
```

Unlike view controllers, outlets cannot be Control-dragged from the storyboard to a view's header file. Instead, we need to manually declare them first. We're also declaring a method to configure our cell—changing the contents of its labels based on the WeightEntry and WeightUnit arguments.

Switch to the implementation file. We'll start by synthesizing our properties.

```
@synthesize weightLabel=_weightLabel;
@synthesize dateLabel=_dateLabel;
```

Then implement configureWithWeightEntry:defaultUnits:.

```
- (void)configureWithWeightEntry:(WeightEntry*)entry
                     defaultUnits:(WeightUnit)unit {
  self.weightLabel.text = [entry stringForWeightInUnit:unit];
  self.dateLabel.text =
    [NSDateFormatter
      localizedStringFromDate:entry.date
```

```
        dateStyle:NSDateFormatterShortStyle
        timeStyle:NSDateFormatterShortStyle];
}
```

Here, we use our `WeightEntry`'s `stringForWeighInUnit:` method to set the `weightLabel` outlet with a correctly formatted weight string. Next, we use `NSDateFormatter` to create a properly localized date string using the short date and short time formats. We then assign this to our `dateLabel` outlet.

Now, let's open the storyboard and zoom in on our history view. Select the prototype cell and switch to the Identity inspector. Set the cell's class to `HistoryCell`. Then switch back to the Attributes inspector. Make sure the Accessory attribute is set to Disclosure Indicator. This will add a gray chevron on the right side of our cell.

Xcode provides two built-in accessories with very similar functions. Both the Disclosure Indicator and the Detail Disclosure indicate that the application has additional information related to this row. However, there are slight differences, both in the way they operate and in their intended use.

Detail Disclosure creates a round blue button with a white chevron. When the user taps the button, it should navigate to a detail view for the selected item. The Disclosure Indicator, on the other hand, just provides the gray chevron image. Here, the user must select the row itself, and they are then navigated to a sublist (usually containing additional options).

Arguably, Health Beat should use Detail Disclosure accessories—but I feel that having users select the row, not the disclosure button, works better. Besides, our detail view is a list (of sorts), so it's not wholly inappropriate, and even Apple isn't 100 percent consistent with their accessories.

Now, drag out two labels. Set the first label's title to Weight. Make it 100 points wide, and set the font to 18-pt System Bold. Then drag it until it is vertically centered along the cell's left margin. In the Size inspector, lock its Autosizing position to the top and the left side.

FIGURE 4.21 The finished history cell

Make the second label right-aligned 12-pt System Italic with a light gray text color. Set its title to Short Date and Time. Then align it with the Weight label, stretched so it fills the area between the Weight label and the Disclosure Indicator accessory. Its Autosizing position should be locked to the top and the right side (**Figure 4.21**).

Now, right-click the prototype cell and draw the connections from the date Label outlet to our Short Date and Time label. Draw a second connection from the weightLabel outlet to our Weight label. With that, our cell prototype is ready, and we just need to finish the HistoryViewController.

Let's start by importing our HistoryCell class at the top of HistoryViewController.m.

```
#import "HistoryCell.h"
```

Now we need to clean up our temporary code. Our history list should only have a single section, so numberOfSectionsInTableView: should still return 1. However, we need a number of rows equal to the number of entries in our weight history. Modify tableView:numberOfRowsInSection: to return this value.

```
- (NSInteger)numberOfSectionsInTableView:(UITableView *)tableView
{
    // We only have a single section.
    return 1;
}
- (NSInteger)tableView:(UITableView *)tableView
  numberOfRowsInSection:(NSInteger)section
{
    // Return the number of entries in our weight history.
    return [self.weightHistory.weights count];
}
```

Next, navigate to the tableView:cellForRowAtIndexPath: method, and modify this method as shown.

```
- (UITableViewCell *)tableView:(UITableView *)tableView
        cellForRowAtIndexPath:(NSIndexPath *)indexPath
{
    static NSString *CellIdentifier = @"History Cell";
    HistoryCell *cell =
        [tableView dequeueReusableCellWithIdentifier:
         CellIdentifier];
    // Configure the cell...
    WeightEntry* entry =
        [self.weightHistory.weights objectAtIndex:indexPath.row];
    [cell configureWithWeightEntry:entry
                      defaultUnits:self.weightHistory.defaultUnits];
    return cell;
}
```

It's important to understand how table view cells work. We want to make our tables as efficient as possible, and there's no point creating 10,000 separate cells if only ten of them can fit on the screen at a time. Therefore, when a cell scrolls off the screen, we should recycle it, reusing it the next time we need a new cell. Fortunately, UIKit can automatically do this for us.

To support cell reuse, we create a unique identifier for our cells. This is particularly important if you have different cells with different formats or even different classes. Each format needs its own identifier. When we need a new cell, we check to see if we have any available, unused cells by calling `dequeueReusableCell WithIdentifier:` and passing in our cell identifier.

Before iOS 5, if this method couldn't find an unused cell, it simply returned `nil`. We then had to create a new instance ourselves. In the simplest cases, this was not too difficult; however, if our table had a number of different cell types, the code could rapidly grow complex. Fortunately, iOS 5 has automated much of this for us.

As long as we're using a cell prototype from our storyboard, or a cell from a nib that we've registered using `registerNib:forCellReuseIdentifier:`, the `dequeueReusableCellWithIdentifier:` method will always returns a valid cell object. It will still reuse an existing cell, if possible; however, if nothing's available, it will automatically create a new cell for us.

As you can see, this greatly simplifies our `tableView:cellForRowAtIndexPath:` method. When we modified this method, we deleted more code than we added.

Our code grabs a `HistoryCell` instance using our `HistoryCellIdentifier` constant. This, of course, matches the identifier set in our storyboard. Then we get the `WeightEntry` that corresponds with the current row, and we pass that weight entry and our default units value into the cell's `configureWithWeightEntry: defaultUnits:` method. This, in turn, properly sets the text in the cell's labels.

If you run the application now, you can enter new weight values; however, they may not appear in the history view. This is because our application doesn't yet update the history view when our model changes. Let's fix that.

RESPONDING TO CHANGES IN THE MODEL

Navigate back to the top of the file, and add the following extension before the @implementation block:

```
@interface HistoryViewController()
- (void)reloadTableData;
- (void)weightHistoryChanged:(NSDictionary*) change;
@end
```

This defines two private methods. The first, reloadTableData, will reload the entire table. We will call this whenever the default weight unit changes, since we will need to rewrite all the weight strings in all the cells.

The second method, weightHistoryChanged:, will be called whenever a Weight Entry is added to or removed from our history. In this case, we want to modify only the affected cells (adding or removing individual cells as needed).

Now, navigate to the viewDidLoad method and modify it as shown here:

```
- (void)viewDidLoad
{
    [super viewDidLoad];
    // Uncomment the following line to preserve
    // selection between presentations.
    // self.clearsSelectionOnViewWillAppear = NO;


    // Uncomment the following line to display an Edit button
    // in the navigation bar for this view controller.
    // self.navigationItem.rightBarButtonItem = self.editButtonItem;
    // Register to receive KVO messages when the weight history
    // changes.
    [self.weightHistory addObserver:self
                        forKeyPath:KVOWeightChangeKey
                           options:NSKeyValueObservingOptionNew
```

```
                                context:nil];
        // Register to receive messages when the default units change.
        [[NSNotificationCenter defaultCenter]
            addObserver:self
                selector:@selector(reloadTableData)
                    name:WeightHistoryChangedDefaultUnitsNotification
                  object:self.weightHistory];
}
```

The addObserver:forKeyPath:options:context: method registers our History
ViewController as an observer of our weight history. Our controller will receive
a notification whenever the list of weight entries changes. Notice that the KVO
WeightChangeKey actually points to the private weightHistory property (see "The
WeightHistory Class" in Chapter 3). We could observe the public weights property,
but unfortunately, because it's a virtual property we only receive a general notification that the array has changed—we don't get any additional information about
the change. When we observe the weightHistory array directly, we get additional
information about the type of change and a list of the actual indexes that changed.

In many ways, using the KVOWeightChangeKey really lets us break the Weight
History class's encapsulation. In my opinion, this is not necessarily ideal, but by
using a public variable for the key, we are essentially blessing this backdoor access.
We are promising that we won't change the underlying implementation without
also changing KVOWeightChangeKey to match.

Realistically, however, we should change the WeightHistory code to manually
throw the correct KVO notifications for the weights property and just get rid of
the backdoor access. However, I wanted to show how to automatically generate
KVO notifications using the keyPathsForValuesAffecting<key> method. This has
the fortunate side effect of also highlighting some of the limits of this approach.

The addObserver:selector:name:object: method registers our controller to
receive WeightHistoryChangedDefaultUnitsNotification messages from our
model (and only from our model). When a matching notification is found, the
notification center will call our reloadTableData method directly.

Next, we need to remove our observers when the view unloads. Modify the viewDidUnload method as shown here:

```
- (void)viewDidUnload
{
    [self.weightHistory removeObserver:self
                            forKeyPath:KVOWeightChangeKey];


    [[NSNotificationCenter defaultCenter] removeObserver:self];
    [super viewDidUnload];
}
```

This shows another difference between KVO and notifications. For KVO, we must remove each observer/key pair separately. For notifications, we have a convenience method that removes all notifications for a given observer.

Now we must respond to the notifications. We need to implement the observeValue ForKeyPath:ofObject:change:context: method and our two private methods, reloadTableData and weightHistoryChanged:.

```
#pragma mark - Notification Methods
- (void)observeValueForKeyPath:(NSString *)keyPath
                      ofObject:(id)object
                        change:(NSDictionary *)change
                       context:(void *)context    {
    if ([keyPath isEqualToString:KVOWeightChangeKey]) {
        [self weightHistoryChanged:change];
    }
}
```

All KVO notifications call the observer's observeValueForKeyPath:ofObject: change:context: method. Here, we simply check to ensure that the notification's key path matches the KVOWeightChangeKey. If that is the case, we call the weight HistoryChanged: method, passing in the change dictionary. We could process the

changes here, but I like to keep the ObserveValueForKeyPath:ofObject:change
:context: method as clean and simple as possible, typically using it to dispatch
out to other methods. After all, this method will grow increasingly complex if we
start adding new KVO notifications.

```
- (void)weightHistoryChanged:(NSDictionary*) change {
    // First extract the kind of change.
    NSNumber* value = [change objectForKey:NSKeyValueChangeKindKey];
    // Next, get the indexes that changed.
    NSIndexSet* indexes =
        [change objectForKey:NSKeyValueChangeIndexesKey];
    NSMutableArray* indexPaths =
        [[NSMutableArray alloc] initWithCapacity:[indexes count]];
    // Use a block to process each index.
    [indexes enumerateIndexesUsingBlock:
        ^(NSUInteger indexValue, BOOL* stop) {
        NSIndexPath* indexPath =
            [NSIndexPath indexPathForRow:indexValue inSection:0];
        [indexPaths addObject:indexPath];
    }];
    // Now update the table.
    switch ([value intValue]) {
        case NSKeyValueChangeInsertion:
            // Insert the row.
            [self.tableView insertRowsAtIndexPaths:indexPaths
                withRowAnimation:UITableViewRowAnimationAutomatic];
            break;
        case NSKeyValueChangeRemoval:
            // Delete the row.
            [self.tableView deleteRowsAtIndexPaths:indexPaths
```

```
            withRowAnimation:UITableViewRowAnimationAutomatic];
        break;
    case NSKeyValueChangeSetting:
        // Index values changed...just ignore.
        break;
    default:
        [NSException raise:NSInvalidArgumentException
            format:@"Change kind value %d not recognized",
            [value intValue]];
    }
}
```

The KVO change dictionary becomes particularly useful when we are monitoring collections. It contains information on both the type of change that occurred and the affected indexes. In our weightHistoryChanged method, we start by extracting the type of change. There are four possible types: inserts, removals, replacements, and the somewhat oddly named "setting" changes.

The first two should be obvious. You are adding or deleting one or more elements in the collection. Replacement merely means you are changing the value at a given index in the collection. Setting changes mean you are changing the value of the key path itself. Usually, this occurs when you change the property's value. For a collection, that means replacing the current collection with an entirely new one.

Next, we extract the set of affected indexes. Notice that the change dictionary returns an NSIndexSet. However, we need an NSArray of NSIndexPaths. We therefore need to convert our indexes.

Here, we're using a block to iterate over our index set. The enumerateIndexes UsingBlock: method takes each index in the index set and passes it to the provided block. The block should have two arguments: an NSUInteger representing the current index, and a pointer to a BOOL. The pointer is an output-only argument. Setting its value to YES will stop the enumerations, causing enumerateIndexes UsingBlock: to return.

Our block simply takes the index and converts it to an index path. When dealing with UITableViews, the index path contains both the row and the section of a particular entry. Our table has only one section, so we just hard-code the section index to 0. The block then adds the new NSIndexPath to our indexPaths array. Notice how our block can access and modify objects in the same lexical scope. For more information on blocks, see "Blocks" in Chapter 2.

Finally, we update the table. We are primarily concerned with insertions and removals. If either of these occurs, we modify the corresponding rows in the table. We should not get any replacement changes, but we could see an accidental setting change (for example, when the model's history array is deallocated); however, we can safely ignore these. For anything else, we throw an exception.

As you can see, this method only modifies the table rows that actually changed. Additionally, we animate our changes using UITableViewRowAnimationAutomatic. This tells the system to automatically select an animation style that will look good, based on the type of table view and the cell's location within the table. In general, you should use automatic animation unless you have an overriding reason to use something else. This helps maintain consistency across applications.

Unfortunately, the new rows are inserted while the table view is offscreen, so the animation will finish before we can navigate to the history view. However, you will get to see the removals once we add editing support.

Our last private method is simply a wrapper around the table view's reload Data method.

```
- (void)reloadTableData {
    [self.tableView reloadData];
}
```

This raises the question, why don't we have the table view observe the Weight HistoryChangedDefaultUnitsNotification and let the notification center call its reloadData method directly? While this would simplify our HistoryView Controller class, it creates a subtle bug.

We still need to remove our table view from the observer list before it is deallocated. Unfortunately, our viewDidUnload method occurs after the view has already been released. Worse yet, if we accidentally try to access self.tableView in the viewDidUnload method, we will actually force the view to reload. Since viewDidUnload is only called during memory shortages, grabbing additional memory to rebuild our table view could cause our app to crash. At the very least, it would short-circuit our controller's attempt to free up some unneeded memory.

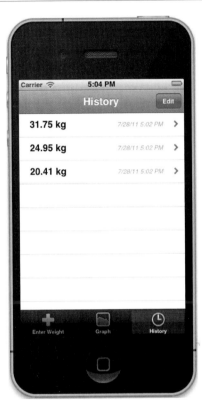

FIGURE 4.22 Automatically updating when the default units change

Using the view controller as the observer lets us cleanly register and unregister ourselves for notifications, even if we do end up just dispatching the call back to the table.

OK, run the application again. Try adding a few dates. You should see them appear in the history list, with the most recent weight at the top. Try switching from pounds to kilograms and back. The history view should update automatically (**Figure 4.22**).

EDITING THE HISTORY VIEW

Now that we can add new weights, we really need a way to remove them. The easiest option is to enable editing in the table view. To do this, we just need to add our controller's edit button to the navigation bar. The code is already located in viewDidLoad. We just need to uncomment it. While we're at it, let's delete the rest of the comments.

```
- (void)viewDidLoad
{
    [super viewDidLoad];
    self.navigationItem.rightBarButtonItem = self.editButtonItem;
    // Register to receive KVO messages when the weight history
    // changes.
    [self.weightHistory addObserver:self
                         forKeyPath:KVOWeightChangeKey
                            options:NSKeyValueObservingOptionNew
                            context:nil];
    // Register to receive messages when the default units change.
    [[NSNotificationCenter defaultCenter]
        addObserver:self
           selector:@selector(reloadTableData)
               name:WeightHistoryChangedDefaultUnitsNotification
             object:self.weightHistory];
}
```

Pressing the edit button puts the table view in editing mode. By default, this displays a Delete icon beside each row. You can modify this behavior using several UITableViewDelegate methods, but for our case, the default behavior is exactly what we want.

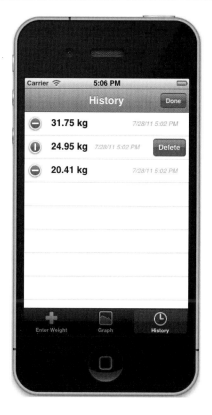

FIGURE 4.23 Editing the table

Go ahead and run the app now. Enter a few weights, and then put the history view in edit mode. If you press one of the Delete icons, it will bring up a red confirmation button. However, pressing the confirmation button doesn't do anything (**Figure 4.23**).

We still need to respond to the edit commands by both removing the row from the table and removing the corresponding WeightEntry from our model. To do this, uncomment and modify the tableView:commitEditingStyle:forRow AtIndexPath: method.

```
- (void)tableView:(UITableView *)tableView
    commitEditingStyle:(UITableViewCellEditingStyle)editingStyle
    forRowAtIndexPath:(NSIndexPath *)indexPath {
    if (editingStyle == UITableViewCellEditingStyleDelete) {
        [self.weightHistory removeWeightAtIndex:indexPath.row];
    }
}
```

Here we just verify that we are deleting an object. Then we remove the selected object from our weightHistory. That's it. We've already built in support for removing table rows when entries are deleted from our model. Our existing notifications will trigger that code automatically. Additionally, we never add new entries from within the table view, so we don't need to check for inserts here.

And that's it. Build and run the application. Try adding and deleting weights. If everything works correctly, remember to commit your changes.

There's a lot more to editing table views, of course. If you really want, you can add the ability to reorder the weights (though I don't know why we would want that feature for this project). You could also add new weights directly from the table view. You can even allow multiple selections using UITableView's allows MultipleSelections and allowsMultipleSelectionsDuringEditing properties. However, I'll leave those as homework.

FIGURE 4.24 After converting to a grouped static table

There is still one piece left to implement. When the user selects one of the weights, we want to display detailed information about our weight entry. Unfortunately, once you've listed the weight and the date, there's really not much more you can say about a single `WeightEntry`, so we will fill out our detail view by comparing the selected weight entry with the minimum, maximum, and current monthly average from our `WeightHistory`.

We will also look at using static tables to organize and display our data. Static tables are a very convenient way to display a fixed set of information. We lose a little bit of flexibility in that we cannot change the number, order, or types of rows in our table. However, we can build our entire interface directly in the storyboard. We don't even need to implement a data source for our table.

DESIGNING THE STATIC TABLE VIEW

Open the storyboard and zoom in on the detail view scene. First things first, let's turn it into a static table. Select the table view, then set its Content attribute to Static Cells. We also want to change the Style attribute to Grouped. This should give us a rounded bubble of three blank cells against a striped gray background (**Figure 4.24**).

FIGURE 4.25 Our initial cell design

FIGURE 4.26 Finished detail view interface

Now select and delete all but one of these cells. Select the remaining cell and change its Selection attribute to None. Then, drag out a label and place it in the row. Set its font size to 16pts, center it vertically, and align it with the left margin. Change its text to Monthly Average, and right-align the text. Finally, make sure the cell's Autosizing settings are locked to the top and the left side.

Next, drag out a text field and position it so it's centered vertically. Stretch it so it fills the space between our label and the row's right margin. Its Autosizing settings should be locked to the left, right, and top, with horizontal scaling enabled. Finally, deselect the text field's Enabled attribute. This will make the text field `readonly`. We can use it to display text, but the users won't be able to edit it (**Figure 4.25**).

There's a nice benefit to creating cells in our storyboard. Once we've designed one, we can copy it to create the others. This is a very easy way to create a number of controls, while keeping them all the same size and properly aligned.

Select the Table View section, and then change its Rows attribute to 2. We should now have two identical rows grouped together. While we're here, change the Header attribute to Weight Entry.

Now select the table view itself. Change the Sections attribute to 2. This gives us two groups of two rows each. Notice that this copies everything, including the header. To modify the bottom section, select it and change its header to Statistics. Change its Rows attribute to 3. Now go through each row and set the label text. Starting at the top, they should be Weight, Date, Monthly Average, Loss from Max, and Gain from Min. When you're done, the interface should match **Figure 4.26**.

Now let's create outlets for all our text views. Open the Assistant editor and make sure the DetailViewController.h file is showing. Control-drag from each text field to the header file. Name the outlets weightTextField, dateTextField, averageTextField, lossTextField, and gainTextField, respectively.

Now, switch back to the Standard editor and open DetailViewController.m. First things first, we no longer need a data source. Delete the following methods: numberOfSectionsInTableView:, tableView:numberOfRowsInSection:, and tableView:cellForRowAtIndexPath:.

Finally, we need to fill in our text fields with actual data. We will do this in the viewWillAppear: method. This lets us update the displayed values each time the view appears. However, this method gets a bit long, so let's examine it in chunks.

```
- (void)viewWillAppear:(BOOL)animated {
    [super viewDidAppear:animated];
    WeightUnit unit = self.weightHistory.defaultUnits;
    WeightEntry* currentEntry =
        [self.weightHistory.weights objectAtIndex:
        self.selectedIndex];
    CGFloat weight = [currentEntry weightInUnit:unit];
    // If the entry is within the same month.
    NSDate* startOfMonth;
    NSTimeInterval monthLength;
    [[NSCalendar currentCalendar] rangeOfUnit:NSMonthCalendarUnit
                                    startDate:&startOfMonth
                                     interval:&monthLength
                                      forDate:currentEntry.date];
```

First, we get some basic values. We grab the default unit value and the WeightEntry for the currently selected index. Then we extract the weight from our entry for the given unit.

Once we have the basic data, we want to calculate the start and length of the current month. We do that using the NSCalendar rangeOfUnit:startDate:interval:forDate: method. Notice that the startDate and interval are output-only arguments. You select a date and a calendar unit, and the method calculates the start and interval values for you.

```
CGFloat minWeight = CGFLOAT_MAX;
CGFloat maxWeight = CGFLOAT_MIN;
int monthlyCount = 0;
CGFloat monthlyTotal = 0.0f;
for (WeightEntry* entry in self.weightHistory.weights) {
    CGFloat sampleWeight = [entry weightInUnit:unit];
    if (sampleWeight < minWeight) minWeight = sampleWeight;
    if (sampleWeight > maxWeight) maxWeight = sampleWeight;
    // Check to see if it's in the same month.
    NSTimeInterval timeFromStartOfMonth =
        [entry.date timeIntervalSinceDate:startOfMonth];
    if (timeFromStartOfMonth > 0 &&
        timeFromStartOfMonth <= monthLength) {
        monthlyTotal += sampleWeight;
        monthlyCount++;
    }
}
CGFloat monthlyAverage = monthlyTotal / (float)monthlyCount;
```

Next, we iterate over the weight history, looking for the minimum and maximum weight values. We also use the timeIntervalSinceDate: method to calculate the number of seconds between our startOfMonth date and the given WeightEntry's date. If this is a positive number (meaning the weight entry occurred after the month began) and it is less than our `monthLength` interval, then it falls within the month in question. We add the weight to our monthly total, and we increment our monthly count.

Once we have iterated over the entire history list, we calculate the monthly average from our total and count.

```
// Now fill in our values.
self.weightTextField.text =
    [WeightEntry stringForWeightInLbs:weight inUnit:unit];
if (weight < monthlyAverage) {
    self.weightTextField.textColor = [UIColor colorWithRed:0.0f
                                                green:0.5f
                                                 blue:0.0f
                                                alpha:1.0f];
}
if (weight > monthlyAverage) {
    self.weightTextField.textColor = [UIColor colorWithRed:0.5f
                                                green:0.0f
                                                 blue:0.0f
                                                alpha:1.0f];
}
self.dateTextField.text =
[NSDateFormatter
 localizedStringFromDate:currentEntry.date
 dateStyle:NSDateFormatterShortStyle
 timeStyle:NSDateFormatterShortStyle];
self.averageTextField.text =
    [WeightEntry stringForWeightInLbs:monthlyAverage
                           inUnit:unit];
self.lossTextField.text =
```

FIGURE 4.27 Filling in the detail view

```
    [WeightEntry stringForWeightInLbs:maxWeight -
        weight inUnit:unit];
  self.gainTextField.text =
    [WeightEntry stringForWeightInLbs:weight -
        minWeight inUnit:unit];
}
```

Here we fill in our text fields. Again, we use the stringForWeightInLbs:inUnit: class method to generate properly formatted and localized weight strings. The only catch here is the weightTextField. If the current WeightEntry's weight is less than the monthly average, we set the text color to dark green. If it is greater than the monthly average, we set it to dark red. Here, we are using custom colors by specifying their RGBA values (**Figure 4.27**).

There's one last step. Modify shouldAutorotateToInterfaceOrientation: so that it returns YES, allowing us to rotate into any orientation.

```
- (BOOL)shouldAutorotateToInterfaceOrientation:
    (UIInterfaceOrientation)interfaceOrientation
{
    return YES;
}
```

DISPLAYING TEXTUAL OUTPUT

There are a number of different ways we could display textual output in iOS. We have already seen two: UILabels and UITextFields. These are useful when you're displaying relatively short pieces of text in a more-or-less static layout. The UITextView gives us a little more flexibility, letting us enter multi-line blocks of text. Like the others, we can set the font type, size, and text color. However, we must use the same settings for the entire text view.

What if we want more-complex text? Something with headers and body text? Something that uses bolds, italics, and different colors to draw and focus attention? After all, the Mac has historically had great text-layout capabilities. In the '90s, the Mac was at the forefront of the desktop publishing revolution. Therefore, you would expect iOS would have inherited some of this tradition. Unfortunately, there seems to be an odd gap in the technology here.

There are a number of different technologies, each with their own strengths and weaknesses. Some, like NSString's UIStringDrawing category, provide useful methods for drawing strings onto the screen—but like the UILabels and UITextFields, these are really only suited for short labels. The Core Animation CATextLayer and Core Graphics text support also fall into this category—useful for some corner cases, but not a general solution.

To do real formatted text, we have two main options: use a UIWebView or build it ourselves using the Core Text framework.

continues on next page

The UIWebView represents the high-level approach. Here, we lay out our text using HTML and CSS. We then load this into the Web view to display it. This has a number of advantages. You get full copy-paste support for free. You can also leverage any existing Web development experience you might have. You can incorporate images and other media. The UIWebView supports a wide range of (non-Flash) Web technologies, including JavaScript. You can even communicate between your native Objective-C code and the JavaScript running in your Web view, producing a hybrid application. In fact on iOS 5, with a little help from contentsEditable and execCommand, you can easily build a fully featured rich text editor.

The main disadvantage is that the UIWebView is an infamous memory hog. And it's true; the system performs a lot of behind-the-scenes setup when you instantiate your first Web view. This can cause a noticeable lag when first displaying a Web view. However, this reputation may be a little unfair. You can often hide the initial startup cost by pre-loading your Web view, and once the initial setup is done, the performance really isn't as bad as most people think.

Core Text, on the other hand, provides a full-throttled, high-octane, pedal-to-the-metal text system. It is designed for high performance and ease of use. It can also provide higher quality typographical controls—especially on older devices (kerning and ligatures were not available in the UIWebView before iOS 5).

Core Text is particularly well suited for paging apps, where the Web view more naturally supports scrolling apps. Core Text is also tightly integrated with Core Graphics, giving us the power to perform a wide range of drawing tasks.

On the downside, because it's a low-level library you will have to do most of the work yourself. There's no support for other media, and there's no support for copy-paste. This last point is particularly important. The iOS copy-paste system acts as a gateway to a lot of really interesting controls. As developers, we can add our own items into the copy-paste menu, which lets us include support for everything from highlighting the selected text to looking up keywords in Wikipedia.

My basic advice is to always use a UIWebView when you can. They can be frustrating at times, but you get so much bang for your buck. Only consider switching to Core Text when you absolutely need the additional power.

You can find more information on both of these technologies in Apple's documentation. See the Text Web and Editing Programming Guide for iOS, and the Core Text Programming Guide. You can also find some execCommand documentation (for editing rich text in a Web view) at https://developer.mozilla.org/en/rich-text_editing_in_mozilla.

WRAPPING **UP**

That's it. Run the application. Try adding a few weight entries. Move to the history view and then select a few entries from the list. Rotate both the history view and the detail view to make sure they work in all orientations. If everything's working fine, commit your changes.

That finishes off two of our three views. In the next chapter, we will look at creating a custom view for our `GraphViewController`. In Chapter 6, we will learn how to save both our application date and our user defaults.

5

DRAWING
CUSTOM **VIEWS**

In this chapter, we will build a simple line graph that shows how the user's weight changes over time. Both the weight axis and the time axis will scale to fill all available space. We will also draw labeled reference lines to help the user interpret the graph.

Most of this chapter focuses on performing custom drawing within our UIViews. We will look both at UIKit's drawing methods and at the underlying Core Graphics framework. We will also examine how the iOS SDK manages the difference in resolution between regular and Retina displays.

BUILDING GRAPHSTATS

Let's start by creating the `GraphStats` class. This class will process an array of `WeightEntries` and calculate some simple statistics about the collection. These include: starting date, ending date, duration, minimum weight, maximum weight, and weight span. `GraphStats` will also provide a block-based method for iterating over all the `WeightEntries` in the collection.

Create a new NSObject subclass in the Views group. Name it `GraphStats`. Then open `GraphStats.h` and make the following changes:

```objc
#import <Foundation/Foundation.h>

@class WeightEntry;

@interface GraphStats : NSObject

@property (strong, nonatomic, readonly) NSDate* startingDate;

@property (strong, nonatomic, readonly) NSDate* endingDate;

@property (assign, nonatomic, readonly) NSTimeInterval duration;

@property (assign, nonatomic, readonly) CGFloat minWeight;

@property (assign, nonatomic, readonly) CGFloat maxWeight;

@property (assign, nonatomic, readonly) CGFloat weightSpan;

- (id)initWithWeightEntryArray:(NSArray*)weightEntries;

- (void)processWeightEntryUsingBlock:(void (^)(WeightEntry*)) block;

@end
```

The `GraphStats` class acts as a wrapper around an array of `WeightEntry` objects. We start by adding a forward declaration for the `WeightEntry` class. Then we add six readonly properties. These give us access to our calculated values, like the starting date of the array or the maximum weight value. Next, we declare our designated initializer. Not surprisingly, it consumes an array of `WeightEntry` objects.

We will create `GraphStats` as a non-mutable class. We pass in our `WeightEntry` array when we first instantiate the object, and the weights cannot change over the object's lifetime. If you need to add or remove a weight, you must create an entirely new `GraphStats` object. This greatly simplifies our code. For example, we can bulk-calculate all the property values during our initialization step, and we never need to change them.

Of course, you never get something for nothing. This approach makes updates more computationally expensive. My recommendation is to go with the simplest approach. Once the application is working, we can perform usability testing and profiling to determine if there's an actual performance problem.

After our designated initializer, we declare the processWeightEntryUsingBlock: method. This will provide access to the underlying array, allowing us to iterate over all the individual WeightEntry values.

Next, open GraphStats.m. We need to import the WeightEntry header and then add the following extension before the @implementation block:

```
#import "GraphStats.h"

#import "WeightEntry.h"

@interface GraphStats()

@property (copy, nonatomic) NSArray* entries;

@property (strong, nonatomic, readwrite) NSDate* startingDate;

@property (strong, nonatomic, readwrite) NSDate* endingDate;

@property (assign, nonatomic, readwrite) NSTimeInterval duration;

@property (assign, nonatomic, readwrite) CGFloat minWeight;

@property (assign, nonatomic, readwrite) CGFloat maxWeight;

@property (assign, nonatomic, readwrite) CGFloat weightSpan;

- (void)processArray:(NSArray*)weightEntries;

@end
```

Here, we add a property to hold our array of WeightEntries. Notice that we copy the array, we do not hold onto the original. This prevents events from accidentally modifying our entries. Adding or removing an entry from the original array has no effect on our copy.

Next, we redeclare our readonly properties, making them readwrite. We also add a private helper method to process our array—this will perform the actual calculations needed to fill our public properties.

With the extension in place, we still have to synthesize our properties:

```
@synthesize entries = _entries;
@synthesize startingDate = _startingDate;
@synthesize endingDate = _endingDate;
@synthesize duration = _duration;
@synthesize minWeight = _minWeight;
@synthesize maxWeight = _maxWeight;
@synthesize weightSpan = _weightSpan;
```

Now, let's implement the designated initializer and override the superclass's designated initializer, as shown here:

```
// Designated Initializer.
- (id)initWithWeightEntryArray:(NSArray*)weightEntries {
    if ((self = [super init])) {
        [self processArray:weightEntries];
    }
    return self;
}
// Superclass's Designated Initializer.
- (id)init {
    // Create with an empy array.
    return [self initWithWeightEntryArray:[NSArray array]];
}
```

We've had a lot of practice with designated initializers, so these should seem familiar by now. The initWithWeightEntryArray: method calls the processArray: helper method, while init simply defaults back to the designated initializer and passes in an empty array. That's it.

Now, let's implement the processWeightEntryUsingBlock: method.

```
- (void)processWeightEntryUsingBlock:
(void (^)(WeightEntry*)) block {
    for (WeightEntry* entry in self.entries) {
        block(entry);
    }
}
```

As you can see, we iterate over the array, passing each WeightEntry object to the provided block. This is a convenient technique for exposing some access to an internal collection. Anyone using our class can iterate over the entire array—but they are never given access to the array itself.

Finally, we need to add our private helper method, processArray:. This gets a bit long, so let's take it in small steps.

```
#pragma mark - private methods
- (void)processArray:(NSArray*)weightEntries {
    self.entries = weightEntries;
    // Handle the edge case where we have no
    // dates in our array.
    if ([weightEntries count] == 0) {
        NSDate* date = [NSDate date];
        self.startingDate = date;
        self.endingDate = date;
        self.duration = 0.0f;
        self.minWeight = 0.0f;
        self.maxWeight = 0.0f;
        self.weightSpan = 0.0f;
        return;
    }
```

Here, we assign the `weightEntries` argument to our entries property. As we discussed earlier, this is a copy property, so it will make a new copy of the entire array. This prevents others from accidentally changing the array out from under us.

Next, we handle the corner case where the `weightEntries` argument is empty. Here, we create a new `NSDate` object set to the current date and time. We assign this date object to both the starting date and the ending date (ensuring that these values are the same). Then we set everything else to zero. Finally, we just return without doing any additional calculations.

```
// The weight entries are in order from newest to oldest.
// Ending date is stored in the first entry.
id myEntry = [weightEntries objectAtIndex:0];
self.endingDate = [myEntry date];
// Starting date is stored in the last entry.
myEntry = [weightEntries lastObject];
self.startingDate = [myEntry date];
self.duration =
[self.endingDate timeIntervalSinceDate:self.startingDate];
```

From here on, we know that we have at least one `WeightEntry` in our array, so we start calculating the start and end dates. While we could scan over the entire array looking for the entries with the earliest and latest dates, this is not necessary. If you remember, our code in Chapter 4 kept our weights in strict date order. The newest entry is always at the front of the array, the oldest at the end. Knowing this, we can just grab those values directly.

We calculate the array's duration by calling `timeIntervalSinceDate:`. This gives us an `NSTimeInterval` containing the number of seconds between the two dates. The duration is a positive number if the calling date occurs later than the argument date. If it's earlier, `timeIntervalSinceDate:` returns a negative number.

```
    self.minWeight = CGFLOAT_MAX;
    self.maxWeight = CGFLOAT_MIN;
    for (id currentEntry in weightEntries) {
        CGFloat weight = [currentEntry weightInLbs];
        if (weight < self.minWeight) self.minWeight = weight;
        if (weight > self.maxWeight) self.maxWeight = weight;
    }
    self.weightSpan = self.maxWeight - self.minWeight;
}
```

Finally, we iterate over all the WeightEntries and look for the minimum and maximum weights. We then calculate the weight span by subtracting the minimum from the maximum.

Next up, we need to create our GraphView. Right-click the Views group and select New File. When the "Choose a template" panel appears, make sure the iOS > Cocoa Touch templates are selected, choose the Objective-C class, and click Next. Name our class GraphView, make it a subclass of UIView, and click Next again. In the final panel, simply accept the defaults and click Create.

Now open our storyboard and zoom in on the graph view controller scene. Select the view and switch to the Identity inspector. Change the Class setting to GraphView (**Figure 5.1**). That's it. We're now using our very own custom view.

Of course, it doesn't do anything yet. Let's fix that. Switch to the Attributes tab. Set the Background attribute to Dark Gray Color. Then open GraphView.h and modify it as shown here:

```objc
#import <UIKit/UIKit.h>
#import "WeightEntry.h"

@interface GraphView : UIView

@property (nonatomic, assign) CGFloat margin;
@property (nonatomic, assign) CGSize cornerRadius;
@property (nonatomic, strong) UIColor* graphBorderColor;
@property (nonatomic, strong) UIColor* graphFillColor;
@property (nonatomic, assign) CGFloat graphBorderWidth;
@property (nonatomic, strong) UIColor* gridColor;
@property (nonatomic, assign) CGFloat gridSquareSize;
@property (nonatomic, assign) CGFloat gridLineWidth;
@property (nonatomic, strong) UIColor* trendLineColor;
@property (nonatomic, assign) CGFloat trendLineWidth;
@property (nonatomic, strong) UIColor* referenceLineColor;
@property (nonatomic, assign) CGFloat referenceLineWidth;
@property (nonatomic, strong) UIColor* textColor;
@property (nonatomic, assign) CGFloat fontSize;

- (void)setWeightEntries:(NSArray*)weightEntries
              andUnits:(WeightUnit)units;

@end
```

As you can see, we're declaring a slew of properties that control the graph's appearance. This has a couple of advantages. First, it makes the code easier to maintain. We can create a single method that defines all the default values. Then, if we want to make a change, we don't have to chase down every instance where that value is used, we simply modify the default value instead. These properties also let us customize the view's appearance at runtime. Our GraphViewController just needs to modify these properties before the view appears onscreen.

After the properties, we also declare the setWeightEntries:andUnits: method. The controller will use this to pass in data from our model.

Once the header is finished, switch to the implementation file. Here, we need to import GraphStats.h and then declare a private property to hold our GraphStats object and our units value. We also declare a number of private helper methods. These will draw the different parts of our user interface.

```
#import "GraphStats.h"

@interface GraphView()

@property (nonatomic, assign) WeightUnit units;

@property (nonatomic, strong) GraphStats* graphStats;

- (void)setDefaults;

- (void)drawSingleEntryTrendLine;

- (void)drawTrendLine;

- (void)drawReferenceLineWithLabel:(NSString*)label
                              font:(UIFont*)font
                               atY:(CGFloat)y
               withTextWidthOffset:(CGFloat)xOffset;

- (CGPoint) coordinatesForEntry:(WeightEntry*)entry
                       inBounds:(CGRect)bounds;

@end
```

Next, we synthesize all the properties:

```
@synthesize margin = _margin;
@synthesize cornerRadius = _cornerRadius;
@synthesize graphBorderColor = _graphBorderColor;
@synthesize graphFillColor = _graphFillColor;
@synthesize graphBorderWidth = _graphBorderWidth;
@synthesize gridColor = _gridColor;
@synthesize gridSquareSize = _gridSquareSize;
@synthesize gridLineWidth = _gridLineWidth;
@synthesize trendLineColor = _trendLineColor;
@synthesize trendLineWidth = _trendLineWidth;
@synthesize referenceLineColor = _referenceLineColor;
@synthesize referenceLineWidth = _referenceLineWidth;
@synthesize textColor = _textColor;
@synthesize fontSize = _fontSize;
@synthesize units = _units;
@synthesize graphStats = _graphStats;
```

Now let's implement our default initializer. Unlike most of the other classes we've seen so far, GraphView uses the same designated initializer as its superclass. This means we do not need a separate method just to override the superclass's initializer.

On the other hand, we will want to override our class's initWithCoder: method. We will discuss initWithCoder: in more detail in Chapter 6, when we discuss loading and saving files. For now, just understand that loading a view from a nib file (and by extension, loading from a storyboard) does not call the view's designated initializer, it calls initWithCoder: instead.

```
- (id)initWithFrame:(CGRect)frame
{
    self = [super initWithFrame:frame];
    if (self) {
        [self setDefaults];
    }
    return self;
}
- (id)initWithCoder:(NSCoder *)aDecoder {
    self = [super initWithCoder:aDecoder];
    if (self) {
        [self setDefaults];
    }
    return self;
}
```

In both cases, we simply call the superclass's version and then we call the setDefaults method.

Next, let's set the default values for our drawing:

```
#pragma mark - Default Values
- (void)setDefaults {
    _units = LBS;
    _margin = 5.0f;
    _cornerRadius = CGSizeMake(20.0f, 20.0f);
    _graphBorderColor = [UIColor blackColor];
    _graphFillColor = [UIColor lightGrayColor];
    _graphBorderWidth = 2.0f;
    _gridColor = [UIColor colorWithRed:0.0f
                                green:1.0f
                                 blue:1.0f
                                alpha:1.0f];
    _gridSquareSize = 20.0f;
    _gridLineWidth = 0.25f;
    _trendLineColor = [UIColor redColor];
    _trendLineWidth = 4.0f;
    _referenceLineColor = [UIColor lightTextColor];
    _referenceLineWidth = 1.0f;
    _textColor = [UIColor lightTextColor];
    _fontSize = 10.0f;
}
```

Here we set a slew of color, line width, and other values for our drawing code. We will look at these in more depth when they are actually used.

Next, implement the setWeightEntries:andUnits: method as shown here:

```
#pragma mark - Setting the weight data
- (void)setWeightEntries:(NSArray*)weightEntries
               andUnits:(WeightUnit)units {
    self.graphStats =
    [[GraphStats alloc] initWithWeightEntryArray:weightEntries];
    self.units = units;
    [self setNeedsDisplay];
}
```

Here, we start by instantiating a new GraphStats object using the weightEntries argument. We then assign that object to our graphStats property. We also set the units property and call setNeedsDisplay.

The setNeedsDisplay method tells the system that the view's content has changed and needs to be redrawn. Notice that setNeedsDisplay does not trigger an immediate redrawing. Instead, the system just records the request and allows setNeedsDisplay to return. Then, during the next draw cycle, the view redraws itself.

PERFORMING CUSTOM DRAWING

Now we get to the heart of this chapter: drawing our user interface.

When UIKit needs to draw a view (either entirely or just in part), it creates a graphics context whose origin matches the view's bounds (e.g., {0.0, 0.0} is located at the top left corner of the view). It also applies any transforms necessary to make the context match the view (rotation, scaling, etc.). Then, it calls the view's drawRect: method.

Of course, the default UIView's drawRect: method doesn't do anything at all, but we can override it to customize our view's appearance.

Please note, this is not the only way to draw a view. If you just want to change the background color, you do not need to implement drawRect:. Just change the view's backgroundColor property. The rest is automatic.

At the other extreme, if you are drawing the content directly in the view's layer, or if you plan to use OpenGL ES for your drawing, you do not need to override the drawRect: method. These approaches have their own drawing techniques.

Still, if you plan to use the native drawing technologies in Core Graphics and UIKit, drawRect: is your best friend.

In our view, we will draw a simple graph. The y-axis will represent our weights; the x-axis will represent time. We will dynamically scale both axes to cover the full range from our array of WeightEntries. We will also draw a grid in the background, and reference lines to mark the maximum and minimum values. Finally, we will lay the weight's trend line over this background information.

Obviously, this isn't the best possible graph. Even small changes in weight can appear huge because of the autoscaling. A better approach would more intelligently select the scale so that it uses the entire space effectively, still shows the entire trend line, and also minimizes the natural daily variances. Additionally, we really should label both axes, not just the weights, and the reference lines should be spaced evenly throughout this range (every 2 pounds, 5 pounds, 10 pounds, whatever). It would also be nice if they aligned with the background grid.

Still, our quick and dirty implementation is relatively straightforward, while letting us explore a number of useful drawing techniques. So go ahead and uncomment the drawRect: method.

In theory, the first time this method is called, the rect argument should be set to the view's bounds, letting you fill the entire view. Subsequent calls may then only ask to redraw a small portion of that view. In practice, however, unless you are changing your view and explicitly calling setNeedsDisplay or setNeedsDisplayInRect:, you will probably only draw the view once. UIKit caches and reuses this original drawing.

The UIView draws onto its CALayer and then displays the CALayer as needed. As a result, we can resize the view, flip it, fade it in and out, and even cover it up and reveal it again without needing to redraw it.

If you are updating your view, you should try to make the update rectangle as small as possible. The system will automatically set the current context's clipping path to match the update rectangle. This prevents us from accidentally drawing outside the update rectangle. Still, we should avoid performing any unnecessary drawing, especially when frequently updating our views, since these can create significant performance bottlenecks.

In complex views, you often want to separate the content using multiple views or layers—one contains the static content, the others contain different dynamic elements. This allows us to selectively redraw only those elements that actually change.

In our case, the entire view is static; it should be drawn only once, when the system first displays it. This means we can safely ignore the rect argument and just draw the entire view. If, by some chance, the system happens to update just a portion of our view, everything will still work properly. Yes, we might waste a little computational effort trying to draw outside the clipping path—but those drawing commands are ignored and don't actually affect the application's appearance. Remember, there's no point in optimizing our code for edge cases that never occur in practice.

Also, notice that we don't ever draw our view's backgroundColor. The system automatically handles this for us before calling our drawRect: method. However, since our custom drawing code does not fill the entire view, we must either set a non-opaque background color or change our view's opaque property to NO. Anything else may result in unpredictable drawing errors.

CORE GRAPHICS VS. UIKit DRAWING

Our custom drawing code will use a combination of Core Graphics drawing functions and UIKit drawing methods. These methods and functions are (for the most part) completely compatible. In fact, the UIKit methods typically use Core Graphics functions to perform the actual drawing. Many duplicate methods exist between the two frameworks. For example, we set our current context's fill color using [self.graphFillColor setFill]. Alternatively, we could have called the Core Graphics function CGContextSetFillColorWithColor(context, self.graphFillColor.CGColor) instead.

Notice that there is an important difference here: UIKit uses UIColor classes, while Core Graphics uses CGColorRefs. Also, the UIKit methods implicitly use the current graphics context. Most Core Graphics methods require an explicit reference to the context. Still, while the details may differ, the end results are the same.

```
#pragma mark - drawing
- (void)drawRect:(CGRect)rect {
    // Calculate bounds with margin.
    CGRect innerBounds =
        CGRectInset(self.bounds, self.margin, self.margin);
    // Fill in the rounded rectangle.
    UIBezierPath* graphBorder =
        [UIBezierPath bezierPathWithRoundedRect:innerBounds
        byRoundingCorners:UIRectCornerAllCorners
        cornerRadii:self.cornerRadius];
    [self.graphFillColor setFill];
    [graphBorder fill];
```

Here we use the CGRectInset() method to create a smaller rectangle centered in the view's bounds. We use the margin property to determine the spacing between the inner bounds and the view's bounds. We set the default margin to 5.0f, so there should be a 5-point gap on all sides (left, right, top, and bottom).

Next, we use the bezierPathWithRoundedRect:byRoundingCorners:corner Radii: convenience method to create a UIBezierPath. The UIBezierPath class lets us create a series of straight and curved line segments, then draw that path to the current context. Paths can be open or closed. You can build them either one line segment at a time, or you can use one of the convenience methods to create common shapes: rectangle, oval, arc, or in this particular case a rounded rectangle. Once we have our rounded rectangle, we set the current context's fill color, using the graphFillColor property, and then we fill it in.

Core Graphics and UIKit support two basic drawing operations: fills and strokes. A fill operation paints the inside of a region or shape; a stroke draws the outline. Our context can have separate stroke and fill colors but can have only one fill or stroke color at a time (not including fill patterns and gradients).

```
// Save the current context.
CGContextRef context = UIGraphicsGetCurrentContext();
CGContextSaveGState(context);
// Limit drawing to inside the rounded rectangle.
[graphBorder addClip];
```

This step is short, but it's worth talking about in detail. Each graphics context maintains a stack of states. The states record a number of the graphics context's parameters. These include the following:

- Current transformation matrix
- Clip region
- Image interpolation quality
- Line width
- Line join
- Miter limit
- Line cap
- Line dash
- Flatness
- Should anti-alias
- Rendering intent
- Fill color space

- Stroke color space
- Fill color
- Stroke color
- Alpha value
- Font
- Font size
- Character spacing
- Text drawing mode
- Shadow parameters
- Pattern phase
- Font smoothing parameter
- Blend mode

Some of these, like the stroke or fill color, are simple enough to set and reset manually. In other cases, it may not be so easy to undo your changes. Look at the clipping path. Both the UIKit methods and the Core Graphics functions offer ways of adding shapes to the current clipping path; however, there's no way to remove them.

The graphics context's stack of states gives us an easy way to quickly undo a large number of changes. We can even roll back those hard-to-fix changes. By calling CGContextSaveGState() and CGContextRestoreGState(), we can push and pop the current state onto and off of the state stack.

In this particular case, we want to add the rounded rectangle to the clipping path (thus limiting all drawing to the inside of our rounded rectangle). However, we will still want to draw outside the rectangle later on. Therefore, we must save the state before we alter the clipping path.

NOTE: You only need to use CGContextSaveGState() and CGContextRestoreGState() if you plan to undo state changes within your own drawing code. The system automatically creates a new graphics context each time a view is drawn. Any changes you make will not persist beyond the current draw cycle and the current view.

```
// Draw graph paper background.
[self.gridColor setStroke];
CGContextSetLineWidth(context, self.gridLineWidth);
// Draw horizontal.
CGFloat y = innerBounds.origin.y + self.gridSquareSize;
while (y < innerBounds.origin.y + innerBounds.size.height) {
    CGPoint segments[] = {CGPointMake(innerBounds.origin.x, y),
        CGPointMake(innerBounds.origin.x +
                    innerBounds.size.width, y)};
    CGContextStrokeLineSegments(context, segments, 2);
    y += self.gridSquareSize;
}
// Draw vertical.
CGFloat x = innerBounds.origin.x + self.gridSquareSize;
```

```
    while (x < innerBounds.origin.x + innerBounds.size.width) {
        CGPoint segments[] = {CGPointMake(x, innerBounds.origin.y),
            CGPointMake(x, innerBounds.origin.y +
                             innerBounds.size.height)};
        CGContextStrokeLineSegments (context, segments, 2);
        x += self.gridSquareSize;
    }
}
```

This snippet draws a grid of horizontal and vertical lines inside our rounded rectangle. We set the stroke color and line width based on our parameters. We then step across the rounded rectangle's bounds, first drawing vertical lines and then drawing horizontal lines.

The actual drawing is done using the CGContextStrokeLineSegments() function. This takes the context, a C-style array of CGPoints, and a count parameter that indicates the number of points in our array. Here, we just use the line's two endpoints. The stroke function draws a straight line connecting those points.

```
    // Now draw the trend line.
    if (self.graphStats.duration == 0.0) {
        [self drawSingleEntryTrendLine];
    }
    else {
        [self drawTrendLine];
    }
```

Next, we check to see if we have an actual trend line (two or more WeightEntries) or just a dot (zero or one WeightEntry). We then call the appropriate helper method.

```
    // Now draw the graph's outline.
    CGContextRestoreGState(context);
    graphBorder.lineWidth = self.graphBorderWidth;
    [self.graphBorderColor setStroke];
    [graphBorder stroke];
}
```

By default, our gridLineWidth is set to 0.25 points. On an older iPhone, this would produce a line a quarter of a pixel wide. On the iPhone 4 (or anything with a Retina display), it would be half a pixel wide. Obviously, you cannot draw less than a single pixel.

UIKit manages this by using anti-aliasing—proportionally blending the drawn line with the background color. Anti-aliasing often makes lines look smoother (especially curved or diagonal lines), but it can also make them appear softer or somewhat fuzzy.

By default, anti-aliasing is turned on for any window or bitmap context. It is turned off for any other graphics contexts. However, we can explicitly set our context's anti-aliasing using the CGContextSetShouldAntiAlias() function. Notice that, if we do this for our graph view, our grid lines will be drawn with a minimum 1-pixel width.

It's also important to realize that the graphics context's coordinates fall in between the pixels. For example, if you draw a 1-point-wide horizontal line at y = 20, on a non-Retina display (iPad or iPhone 3GS or earlier), the line will actually be drawn half in pixel row 19 and half in row 20. If anti-aliasing is on, this will result in two rows of pixels, each with a 50% blend. If anti-aliasing is off, you will get a 2-pixel-wide line. You can fix this by offsetting the drawing coordinates by half a point (y = 20.5). Then the line will fall exactly along the row of pixels.

For a Retina display, the 1-point line will result in a 2-pixel line that properly fills both rows on either side of the y-coordinate. For more information on how Retina displays and scale factors work, see the "Drawing for the Retina Display" sidebar later in this chapter.

And finally, we restore our graphics state, thus removing the rounded rectangle from the clipping path. Then we set the line width and color, and draw the rounded rectangle's border. It's important to draw the border last, placing it over the top of the other drawings. Otherwise, the fill and graph lines would cover its inner edge. Similarly, we have to remove the clipping path, because half the line's width will be drawn outside the path. If we leave the clipping in place, we'll only get the inner half of our border.

Now, let's add stubs for our helper methods. These will let us compile and test our app (**Figure 5.2**).

```
- (void)drawSingleEntryTrendLine {

}
- (void)drawTrendLine {

}
- (void)drawReferenceLineWithLabel:(NSString*)label
```

FIGURE 5.2 Drawing the rounded rectangle and the grid

```
                font:(UIFont*)font
                 atY:(CGFloat)y
     withTextWidthOffset:(CGFloat)xOffset {

}
- (CGPoint) coordinatesForEntry:(WeightEntry*)entry
                   inBounds:(CGRect)bounds {

    return CGPointZero;
}
```

Here we can see the view's dark background, our rounded rectangle, and our grid lines. We just need to draw our reference lines and the actual trend line.

DRAWING FOR THE RETINA DISPLAY

As you probably know, the iPhone 4's Retina display has a 960 x 640 display. This is four times the number of pixels as the earlier models. This could result in a lot of complexity for developers—where we have to constantly test for the screen size and alter our drawing code to match. Fortunately, Apple has hidden much of this complexity from us.

All the native drawing functions (Core Graphics, UIKit, and Core Animation) use a logical coordinate system measured in points. A point is approximately 1/160 of an inch. It's important to note that these points may or may not be the same as the screen's pixels. Draw a 1-point-wide line on an iPhone 3GS, and you get a 1-pixel-wide line. Draw the same line on an iPhone 4, and it is now 2 pixels wide. This also means a full-screen frame is the same size on the iPhone 3GS and the iPhone 4: 320 points by 480 points.

A device's scale factor gives us the conversion between points and pixels. You can access the scale property from the UIScreen, UIView, UIImage, or CALayer classes. This allows us to perform any resolution-dependent processing. However, we actually get a lot of support for free.

- All standard UIKit views are automatically drawn at the correct resolution.
- Vector-based drawings (e.g., UIBezierPath, CGPathRef, and PDFs) automatically take advantage of the higher resolution to produce smoother lines.
- All text is automatically rendered at the higher resolution.

There are, however, some steps we still need to take to fully support multiple screen resolutions. One obvious example occurs when loading and displaying images and other bitmapped art. We need to create higher-resolution copies of these files for the Retina display. Fortunately, UIKit supports automatically loading the correct resolution, based on the image name.

Let's say you have a 20-pixel by 30-pixel image named stamp.png. You need to create a higher-resolution version of this image (40 pixels by 60 pixels), and save it as stamp@2x.png. Add both images to your project. Now, just load the image using the following code:

```
UIImage* stampImage = [UIImage imageNamed:@"stamp"];
```

UIKit will automatically load the correct version for your device.

Similarly, if we are creating bitmaps programmatically, we will want to make sure we give them the correct scale factor. The UIGraphicsBeginImageContext function creates a bitmap-based graphics context with a 1.0 scale factor. Instead, use the UIGraphicsBeginImageContextWithOptions function, and pass in the correct scale (which you can access by calling [[UIScreen mainScreen] scale]).

Core Animation layers may also need explicit support. Whenever you create a new CALayer (one that is not already associated with a view), it comes with a default scale value of 1.0. If you then draw this layer onto a Retina display, it will automatically scale up to match the screen. You can prevent this by manually changing the layer's scale factor and then providing resolution-appropriate content.

Finally, OpenGL ES also uses a 1.0 scale by default. Everything will still draw on the Retina display, but it will be scaled up and may appear blocky (especially when compared to properly scaled drawings). To get full-scale rendering, we must increase the size of our renderbuffers. This, however, can have severe performance implications. Therefore, we must make these changes manually. Changing a view's contentScaleFactor will automatically alter the underlying CAEAGLLayer, increasing the size of the renderbuffers by the scale factor.

It is also important to test your drawing code on all the devices you intend to support. Drawing a 0.5-point-wide line may look fine on an iPhone 3GS but appear too thin on an iPhone 4. Similarly, higher-resolution resources use more memory and may take longer to load and process. Still, using a logical coordinate system greatly simplifies creating custom drawing code that works across multiple resolutions.

DRAWING A SINGLE-ENTRY TREND LINE

Now we need to implement our helper methods. Let's start by drawing a dot when we only have a single entry. This also works when we don't have any entries at all, since the GraphStats will return a duration of 0.0 and a weight of 0.0f.

```
- (void)drawSingleEntryTrendLine {
    NSAssert2(self.graphStats.minWeight ==
    self.graphStats.maxWeight,
            @"If there's only one entry the minimum weight "
            @"(%1.2f) should equal the maximum (%1.2f)",
            self.graphStats.minWeight, self.graphStats.maxWeight);
```

We start with a quick sanity check. We should only call the drawSingleEntry TrendLine method when the GraphStats object has zero or one WeightEntries. In either case, the minimum and maximum weights should have the same value.

We can use NSAssert (and its variants) to verify this assumption. NSAssert takes two arguments: the first is an expression, the second is an NSString. By default, the macro evaluates the expression. If the result is false, NSAssert throws an NSInternalInconsistencyException, using the string in the error message.

NSAsserts can help when debugging, testing, and hardening our code. However, we may not want to include these checks in our final release builds. Fortunately, we can easily disable these checks. Simply define an NS_BLOCK_ASSERTIONS preprocessor macro, and the compiler won't include the NSAsserts.

By default, Xcode 4.0 automatically disables NSAsserts when you are making release builds. This means we can use as many NSAsserts as we want when developing and testing. We don't need to worry about them adversely affecting our final product.

Generously sprinkling asserts through your code can greatly help improve your application's reliability. If a method should take only positive numbers, use an assert to verify that fact. It's better to crash the application with a reasonable error message than to let it lumber forward in an undefined state.

Of course, there is some debate about whether it's better to use Cocoa's NSAssert macro or C's assert() function. While they largely do the same thing, they have two main differences. The assert() method does not take an error string as an argument. Using NSAssert with well-defined error messages can make it a lot easier to debug your code. On the other hand, assert() is guaranteed to halt your application—NSAssert might not.

NSAssert typically throws an exception, but you can change this behavior by creating a custom NSAssertionHandler subclass. In practice, however, this is almost never done. More commonly, problems might occur when a third-party library accidentally catches and then silently discards your NSInternalInconsistencyException, masking the error from you. This means you might have an assert fail but never actually see it.

Personally, I prefer the richer messages afforded by NSAssert. After all, you can always set a breakpoint to catch exceptions, so they can't really hide from you—at least, not during development. And, if it becomes a real concern, you can always implement a custom NSAssertionHandler to work around the problem.

Another great source of Internet arguments is the debate over stripping your asserts from your release code. Unless they are actively hurting your performance, there are good arguments both for taking them out and for leaving them in. I must admit, I usually take the path of least resistance. Previous versions of Xcode did not automatically strip the NSAsserts; Xcode 4 does. Most of the time, I'm just not sufficiently motivated to actually go out and modify the behavior either way.

```
// Find the center of the screen.
CGFloat x = self.bounds.size.width / 2.0f;
CGFloat y = self.bounds.size.height / 2.0f;
CGFloat weight = self.graphStats.minWeight;
```

After passing the sanity check, we generate some useful values. We calculate the x- and y-coordinates for the center of the graph view. Then we grab the weight value. Since we only have one value, we can just use the GraphStats minimum weight—there's no need to access the individual WeightEntry objects.

```
NSString* label =
    [WeightEntry stringForWeightInLbs:weight inUnit:self.units];
UIFont* font = [UIFont boldSystemFontOfSize:self.fontSize];
CGSize textSize = [label sizeWithFont:font];
[self drawReferenceLineWithLabel:label
                            font:font
                             atY:y
            withTextWidthOffset:textSize.width];
```

Now we're getting into the nitty-gritty. We start by creating a label string from our weight. As always, this will include the properly formatted number and the unit label. We then request the bold system font based on our current fontSize property. We can use the font to calculate the bounding box needed to draw our string. Simply call the sizeWithFont: method from NSString's UIStringDrawing extension.

With the string, font, y-coordinate, and text width in hand, we can call the drawReferenceLineWithLabel:font:atY:withTextWidthOffset: helper function. We will look at this function in a bit, but basically it will draw our text label at the specified y-coordinates along the left margin. This is followed by a small space (based on the text width offset and our margin property), and then a thin horizontal line is drawn stretching to the right margin.

```
UIBezierPath* trendLine = [UIBezierPath bezierPath];

trendLine.lineWidth = self.trendLineWidth;

trendLine.lineCapStyle = kCGLineCapRound;

[trendLine moveToPoint:CGPointMake(x, y)];

[trendLine addLineToPoint:CGPointMake(x + 1, y)];

[self.trendLineColor setStroke];

[trendLine stroke];
}
```

Finally, we draw our trend line—or actually our trend point. While we could have used the UIBezierPath to create an actual circle, we wanted our trend point to match a multiple-entry trend line as closely as possible. The easiest way to do this is to just draw a very short line.

Here, we create our Bezier path. We set the line width based on our trendLine Width property. This is 4 points wide by default. We then set the line cap style to round caps. This defines the shape of the line's endpoints. We then move the cursor to the center of the view and create a 1-point-long line.

Finally, we set the line's color, based on our trendLineColor property, and draw the line. By drawing a very short, wide line with round end caps, we create a nice little dot that will perfectly match the actual lines we will draw in our next helper method.

DRAWING THE FULL TREND LINE

While similar to the previous method in many ways, drawTrendLine adds a few layers of complexity. Here, we're going to draw two labeled reference lines. One corresponds to the minimum weight, one to the maximum. We will also need to coordinate their appearance, so even though the weight labels may have different widths, the left edge of the reference lines remains properly aligned. Finally, we need to dynamically size our graph so our trend line fills the bulk of the view.

Again, because of the length of this method, we will look at it in smaller chunks.

```
- (void)drawTrendLine {
    // Draw the reference lines.
    UIFont* font = [UIFont boldSystemFontOfSize:self.fontSize];
    CGFloat textPadding = font.lineHeight / 2.0f;
    CGFloat topY = self.margin * 2 + textPadding;
    CGFloat bottomY = self.bounds.size.height - topY;
```

We start by requesting the bold system font again. Then we calculate a text Padding variable based on half the font's height. We then use this value and our margin property to calculate a safe upper and lower limit for our reference lines. After all, we don't want to cut off the tops and bottoms of our labels.

```
    NSString* topLabel =
        [WeightEntry stringForWeightInLbs:self.graphStats.maxWeight
                                   inUnit:self.units];
    NSString* bottomLabel =
        [WeightEntry stringForWeightInLbs:self.graphStats.minWeight
                                   inUnit:self.units];
    CGSize topTextSize = [topLabel sizeWithFont:font];
    CGSize bottomTextSize = [bottomLabel sizeWithFont:font];
    // Get the maximum width.
    CGFloat textOffset =
        topTextSize.width > bottomTextSize.width ?
```

```
                  topTextSize.width: bottomTextSize.width;
[self drawReferenceLineWithLabel:topLabel
                            font:font
                             atY:topY
            withTextWidthOffset:textOffset];
[self drawReferenceLineWithLabel:bottomLabel
                            font:font
                             atY:bottomY
            withTextWidthOffset:textOffset];
```

Next, we create our weight labels for the top and bottom reference lines. As stated earlier, the top line will be our maximum weight, while the bottom will be our minimum weight. We then calculate the size of each of these.

Here we use C's ternary conditional operator to determine the maximum width (see "Operators" in Chapter 2). This expression says that if the top width is greater than the bottom width, we use the top width. Otherwise we use the bottom.

Finally, we call our helper method to draw the two reference lines. Notice that we use the same textOffset for both of them.

```
CGFloat startX = self.margin * 4 + textOffset;
CGFloat endX = self.bounds.size.width - (self.margin * 3);
UIBezierPath* trendLine = [UIBezierPath bezierPath];
trendLine.lineWidth = self.trendLineWidth;
trendLine.lineCapStyle = kCGLineCapRound;
trendLine.lineJoinStyle = kCGLineJoinRound;
// Get starting point.
CGRect graphBounds =
    CGRectMake(startX, topY, endX - startX, bottomY - topY);
```

Here, we want to make sure the graph starts well to the right of our labels. So, we utilize our textOffset variable and our margin property to calculate the starting and ending x-coordinates.

Once we have the start and end x-coordinates, we create an empty UIBezierPath. This will hold our trend line. We set the width based on our trendLineWidth property and then give it rounded caps and joins. We discussed the caps earlier. Joins define the shape of the corners where two line segments connect.

As the last step in this snippet, we create a rectangle based on our startX, endX, topY, and bottomY values.

```
// Process all the entries.
[self.graphStats processWeightEntryUsingBlock:
 ^(WeightEntry* entry) {
    CGPoint point =
        [self coordinatesForEntry:entry inBounds:graphBounds];
    if (trendLine.empty) {
        // If we don't have any points,
        // move to the starting point.
        [trendLine moveToPoint:point];
    }
    else {
        // Otherwise, draw a line to the next point.
        [trendLine addLineToPoint:point];
    }
}];
[self.trendLineColor setStroke];
[trendLine stroke];
}
```

Finally, we use our processWeightEntryUsingBlock: method to process all the WeightEntries in our GraphStats object (see "Building GraphStats" at the beginning of this chapter).

We start by calling the coordinatesForEntry:inBounds: helper method to calculate the entry's coordinates within our selected bounds. Then, if our Bezier path is empty, we move the cursor to the starting point. Otherwise, we add a new line segment stretching from the current cursor location to the provided point. This also updates the cursor's location to the new point.

Once the path is complete, we set the stroke color and draw it.

DRAWING THE REFERENCE LINES AND LABELS

Now let's implement the reference line helper method:

```
- (void)drawReferenceLineWithLabel:(NSString*)label
                              font:(UIFont*)font
                               atY:(CGFloat)y
                  withTextWidthOffset:(CGFloat)xOffset {
    // Set x-coordinate.
    CGFloat x = self.margin * 2.0f;
    [self.textColor setFill];
    [label drawAtPoint:CGPointMake(x, y - (font.lineHeight / 2.0f))
            withFont:font];
    x += self.margin + xOffset;
    UIBezierPath* referenceLine = [UIBezierPath bezierPath];
    referenceLine.lineWidth = self.referenceLineWidth;
    [referenceLine moveToPoint:CGPointMake(x, y)];
    [referenceLine addLineToPoint:
        CGPointMake(self.bounds.size.width -
            (self.margin * 2.0f), y)];
    [self.referenceLineColor setStroke];
    [referenceLine stroke];
}
```

We start by creating an x-coordinate that is inset by twice the `margin` property—once to bring us to the edge of the rounded rectangle, then once more to give us a nice margin inside it. Notice that we are using the same margin value for all the margins: the distance between the view's bounds and the round rectangle, the distance between the left side of the round rectangle and our reference label, and the distance between the reference label and the reference line. We could have used different margin parameters, but this simplifies the code and provides a clean, uniform appearance.

We then set the fill color to our `textColor` property, and draw our text using the `UIStringDrawing` `drawAtPoint:withFont:` method. This draws a single line of text whose upper-left corner is the given point. Notice that this method uses the text drawing mode and colors from the current context; however, you do not need to set the context's font. The `drawAtPoint:withFont:` method manages the font for you automatically.

By default, text is drawn using only the fill color. You can change this if you want by calling the Core Graphics `CGContextSetTextDrawingMode()` method to add outlines (as well as other drawing effects).

Additionally, we want our text to be vertically centered on the y-coordinate. Notice how we offset the drawing point by subtracting half the font's line height from our y-coordinate. This moves the label up, centering its bounding box appropriately.

Next, we move the x-coordinate in by using our text width offset and margin. We create our path, a single horizontal line segment that runs from the x- and y-coordinates to the right margin. We set the line width and color, and then we draw the line.

This approach is somewhat different from the one we used to draw the grid lines. Here, we are using UIKit's `UIBezierPath`. There, we used Core Graphics' `CGContextStrokeLineSegments()` function. As we said earlier, there are a number of duplicate (or near-duplicate) methods between the two frameworks. This often gives us several different ways to accomplish the same basic task. You can pick whichever approach works best in your particular application.

CALCULATING A WEIGHT ENTRY'S COORDINATES

This method takes a weight entry and the bounds for our trend line. We then calculate the coordinates for that entry within those bounds.

```
- (CGPoint) coordinatesForEntry:(WeightEntry*)entry
                     inBounds:(CGRect)bounds {
    NSTimeInterval secondsAfterStart =
        [entry.date timeIntervalSinceDate:
          self.graphStats.startingDate];
    CGFloat x = (float)secondsAfterStart /
                (float)self.graphStats.duration;
    x *= bounds.size.width;
    x += bounds.origin.x;
    CGFloat y = 1.0f - (entry.weightInLbs -
        self.graphStats.minWeight) /
        self.graphStats.weightSpan;
    y *= bounds.size.height;
    y += bounds.origin.y;
    return CGPointMake(x, y);
}
```

We start by calculating our x-coordinates. The x-coordinates should be based on the entry's date. The starting date should be at the left edge of the bounds; the end date along the right.

We start by using timeIntervalSinceDate: to calculate the number of seconds since our GraphStats starting date. We then divide this by the duration of the GraphStats. This gives us a number from 0.0 to 1.0, where 0.0 is the starting date and 1.0 is the ending date. We convert this to the actual x-coordinate by multiplying it by the bound's width and then adding the bound's x-offset.

Next, we do the same thing for the y-coordinates. This time the maximum weight should be at the top of the graph's bounds, the minimum weight at the bottom. The math is basically the same as above—with one small change. We need to invert the y-coordinates.

FIGURE 5.3 Zero-entry graph

The expression, (entry.weightInLbs - self.graphStats.minWeight) / self.graphStats.weightSpan, returns a value from 0.0 to 1.0, with the maximum weight as 1.0. To print at the top, we need the maximum weight to be 0.0 instead. To do that, we simply subtract it from 1.0.

That's it. Calculate the two coordinates, shove them into a CGPoint, and we're done.

Run the project and navigate over to the graph view (**Figure 5.3**). Of course, a graph with no elements isn't very interesting. Notice how the reference line defaults to 0.0 lbs. We have our red dot in the center of our view. Other than that, there's not a lot to report here.

Add another weight and navigate back to the graph. Nothing's changed. Change the units and navigate back. Still nothing. Clearly the controller isn't passing along our model information. Let's fix that.

FINISHING THE CONTROLLER

Open GraphViewController.m. Let's start by importing our GraphView class. We also need to add string constants for observing our weight list and units.

```
#import "GraphViewController.h"
#import "GraphView.h"
#import "WeightHistory.h"
static NSString* const WeightKey = @"weights";
static NSString* const UnitsKey = @"defaultUnits";
```

Next, uncomment the viewDidLoad method and make the following changes:

```
- (void)viewDidLoad
{
    [super viewDidLoad];
    id graphView = self.view;
    [graphView setWeightEntries:self.weightHistory.weights
                       andUnits:self.weightHistory.defaultUnits];
    // Watch weight history for changes.
    [self.weightHistory addObserver:self
                         forKeyPath:WeightKey
                            options:NSKeyValueObservingOptionNew
                            context:nil];
    [self. weightHistory addObserver:self
                          forKeyPath:UnitsKey
                             options:NSKeyValueObservingOptionNew
                             context:nil];
}
```

First, we grab a reference to our custom view and set the view's weight entries and default units.

There are three common idioms for letting a view controller access a custom view's properties and instance methods. One is to just cast the view pointer whenever you need it.

```
[(MyView*) self.view setMyProperty:myValue];
```

This works, but casting is ugly and I try to avoid it wherever possible.

A second approach involves creating a `readonly` property to access the custom view, encapsulating the cast in the property's getter. For example, look at the `UITableViewcontroller`. This has both a `view` and a `tableView` property. The `tableView` just calls `view` and casts the result before retuning it. This approach requires a bit more code to set up, but it produces very clean results.

```
self.myView.myProperty = myValue;
```

The third option is the one we use here. We leverage Objective-C's dynamic nature to avoid explicitly casting our results. Instead, we assign the `self.view` property to an `id` variable. We can then call any methods we want without getting any compiler warnings. It's not as nice as the `readonly` property, but it's a lot quicker for a one-off solution.

The only downside is that we cannot use the property's dot notation on `id`s. We must call the accessor methods instead.

We've passed our original data to our view, but we still need to detect updates. To do this, we register our controller for KVO notifications. We've seen this before, so there shouldn't be any big surprises (see "Responding to Changes in the Model" in Chapter 4). There are, however, two small surprises. First, we are observing our model's `weights` virtual property—not the `weightHistory` property. Unlike our history view, we don't need to know the details of the change. If we see any change at all, we simply redraw the whole view. So, observing the `weights` property works perfectly well.

Additionally, we are using KVO to observe our `defaultUnits` property directly, instead of going through the notification center like we did in Chapter 4. We will see why in a second.

As always, anything we set up in `viewDidLoad` needs to be torn down in `viewDidUnload`. We added our controller as an observer, so now we must remove it.

```
- (void)viewDidUnload
{
    [super viewDidUnload];
    [self.weightHistory removeObserver:self forKeyPath:WeightKey];
    [self.weightHistory removeObserver:self forKeyPath:UnitsKey];
}
```

And we still need to catch these notifications. Remember, all KVO notifications go through the observeValueForKeyPath:ofObject:change:context: method. Let's implement that now.

```
- (void)observeValueForKeyPath:(NSString *)keyPath
                      ofObject:(id)object
                        change:(NSDictionary *)change
                       context:(void *)context {
    if ([keyPath isEqualToString:WeightKey]||
        [keyPath isEqualToString:UnitsKey]) {
        id graphView = self.view;
        [graphView
          setWeightEntries:self.weightHistory.weights
          andUnits:self.weightHistory.defaultUnits];
    }
}
```

Having all KVO notifications route through the same method is usually a disadvantage, but this time it actually helps simplify things. If we receive a change notification, we just verify that it matches one of our two keys. If there is a match—we don't even care which one—we call setWeightEntries:andUnits:, resetting both of them. Also, remember that setWeightEntries:andUnits: automatically calls setNeedsDisplay, causing our view to redraw itself.

FIGURE 5.4 Single-entry trend line

FIGURE 5.5 Displaying a multi-entry graph

Run the application again. Look at the empty graph, and then add a single weight. The graph's weight label should change when you navigate back to it (**Figure 5.4**).

Keep adding weights and see how the graph changes. Try switching between units; the reference line labels should change automatically (**Figure 5.5**).

So far, everything looks good, but there's still one small problem. Try rotating the application. The good news is that our view does not need to be redrawn. The system automatically stretches and squeezes its layer to fit. The bad news—this is obviously not what we want (**Figure 5.6**).

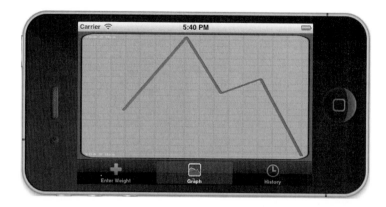

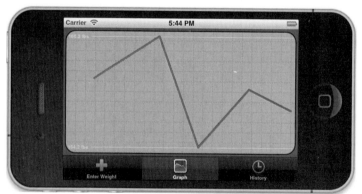

Fortunately, there's an easy fix. Our view controller already receives a will AnimateRotationToInterfaceOrientation:duration: message when the view rotates. We just need to override this method and ask the view to redraw itself.

```
- (void) willAnimateRotationToInterfaceOrientation:
    (UIInterfaceOrientation) toInterfaceOrientation
    duration:(NSTimeInterval)duration {
    [self.view setNeedsDisplay];
}
```

Now run the application again. Add a few weights, and try to rotate it (**Figure 5.7**). If everything is working properly, commit these changes.

WRAPPING **UP**

In this chapter, we examined different techniques for drawing custom user interface elements. This included a discussion of how UIKit manages the drawing of views, a look at the differences between UIKit and Core Graphics, and some sample code demonstrating drawing techniques from both libraries. However, all the examples in this chapter focused on drawing a static view—a view whose contents rarely changed.

We will take this one step further in Chapter 8, where we will look at custom-drawing a dynamic interface—an interface that is constantly changing. We will also look at incorporating Core Animation to move otherwise static UI elements onto and off of our screen. Finally, we will combine our custom drawing with custom event handling to create our own controls.

In the meantime, Chapters 6 and 7 will focus on saving our user information. Chapter 6 will look at techniques for saving our data model both to disk and to our iCloud storage. Then, in Chapter 7, we will replace our current model with a Core Data-based model.

6

LOADING AND SAVING DATA

This chapter will focus on loading and saving data. We will begin with a brief discussion of iOS's local file system and then look at how documents can be shared across multiple devices using iCloud. We will then expand Health Beat to save and load application data and our user preferences to the cloud. Finally, we will add a custom preferences page to the Settings app, letting us view and change Health Beat's default settings.

THE iOS FILE SYSTEM

Always remember, iOS is not a desktop operating system. Some of the things we take for granted on desktop machines are impossible, inappropriate, or at least very difficult in iOS. The file system is a great example of this. Where the desktop often displays dialog boxes to open and save files, forcing the user to search through a forest of directories, iOS goes to great lengths to hide the underlying file system, both from the user and from the applications themselves.

This provides two main benefits. For the user, this greatly simplifies the experience. You don't need to worry about where files are stored or how to find them. Your application handles all of this transparently. For the applications, limiting access to the file system greatly improves system security. Each application is limited to its own sandbox. The application can freely open and save files within this sandbox, but it cannot touch anything outside these carefully defined boundaries. This protects both your data and the system files from accidental (or worse yet, malicious) alterations. Unfortunately, it also makes sharing files between applications somewhat difficult. The communication channels between applications are few and tightly controlled.

GENERATING DIRECTORY PATHS

Within the application sandbox, iOS sets aside specific directories for different types of use. These include the Document, Temporary, Caches, and Application Support directories.

The Document directory stores our application's documents—basically, any user-generated data. When writing a text editor, this is where we save the user's text files. When designing a game, this is where we store the saved game files. For Health Beat, this is where we save our `WeightHistory`.

The Temporary directory provides a handy location for storing information that does not need to survive past the current session. This often includes the scratch space needed for large calculations and similar transient uses. It's best to actively delete these files when they are no longer needed; however, the system will periodically clear out the Temporary directory when our application is not running.

The Caches directory also stores temporary information; however, this directory focuses on caching data to improve performance. Most of the time this means saving information that we may need to reuse, especially information that takes a long time or a lot of computational effort to re-create.

You are probably familiar with caches from Web browsers. The browser caches a page after downloading it. The next time you try to view that page, it simply loads the file from disk instead of downloading it again.

Caches also differ from temporary files in one other important way—caches typically persist beyond the current session. After all, a Web browser doesn't clear out its cache each time it launches. However, this data may be automatically deleted if the device is running out of disk space, so we cannot depend on the contents of this directory staying around forever.

Last, we have the Application Support directory. This is essentially used to hold everything else. This can include data files that the application needs to run, modifiable copies of resources from our application bundle, or even additional content from in-app purchases. It should not be used to store anything that more properly belongs in the Document, Caches, or Temporary folders.

It's important to remember that your application can both read and write to the Application Support directory. If you just need to read a resource file, then you should probably load it directly from the application bundle (see the "Reading Resource Files" sidebar for more information).

On the other hand, the Application Support directory and the application bundle often work in tandem. The application checks to see if the support directory has a desired data file. If it does, the application loads the file and proceeds as normal. However, if it does not, the application copies the default data file from the application bundle and then loads it. The application can then modify the version in the Application Support directory, but the original copy in the application bundle remains untouched. This is a great way to handle user-modifiable templates and similar resources.

To be a good iOS citizen, our application should try to respect these categories and save our files in the proper locations. Of course, to do this we need either a path or a URL that points to the correct directory.

While iOS provides a number of ways to programmatically generate these paths, Apple recommends using the `NSTemporaryDirectory()` function for temporary files and either the `NSSearchPathForDirectoriesInDomains()` function or one of `NSFileManager`'s URL-based methods (`URLsForDirectory:inDomains:` or `URLForDirectory:inDomain:appropriateForURL:create:error:`) for persistent data.

HOW THE SYSTEM MANAGES DIRECTORIES

iOS manages the various directories differently. Deciding where a file should be stored often depends on knowing how the system will handle that file. The following list covers most of the common system-level tasks and how they interact with the different directories.

SHARING FILES WITH iTUNES

If the `UIFileSharingEnabled` key is set in the application's `Info.plist`, then everything inside the Document directory appears in iTunes. Users can add or delete files from iTunes, modifying the content stored on the device.

Unfortunately, many applications produce or consume files that are intended for sharing (PDFs, text files, image files, etc.) but may store their internal state in a proprietary binary format. Typically, we don't want to share these proprietary files with iTunes.

Ideally, we should save this private data in another location. If it is simply application data (not a user document), then we can safely stash it in the Application Support directory. If, on the other hand, it really is a private version of the user's document, then we probably want to create a custom directory to hold it. Apple recommends using `<Application_Home>/Library/Private Documents` for these cases.

The system does not share anything within the Temporary, Caches, or Application Support directories with iTunes.

BACKING UP FILES

iOS backs up all files in the application sandbox except the application bundle, the Temporary directory, and the Caches directory. Specifically, the Document and Application Support directories are backed up, as are any custom directories not located in Temporary or Caches (e.g., the Private Documents directory mentioned previously).

With iOS 5, these files may be backed up using either iTunes or iCloud, depending on the user's settings. Unfortunately, this means that anything placed in the Document or Application Support directories could eat up part of the user's free 5 GB iCloud space. This means we have to be very careful not to save too much data to these directories.

Apple currently appears to be cracking down on applications that save large files to either the Document or Application Support directories. This is especially true of any files downloaded from the Internet. As a rule of thumb, all downloaded content (at least, any significant amount of downloaded content) should be saved to the Caches file. Obviously, this could create a problem, since files in the Caches folder may be cleared whenever the device runs low on disk space.

Imagine the following situation: A user downloads a number of maps for a GPS app before hopping on an international flight. The application saves these files to the Caches folder. Next, the user downloads an audio book. This uses up most of the device's available space, triggering a low disk space warning. In response, iOS clears all the Caches folders. When the user gets off the plane, they will discover that they no longer have the maps they needed—and without an international data plan, there's no good way to download replacements.

Developers are currently talking with Apple about this issue, so don't be surprised if this policy is refined as iCloud usage matures.

FILES COPIED DURING UPDATES

When you update an application, the new application is saved to the device's drive. Then, some files are copied from the old application to the new one. Finally, the old application is deleted.

All files within the Document folder and within <Application_Home>/Library/ are copied during an application update. This means the Application Support and Caches directories are both copied, as are any custom directories within <Application_Home>/Library/ (e.g., the Private Documents directory mentioned previously).

The Temporary directory is not copied.

`NSTemporaryDirectory()` simply returns an `NSString` containing the path to your application's Temporary directory. On the device, this will have the following format:

```
/private/var/mobile/Applications/
→  8BE8C8F8-D259-4E35-A515-1F5DE7E0E411/tmp/
```

On the simulator, the path points to something like the following:

```
/var/folders/30/30GdsGkgF6mT1duyW7yCsk+++TI/-Tmp-/
```

`NSSearchPathForDirectoriesInDomains()`, on the other hand, takes three arguments—an `NSSearchPathDirectory`, an `NSSearchPathDomainName`, and a `BOOL`. It then returns an `NSArray` of `NSString` paths matching your arguments.

The `NSSearchPathDirectory` specifies the type of directory that you are looking for. The `NSSearchPathDomainName` value describes where you should look (system files, user files, etc.). The `BOOL` determines whether the tilde (~) in the returned paths is expanded.

In Mac OS X (and most UNIX systems), the tilde represents the current user's home directory. On iOS, it refers to the application's sandboxed directory.

Remember, these methods were originally developed for Mac OS X on the desktop, which has a much more open and much richer file system. As a result, there are a large number of legal arguments that sound intriguing but that, quite honestly, don't do anything useful on iOS.

Additionally, the desktop version often finds multiple matching directories (particularly when searching across all domains). Because of this, `NSSearchPath ForDirectoriesInDomains()` returns an `NSArray` of `NSStrings`. In iOS, there is usually only one possible path for each directory, so we simply grab the first path (or equivalently the last path) from the list.

The bottom line is that, of all the possible domain and directory combinations, we really only use three search path directories when developing iOS applications: `NSDocumentDirectory`, `NSCachesDirectory`, and `NSApplicationSupportDirectory`. As you might guess, these correspond to our Document, Caches, and Application Support directories. In all three cases, `NSSearchPathForDirectoriesInDomains()` must use the `NSUserDomainMask`, as shown below:

```
// Document Directory
NSArray* documentPaths =
```

```
NSSearchPathForDirectoriesInDomains(NSDocumentDirectory,
                                    NSUserDomainMask,
                                    NO);
NSString* documentPath = [documentPaths objectAtIndex:0];
// Caches Directory
NSArray* cachePaths =
NSSearchPathForDirectoriesInDomains(NSCachesDirectory,
                                    NSUserDomainMask,
                                    NO);
NSString* cachePath = [cachePaths objectAtIndex:0];
// Application Support Directory
NSArray* supportPaths =
NSSearchPathForDirectoriesInDomains(NSApplicationSupportDirectory,
                                    NSUserDomainMask,
                                    NO);
NSString* supportPath = [supportPaths objectAtIndex:0];
```

These return the following path strings:

```
~/Documents
```

```
~/Library/Caches
```

```
~/Library/Application Support
```

The tilde expands to the application's directory. In the simulator, this would return a string similar to the following:

```
/Users/rich/Library/Application Support/iPhone Simulator/4.3/
→ Applications/B928F481-FAE4-4A11-965D-82DCF6799060
```

On the device, it expands to look like this:

```
/var/mobile/Applications/8BE8C8F8-D259-4E35-A515-1F5DE7E0E411
```

READING RESOURCE FILES

We often need to include resource files in our application. Typically, these include the images and sounds that our application will use—but they don't need to be limited to these. Any type of support data files could be included.

We start by adding the resource files to our project. We saw this in the "Adding Images" section of Chapter 3 when we added the graph.png and plus.png files to our application. These files are then included in our application's main bundle.

We can then generate a path to these resources using the NSBundle class. This is a two-step process. First we get a reference to the main bundle by calling [NSBundle mainBundle], and then we use the bundle's pathForResource:ofType: method (or one of its variants) to get the path. For example, to get the path to the graph.png file, we would use the following:

```
NSBundle* bundle = [NSBundle mainBundle];

NSString* path = [bundle pathForResource:@"graph" ofType:@"png"];
```

Other classes also support loading resource files directly from the main bundle. For example, UIImage has the imageNamed: convenience method.

In iOS 4.0 or later, we can provide device-specific resource files, using specially formatted filenames. When we search for a path, we will automatically get the correct resource for our current device. Device-specific filenames use the following format:

```
<base name><device string>.<extension>
```

Here, <device string> should be either ~iphone or ~ipad. For example, to provide device-specific versions of our graph.png file, we could add two files: a lower-resolution version named graph~iphone.png and a higher-resolution version named graph~ipad.png. We then use the code shown above to generate the path—it will automatically load the correct version for our device.

Many of the image-loading methods also support automatically loading higher-resolution images on Retina display devices by appending @2x to the <base name>, producing filenames like graph@2x.png. For more information, see Apple's iOS Application Programming Guide.

Finally, remember that all files in the main directory are readonly. If your application needs to modify these files, you must copy them to another directory first.

When working with iOS 4.0 or later, you should probably use NSFileManager's URLsForDirectory:inDomain: or URLForDirectory:inDomain:appropriateForURL:create:error: methods instead of NSSearchPathForDirectoriesInDomains().

URLsForDirectory:inDomain: works similarly to the NSSearchPathFor DirectoriesInDomains() function, but it returns an array of NSURLs instead of an array of NSStrings. URLForDirectory:inDomain:appropriateForURL:create:error: just returns a single NSURL—making it even more convenient to use—but it has a few additional arguments we'll need to set before we call it. Still, we will get a chance to see it in action in the "Loading iCloud Documents" section.

Most of the time, it doesn't matter which format we use. Most methods that deal with the file system have parallel versions for both URLs and raw file-names. Yes, we will occasionally run across a method that only accepts one form or the other, but these are getting increasingly rare. Besides, it's relatively easy to convert the paths from NSURL to NSString and back again.

In fact, the most important difference is that URLs are more flexible than string-based paths. NSURL can refer to both locally stored and remote files. This can be particularly useful if our application deals with both types of data. For example, if the app downloads a file from a URL and then caches a local copy for later use, we could use the same code to load and process both files—we just need to change the NSURL's address.

USING PATHS

So once you have the path to a file or directory, what can you do with it?

Well, NSString has a number of methods for manipulating paths. For example, stringByAppendingPathComponent: adds a subdirectory or filename to an existing path. stringByDeletingLastPathComponent: lets us move back up the directory tree. NSURL has a parallel set of path manipulation methods, letting us easily manipulate URLs as well.

NSFileManager also provides a number of useful methods for querying and manipulating the file system. For example, the following code explores a given path. If it points to a file, it will print out information about that file. If it points to a directory, it will get a list of the entire directory's contents and then recursively explore each item in the list.

```objc
- (void)explorePath:(NSString*)path {
    // Access singleton file manager.
    NSFileManager* fileManager = [NSFileManager defaultManager];
    BOOL isDirectory;
    // If the file doesn't exist, display an error
    // message and return.
    if (![fileManager fileExistsAtPath:path
                           isDirectory:&isDirectory]) {
        NSLog(@"%@ does not exist", path);
        return;
    }
    // If it's not a directory, print out some information
    // about it.
    if (!isDirectory) {
        NSString* fileName = [path lastPathComponent];
        NSMutableString* permissions =
        [[NSMutableString alloc] init];
        if ([fileManager isReadableFileAtPath:path]) {
            [permissions appendString:@"readable "];
        }
        if ([fileManager isWritableFileAtPath:path]) {
            [permissions appendString:@"writable "];
        }
        if ([fileManager isExecutableFileAtPath:path]) {
            [permissions appendString:@"executable "];
        }
        if ([fileManager isDeletableFileAtPath:path]) {
            [permissions appendString:@"deletable"];
```

```
        }
        if ([permissions length] == 0) {
            [permissions appendString:@"none"];
        }
        NSLog(@"File: %@ Permissions: %@", fileName, permissions);
        return;
    }
    // If it is a directory, print out the full path and then
    // recurse over all its children.
    NSLog(@"Directory: %@", path);
    NSArray* childPaths =
    [fileManager contentsOfDirectoryAtPath:path error:nil];
    for (NSString* childPath in childPaths) {
        [self explorePath:
        [path stringByAppendingPathComponent:childPath]];
    }
}
```

We start by getting a reference to the default file manager. Then we check to see if a file or directory exists at the provided path. If we have a regular file, we extract the filename from the path and then query the file manager about the file's permissions: Can we read, write, execute, or delete the file? Once we're done, we print out this information.

If it's a directory, we call contentsOfDirectoryAtPath:error: to get an array containing the directory's contents. This performs a shallow search. It gives us the names of all the subdirectories, files, and symbolic links within the provided directory; however, it does not return the contents of those subdirectories, traverse the links, or return the current (".") or parent ("..") directories.

We then iterate over this array, recursively calling explorePath: on each entry. Note that the strings in the array represent just the file and directory names, not the complete path. We must append these names to our path to create a new valid path.

We can use this method to explore our entire application's sandbox by calling it as shown below:

```
[self explorePath:[@"~" stringByExpandingTildeInPath]];
```

Here, we start with the tilde, which represents the root directory of our application's sandbox. However, many of NSFileManager's methods require the fully expanded path. We can get that by calling NSString's stringByExpandingTilde InPath method.

I highly recommend reading through the full documentation for NSfileManager before doing any serious file system work. There are a wide range of methods to help you move, delete, and even create files, links, and directories.

NOTE: While explorePath: demonstrates a number of NSFileManager and NSString methods, it is not really the best way to iterate over a deep set of nested directories. For production code, I recommend instead using enumeratorAtPath: or enumeratorAtURL:includingPropertiesForKeys: options:errorHandler:.

While all this path manipulation and exploration is fun, ultimately we need to save or load our data. Cocoa provides a number of options for us. Many classes have methods both for initializing objects from a file and for saving objects directly to a file. This includes NSString (for text files) and UIImage (for image files), as well as many of the collection classes (for collections of supported objects) and even NSData (for raw access to a file's bytes).

These methods are often useful for quick tasks; however, saving an entire application's state may require something a bit more robust. Here, we could use one of NSCoder's subclasses to save and load entire hierarchies of objects. Our only restriction is that all the objects in the hierarchy must adopt the NSCoding protocol. Typically this means using the NSKeyedArchiver and NSKeyedUnarchiver classes to perform our serialization, while adding the initWithCoder: and encodeWithCoder: methods to our custom classes.

Alternatively, we can use database technologies, such as SQLite or Core Data with an SQLite-based store, to persist our application's data. While NSCoding forces us to save and load an entire file at a time, SQLite and Core Data let us work with smaller, discrete chunks of data. Of course, this comes at a cost. These technologies tend to be a bit more complex. Still, we will look at Core Data in more depth in Chapter 7.

MANAGING USER PREFERENCES

Preferences are a special type of data. They define how an application operates. How large are the fonts? How responsive is the gyroscope? How loud is the background music? While the users often change these values, the application needs some sort of default to start out with. As a result, we often refer to preferences as defaults (or user defaults).

Typically, applications save their preferences separately from the rest of their data. You can change the background music volume without affecting your saved games—and when you switch from one saved game to another, the background music volume probably shouldn't change.

Furthermore, preferences may represent both the explicit and the implicit settings for our application. Explicit preferences are exposed to the user, either in the Settings app or within the application itself. We display a set of options and let the user make their own selections. If the user wants to change the background music volume, we present a slider and let them adjust it.

Implicit preferences, on the other hand, are inferred from the user's actions. In most cases, we simply watch what the user is doing and record it. This could include recording the last site visited in a Web view or the last page read in an e-book reader. Implicit preferences could even include the state of the user interface: What tab did the user have open? What views are currently stored in their navigation controller's stack? (See "Saving Health Beat's State" for more information about the interface's state.)

Like any other data, iOS has a specific directory for saving user preferences. In this case, it's the Library/Preferences directory. However, we should never need to touch this path directly. Instead, we should use the NSUserDefaults class (or, alternatively, Core Foundation's CFPreferences API).

NSUserDefaults gives us programmatic access to the user's defaults database. This stores information in key-value pairs. To use this class, simply access the shared object using the standardUserDefaults class method. Then you can call a variety of methods to set and retrieve values for the specified keys. All of the changes are cached locally to improve performance.

You can call the synchronize method to force updates. This both writes local changes to disk and updates the local values from disk. However, the system will automatically synchronize itself periodically, so you only need to call synchronize when you want to programmatically force an update.

But wait, there's more. This NSUserDefaults interface is only the beginning. We can also add a Settings.bundle to our application. This allows us to configure a custom preferences page in the device's Settings application. This page uses the same defaults database as the NSUserDefaults class, allowing us to freely mix both in-app and Settings-based user defaults.

The Settings application provides a convenient, centralized location for many preferences. In many ways, it is better than designing your own in-application settings. You don't need to build the interface or find a way to fit it into the application's workflow. You just configure the Settings.bundle's .plist file, and iOS handles the rest.

Unfortunately, Settings pages have a serious drawback: They aren't part of the actual application, so it's easy to forget about them. I can only speak for myself, but I'd like to think I'm reasonably technically savvy. Still, I rarely remember to check Settings after installing a new app. When I do remember, it's only after I've spent hours searching for an in-app way to change the default behavior.

General wisdom says that the Settings app should be used for settings that the user makes once and then largely leaves alone. In-app settings should be used for things the user often changes while working with the app. However, there's no clear dividing line between these two. In practice, the Settings app has a relatively limited range of controls. This may force the decision for us. In addition, in-app settings can be a lot more intuitive and easier to find. Of course, that relies on your ability to add them to your application's interface in a manner that is both unobtrusive and helpful. That's a lot easier said than done.

We will look at both using NSUserDefaults and using a Settings.bundle in "Saving User Defaults," later this chapter.

SAVING TO iCLOUD

With the release of iOS 5, Apple has given us a new way to store our document's data. Instead of stashing the information in our device's local file system, we can share it using iCloud.

iCloud is a new set of services and APIs that enable automatically sharing data among different devices. It provides a local directory, the iCloud container, where our device can read and write its data. The system then automatically syncs all the data in our container with our iCloud storage area. The truth is in the cloud—the system keeps the most current version in our iCloud storage, pushing updates back to our devices as needed.

This has several benefits. First, all our data is safely backed up remotely. If something bad happens to the local copy (for example, you accidentally drop your phone in the toilet), we can simply download the file again from the cloud.

Our data is also available on all our devices. Create a file on your Mac at home. Edit it on your iPad while sitting at a café. Show it to your friends on your iPhone. You can even access it from your PC at work. Your data is everywhere.

Enabling this ubiquitous access requires shuffling around a fair number of bits. Fortunately, iCloud uses several techniques for minimizing bandwidth usage. First, it stores both the file itself as well as metadata about the file. When a file is created, the system uploads both the metadata and the file to the cloud. iCloud then pushes the updated metadata to all devices associated with that iCloud account—alerting them to the change. The actual file is only pulled down to a device when it is actually needed. Most of the time this happens transparently, though iCloud provides API calls to both monitor and trigger the download of non-local files.

iCloud also tries to minimize the amount of data it needs to upload and download. It will automatically break your application's data into chunks and—when possible—only upload and download the chunks that actually change. iCloud will also transmit data peer-to-peer across the local Wi-Fi network whenever possible. Still, as developers, we need to be careful about what we store and how often we perform updates.

Finally, it's important to note that iCloud is not a general communication channel. We can share containers among a relatively small suite of related applications. For example, we probably want to share data between the lite and pro versions of our app. We can also publish URLs that allow others to copy data from our iCloud containers. However, we cannot create a communal container for other, third-party developers to access. We also cannot share cloud data across multiple users.

iCloud is designed to allow a closely related set of applications to share their data and preferences across all the devices associated with a single account. That's all. Don't try to force it to do things that it cannot.

iCloud's APIs can be broken into two general categories: iCloud document storage and iCloud key-value storage.

iCLOUD DOCUMENT STORAGE

We should primarily use iCloud document storage to store any user-created documents. We may also use it to store other internal application data—but we have to be a little careful here. We want to minimize the amount of data we're uploading and downloading to the cloud. That means we should avoid uploading cached data or anything that the application could easily re-create.

iCloud document storage supports both files and packages and is only limited by the amount of available memory in the user's iCloud account. To enable document storage, we first have to add an entitlements file and then set our ubiquity container identifiers. These define the different iCloud containers available to our application. We need at least one application-specific container, but we may include additional shared containers.

Then, early in our application, we need to call NSFileManager's URLForUbiquity ContainerIdentifier: method to determine if iCloud is enabled. It's true that everyone using iOS 5 has a free 5 GB iCloud account; however, that doesn't mean that the user actually set up their account. Some users might not understand iCloud. They may have skipped those steps when setting up their device. Others may deliberately disable their account—especially if they're worried about incurring additional bandwidth costs or increasing the drain on the battery. Bottom line, we cannot assume that iCloud is enabled. We must always check.

URLForUbiquityContainerIdentifier: also has a secondary purpose. It extends our application's sandbox to the specified container. Until this method is called, we cannot read or write into the container. Therefore, we must call URLFor UbiquityContainerIdentifier: before using any other iCloud APIs.

Next, we need to access our file. If we're creating a new file, we start by saving it in our application's sandbox and then using NSFileManager's setUbiquitous: itemAtURL:destinationURL:error: to move it to the cloud. If we want to open an existing file, we search for its current URL using NSMetadataQuery. We shouldn't store and reuse the iCloud URLs in our app, since the file's location may change.

We also have to be careful how we access our file. We must use an `NSFile Coordinator` to read or write any files in our iCloud container. The coordinator manages access to our data, ensuring that no process is trying to read our data while another is modifying it. However, within a coordinated block, our iCloud containers can be treated just like any other directory. We can read, write, create, delete, move, or rename files and directories using regular `NSFileManager` methods.

Finally, we need to make sure we receive notifications about the changes to our files. Any class that allows users to view or edit things inside the iCloud container must also implement the `NSFilePresenter` protocol. This protocol allows us to monitor the data's state and respond to changes as needed. This includes loading a new version of the data when changes are made remotely, or managing conflicting versions as they are detected. `NSFilePresenters` also work hand in hand with the `NSCoordinators` to ensure that all running copies of your application have the correct, up-to-date version of the file when they need it. For example, an `NSCoordinator` may ask another process's `NSFilePresenter` to save its changes before it creates a coordinated block.

As you can see, working with iCloud documents can get quite complex. Fortunately, iOS 5 also provides the `UIDocument` abstract class. While this doesn't make using iCloud simple, it does manage many of the details for us.

THE UIDOCUMENT ABSTRACT CLASS

The `UIDocument` automates many of the tedious and complex details in managing a document's data. For example, it automatically saves and loads data on a background thread. This prevents our user interface from locking up whenever it has to access large files.

The `UIDocument` uses a saveless user model. Users never need to explicitly save their documents. Instead, as developers, we let the document know whenever its data has changes. `UIDocument` caches these changes, waiting for an opportunity to write them back to disk. If possible, it takes advantage of lulls in the application, writing its data during idle moments. However, `UIDocument` will also save all its changes before the application goes into the background.

We can use `UIDocument` for both standard files and iCloud storage. It adopts the `NSFilePresenter` protocol and will automatically reload the document's data whenever it detects a remote update. It also wraps its reading/writing code in `NSFileCoordinators`, ensuring safe access to our data.

Despite all this, there are still a few tasks we need to perform on our own. For example, we must tell the document how to save and load its data. We also need to monitor the document's state and respond to version conflicts and other errors. As we will see, these are not trivial tasks. Still, without UIDocument we'd have a lot more work on our hands.

To use UIDocument, we need to create a subclass and implement two methods: contentsForType:error: and loadFromContents:ofType:error:. The contentsForType:error: method takes a snapshot of our document's model and returns it as either an NSData or NSFileWrapper object—allowing us to support saving to either files or packages, respectively. The UIDocument will then atomically save this data on a background thread. Similarly, when loading new data UIDocument reads our information on a background thread, then calls loadFromContents:ofType:error:. Again, we may receive either an NSData or an NSFileWrapper. We use this method to update our document's model and then refresh the user interface, if necessary. Both of these methods take an NSString argument indicating the document's Uniform Type Identifier. This allows us to read and write multiple formats.

Next, in our application we need to alert the document to any changes in our model. There are two ways to do this. Most simply, we can call the document's updateChangeCount method. This lets the document know that it has unsaved changes. Alternatively, we could register an undo action with UIDocument's built-in NSUndoManager. While this is a little more complicated, it also enables full undo/redo support. For this reason, we should use the undo manager whenever possible.

We will get more experience both subclassing and using UIDocument later this chapter.

iCLOUD KEY-VALUE STORAGE

iCloud key-value storage provides a simpler interface for saving data in the cloud. Unfortunately, it is also more restricted. Key-value storage is intended for non-critical configuration data. In many ways, it parallels the NSUserDefaults. It can only store a limited amount of data—up to 64 kilobytes per app—and can only store simple property-list data types: numbers, dates, strings, arrays, dictionaries, and so on. Finally, it does not have any conflict resolution—the last save always wins.

As in iCloud document storage, we need to set up the key-value store identifier in our application's entitlements. Once that is done, we simply access the shared NSUbiquitousKeyValueStore. We then call the store's instance methods to read and write our data. All changes are initially cached in memory. We must call synchronize to save these changes to disk. The system will then automatically sync the data from our local container with iCloud.

> **NOTE:** Syncing the NSUbiquitousKeyValueStore does not force the system to upload its changes to iCloud immediately. Indeed, the system may deliberately delay uploading, especially when our application makes frequent changes. The more frequent the updates, the longer the delay.

In general, we should not use iCloud key-value storage to save user-generated data. It's really intended for syncing user preferences. In fact, we shouldn't use it to replace NSUserDefaults. Instead, our applications should still use NSUserDefaults to manage their preferences locally. We simply use key-value storage to sync these preferences across multiple devices.

We will see how NSUserDefaults and iCloud key-value storage work hand in hand in the "Saving User Defaults" section, later this chapter.

SAVING HEALTH BEAT'S STATE

When we talk about saving the state of the application, we are really talking about two things. The first is saving the application's data. In well-designed MVC applications, this means saving the model.

However, we can also talk about saving the state of the interface. For example, which tab did the user have open? Which page did they navigate to last? What views are currently stored in their navigation controller's stack?

Desktop applications often ignore the interface's state, focusing entirely on the application's data. However, the same is not true for iOS. Most users expect well-designed, polished applications to provide a smooth, seamless interaction. We should be able to leave the application to do other work. When we come back, everything should still be exactly where we left it.

Admittedly, this was somewhat more important before multitasking and fast task-switching. Before iOS 4.0, if you wanted to let your users jump quickly between two applications, you needed to both save your interface's state and optimize your application to load quickly. Now, this is largely handled automatically. When you switch tasks, your application goes into the background. As long as it isn't terminated (e.g., due to a low memory warning), everything will remain the same once the app resumes. Still, saving the interface's state can add a nice bit of polish and consistency to your app.

On the other hand, robotically saving your application's state isn't always the best option. You should think about how your users will use your application, and try to make their experience as streamlined and intuitive as possible. Additionally, make sure you aren't saving bad information. For example, if a document-based application crashes while trying to open a file, you don't want it to try to open the same file the next time you launch. This would render your application unusable, forcing your user to delete the entire application and reinstall—losing all their information.

NOTE: Once we decide to save our interface's state, we still need to determine where and how to save it. In most cases, we shouldn't mix the user interface data with our application's model. Instead, we could create a second file inside the Application Support directory and store the interface state there. Alternatively, we could just treat the interface data as an implicit user preference. It's not something we want to expose in the Settings app, but it can be a nice fit for NSUserDefaults.

In Health Beat, the user will generally open the application and enter a new weight. We want to make this as quick and easy as possible. Therefore, instead of saving and restoring the user's last position, we should always open to the enter weight view. Fortunately, this means we don't need to save our interface's state; we can focus on our model.

Unfortunately, before we can do that, we have to prepare our application to support iCloud.

PREPARING THE APPLICATION

Before we begin using iCloud storage, we have to make sure our provisioning profile has iCloud support enabled. In most cases, Xcode will handle this automatically. Since the iOS 5 release, the generic app id (and therefore the default provisioning profile created by Xcode) will have iCloud enabled. However, if you set up your development tools prior to the iOS 5 release, you may need to refresh your provisioning profile.

Next, we need to set the entitlements for our application. As mentioned previously, we need an entitlements file with two iCloud identifiers. The first is for document storage, the second for key-value storage. The entitlements provide a measure of security for your application, ensuring that your documents are only accessible by your own apps. Additionally, the system uses the entitlements to identify your application's documents and distinguish them from other documents within iCloud storage.

The entitlements file contains a number of key-value pairs. For document storage, the com.apple.developer.ubiquity-container-identifiers key should contain an array of strings representing bundle identifiers for applications created by our team. All bundle identifiers use the following format: <DEVELOPER_ID>.<BUNDLE_ IDENTIFIER>. Here <DEVELOPER_ID> is the unique ten-character identifier associated with your individual or team account. You can find this by viewing your account information at Apple's Developer Member Center (http://developer.apple.com/ membercenter). <BUNDLE_IDENTIFIER> is the target application's identifier.

We do not have to use the bundle identifier for our current application. For example, a lite app may use the pro app's bundle identifier, guaranteeing continued access to the files after the user upgrades. We can also use multiple identifiers, giving us access to a number of different containers. While the first bundle identifier must be explicitly defined, any secondary identifiers can use wildcards. This lets us implicitly refer to a number of applications without having to list them individually.

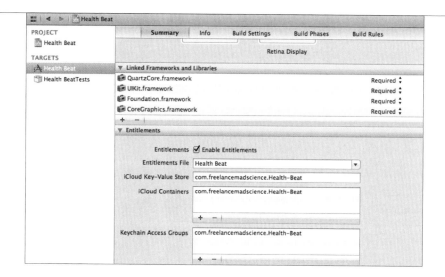

FIGURE 6.1 Setting the entitlements

For key-value storage, we need to define the com.apple.developer.ubiquity-kvstore-identifier key. This takes a single bundle identifier—we cannot use multiple containers. Most of the time this should match our primary document storage key.

As you can see, finding and setting the bundle identifiers can require a bit of work. Fortunately, there's a very easy way to automatically generate your Entitlements file and set up both document and key-value storage. In the Project navigator, select the Health Beat application icon. Then, in the Editor area, make sure that both the Health Beat target and the Summary tab are selected. Scroll down until you find the Entitlements settings, and select the Enable Entitlements checkbox. This will automatically fill in the iCloud Key-Value Store and iCloud Containers settings with the bundle identifier for the current target (**Figure 6.1**).

Next, we want to set up the document types and exported Uniform Type Identifiers (UTIs). This lets us to define a unique UTI for our application. Unfortunately, this won't do much for us right now. However, it will let us properly label our application's iCloud data when we submit the application using iTunes Connect.

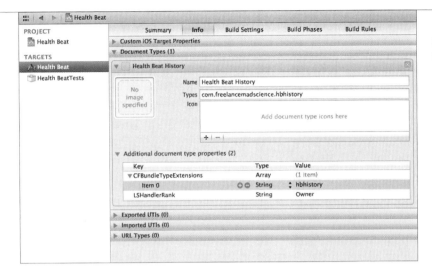

FIGURE 6.2 Setting the document type

With the application icon and Health Beat target still selected, click the Info tab. Now, click the Add icon and select Add Document Type from the pop-up menu. This will create a single untitled document type. Expand the document type and make the following changes. Enter **Health Beat History** in the Name field. Enter **com.freelancemadscience.hbhistory** in the Types field. Next, expand "Additional document type properties," add a CFBundleTypeExtensions key, and set its Type to Array. Next, add an LSHandlerRank key and set its Value to Owner. Finally, expand CFBundleTypeExtensions and add a single string sub-item named hbhistory.

We don't need to worry about creating document icons. iOS will automatically create our icons based on our application icons (see Chapter 9). If you want additional information on creating document-specific icons, check out the section "Custom Icon and Image Creation Guidelines" in Apple's iOS Human Interface Guidelines.

The entry should now match **Figure 6.2**.

Since we've defined a custom document type, we must now export it. Click the Add button again and select Add Exported UTI. Then expand the untitled UTI. Type **Health Beat History** in the Description field and **com.freelancemadscience .hbhistory** in the Identifier field. Now expand "Additional exported UTI properties," add a UTTypeTagSpecification key, and set its Type to Dictionary. Expand the dictionary, add a public.filename-extension sub-key, and set its Type to Array. Finally, expand the array and add a single item to it. Set this item's Value to **hbhistory**. The exported UTI should now match **Figure 6.3**.

FIGURE 6.3 Setting the exported UTI

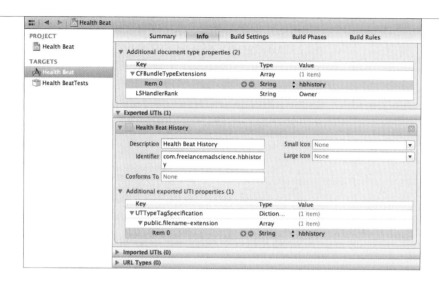

We will still need to create an iCloud display set before we can submit our app to the iTunes Store. This will define how our documents appear when users view them in the Settings app. Unfortunately, this is beyond the scope of this book, but for more information, check out "iCloud Display Sets" in the iTunes Connect Developer Guide.

For now, let's move on and create our UIDocument subclass.

CREATING A UIDOCUMENT SUBCLASS

In our case, saving our model really means saving our WeightHistory object. Obviously, we want to take advantage of iCloud storage—and the easiest way to do that is to use a UIDocument. Fortunately, we can make WeightHistory a subclass of UIDocument with a minimum of fuss.

Open WeightHistory.h and modify our interface declaration as shown:

```
@interface WeightHistory : UIDocument
```

Here, we just change our WeightHistory's subclass from NSObject to UIDocument. While we're at it, go ahead and remove the defaultUnits property. After all, we're going to move that to NSUserDefaults eventually. That's it. Of course, the implementation file will take a bit more work.

Open WeightHistory.m and clean things up a bit. We need to remove all traces of our defaultUnits property. Delete the line to @synthesize defaultUnits as well as deleting the entire setDefaultUnits: method.

We also need to replace the init method with a new designated initializer:

```
#pragma mark - initialization
- (id)initWithFileURL:(NSURL *)url
{
    self = [super initWithFileURL:url];
    if (self) {
        _weightHistory = [[NSMutableArray alloc] init];
    }
    return self;
}
```

We're still overriding our superclass's designated initializer. The name has changed and it takes an argument—but since we just pass the argument on to the superclass, it doesn't affect our implementation. Also, we've deleted the code that initialized our _defaultUnits property. Other than that, everything's the same.

Now we just need to implement a few required features. Specifically, we need to override the UIDocument methods to save and load our data. We need to change our weightHistory accessors, letting us alert the superclass whenever a change is made. Finally, we need to deal with version conflicts whenever they arise.

SAVING AND LOADING THE DOCUMENT

The easiest way to save and load our UIDocument is to simply convert our model into an NSData instance. This isn't absolutely required. UIDocument has a number of methods we could override to more fully customize our saving and loading code—but we should try to use simple NSData or NSFileWrapper objects whenever possible.

Currently, our WeightHistory class has a single instance variable: our weight History mutable array. So how do we convert an array into an NSData object? A quick glance at the class references for NSMutableArray and NSData doesn't reveal any obvious methods for converting one into the other; however, NSMutableArray does adopt the NSCoding protocol. This means we can load and save our array using a keyed archiver—and keyed archivers can read and write to NSData objects (or directly to files, for that matter).

There's just one catch: All the objects in our array must also adopt the NSCoding protocol. Unfortunately, our WeightEntry class does not. Fortunately, this is easy to fix. Let's start by adding the protocol to WeightEntry's interface:

```
@interface WeightEntry : NSObject <NSCoding>
```

Then open the implementation file and define the keys that we will need. Place these before the @implementation block.

```
static NSString* const WeightKey = @"WeightHistoryWeightInLbs";
static NSString* const DateKey = @"WeightHistoryDate";
```

Now we need to implement NSCoding's required methods. First, let's implement the encodeWithCoder: method.

```
#pragma mark - NSCoding Methods
- (void)encodeWithCoder:(NSCoder *)encoder {
    [encoder encodeFloat:self.weightInLbs forKey:WeightInLbsKey];
    [encoder encodeObject:self.date forKey:DateKey];
}
```

This is relatively straightforward. When saving an object hierarchy, each object's encodeWithCoder: method is called in turn. The object is responsible for saving all of its non-transient internal data. In our case, we simply save our data using our WeightInLbsKey and DateKey.

Next, implement the initWithCoder: method.

```
- (id)initWithCoder:(NSCoder *)decoder {
    self = [super init];
    if (self) {
        _weightInLbs = [decoder decodeFloatForKey:WeightInLbsKey];
        _date = [[decoder decodeObjectForKey:DateKey] retain];
    }
    return self;
}
```

We actually saw `initWithCoder:` in "Building a Custom View" in Chapter 5. `GraphView` used it when loading from a nib file. As it turns out, the system uses `NSCoding` to store and load nibs.

In many ways, `initWithCoder:` mirrors our designated initializer. If the super-class adopts the `NSCoding`, we should call the superclass's `initWithCoder:` method. Just like our designated initializer, we assign the return value from the superclass's `initWithCoder:` method to `self`. As long as `self` is a valid object (not equal to `nil`), we decode the rest of our data using our keys and assign those values to our instance variables. Then we return `self`.

In `WeightEntry`, our superclass (`NSObject`) does not adopt `NSCoding`. As a result, we cannot call `[super initWithCoder: decoder]`. Instead, we call the superclass's designated initializer.

In both cases, this bypasses our class's designated initializer. Therefore, we need to make sure our `initWithCoder:` class duplicates any of the setup and configuration steps performed in the designated initializer. `initWithWeight:units:forDate:` sets both the `_weightInLbs` and `_date` instance variables, so we do the same thing here. In fact, `initWithCoder:` is a bit simpler. We know that the weights are always saved in pounds, so we don't need the extra logic to convert from kilograms.

If you look at our `GraphView` class, you will see a similar relationship. Both `initWithFrame:` and `initWithCoder:` call `[self setDefaults]`. Again, `initWithCoder:` duplicates our designated initializer's configuration steps.

With that out of the way, we can now override `UIDocument`'s `contentsForType:error:` and `loadFromContents:ofType:error:` methods.

```
#pragma mark - iCloud Methods
- (id)contentsForType:(NSString *)typeName
    error:(NSError **)outError {
    return [NSKeyedArchiver archivedDataWithRootObject:
            self.weightHistory];
}
```

USING KEYED ARCHIVES

When using NSKeyedArchiver or NSKeyedUnarchiver, all the objects and values are given a key to identify them. These keys must be unique within the scope of the current object being saved or loaded. Therefore, if you are creating a public class that might be subclassed in the future, you should add a prefix to your keys to prevent collisions with any possible future subclasses. Additionally, you should avoid starting your keys with $, NS, or UI, since these are used by the system. Apple's documentation recommends appending the full class name to the front of the key.

While the keys add a little complexity, they give us considerable flexibility when loading our data. We can load the data in any order and even selectively choose which data to load. This gives us better support for forward and backward compatibility should our data structure change, letting us easily add or remove keyed values from our archives.

Keyed archives are easy to use. You can store an object hierarchy into an NSData object by calling the NSKeyedArchiver's archivedDataWithRootObject: class method. You save it to disk by calling archiveRootObject:toFile: instead.

The system will take your root object and call its encodeWithCoder: method, passing in a properly formatted NSKeyedArchiver object. The keyed archive contains a number of methods that you can use to store raw C values (e.g., encodeBool:forKey:, encodeInt:forKey:, and encodeFloat:forKey:). It also includes a method for encoding other objects, unsurprisingly named encodeObject:forKey:. These children objects must also adopt the NSCoding protocol. The system then calls their encodeWithCoder: method, passing along the keyed archive, until the entire object hierarchy is saved.

Unarchiving works the same way. Simply call NSKeyedUnarchiver's unarchiveObjectWithData: or unarchive ObjectWithFile: method. This will build the object hierarchy, calling initWithCoder: on each object, and then return the root object.

The archivers are smart enough to notice when your object graph has multiple references to the same object, and they will correctly save or load just one version of the object with all the references properly linking to that object. This means we can make our object graph as complex as we like. We don't need to worry about loops or circular references.

However, for the sake of performance, we want to minimize the number of objects we save and load. Unless the operations are computationally intense, you should manually set, calculate, or create any values that you can, and save and load only those values that you absolutely must. If your object graph has multiple references to the same object, there is a good chance that you could save and load the object once, and assign all the other references manually.

Here, we simply call the NSKeyedArchiver's `archivedDataWithRootObject:` method to create our NSData object. The keyed archiver does all the hard work for us.

```
- (BOOL)loadFromContents:(id)contents
                  ofType:(NSString *)typeName
                   error:(NSError **)outError {
    self.weightHistory =
    [NSKeyedUnarchiver unarchiveObjectWithData:contents];
    // Clear the undo stack.
    [self.undoManager removeAllActions];
    return YES;
}
```

This is almost as simple. We call NSKeyedUnarchiver's `unarchiveObjectWith Data:` method to convert the NSData object back into our history array. In addition, we clear all the undo actions from our undo stack (we will look at undo support in the "Enabling Undo Support" section), and we return YES to indicate that we have successfully loaded our data.

> **NOTE:** While we use NSKeyedArchiver and NSKeyedUnarchiver in this example, NSCoder also has an older set of concrete subclasses: NSArchiver and NSUnarchiver. These archives do not use keys to save and load their objects and values. Instead, they must load the data in the same order they saved it. In general, you should avoid using these whenever possible. They have been replaced by the keyed archives for iOS and all versions of Mac OS X 10.2 and later.

We could add additional error checking to these methods (e.g., catching the NSKeyedUnarchiver's NSInvalidArchiveOperationException), but to be honest, all the error-prone operations are already managed by the UIDocument class. If we have any problems in these methods, it's undoubtedly due to an error on our part—and that's something we should detect and fix during development.

Next up, we need to alert our UIDocument superclass whenever our model changes.

TRACKING CHANGES

UIDocument uses a saveless model. This means we never ask the document to save. Instead, we let the document know whenever our model changes. The document then automatically saves itself as needed. Furthermore, the best way to alert the UIDocument to changes is to register an undo action with the document's undo manager.

When we register an undo action, we need to tell our application how to undo the change we just made. In Health Beat, we are only adding and deleting entries from the history. This means that our undo actions may need to know both the WeightEntry involved in the change and its index in our history array. Let's create an object to encapsulate that data.

Since we're only going to use this data inside our WeightHistory class, let's declare it as a private class. With WeightHistory.m still open, add the following code before the @implementation block:

```
// Private class, used to store undo information.
@interface UndoInfo : NSObject
@property (strong, nonatomic) WeightEntry* weight;
@property (assign, nonatomic) NSUInteger index;
@end
@implementation UndoInfo
@synthesize weight = _weight;
@synthesize index = _index;
@end
```

This simply creates a new class, UndoInfo, with two parameters: our WeightEntry and our index. Now let's look at the methods that actually modify our model. Let's start with the addWeight: method.

```
- (void)addWeight:(WeightEntry*)weight {
    // Manually send KVO messages.
    [self willChange:NSKeyValueChangeInsertion
      valuesAtIndexes:[NSIndexSet indexSetWithIndex:0]
            forKey:KVOWeightChangeKey];
```

```
// Add to the front of the list.
[self.weightHistory insertObject:weight atIndex:0];
// Manually send KVO messages.
[self didChange:NSKeyValueChangeInsertion
valuesAtIndexes:[NSIndexSet indexSetWithIndex:0]
        forKey:KVOWeightChangeKey];
// Now set the undo settings...this will also trigger
// UIDocument's autosave.
UndoInfo* info = [[UndoInfo alloc] init];
info.weight = weight;
info.index = 0;
[self.undoManager
 registerUndoWithTarget:self
 selector:@selector(undoAddWeight:)
 object:info];
NSString* name =
[NSString stringWithFormat:@"Remove the %@ entry?",
[weight stringForWeightInUnit:getDefaultUnits()]];
[self.undoManager setActionName:name];
}
```

Here, we instantiate an UndoInfo object and set its weight and index properties. We're adding the weight object at index 0, so we will want to remove it from the same location. Next, we register our undo action. We tell the system to call the undoAddWeight: method and pass in our info object. Then we create a name for our undo action and set the undo manager's action name.

Setting an action name labels the action at the top of the undo stack (i.e., the next action to be undone). The Mac OS X desktop uses this string at the top of the Edit menu in the Undo, Redo, and Repeat menu items. For example, my Edit menu currently says Undo Typing and Repeat Typing. My current action name is therefore Typing.

Unlike the desktop version, iOS does not have a built-in use for the action names. Instead, we will hijack these names to pass message strings back to our undo method.

There are two problems with this code. Both the undoAddWeight: method and the getDefaultUnits() function are undefined. We'll add undoAddWeight: later this section, but getDefaultUnits() will have to wait until the "Saving User Defaults" section.

Next, make similar changes to removeWeightAtIndex:.

```
- (void)removeWeightAtIndex:(NSUInteger)weightIndex {
    // Grab a reference to the weight before we delete it.
    WeightEntry* weight =
    [self.weightHistory objectAtIndex:weightIndex];
    // Manually send KVO messages.
    [self willChange:NSKeyValueChangeRemoval
      valuesAtIndexes:[NSIndexSet indexSetWithIndex:weightIndex]
            forKey:KVOWeightChangeKey];
    // Remove the weight.
    [self.weightHistory removeObjectAtIndex:weightIndex];
    // Manually send KVO messages
    [self didChange:NSKeyValueChangeRemoval
    valuesAtIndexes:[NSIndexSet indexSetWithIndex:weightIndex]
            forKey:KVOWeightChangeKey];
    // Now set the undo settings...this will also trigger
    // UIDocument's autosave.
    UndoInfo* info = [[UndoInfo alloc] init];
    info.weight = weight;
    info.index = weightIndex;
    [self.undoManager
      registerUndoWithTarget:self
      selector:@selector(undoRemoveWeight:)
```

```
    object:info];
    NSString* name =
    [NSString stringWithFormat:@"restore the %@ entry?",
     [weight stringForWeightInUnit: getDefaultUnits()]];
    [self.undoManager setActionName:name];
}
```

Here we grab a reference to the weight entry that we're going to delete before we actually remove it. We use the undoRemoveWeight: selector instead of undoAdd Weight:, and we use a slightly different action name, but otherwise the steps are the same.

Now we need to implement the missing methods for our actions. Let's start by declaring them in our class extension.

```
@interface WeightHistory()
@property (nonatomic, strong) NSMutableArray* weightHistory;
- (void) undoAddWeight:(UndoInfo*)info;
- (void)undoRemoveWeight:(UndoInfo*)info;
@end
```

Now we can implement them, starting with undoAddWeight:.

```
#pragma mark - Undo Methods
- (void) undoAddWeight:(UndoInfo*)info {
    // Manually send KVO messages.
    [self willChange:NSKeyValueChangeRemoval
     valuesAtIndexes:[NSIndexSet indexSetWithIndex:info.index]
            forKey:KVOWeightChangeKey];
    // Add to the front of the list.
    [self.weightHistory removeObjectAtIndex:info.index];
    // Manually send KVO messages.
    [self didChange:NSKeyValueChangeRemoval
```

```
                valuesAtIndexes:[NSIndexSet indexSetWithIndex:info.index]
                        forKey:KVOWeightChangeKey];
    }
```

Here we simply remove the object that we added. Of course, we have to bracket this change with the proper KVO messages. As you can see, this is simply the inverse of the addWeight: method. Actually, it's even simpler, since we don't need to tell our document about this change.

The undoRemoveWeight: method is similar.

```
- (void)undoRemoveWeight:(UndoInfo*)info {
    // Manually send KVO messages.
    [self willChange:NSKeyValueChangeInsertion
     valuesAtIndexes:[NSIndexSet indexSetWithIndex:info.index]
            forKey:KVOWeightChangeKey];
    // Add to the front of the list.
    [self.weightHistory insertObject:info.weight
                             atIndex:info.index];
    // Manually send KVO messages.
    [self didChange:NSKeyValueChangeInsertion
     valuesAtIndexes:[NSIndexSet indexSetWithIndex:info.index]
            forKey:KVOWeightChangeKey];
    }
```

NOTE: You can limit the size of the undo stack by calling the NSUndoManager's setLevelsOfUndo: method. This is a great way to reduce the memory footprint while still adding undo support. For example, calling [self.managed ObjectContext.undoManager setLevelsOfUndo:1] will only allow us to undo the last action—but it will greatly reduce the amount of memory used by our system.

Again, we simply insert the object back at its previous index, bracketing the change with KVO notifications.

So far, we've just added actions to our undo queue. We haven't actually triggered any of these undo actions. That will have to wait until the "Enabling Undo Support" section. For now, this is sufficient. Adding these actions to the undo queue will alert our document to the changes. Our document will then save itself at the next opportune moment.

MERGING CONFLICTING VERSIONS

There's a simple rule. If you're using iCloud storage, then you must be prepared to handle conflicts. Conflicts occur when the cloud storage receives contradicting updates. This typically happens when one device saves a change, and then a second device saves a different change before receiving the first update.

In most cases, this should rarely occur. Sure, I want to have the same data on my iPhone, my iPad, and my Mac—however, I'm probably not going to run the same application on two different devices at the same time. If I make a change on my phone, there should be plenty of time for the update to reach my Mac before I open the file there.

However, remember how iCloud works. Each application saves and reads to a local file. The system then syncs this file with the cloud. There may be times when the system is unable to sync these changes—for example, if the device is in Airplane mode or if it's located in the Wi-Fi–less sub-basement of an office building. In both cases, the user can still access and edit any documents on their device. Any changes they make will be saved locally but won't be synced to the cloud. Furthermore, devices can be shut off. They can run out of power. There are any number of reasons why an update may be delayed, creating potential for conflicts.

Most importantly, if it can happen, it will happen—guaranteed. We have to be prepared to handle it.

There are three basic approaches to managing conflicts. The simplest is to let the last change win. From a developer's standpoint, this is by far the easiest solution to implement. We just mark all the conflicting versions as resolved and then delete them. Done and done. However, it has a rather large downside. While this may work fine in many cases, we risk accidentally deleting some of our user's data. And that would be a bad thing.

KNOW WHEN TO LOAD THEM, KNOW WHEN TO SAVE THEM

Unlike desktop applications, iOS apps shouldn't have a Save button. Instead, the application automatically saves its state at the appropriate times. Of course, that raises the question, what are the appropriate times?

Traditionally, there have been two basic approaches. The first involves waiting and saving the application's entire state (or at least all the changes) just before it goes into the background or terminates. The second involves saving each change as soon as the user makes it. They both have their advantages and disadvantages.

It is often simpler to wait and save everything at once. This can greatly reduce the number of times you need to write to disk, and it can streamline and simplify your code. This is especially true when you are using NSCoding to persist a large object hierarchy. You cannot save just part of the object hierarchy—it's an all or nothing procedure, and you probably don't want to save your whole data file every time you make a tiny little change.

On the other hand, iOS applications need to be able to transition quickly to the background. In general, we have about 5 seconds to save our data. In practice, we want to stay well short of that. We don't want to accidentally lose user data because it took a fraction of a second longer than we expected. If our application needs to save a large amount of data, we may need to find ways to split it up and save off portions as the application is running, rather than leaving everything until the end.

Additionally, even though well-made iOS applications tend to be more reliable than their desktop counterparts, they still crash. If you're bulk-saving your application's data, your users will lose all their work from the current session.

Saving as you go helps to spread the computational cost over the application's entire life cycle. In general, this prevents any noticeable lags as the application loads or saves a large chunk of data. In practice, this can be harder to achieve. We often intend to load only one or two entries—but if they refer to other entries, which refer to still other entries, we may accidentally pull in a much larger chunk of data.

You will typically need to use some sort of database or database-like technology to support a save-as-you-go approach. I highly recommend using Core Data, but SQLite is also well supported. You can also find a number of third-party solutions that are worth considering.

On the downside, loading and saving as you go can easily become more complex and harder to maintain, especially if your persistence code ends up scattered throughout your model rather than concentrated in a couple of methods.

Additionally, you need to make sure your application's data does not end up in an inconsistent state if your application stops unexpectedly. For example, if a typical task involves several steps, you might want to wait until the entire task is finished before saving your application. If your application crashes in the middle of a task, saving after each step could leave a half-finished, malformed task in your database.

Fortunately, UIDocument simplifies all of this. We no longer need to worry about when our document will be saved. UIDocument handles this for us.

Unfortunately, we still need to give some thought to our data.

If we use NSData objects in our contentsForType:error: and loadFromContents:ofType:error: methods, our data will be saved in a flat file. This means it must save and load our entire model, even if we only make a slight change. UIDocument tries to do its best. It will cache changes when it can, waiting for a lull in the application's activities, and then perform the save operation on a background thread. Still, it is an all-or-nothing procedure.

In some cases, we can fix this by using an NSFileWrapper instead. NSFileWrapper allows us to save our data as a file package. This means we're saving a directory, which can contain any number of files and subdirectories. More importantly, our document can save and load the individual files within our directory independently of each other. If we have data that can be easily partitioned into separate files, then switching to an NSFileWrapper may produce significant performance improvements when saving and loading our documents.

The second approach is to show the user the different versions and let them select the one to use. This has one major advantage—the user is in complete control. They get to decide exactly what happens to their data. However, it has several problems as well. First, it's much harder to design. In some cases, it may be extremely difficult to display the differences between versions in any meaningful way. Also, it requires user intervention, and that means that instead of using your app to get work done, they're forced to waste their time solving conflicts. Finally, we still risk losing user data. Anytime we pick one version over another, something may get lost.

The best approach is to merge all the conflicting versions. Unfortunately, this may not be possible for all documents in all situations—but if you can do it, you probably should. In our case, merging is relatively easy. We can simply take the union of all the entries across all versions. Yes, this may cause a deleted weight entry to reappear—but we're not going to lose any information. The user can always delete it again if they really want to.

Unfortunately, as we will soon see, relatively easy is not the same as actually easy.

To start with, we need to monitor changes in our document's state. In particular, we are looking for a UIDocumentStateInConflict flag. Let's start by registering our subclass for notifications. Add the following code to initWithFileURL:.

```
// Set an initial defaults.
_weightHistory = [[NSMutableArray alloc] init];
// Monitor document state.
[[NSNotificationCenter defaultCenter]
 addObserver:self
 selector:@selector(documentStateChanged:)
 name:UIDocumentStateChangedNotification
 object:self];
```

Here, we register to receive UIDocumentStateChangeNotifications, calling documentStateChanged: whenever any occur. Of course, whenever we register for notifications, we also need to unregister. We can override our class's dealloc method to unregister before our WeightHistory instance is deleted.

```
- (void)dealloc {
    // Unregister for notifications.
    [[NSNotificationCenter defaultCenter]
     removeObserver:self
     name:UIDocumentStateChangedNotification
     object:self];
}
```

Next, we have to create the documentStateChanged: method. Again, declare it in WeightHistory's class extension. Actually, we're going to need four different methods before we're done. We may as well declare them all.

```
@interface WeightHistory()
@property (nonatomic, strong) NSMutableArray* weightHistory;
- (void) undoAddWeight:(UndoInfo*)info;
- (void)undoRemoveWeight:(UndoInfo*)info;
- (void)documentStateChanged:(NSNotification*)notification;
- (void)resolveConflictsWithCurrentURL:(NSURL*)currentURL
            coordinator:(NSFileCoordinator*)coordinator;
- (void)mergeCurrentHistory:(NSMutableArray*)currentHistory
    withConflictingVersion:(NSFileVersion*)version
              coordinator:(NSFileCoordinator*)coordinator;
- (void)saveMergedHistory:(NSArray*)currentHistory
                  ToURL:(NSURL*)url
            coordinator:(NSFileCoordinator*)coordinator
            oldVersions:(NSArray*)oldVersions;
@end
```

Now, let's implement documentStateChanged:.

```
#pragma mark - Resolve Conflicts
- (void)documentStateChanged:(NSNotification*)notification {
    UIDocumentState state = self.documentState;
    if (state & UIDocumentStateInConflict) {
        NSURL* url = self.fileURL;
        NSURL* currentURL =
        [[NSFileVersion currentVersionOfItemAtURL:url] URL];
        NSFileCoordinator* coordinator =
        [[NSFileCoordinator alloc] initWithFilePresenter:self];
        dispatch_queue_t backgroundQueue =
        dispatch_get_global_queue(DISPATCH_QUEUE_PRIORITY_DEFAULT,
                                  0);
        dispatch_async(backgroundQueue, ^{
            [self resolveConflictsWithCurrentURL:currentURL
            coordinator:coordinator];
        });
    }
}
```

It's important to note that UIDocument represents its states using a bit field. Multiple state bits can be turned on at one time. Therefore, we need to use a bitwise AND operator to check for the state we're interested in. If the UIDocumentStateInConflict flag is set, we move on to resolve the conflict.

We start by using NSFileVersion to get access to the URL of our current version. Then we create an NSFileCoordinator. You may remember that UIDocument automatically creates NSFileCoordinators for all the regular file loads and saves—but we need to do a bit of digital bushwhacking here, so we have to handle the file coordination ourselves.

We pass our WeightHistory object as the file presenter. This means our Weight History class won't receive any notifications about changes made during our coordinated blocks. In general, this is exactly what we want—but it also means we may need to update the UI manually once we're done.

Finally, we call the resolveConflictsWithCurrentURL:coordinator: method on a background queue. It's very important to use a background thread here. Obviously, from a performance standpoint, we never want to do any file input/output operations in the main thread—that could dramatically hurt our user interface's performance. Instead, we should always read and write data in the background. More pragmatically, however, creating coordination blocks on the main thread can cause the application to deadlock. We definitely don't want that.

Next, let's look at resolveConflictsWithCurrentURL:coordinator:.

```
- (void)resolveConflictsWithCurrentURL:(NSURL*)currentURL
            coordinator:(NSFileCoordinator*)coordinator {
    NSError* error;
    [coordinator
     coordinateReadingItemAtURL:currentURL
     options:0
     writingItemAtURL:currentURL
     options:NSFileCoordinatorWritingForMerging
     error:&error
     byAccessor:^(NSURL *inputURL, NSURL *outputURL) {
        // Load our data.
        NSData* data =
        [NSData dataWithContentsOfURL:inputURL];
        NSMutableArray* currentHistory =
        [NSKeyedUnarchiver unarchiveObjectWithData:data];
        // Read in all the old versions.
        NSArray* unresolvedVersions =
```

```
     [NSFileVersion
      unresolvedConflictVersionsOfItemAtURL:inputURL];
     // Merge the histories.
     for (NSFileVersion* version in unresolvedVersions) {
         [self mergeCurrentHistory:currentHistory
         withConflictingVersion:version
         coordinator:coordinator];
     }
     // Sort the current history.
     NSSortDescriptor* sortByDate =
     [NSSortDescriptor sortDescriptorWithKey:@"date"
                                     ascending:NO];
     [currentHistory sortUsingDescriptors:
         [NSArray arrayWithObject:sortByDate]];
     // Save the changes.
     [self saveMergedHistory:currentHistory
                    ToURL:outputURL
             coordinator:coordinator
             oldVersions:unresolvedVersions];
     }]; // Current File Read/Write block.
 if (error != nil) {
     NSLog(@"*** Error: Unable to perform a coordinated "
         @"read/write on our current history! %@ ***",
         [error localizedDescription]);
 }
}
```

Here, we start by creating a coordinated block for both reading and writing from the current URL. All the coordinated block methods work similarly. We pass in a URL and set some options that define the type of read or write operation we're going to perform, and then we pass it a block. The coordinator makes sure the system is in a good state. This may involve asking file presenters in other processes to perform their own read or write operations. For example, the NSFileCoordinatorWriting ForMerging option forces all relevant file presenters to save their changes before the coordinated write operation can begin. This helps ensure we have the most recent version of our file before we begin making changes.

Next, the coordinator tries to get a lock on the file. The system usually allows multiple concurrent read operations, while write operations require exclusive access to the file. This means a write operation will block until all the currently executing read or write operations are finished. Then, once the write block starts running, no other read or write operation can begin until it's done.

Unlike many block-based APIs, the system executes all the coordinated block operations synchronously. This means it will execute our block argument before the method returns. This makes it much easier to chain together a series of read and write operations. Also note that we provide a URL when creating our coordinated block. The system then passes a URL argument to our block. We should always use the block's URL argument when accessing our files. After all, the file may move as part of another file presenter's write operation. So, our original URL may no longer be valid by the time our block runs.

> **NOTE:** We only need to coordinate our reads and writes with the other processes on our device. We're not coordinating between devices. Typically, for iOS devices we just need to coordinate with our local iCloud sync service. Therefore, creating a coordinated block on my iPhone may force the phone's iCloud service to write its changes to disk (possibly forcing it to download an updated copy of the file), but it won't affect any of the processes running on my iPad.

Even among the coordinated blocks, coordinateReadingItemAtURL:options: writingItemAtURL:options:error:byAccessor: is somewhat odd. This requests a read operation that needs to coordinate with a write operation. In our case, we want to read the current document, update it, and then write it again. Despite the name, it is really just an intelligent read block. We cannot perform write operations directly inside it. Instead, we must create a nested write block and perform our write operations there.

In our code, we load the history array from our current version. Then we get a list of all the conflicting versions. We iterate over these versions, calling mergeCurrent History:withConflictingVersion:coordinator: with each of the conflicting versions. As we will see shortly, this will make sure our current version contains all the entries from all the conflicting versions.

Unfortunately, the merge process may leave our history array out of order. So, we sort it by date. We create a sort descriptor, which uses key-value coding to access our weight entries' date property and sorts them in descending order.

Finally, we call saveMergedHistory:toURL:coordinator:oldVersions: to save our new, merged history and then clean up all the old, conflicted versions. Note that internally, this method will create the nested coordinated write block.

Now let's look at mergeCurrentHistory:withConflictingVersion:coordinator:.

```
- (void)mergeCurrentHistory:(NSMutableArray*)currentHistory
       withConflictingVersion:(NSFileVersion*)version
                coordinator:(NSFileCoordinator*)coordinator {
    NSError* readError;
    [coordinator
    coordinateReadingItemAtURL:version.URL
    options:0
    error:&readError
    byAccessor:^(NSURL *oldVersionURL) {
        NSData* oldData =
        [NSData dataWithContentsOfURL:oldVersionURL];
        NSArray* oldHistory =
        [NSKeyedUnarchiver unarchiveObjectWithData:oldData];
        [currentHistory unionWith: oldHistory];
    }];
    if (readError) {
```

```
        NSLog(@"*** Error: Unable to perform a coordinated read "
            @"on a previous version! %@ ***",
            [readError localizedDescription]);
    }
}
```

While this looks somewhat complex, really we're just creating another coordinated read block. Inside that block, we read the data from the specified conflicted version. We then call NSMutableArray's unionWith: method to combine the two history arrays.

There's only one tiny catch. NSMutableArray doesn't have a unionWith: method. No problem. We'll just add one.

In the Project navigator, right-click the Model group and select New File. In the template panel, select iOS > Cocoa Touch > Objective-C Category. Name it **Union**, and make sure it's a category on the NSMutableArray.

Next, open NSMutableArray+Union.h, and define our unionWith: method.

```
#import <Foundation/Foundation.h>

@interface NSMutableArray (Union)

- (void)unionWith:(NSArray*)array;

@end
```

Switch to the implementation file, and add the method as shown:

```
- (void)unionWith:(NSArray*)array {
    NSMutableArray* toAdd =
    [[NSMutableArray alloc] initWithCapacity:[array count]];
    for (id entry in array) {
        if (![self containsObject:entry]) {
            [toAdd addObject:entry];
        }
    }
}
```

```
    for (id entry in toAdd) {
        [self addObject:entry];
    }
}
```

Here our mutable array iterates over all the items in the incoming array. We check to see if the mutable array contains each item. If it doesn't, we save a reference to the item, then add it to the mutable array.

Again, there's one small catch. Our WeightEntry's default implementation will simply compare the object pointers. However, since our arrays were loaded from disk, we will undoubtedly have different WeightEntry instances that actually contain the same value (same data and weightInLbs). We need to override the default isEqual: method and provide an implementation that performs a deep comparison.

Switch to the WeightEntry.m file and add a new isEqual: method.

```
#pragma mark - Equality
- (BOOL)isEqual:(id)object {
    if (![object isKindOfClass:[WeightEntry class]]) return NO;
    return [self.date isEqual:[object date]] &&
            (self.weightInLbs == [object weightInLbs]);
}
```

We start by verifying that our incoming object argument belongs to the Weight Entry class. If it does, we simply compare the date and weightInLbs properties. If they are both the same, we return YES. Otherwise, we return NO.

That's simple enough. However, whenever we override the isEqual: method we also need to override the hash method.

```
- (NSUInteger)hash {
    size_t size = sizeof(NSUInteger);
    NSUInteger weight = (int)self.weightInLbs * 100;
    return [self.date hash] ^ (weight << (size / 2));
}
```

The hash method returns an integer. We use these values as the object's address in a hash table or similar collection. Ideally, each unique object should return a unique hash value. More importantly, if two objects are equal they must return the same hash value.

Our calculation simply converts our weight value to an integer and shifts it over by half the integer's size. We then combine it with the date's hash using the bitwise XOR operator. This should provide a reasonably good hash value. Our weight values should be (relatively speaking) low values—so shifting it won't lose any information.

I don't know how NSDate implements its hash method. A simple implementation would just convert the internal NSTimeInterval to a hash value. This means the lowest bits may be the most important—we shouldn't alter them. However, a more thorough implementation would create more-random hash values (ensuring that date objects get more evenly spread over the available hash space). In that case, it doesn't really matter which bits we alter.

Either way, we don't need high-performance hashing, so this implementation will work fine. OK, let's get back to WeightHistory.m. First things first, we need to import our new category.

```
#import "NSMutableArray+Union.h"
```

Now we still have to save our merged data. This gets a bit long, so let's take it one step at a time.

```
- (void)saveMergedHistory:(NSArray*)currentHistory
                    ToURL:(NSURL*)url
              coordinator:(NSFileCoordinator*)coordinator
              oldVersions:(NSArray*)oldVersions {
    NSError* writeError;
    [coordinator
     coordinateWritingItemAtURL:url
     options:NSFileCoordinatorWritingForMerging
     error:&writeError
     byAccessor:^(NSURL *outputURL) {
```

```
NSData* dataToSave =
[NSKeyedArchiver
 archivedDataWithRootObject:currentHistory];
NSError* innerWriteError;
BOOL success = [dataToSave
                writeToURL:outputURL
                options:NSDataWritingAtomic
                error:&innerWriteError];
```

Here, we create our coordinated write block and save our currentHistory array. We do this as a two-step process. First, we use an NSKeyedArchiver to create an NSData object from our array. Then we save the NSData to disk. We could have used the keyed archiver to perform this in one step—but doing it this way gives us more-informative error messages.

```
if (success) {
    // Mark the conflicting versions as resolved.
    for (NSFileVersion* version in oldVersions) {
        version.resolved = YES;
    }
    // Remove old versions.
    NSError* removeError;
    BOOL removed =
    [NSFileVersion
     removeOtherVersionsOfItemAtURL:outputURL
     error:&removeError];
    if (!removed) {
        NSLog(@"*** Error: Could not erase outdated "
              @"versions! %@",
              [removeError localizedDescription]);
    }
```

If we successfully save the merged data, we mark all the conflicting versions as resolved. This means they will no longer appear in any future reports about conflicts. Then we remove the old versions. It's important to note that removing old versions must be performed within a coordinated write block. We also deliberately delay modifying the conflicting versions until we're sure the conflict is completely resolved.

```
// And reload our document.
NSError* reloadError;
BOOL reloaded = [self readFromURL:self.fileURL
                             error:&reloadError];
if (!reloaded) {
    NSLog(@"*** Error: Unable to reload our "
           @"UIDocument! %@ ***",
           [reloadError localizedDescription]);
}
```

Now, we force our UIDocument to reload itself. In the normal day-to-day operations of a UIDocument subclass, we never call readFromURL:error: directly. Instead, the system calls this method whenever it needs to load our document. This is, however, a somewhat exceptional situation. So far, we've been reading and writing our data directly to disk—we haven't involved the UIDocument at all. As a result, it doesn't know anything about the changes we've made. By calling readFromURL:error: here, we force our document to update itself.

Also note that we don't need a coordinated read block here. We're still inside our original read block. Yes, we're using the write block's URL, but this should be the most up-to-date URL pointing back to our original file. So we should be good to go.

```
} else {
    NSLog(@"*** Error: Unable to save our merged "
           @"history! %@ ***",
           [innerWriteError localizedDescription]);
}
```

```
    }];
    if (writeError != nil) {
        NSLog(@"*** Error: Unable to perform a coordinated write "
            @"on our merged version: %@ ***",
            [writeError localizedDescription]);
    }
}
```

The rest of this is simply error handling. Honestly, we're not doing much, just logging the error to the console. Still, if we do run into any problems, the conflicts will simply linger. The next time our file is modified, it will trigger the conflict notification again, and we can try one more time to merge everything.

That's it. We've implemented all of our WeightHistory's basic features. Next, let's look at the procedures involved in creating and opening our document.

LOADING iCLOUD DOCUMENTS

Health Beat is a single-document application. This makes managing our files a little complicated. When the application launches, we need to search for any existing documents. If we find an existing document, we open it. If not, we create a new document and save it to disk.

NOTE: In this version of Health Beat, we automatically upload the file to iCloud if we can. However, this isn't the best design. Each user only has 5 GB of free iCloud document storage. We really should ask the user before using up some of that space. Furthermore, they should be able to change their mind later on, moving their files back and forth as necessary. Unfortunately, this makes the application a lot more complex. I will leave that as an extra-credit assignment for the truly determined reader.

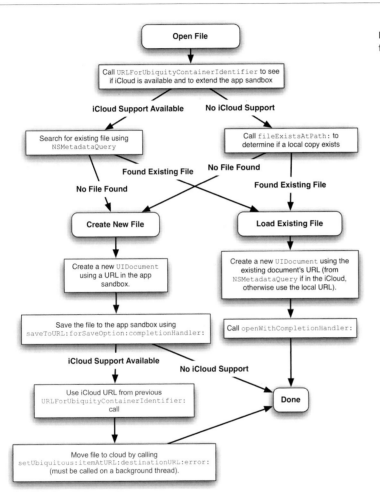

FIGURE 6.4 Opening the document

To further complicate things, documents may be stored either in the local sandbox or in iCloud storage. We need a slightly different procedure for searching, opening, and saving at each location. In fact, all the possible permutations can get quite complex. **Figure 6.4** shows the basic steps we need to follow.

OK, I have some good news and some bad news. The good news is that we can hide all this complexity behind a single `WeightHistory` convenience method. This will allow us to open (or create if necessary) our file with a single method call. The bad news is that we still have to write all this code.

Well, there's no sense in delaying the inevitable. Let's jump right in.

Let's start by creating a few helper methods. Still working in the WeightHistory implementation file, declare a string constant to hold our filename. Be sure to place this before the @implementation block.

```
static NSString* const FileName = @"health_beat.hbhistory";
```

Now find the WeightHistory class extension, and declare three private helper methods.

```
+ (NSURL*)localURL;

+ (NSURL*)cloudURL;

+ (BOOL)isCloudAvailable;
```

Then implement the methods as shown:

```
#pragma mark - Convenience Methods
+ (NSURL*)localURL {
    static NSURL* sharedLocalURL;
    static dispatch_once_t onceToken;
    dispatch_once(&onceToken, ^{
        NSError* error;
        NSURL* documentDirectory =
        [[NSFileManager defaultManager]
          URLForDirectory:NSDocumentDirectory
          inDomain:NSUserDomainMask
          appropriateForURL:nil
          create:NO
          error:&error];
        if (documentDirectory == nil) {
            [NSException
              raise:NSInternalInconsistencyException
              format:@"Unable to locate the local document "
```

```
                @"directory, %@",
                [error localizedDescription]];
        }
        sharedLocalURL = [documentDirectory
        URLByAppendingPathComponent:FileName];
    });
    return sharedLocalURL;
}
```

This method calculates the URL for a locally stored data file; however, there's a little bit of fancy footwork going on here. The dispatch_once() block is guaranteed to only run one time. This will calculate the local URL and assign it to the static sharedLocalURL variable. The next time through, our method will simply use the version previously stored in sharedLocalURL.

To calculate the directory, we call NSFileManager's URLForDirectory:inDomain:appropriateForURL:create:error: method and request the URL for our application's Document directory. We then calculate the sharedLocalURL by appending our filename to the end of our directory URL.

There's no good reason why this request should fail. If it returns an error, we've almost certainly made a mistake somewhere in our code. Therefore, we simply throw an exception. This will help us find the mistake during development, making sure we fix it.

```
+ (NSURL*)cloudURL {
    static NSURL* sharedCloudURL;
    static dispatch_once_t onceToken;
    dispatch_once(&onceToken, ^{
        NSFileManager* fileManager =
        [NSFileManager defaultManager];
        NSURL* containerURL =
        [fileManager URLForUbiquityContainerIdentifier:nil];
        if (containerURL) {
```

```
            NSURL* documentURL =
            [containerURL URLByAppendingPathComponent:@"Documents"];
            sharedCloudURL =
            [documentURL URLByAppendingPathComponent:FileName];
        } else {
            sharedCloudURL = nil;
        }
    });
    return sharedCloudURL;
}
```

This method returns the default URL for our document in the iCloud storage container. In many ways, this mirrors our `localURL` method. The difference is that we get the container URL by calling `URLForUbiquityContainerIdentifier:`.

`URLForUbiquityContainerIdentifier:` takes a string argument, which needs to match the ID of the container we wish to access. Alternatively, by passing in `nil`, we're telling the system to automatically use the first ID from the list of iCloud storage IDs in our entitlements. Therefore, unless we are actively using multiple containers, we can always just pass `nil`.

`URLForUbiquityContainerIdentifier:` returns the URL for the requested container. Actually, it performs three very important functions. First, it checks to see if iCloud support is available. If the user never set up their iCloud account, or if they deliberately disabled Documents & Data support, this method will return `nil`. Next, it extends the document's app sandbox to include the requested container. This lets us read and write into the container. Finally, once everything else is done, it returns our container's URL.

NOTE: Remember, we need to make sure we call `URLForUbiquity ContainerIdentifier:` early in our application's life cycle to trigger these secondary effects. If we don't extend the application's sandbox, all other attempts to access iCloud data will fail.

We then create a URL that points to the Documents folder inside the container, and finally a URL that points to our file inside the Documents folder. Remember, all the files inside the iCloud container's Documents folders are shown as individual files. The user can manage these files inside the Settings app (iCloud > Storage & Backup > Manage Storage). They can see the file's name and the file size, and they can delete individual files if they wish.

Anything saved directly into the container (not in the Documents folder) is hidden. The user can only see the total memory usage and must delete all the data at once.

In our case, it doesn't make a huge difference. We will only ever have a single data file. However, it's usually best to save documents into the Documents folder.

Finally, this method will return nil if iCloud support is disabled.

> **NOTE:** We will only use the cloudURL to move documents into iCloud storage. Never use it to access iCloud files directly. After all, even if we know the file's in the cloud, it might not have downloaded to this particular device. Furthermore, other processes may move the file, changing its URL. Therefore, when opening files from within iCloud, we must always use NSMetadataQuery to search for the document's current location.

```
+ (BOOL)isCloudAvailable {
    return [self cloudURL] != nil;
}
```

Finally, isCloudAvailable simply calls cloudURL and checks to see if it returns nil. If it did, iCloud support is not available and this method returns NO. Otherwise, this method returns YES.

Now let's create our accessWeightHistory: convenience method. Open WeightHistory.h and declare the method as shown:

```
+ (void)accessWeightHistory:(historyAccessHandler)completionHandler;
```

We also need to define the historyAccessHandler type. This will be a callback block that takes two arguments: a BOOL value indicating the access operation's success or failure, and a WeightHistory object. We're going to create a number of functions that use historyAccessHandler blocks. So explicitly creating a block type will simplify our code and make it easier to read.

Add the following code before WeightHistory's @interface block:

```
@class WeightHistory;

typedef void (^historyAccessHandler)

(BOOL success, WeightHistory* weightHistory);
```

The WeightHistory forward declaration lets us get around a chicken-and-egg problem here. The typedef line defines our historyAccessHandler block type. However, the block type refers to the WeightHistory class; therefore, the class needs to be defined first. On the other hand, our WeightHistory class also refers to the historyAccessHandler type; therefore, historyAccessHandler must also be defined first. Fortunately, the forward declaration lets us have it both ways.

Now, go back to WeightHistory.m. We will also need to declare a number of private helper methods. Add the following lines to the WeightHistory class extension.

```
+ (void)queryForCloudHistory:(historyAccessHandler)accessHandler;

+ (void)processQuery:(NSMetadataQuery*)query
        thenCall:(historyAccessHandler)accessHandler;

+ (void)createCloudDocumentAtURL:(NSURL*)url
        thenCall:(historyAccessHandler) accesshandler;

+ (void)loadCloudDocumentAtURL:(NSURL*)url
        thenCall:(historyAccessHandler)accessHandler;
```

Now let's start implementing our methods:

```
+ (void)accessWeightHistory:(historyAccessHandler)accessHandler {
    NSURL* url;
    if ([self isCloudAvailable]) {
        [self queryForCloudHistory:accessHandler];
    } else {
        NSFileManager* fileManager =
```

```
        [NSFileManager defaultManager];
        url = [self localURL];
        WeightHistory* history = [[self alloc] initWithFileURL:url];
        if ([fileManager fileExistsAtPath:[url path]]) {
            [history openWithCompletionHandler:^(BOOL success) {
                accessHandler(success, history);
            }];
        } else {
            [history saveToURL:url
              forSaveOperation:UIDocumentSaveForCreating
             completionHandler:^(BOOL success) {
                accessHandler(success, history);
            }];
        }
    }
}
```

This method will asynchronously create our WeightHistory object. If we can find a health_beat.hbhistory file, we should load our data from that file. Otherwise, we should create a new health_beat.hbhistory file. Additionally, instead of returning our newly initialized WeightHistory, we will pass the result back using our historyAccessHandler block. This gives us a lot of flexibility when creating our WeightHistory. We can pass the block from method to method until either we successfully create our WeightHistory or we run into an error and the operation fails. At which point, we call the historyAccessorBlock and pass in our results.

If we had any errors while opening or creating our file, we will pass NO as the success argument. Otherwise, we will pass YES for success and pass a reference to our fully instantiated WeightHistory object for the weightHistory argument.

Of course, the devil's in the details. We start by calling isCloudAvailable. As mentioned, this checks to see if the device supports iCloud storage. If it does, this method call will also prepare the iCloud container for use.

If we have access to iCloud storage, we need to search for our file. This procedure can get a little bit complicated, so we'll move it into its own method. For now, just call queryForCloudHistory: to kick off the search, and pass in our historyAccessHandler.

If iCloud is not available, we can create our WeightHistory object immediately. Then we check to see if the history file already exists in our local sandbox. If we find the file, we call openWithCompletionHandler: to open it. Otherwise, we call saveToURL:forSaveOperation:completionHandler: to create a new file.

These are the standard UIDocument methods for opening and creating files. For our save operation, we want to pass in the UIDocumentSaveForCreating argument. This makes sure that the system creates the proper NSFileCoordinator blocks before it performs its save operation. Alternatively, we would use UIDocumentSaveForOverwriting if we wanted to force our document to save its changes.

In both cases, when the file access operation is finished, the UIDocument method will call its completion handler block. Inside this block we call our historyAccessHandler, passing in the success argument from our completion handler and our completely initialized WeightHistory object.

Now let's implement queryForCloudHistory:. This is a little bit long, so let's look at it a step at a time.

```
+ (void)queryForCloudHistory:(historyAccessHandler)accessHandler {
    // Search for the file in the cloud.
    NSMetadataQuery* query = [[NSMetadataQuery alloc] init];
    [query setSearchScopes:
        [NSArray arrayWithObject:
            NSMetadataQueryUbiquitousDocumentsScope]];
    // Get all files.
    [query setPredicate:[NSPredicate predicateWithFormat:
                    @"%K like %@",
                    NSMetadataItemFSNameKey,
                    FileName]];
```

Here, we instantiate an NSMetadataQuery object. We will use this to search our iCloud storage for files. We start by setting the search scope. There are two possible scopes: NSMetadataQueryUbiquitousDocumentsScope and NSMetadataQuery UbiquitousDataScope. The first searches inside our iCloud container's Documents folder. The second searches through everything else in the container.

Next, we set the search's predicate. In our case, we're searching for any files named health_beat.hbhistory. Note that the predicate's LIKE string comparison can also accept wildcards. For example, using @"%K like '*.hbhistory'" for our format would match any files ending in .hbhistory.

> **NOTE:** When we enter a string value directly into a predicate format, we need to wrap it in quotes. Both single and double quotes are acceptable. However, when we pass in a string using substitution and the %@ placeholder, the system automatically quotes the string for us. Importantly, strings passed into a %K placeholder are not quoted— which is why we use %K for passing in key names instead of %@.

Additionally, we could use some of the other predicate string comparisons, including BEGINSWITH and ENDSWITH (but not CONTAINS or MATCHES). For more information, check out "String Comparisons" in the Predicates Programming Guide.

```
[[NSNotificationCenter defaultCenter]
   addObserverForName
   NSMetadataQueryDidFinishGatheringNotification
   object:query
   queue:nil
   usingBlock:^(NSNotification* notification) {
     [query disableUpdates];
     [[NSNotificationCenter defaultCenter]
       removeObserver:self
       name:NSMetadataQueryDidFinishGatheringNotification
       object:query];
     [self processQuery:query
```

```
                  thenCall:accessHandler];
        [query stopQuery];
    }];
    [query startQuery];
}
```

Next, we register for notifications from our query object. Queries typically operate over two distinct phases. During the initial search phase, they will gather all the information on documents currently in the iCloud container. Remember, our device will have metadata on all the files in the container; however, the actual files may not be on the device yet.

These results may be returned in batches. The query will post an `NSMetadata QueryGatheringProgressNotification` with each batch. Once the entire search is completed, it posts `NSMetadataQueryDidFinishGatheringNotification` and the query enters its live-update phase. In this phase, the query will continue to monitor our iCloud storage container and will post `NSMetadataQueryDidUpdateNotification` notifications whenever it detects a change.

In our case, we know there's only a single file, so we simply wait for the initial search to complete. However, if an application may have a large number of files, it will be better to process each batch as it arrives.

Once we receive the notification, our system will run our block. Here, we disable updates. Then we remove ourselves as an observer. We call `processQuery:thenCall:` to actually process the query results, and then we shut down our query. Always remember to shut down your queries. You don't want to leave them running any longer than necessary.

Finally, after we're finished registering for notifications, we start our query. Remember, the code is not executed in the order it appears on the screen. This often happens with block-based API. The `startQuery` method is executed well before the notification block. This can be confusing. Just remember that blocks are often called asynchronously—which means the code inside them may be called at some undefined point in the future.

Now let's process the query results.

```
+ (void)processQuery:(NSMetadataQuery*)query
          thenCall:(historyAccessHandler)completionHandler {
    NSUInteger count = [query resultCount];
    id result;
    NSURL* url;
    switch (count) {
        case 0:
            NSLog(@"Creating a cloud document");
            url = [self cloudURL];
            [self createCloudDocumentAtURL:url
                                  thenCall:completionHandler];
            break;
        case 1:
            NSLog(@"Loading a cloud document");
            result = [query resultAtIndex:0];
            url =
            [result valueForAttribute:NSMetadataItemURLKey];
            [self loadCloudDocumentAtURL:url
                                  thenCall:completionHandler];
            break;
        default:
            // We should never have more than 1 file. If this
            // occurs, it's due to a bug in our code that needs
            // to be fixed.
            [NSException
             raise:NSInternalInconsistencyException
             format:@"NSMetadata should only find a single "
```

```
                              @"file, found %d',
                              count];
                  break;
         }
    }
```

Here, we start by checking the number of results returned by our query. If we don't have any results, we simply call createCloudDocumentAtURL:thenCall: to create a new iCloud document.

If our query finds a single match, we open it. We start by accessing the first (and only) result in our query. Then we call valueForAttribute: and pass in NSMetadata ItemURLKey to get the file's URL. Finally, we call loadCloudDocumentAtURL: thenCall: to load the document.

Finally, as a sanity check, if our query finds more than one match we throw an exception. Again, this should never occur during Health Beat's regular operations. If we trigger this notification, it undoubtedly means we made a mistake somewhere else in our code.

We're finally getting to the methods that create and load our iCloud documents. Let's start with createCloudDocumentAtURL:thenCall:. Again, let's take this in steps.

```
+ (void)createCloudDocumentAtURL:(NSURL*)url
         thenCall:(historyAccessHandler)accessHandler{
    WeightHistory* history =
    [[WeightHistory alloc] initWithFileURL:url];
    // First create a local copy.
    [history saveToURL:[self localURL]
      forSaveOperation:UIDocumentSaveForCreating
    completionHandler:^(BOOL success) {
```

Here, we instantiate our WeightHistory object. It doesn't really matter which URL we give it, since we will be moving it shortly. For now, we will use the provided iCloud URL. Then, we save a local copy to our local URL. The rest of this method is executed asynchronously in saveToURL:forSaveOperation:completionHandler:'s completion handler.

```
if (!success) {
    accessHandler(success, history);
    return;
}
// Now move it to the cloud in a background thread.
dispatch_queue_t backgroundQueue =
dispatch_get_global_queue(DISPATCH_QUEUE_PRIORITY_DEFAULT,
                          0);
```

If the save operation is not successful, we simply call our accessHandler and return. Otherwise, we request a background queue that we will use to move our file into the iCloud container. It's important to always move files into iCloud storage on a background thread, otherwise we might cause a deadlock. If you remember, we ran into a similar situation when creating our own file coordination block while resolving conflicts.

```
dispatch_async(backgroundQueue, ^{
    NSFileManager* manager =
    [NSFileManager defaultManager];
    NSError* error;
    BOOL moved = [manager setUbiquitous:YES
                           itemAtURL:[self localURL]
                         destinationURL:url
                              error:&error];
    if (!moved) {
        NSLog(@"Error moving document to the cloud: %@",
            [error localizedDescription]);
    }
    accessHandler(moved, history);
```

```
        });
    }];
}
```

Here, we call NSFileManager's setUbiquitous:itemAtURL:destinationURL: error: method to move our file into iCloud storage.

setUbiquitous:itemAtURL:destinationURL:error: can be used to move files both into and out of iCloud storage. If the setUbiquitous: argument is YES, we're moving into the cloud. If it is NO, we're moving back to the local sandbox. Similarly, itemAtURL: must contain our file's current URL—in our case, the URL in the local sandbox. destinationURL: holds the target URL—in our case, the URL in our iCloud container.

After moving the file, we check for errors. If we had an error, we log it. Then we call our accessHandler, passing in our results.

Apple highly recommends using this general procedure when creating new iCloud documents. First save the document into the local sandbox, and then move it into the cloud. Things get a little complicated because of all the asynchronous callbacks and background queues. But at its heart, that's all we did. Save it locally, and then move it to the cloud.

Finally, we come to our last method. If we find a document in iCloud storage, we load it.

```
+ (void)loadCloudDocumentAtURL:(NSURL*)url
                       thenCall:(historyAccessHandler)accessHandler {
    WeightHistory* history =
    [[WeightHistory alloc] initWithFileURL:url];
    [history openWithCompletionHandler:^(BOOL success) {
        accessHandler(success, history);
    }];
}
```

This time we create a WeightHistory object using the URL returned by our metadata query. We then call openWithCompletionHandler: to load our data file. In the completion handler, we simply call our accessHandler, passing along the completion handler's results.

ASYNCHRONOUSLY ACCESSING THE MODEL

With all that work out of the way, we have a single method that we can call to correctly create our model object. On the surface, it's quite easy to use our new document-based model. Open TabViewController.m and navigate to the viewDidLoad method. Modify it as shown:

```objc
- (void)viewDidLoad {
    [super viewDidLoad];
    [WeightHistory accessWeightHistory:
    ^(BOOL success, WeightHistory *weightHistory) {
        if (!success) {
            // An error occurred while instantiating our
            // history. This probably indicates a catastrophic
            // failure (e.g., the device's hard drive is out of
            // space). We should really alert the user and tell
            // them to take appropriate action. For now, just
            // throw an exception.
            [NSException
             raise:NSInternalInconsistencyException
             format:@"An error occurred while trying to "
                    @"instantiate our history"];
        }
        self.weightHistory = weightHistory;
        // Create a stack, and load it with the view
        // controllers from our tabs.
        NSMutableArray* stack =
        [NSMutableArray arrayWithArray:self.viewControllers];
        // While we still have items on our stack,
        while ([stack count] > 0) {
```

```
// pop the last item off the stack.
id controller = [stack lastObject];
[stack removeLastObject];
// If it is a container object, add its view
// controllers to the stack.
if ([controller
    respondsToSelector:@selector(viewControllers)]) {
    [stack addObjectsFromArray:
        [controller viewControllers]];
}
// If it responds to setWeightHistory, set the
// weight history.
if ([controller
    respondsToSelector:@selector(setWeightHistory:)]) {
    [controller setWeightHistory:
        self.weightHistory];
}
        }
    }];
}
```

Here, we call our accessWeightHistory: convenience method, passing it a block of code that will be executed once our WeightHistory object is properly created. Inside the block, we first check to see if accessWeightHistory: succeeded. If it didn't, we throw an exception.

As the comments suggest, we really should implement more-robust error handling here. There are a number of reasons we might run into errors. Unfortunately, almost all of them are serious issues that probably need some action by the user.

For example, maybe we've released an update to our application that changes the data format, and the user has upgraded the software on some—but not all—of their devices. They might get an error when trying to open the new file format with the old software. Fortunately, the fix is easy. They just need to update the software on all their devices.

Alternatively, their device might be running out of memory, and there simply isn't space to save the iCloud document locally. This can be more complicated. The user will need to delete some of the content off their device, freeing up more space.

In both cases, the best we can do is to try to detect the problem, alert the user, and provide some reasonable suggestions for how they can fix it. We cannot do anything for them directly.

On the other hand, if `accessWeightHistory:` succeeds, we simply assign our new model object to the `weightHistory` property. Then we forward the model object to our other view controllers.

The code that forwards our model is exactly the same as before—however, there's an important difference in timing. In the original version, our model object was created and forwarded synchronously. The system created our `WeightHistory` object and forwarded it to the other view controllers during `TabViewController`'s `viewDidLoad` method.

Our code relied on the fact that the containing view controller's `viewDidLoad` method would execute before the `viewDidLoad` method of the controllers it managed. This means that by the time our content controller's `viewDidLoad` method executed, the content controller already had a valid object stored in its `weightHistory` property.

Unfortunately, now the code runs asynchronously. This means our content view controller's `viewDidLoad` method may run before we pass it a valid model object. We need to make sure they consider this possibility.

For our `EnterWeightViewController`, we just need to make sure the user doesn't try to add a new weight entry until after we receive the `WeightHistory` object. Actually, we will deal with this issue a little bit later. Our `EnterWeightViewController` also needs to monitor our document's state and disable the text field whenever document editing is disabled. We will simply use the same code to disable the text field until we have a valid `WeightHistory` object as well.

For our `GraphViewController`, we can't set ourselves as a key-value observer in the `viewDidLoad` method anymore. Open the implementation file and delete both of the `addObserver:forKeyPath:options:context:` method calls. Similarly, in `viewDidUnload`, delete both of the `removeObserver:forKeyPath:` method calls.

Instead, let's implement a custom setWeightHistory: accessor. This will be called whenever a new WeightHistory object is assigned to the graph view's weightHistory property. We can both set up and tear down our WeightHistory observations here.

```objc
#pragma mark - Custom Accessor
- (void)setWeightHistory:(WeightHistory *)weightHistory {
    // If we're assigning the same history, don't do anything.
    if ([_weightHistory isEqual:weightHistory]) {
        return;
    }
    // Clear any notifications for the old history, if any.
    if (_weightHistory != nil) {
        [_weightHistory removeObserver:self forKeyPath:WeightKey];
    }
    _weightHistory = weightHistory;
    // Add new notifications for the new history, if any,
    // and set the view's values.
    if (_weightHistory != nil) {
        [_weightHistory addObserver:self
                         forKeyPath:WeightKey
                            options:NSKeyValueObservingOptionNew
                            context:nil];
        // If the view is loaded, we need to update it.
        if (self.isViewLoaded) {
            id graphView = self.view;
            [graphView setWeightEntries:_weightHistory.weights
                              andUnits:getDefaultUnits()];
        }
    }
}
```

We start with a little sanity checking. If we're just reassigning the same history object, we don't need to do anything. We just return.

Next, if our old history object is not `nil`, we need to unregister from any KVO notifications. Currently, this should only happen as our application shuts down, so it's not vital. Still, having this code in place could prevent future problems as our application grows and changes.

Finally, as long as we're not assigning a `nil`-value object, we register for KVO notifications. Then, we check to see if our view has loaded. If it has, we update the view.

It's important to check and see if the view has loaded before we modify it. Otherwise, we may force our view to load as soon as we assign the `Weight History`. This would short-circuit the normal lazy-initialization of our view and could waste memory.

Additionally, we've removed the code that previously tracked our default weight units, and we've added another call to the mysterious `getDefaultUnits()` method. We'll deal with both of these issues later, in the section "Saving User Defaults."

While we're at it, we no longer need the `UnitsKey` string constant at the top of the file. Let's delete that. Additionally, our `observeValueForKeyPath:ofObject:change:context:` method only needs to worry about the `WeightKey`. We'll provide an entirely new method for tracking default unit changes in a bit. In the meantime, we can clean up this method.

```
- (void)observeValueForKeyPath:(NSString *)keyPath
                      ofObject:(id)object
                        change:(NSDictionary *)change
                       context:(void *)context {
    if ([keyPath isEqualToString:WeightKey]) {
        id graphView = self.view;
        [graphView setWeightEntries:self.weightHistory.weights
                          andUnits:getDefaultUnits()];
    }
}
```

Next, we need to make similar changes to our HistoryViewController. Start by deleting the notification method calls in both viewDidLoad and viewDidUnload.

```
- (void)viewDidLoad
{
    [super viewDidLoad];
    self.navigationItem.rightBarButtonItem = self.editButtonItem;
}
- (void)viewDidUnload
{
    [super viewDidUnload];
}
```

And add our custom accessor.

```
#pragma mark - Custom Accessor
- (void)setWeightHistory:(WeightHistory *)weightHistory {
    // If we're assigning the same history, don't do anything.
    if ([_weightHistory isEqual:weightHistory]) {
        return;
    }
    // Clear any notifications for the old history, if any.
    if (_weightHistory != nil) {
        [_weightHistory removeObserver:self
                            forKeyPath:KVOWeightChangeKey];
        [[NSNotificationCenter defaultCenter] removeObserver:self];
    }
    _weightHistory = weightHistory;
    // Add new notifications for the new history, if any.
    if (_weightHistory != nil) {
```

```
// Register to receive kvo messages when the weight
// history changes.
[_weightHistory addObserver:self
                forKeyPath:KVOWeightChangeKey
                   options:NSKeyValueObservingOptionNew
                   context:nil];
// If the view is loaded, we need to update it.
if (self.isViewLoaded) {
    [self.tableView reloadData];
}
  }
}
```

The general structure is the same; only the details have changed.

Here, we don't need to modify observeValueForKeyPath:ofObject:change: context:. It already only listens to changes to our WeightHistory. However, we have a different problem to fix.

Whenever our WeightHistory class receives notification of an updated file in iCloud storage, it will download the new file. This causes it to replace its current weightHistory array with an entirely new array. We will receive the notification that this has happened—but we won't process it properly. Our previous implementation of HistoryVewController never had to deal with this type of change. We only worried about additions and deletions.

Let's fix that. Navigate to the weightHistoryChanged: method, and scroll down until you find the NSKeyValueChangeSetting: case. Our current implementation simply ignores this method. Instead, we need to reload our table view. Change the case statement as shown:

```
case NSKeyValueChangeSetting:
    [self.tableView reloadData];
    break;
```

OK, now let's make sure our EnterWeightViewController reacts properly to changes in the document state.

OTHER DOCUMENT STATE CHANGES

UIDocument has four unique state flags, UIDocumentStateClosed, UIDocument StateInConflict, UIDocumentStateSavingError, and UIDocumentStateEditing Disabled, plus UIDocumentStateNormal—which simply means none of the other flags are set.

We've already added support for the UIDocumentStateInConflict to our WeightHistory class—but this is really just the bare minimum we need to make sure our app functions properly. Ideally, we should also alert users whenever we have trouble saving their changes or whenever the document editing is disabled. Document editing, in particular, will be disabled temporarily whenever the application receives an update from iCloud.

In our case, we want to inform the user of these state changes whenever they have the EnterWeightViewController view open. The EnterWeightViewController is our primary interface for modifying our weight history. Ideally, the other views should respond to these notifications as well (e.g., disabling the edit button in the history view whenever document editing is disabled would be nice), but I will leave that as homework.

Let's start by adding a new label to our enter weight scene. Open MainStoryboard .storyboard and zoom in on our enter weight view controller. Drag a label out and position it below the text field. Stretch it until it fills the view from margin to margin, and then set the text attributes to center-aligned, 15-point System Bold font with red text color. Next, change the autosizing settings so that it's locked to the left, right, and top and stretches horizontally. Finally, change the text to **Unable to Save Changes**. It should now match **Figure 6.5**.

Most of the time, we will hide this label, only displaying it when the document enters a UIDocumentStateSavingError state. However, before we can make it appear and disappear, we need access to it in our code. This means we have to link it to an outlet.

Switch to the Assistant editor and make sure the right editor shows EnterWeightViewController.h. Right-click and drag from the label to a space just below the properties. In the pop-up window, make sure it's a strong UILabel outlet, and then set the name to saveWarningLabel.

FIGURE 6.5 Creating a warning for the save error state

Now switch back to the Standard editor, and open EnterWeightViewController.m. We need to make several changes here. Let's start by hiding our warning label. Navigate down to the viewDidLoad method, and add the following line to the bottom:

```
self.saveWarningLabel.alpha = 0.0f;
```

Next, we want to add a custom setWeightHistory: accessor, just as we did for the graph and history view controllers.

```
#pragma mark - Custom Accessor
- (void)setWeightHistory:(WeightHistory *)weightHistory {
    NSNotificationCenter* notificationCenter =
    [NSNotificationCenter defaultCenter];
    // If we're assiging the same history, don't do anything.
    if ([_weightHistory isEqual:weightHistory]) {
        return;
    }
```

```
// Clear any notifications for the old history, if any.
if (_weightHistory != nil) {
    [notificationCenter
    removeObserver:self
    forKeyPath:UIDocumentStateChangedNotification];
}
_weightHistory = weightHistory;
// Add new notifications for the new history, if any,
// and set the view's values.
if (_weightHistory != nil) {
    // Register for notifications.
    [notificationCenter
     addObserver:self
     selector:@selector(updateSaveAndEditStatus)
     name:UIDocumentStateChangedNotification
     object:_weightHistory];
    // Update our save and edit status.
    [self updateSaveAndEditStatus];
}
}
```

This time we're registering and unregistering for the document's UIDocument StateChangedNotification. When we receive this notification, we call our class's updateSaveAndEditStatus method. We also call this method upon receiving a new WeightHistory instance—letting us respond to the document's initial state.

Of course, the updateSaveAndEditStatus method doesn't exist yet. Let's start by declaring it in our EnterWeightViewController's class extension.

```
- (void)updateSaveAndEditStatus;
```

Now, lets walk through the method's implementation a step at a time.

```
#pragma mark - Private Methods
- (void)updateSaveAndEditStatus {
    if (self.weightHistory == nil) {
        // Disable editing.
        [self.weightTextField resignFirstResponder];
        self.weightTextField.enabled = NO;
        return;
    }
```

Here, we check to see if we have a nil-valued weightHistory property. This typically happens when our enter weight scene appears onscreen before our document loads. This happens almost every time the app launches.

We simply make sure our text field is not the first responder, and then we disable the text field. This prevents the user from making any changes until after our WeightHistory document is ready to go.

```
    UIDocumentState state =
    self.weightHistory.documentState;
    if (state & UIDocumentStateSavingError) {
        // Display save warning.
        [UIView
         animateWithDuration:0.25f
         animations:^{
            self.saveWarningLabel.alpha = 1.0f;
        }];
    } else {
        // Hide save warning.
        [UIView
         animateWithDuration:0.25f
```

```
    animations:^{
        Saving Health Beat's State 345
        self.saveWarningLabel.alpha = 0.0f;
    }];
}
```

Now we check the document's `UIDocumentStateSavingError` flag. This flag will be set whenever an error occurs that prevents the document from saving its state. If the flag is set, we use Core Animation to display our warning label. If it is not set, we hide the label.

```
if (state & UIDocumentStateEditingDisabled) {
    // Disable editing.
    [self.weightTextField resignFirstResponder];
    self.weightTextField.enabled = NO;
} else {
    // Enable editing.
    self.weightTextField.enabled = YES;
    [self.weightTextField becomeFirstResponder];
    // Sets the current time and date.
    self.currentDate = [NSDate date];
    self.dateLabel.text =
    [NSDateFormatter
     localizedStringFromDate:self.currentDate
     dateStyle:NSDateFormatterLongStyle
     timeStyle:NSDateFormatterShortStyle];
}
}
```

Finally, we check the document's `UIDocumentStateEditingDisabled` flag. This is set whenever the document is in a state where editing the document is no longer safe. Typically, this happens when the document is loading a remote update, but other events may trigger it as well.

If the flag is turned on, we have our text field resign first responder status, hiding the keyboard. We also disable the text field, preventing the user from making any changes. If the flag is turned off, we enable the text field and set it as the first responder. This causes the keyboard to reappear. We also update our `currentDate` property and the user interface's date label. This helps ensure that our weight entries remain in sequential order.

That wraps up our work with the document; however, we still need to save the user defaults. Fortunately, as you will see, this is much, much easier. Still, this is a good place to take a break. Stretch for a bit, and (as always) commit your changes.

SAVING USER DEFAULTS

We're going to start by storing the default weight units using NSUserDefaults. First, let's define a few functions to simplify our code.

We are just going to write C functions, but we still want them to have full access to our Objective-C classes. So, we need the file to be compiled as if it were Objective-C. The easiest way to do this is to create a new NSObject class and then delete both the class interface and its implementation.

Right-click the Model group and create a new NSObject named WeightUnits. Then open up both the header and implementation file and delete everything except the #import directives. We can even move the Foundation import directive from the header to the implementation file.

Now, in WeightUnits.h, add the following code:

```
typedef enum {
    LBS,
    KG
} WeightUnit;

WeightUnit getDefaultUnits(void);

void setDefaultUnits(WeightUnit value);
```

Here, we're just defining our WeightUnit enum and declaring two accessor functions for our default weights.

Next, switch to the implementation file.

```
#import "WeightUnits.h"

#import <Foundation/Foundation.h>

static NSString* const WeightUnitKey = @"weight_unit";

WeightUnit getDefaultUnits(void) {
    return [[NSUserDefaults standardUserDefaults]
            integerForKey:WeightUnitKey];
}

void setDefaultUnits(WeightUnit value) {
    [[NSUserDefaults standardUserDefaults]
     setInteger:value forKey:WeightUnitKey];
}
```

NSUserDefaults stores values using keys, so we start by defining a static string to use as our key. The getDefaultUnits() function simply accesses the standard user defaults and returns the value associated with our key. setDefaultUnits() saves a new value into the standard user defaults, also using our key.

We will be using these functions in several places throughout our application. So, let's add an #import directive to our precompiled prefix header file. Open Health Beat-Prefix.pch and modify it as shown.

```
#import <Availability.h>

#ifndef __IPHONE_5_0

#warning "This project uses features only available in iOS SDK 5.0
→  and later."

#endif

#ifdef __OBJC__

    #import <UIKit/UIKit.h>

    #import <Foundation/Foundation.h>

    #import "WeightUnits.h"

#endif
```

FIGURE 6.6 Searching for the defaultUnits property

This automatically imports WeightUnits.h into every class in our project, making our accessor functions available everywhere.

Now we need to go through our project and replace every instance of self.weight History.defaultUnits with one of our two accessor functions. To start, switch to the Search navigator (the icon that looks like a magnifying glass in the navigator selector bar) and perform a search for self.weightHistory.defaultUnits (**Figure 6.6**).

Our search has found seven matches. Select each one in turn. If the code is getting the default unit value, replace it with a call to getDefaultUnits().

```
WeightUnit unit = getDefaultUnits();
```

If the matching code is setting a new default unit value, replace it with a call to setDefaultUnits().

```
setDefaultUnits(unit);
```

We also need to delete the WeightUnit typedef from the top of WeightEntry.h. We've already copied it over to WeightUnits.h, and having a duplicate will just cause compilation errors.

Finally, we need to update our UI whenever our default units change. Fortunately, the NSUserDefaults posts an NSUserDefaultsDidChangeNotification whenever its notification changes. We just need to listen for this notification.

In EnterWeightViewController.m, navigate to the viewDidLoad method and add the following code to the bottom of the method.

```
[[NSNotificationCenter defaultCenter]
 addObserverForName:NSUserDefaultsDidChangeNotification
 object:[NSUserDefaults standardUserDefaults]
 queue:nil
 usingBlock:^(NSNotification *note) {
    NSString* title = [WeightEntry stringForUnit:
                          getDefaultUnits()];
    [self.unitsButton setTitle:title
                  forState:UIControlStateNormal];
}];
```

Then, in the viewDidUnload method, we need to unregister our self.

```
[[NSNotificationCenter defaultCenter]
  removeObserver:self];
```

In GraphViewController's viewDidLoad method, register for a similar notification. Remember to unregister in the viewDidUnload method as well.

```
// Register to receive notifications when the default unit changes.
[[NSNotificationCenter defaultCenter]
 addObserverForName:NSUserDefaultsDidChangeNotification
 object:[NSUserDefaults standardUserDefaults]
 queue:nil
 usingBlock:^(NSNotification *note) {
```

```
[graphView
  setWeightEntries:self.weightHistory.weights
  andUnits:getDefaultUnits()];
}];
```

We also want to register our HistoryViewController for notifications as well. Again, add the following to its viewDidLoad method. As always, remember to unregister in the viewDidUnload method.

```
// Register to receive notifications when the user
// defaults change.
  [[NSNotificationCenter defaultCenter]
    addObserver:self
    selector:@selector(reloadTableData)
    name:NSUserDefaultsDidChangeNotification
    object:[NSUserDefaults standardUserDefaults]];
```

Finally, we want to make sure our EnterWeightController view starts with the correct units. Open EnterWeightViewController.m and navigate to the viewWill Appear: method. Add the following code.

```
- (void)viewWillAppear:(BOOL)animated {
    // Sets the current time and date.
    self.currentDate = [NSDate date];
    self.dateLabel.text =
    [NSDateFormatter
      localizedStringFromDate:self.currentDate
      dateStyle:NSDateFormatterLongStyle
      timeStyle:NSDateFormatterShortStyle];
    // Clear the text field.
    self.weightTextField.text = @"";
    [self.weightTextField becomeFirstResponder];
```

```
    [self.unitsButton
    setTitle:[WeightEntry stringForUnit:getDefaultUnits()]
    forState:UIControlStateNormal];
  [super viewWillAppear:animated];
}
```

The project should now build without any errors. Try running it. Add a few weights. Change the default units. Now send the app to the background, and then stop it. Run it again. It should remember both the weight entries and the changed units.

NOTE: Sending the app to the background forces the application to save any pending changes. On the other hand, pressing the Stop button in Xcode will immediately kill the app without giving it a chance to save its state. When testing any document-based project, it's always best to send the app to the background before stopping it.

Try running the app on two devices. Add a new weight to one device, and then send the app to the background. You should see the new entry show up on the second device within about 30 seconds.

Try adding a new weight to both simultaneously. Send both apps to the background, and then bring them back to the foreground. Both apps should initially appear with their own unique set of weights. Then one app will resolve the conflict, changing to display the merged set of weights. A minute or so later, the other app will also change over. The conflict is now resolved.

Note that both copies of our app are successfully syncing their weight history, but they're not syncing the default units. Let's fix that.

IMPLEMENTING iCLOUD KEY-VALUE STORAGE

We want to continue to use the NSUserDefaults to store our preferences locally; however, we can use iCloud key-value storage to sync these defaults between machines. The procedure is simple. We register for notifications about changes to our iCloud key-value storage. If a change occurs, we modify our user defaults to match. Similarly, we monitor our user defaults. If they change, we update the iCloud key-value storage. Furthermore, we can do all of this in our application delegate. Our view controllers already respond to any changes we make to our user defaults.

Open HBAppDelegate.m. At the top of the file, we need to import our WeightEntry class. We also want to define a key to use with iCloud key-value storage.

```objc
#import "WeightEntry.h"
static NSString* const UbiquitousWeightUnitDefaultKey =
@"UbiquitousWeightUnitDefaultKey";
```

Next, let's modify application:didFinishLaunchingWithOptions: to register for our notifications. Let's examine this one chunk at a time.

```objc
- (BOOL)application:(UIApplication *)application
didFinishLaunchingWithOptions:(NSDictionary *)launchOptions {
    // Since the delegate lasts throughout the life of the app,
    // we don't need to unregister these notifications.
    NSUbiquitousKeyValueStore* store =
    [NSUbiquitousKeyValueStore defaultStore];
    NSNotificationCenter* notificationCenter =
    [NSNotificationCenter defaultCenter];
```

So far, we're just getting reference to the default notification center and the default iCloud key-value store.

```objc
    [notificationCenter
      addObserverForName:
      NSUbiquitousKeyValueStoreDidChangeExternallyNotification
      object:store
      queue:nil
      usingBlock:^(NSNotification *note) {
        WeightUnit value =
        (WeightUnit)[store longLongForKey:
            UbiquitousWeightUnitDefaultKey];
        setDefaultUnits(value);
    }];
```

Next, we register for notifications from the iCloud key-value store. When we receive a notification, we grab the value for our key and use it to update our user defaults.

Notice that NSKeyValueUbiquitousStore looks similar to NSUserDefaults, but it does not support the same range of data types. Specifically, the only integer type it supports is the long long. That's a bit of overkill when it comes to storing our WeightUnit values—but it's the only option available. Also, we have to explicitly cast the long long back to our WeightUnit type. This lets the compiler know that we (hopefully) know what we're doing and keeps it from complaining about possible data loss.

```
[notificationCenter
    addObserverForName:NSUserDefaultsDidChangeNotification
    object:[NSUserDefaults standardUserDefaults]
    queue:nil
    usingBlock:^(NSNotification *note) {
        int value = getDefaultUnits();
        NSLog(@"Setting iCloud Value: %@",
                [WeightEntry stringForUnit:value]);
        [store setLongLong:value forKey:
                UbiquitousWeightUnitDefaultKey];
    }];
    [store synchronize];
    return YES;
}
```

Now, we register for notifications about changes to our NSUserDefaults. When a change occurs, we get the current default value and use it to update the value in the cloud.

Finally, once both notifications are set up, we synchronize our cloud storage. This forces the system to post notifications about any changes that might have occurred while the application was turned off. We don't have to synchronize NSUserDefaults, since it already automatically posts those notifications.

FIGURE 6.7 Adding the settings bundle

Similarly, we need to synchronize the iCloud key-value storage whenever our application enters or leaves the background and before our application terminates. Add the following line of code to `applicationDidEnterBackground:`, `applicationWill EnterForeground:`, and `applicationWillTerminate:`. Again, our user defaults handle these synchronizations for us automatically.

```
[[NSUbiquitousKeyValueStore defaultStore] synchronize];
```

That's it. We're now syncing our defaults across the cloud. Unfortunately, it can be a bit difficult to test. Remember, when we sync the iCloud key-value storage, we're only saving data to the local container. The system decides when and how this data will be uploaded to iCloud. To preserve bandwidth, it throttles these changes, delaying updates. The more rapidly we make our changes, the longer the delays become.

In my own testing, I could usually observe one or two changes before the delays became too long and the system seemed to become unresponsive. If I checked again later in the day, both devices would have synced up again. Unfortunately, this is not something that we can easily test in real time during development.

Now we just need to link our user defaults into the system settings.

ADDING SYSTEM SETTINGS SUPPORT

Adding a custom preferences page to the Systems application is actually not too difficult. Right-click the Supporting Files group and select New File. Under iOS > Resource, select Settings Bundle and click Next (**Figure 6.7**). Name the file **Settings**, and click Create.

FIGURE 6.8 The contents of the Settings.bundle file

FIGURE 6.9 The default Root.plist file

Key	Type	Value
▼ Preference Items	Array	(4 items)
▼ Item 0 (Group – Group)	Diction...	(2 items)
Title	String	Group
Type	String	Group
▼ Item 1 (Text Field – Name)	Diction...	(8 items)
Autocapitalization Style	String	None
Autocorrection Style	String	No Autocorrection
Default Value	String	
Text Field Is Secure	Boolean	NO
Identifier	String	name_preference
Keyboard Type	String	Alphabet
Title	String	Name
Type	String	Text Field
▼ Item 2 (Toggle Switch – Enabled)	Diction...	(4 items)
Default Value	Boolean	YES
Identifier	String	enabled_preference
Title	String	Enabled
Type	String	Toggle Switch
▼ Item 3 (Slider)	Diction...	(7 items)
Default Value	Number	0.5
Identifier	String	slider_preference
Maximum Value	Number	1
Max Value Image Filename	String	
Minimum Value	Number	0
Min Value Image Filename	String	
Type	String	Slider
Strings Filename	String	Root

This adds the Settings.bundle file to your application. If you expand this bundle, you will see that it contains an empty English-language localization folder (en.lproj) and a file named Root.plist (**Figure 6.8**).

We've brushed up against property lists (or plists) a few times now. Basically, these files store key-value pairs. However, since the values can include arrays and dictionaries, we can create rather complex data structures. Property list files are commonly used to configure applications in both iOS and Mac OS X.

Xcode displays property lists using a property list editor. Under the surface, however, plists are simply XML files—albeit XML files with a structure designed to be easy to transport, store, or access while still remaining as efficient as possible. For more information, check out Apple's Property List Programming Guide.

The default Root.plist defines a sample preferences page. If you expand all the elements, you will see that it has a single group of settings, somewhat simplistically named Group. Inside this group we have three controls: a text field titled Name, a toggle switch titled Enabled, and an untitled slider. Each of these controls also has an identifier field (name_preference, enabled_preference, and slider_preference). This value corresponds to the key used to access these values from NSUserDefaults (**Figure 6.9**).

FIGURE 6.10 Simulator showing Health Beat's settings

FIGURE 6.11 Default custom preferences page

Let's see this preferences sheet in action. Run the application. This will compile a new copy of your app that includes the Settings.bundle and then upload it to the simulator or device. Once the application launches, go ahead and stop it. Switch to the Systems app. You should now see an entry for Health Beat's settings (**Figure 6.10**).

Tap the Health Beat row and it opens the custom preferences page. It has a single group with three controls, just as we expected (**Figure 6.11**).

Of course, this isn't what we want. We really need a single group named Units, with a single multi-value item that will allow us to choose between pounds and kilograms. Edit the property list file so that it matches the settings shown in **Figure 6.12**.

FIGURE 6.12 Health Beat's Root.plist file

Key	Type	Value
▼ Preference Items	Array	(2 items)
▼ Item 0 (Group – Units)	Diction...	(2 items)
Type	String	Group
Title	String	Units
▼ Item 1 (Multi Value – Weight)	Diction...	(6 items)
Type	String	Multi Value
Title	String	Weight
Identifier	String	weight_unit
▼ Titles	Array	(2 items)
Item 0	String	lbs
Item 1	String	kg
▼ Values	Array	(2 items)
Item 0	Number	0
Item 1	Number	1
Default Value	Number	0
Strings Filename	String	Root

I find it easiest to just delete the four existing items and start fresh. Select the Preference Items key. Plus and minus buttons will appear next to the key name. Press the plus button twice. This will add two new items to the Preference Items array. Expand Item 0. Change the Type entry to Group, and change the Title entry to **Units**.

Next, expand Item 1. Change the Type entry to Multi Value, the Title entry to **Weight**, and the Identifier entry to weight_unit. For this to work correctly, the Identifier entry must match the key we use to access our NSUserDefaults values. In our case, it must match the WeightUnitKey constant we defined at the top of WeightUnits.m. Also, set the Default value to **0**.

Now select the Identifier row, and press the plus button twice. For the first one, select Titles. For the second, select Values. Titles will contain an array of strings. These represent the options that are displayed onscreen. Expand Titles and add two items to it. Set the first value to **lbs** and the second to **kg**.

Now expand Values. These hold the actual values returned when a corresponding title is selected. Again, add two items. Change their Type entries to Number, and set the first to **0** and the second to **1**.

NOTE: Changing preferences in the Settings application does not automatically change the settings in iCloud key-value storage. The user must launch the Health Beat app to force an update to the cloud.

The Settings.bundle property files can get quite complex. Check out Apple's documentation for all the sticky details. In particular, I recommend looking over the Settings Application Schema Reference and reading "Creating and Modifying the Settings Bundle" in the Preferences and Settings Programming Guide.

Run the application again. From the enter weight screen, set the Units value to kilograms. Now put the app in the background and open the Settings app. Navigate to the Health Beat settings. Change the weight back to pounds. Move back to the Health Beat application. The units should have automatically changed to match the value in our Settings app.

There's only one last thread to tie up. We've already registered an undo action every time we add or delete a weight entry. Now we need to finish setting up our undo support.

ENABLING UNDO SUPPORT

Start by opening WeightHistory's header file. The class should adopt the UIAlert ViewDelegate protocol. We also need to declare an undo method.

```objc
@interface WeightHistory : UIDocument <UIAlertViewDelegate>
// This is a virtual property.
@property (nonatomic, readonly) NSArray* weights;
- (void)addWeight:(WeightEntry*)weight;
- (void)removeWeightAtIndex:(NSUInteger)index;
- (void)undo;
+ (void)accessWeightHistory:(historyAccessHandler)completionHandler;
@end
```

Now, switch to WeightHistory.m and implement the undo method as shown:

```objc
- (void)undo {
    if ([self.managedObjectContext.undoManager canUndo]) {
        NSString* title = @"Confirm Undo";
        NSString* message =
        [self.managedObjectContext.undoManager undoActionName];
        UIAlertView* alert = [[UIAlertView alloc]
                                initWithTitle:title
                                message:message
                                delegate:self
                                cancelButtonTitle:@"Cancel"
                                otherButtonTitles:@"Undo",
                                nil];
        [alert show];
        [alert release];
    }
    else {
        NSString* title = @"Cannot Undo";
```

```
            NSString* message = @"There are no changes that "
                                @"can be undone at this time.";
        UIAlertView* alert = [[UIAlertView alloc]
                                initWithTitle:title
                                message:message
                                delegate:nil
                                cancelButtonTitle:@"OK"
                                otherButtonTitles:nil];
        [alert show];
        [alert release];
    }
}
```

iOS typically uses the shake gesture to trigger undo commands; however, it's
very easy to accidentally trigger shake gestures. Therefore, we should have the
user confirm the undo command before we actually perform it.

This method handles that for us. If we have an undo action available, it creates
an alert message using the action name. Otherwise, it displays a message letting
the user know that it cannot undo anything at this time.

Note that our code doesn't actually do anything until the user taps the Undo
button. We catch this in the alertView:didDismissWithButtonIndex: method.

```
# pragma mark - alert view delegate methods
- (void)alertView:(UIAlertView *)alertView
didDismissWithButtonIndex:(NSInteger)buttonIndex {
    // Undo the last action if it is confirmed.
    if (buttonIndex == 1) {
        [self.undoManager undo];
    }
}
```

If the user dismisses an alert view by tapping the second button (which we have previously defined as the Undo button), then we call our undo manager's undo method. That will trigger the undo action currently at the top of the stack.

Finally, we can improve our application's memory management by clearing out the undo stack if we receive a memory warning. Simply implement the application DidReceiveMemoryWarning: method.

```
- (void)applicationDidReceiveMemoryWarning:(UIApplication *)
application {
    // Clear the undo manager.
    [self.undoManager removeAllActions];
}
```

Now, let's modify the HistoryViewController so that it responds to the shake gesture. When this gesture occurs, we'll undo our last action. Fortunately, UIResponder provides support for motion events using the motionBegan:withEvent:, motionEnded:withEvent:, and motionCanceled:withEvent: methods. Our History ViewController, as a UIResponder subclass, inherits these methods.

In general, I prefer to respond to shake events in the motionEnded:withEvent: method. This will occur after the user stops shaking the device—provided the shaking motion was sufficient to trigger an event. This helps prevent accidental shakes.

Implement the method as shown:

```
#pragma mark - Responder Events
- (void)motionEnded:(UIEventSubtype)motion
        withEvent:(UIEvent *)event {
    // Only respond to shake events.
    if (event.type == UIEventSubtypeMotionShake) {
        [self.undoManager undo];
    }
}
```

Here, we check to make sure we have a motion shake event, and then we trigger our document's undo method. Currently, UIEventSubtypeMotionShake is iOS's only motion event, so the check doesn't actually do anything. Still, it helps future-proof our code. Apple may add new motion events to future releases.

This seems too simple to be true, and it is. Run the app, add a new weight entry, and then after it navigates to the history view, shake your phone. Nothing happens. It turns out that motion events are only sent to the first responder. So, we just need to set our controller as the first responder.

First, we have to tell the system that our controller can become first responder, by overriding the canBecomeFirstResponder method. Here, we just need to return YES.

```
- (BOOL)canBecomeFirstResponder {
    return YES;
}
```

Next, we need to set our controller as the first responder when the history view appears and release the first responder when it disappears. We can do this in our viewDidAppear: and viewWillDisappear: methods.

```
- (void)viewDidAppear:(BOOL)animated
{
    [super viewDidAppear:animated];
    [self becomeFirstResponder];
}
- (void)viewWillDisappear:(BOOL)animated
{
    [super viewWillDisappear:animated];
    [self resignFirstResponder];
}
```

That's it. Run the application. Try adding and deleting weights. Navigate to the history view and shake to undo. Everything should work as expected. Don't forget to commit all your changes.

WRAPPING **UP**

We've covered a lot of important ground in this chapter. iCloud is, without a doubt, one of the most important new features in iOS 5. As you've seen, it is also somewhat complicated to implement correctly. In this chapter, we covered the steps needed to implement a UIDocument subclass. We looked at techniques for creating new documents and opening existing documents. We also modified our application to respond to notifications from our document and to merge any conflicts as they arise. We added undo support and autosaving. And we synced our user preferences using iCloud key-value storage.

Our Health Beat application is now functionally complete. We can add and remove weight entries. These entries are saved and synced to all our devices. We can view our history and graph our progress. While the application can undoubtedly be improved, there are no major pieces left to implement.

Next chapter, we will take a step back and replace our application's model with Core Data. As you will see, UIManagedDocument and the Core Data model automatically handle many tedious document management tasks for us.

7

CORE DATA

Core Data is, in many ways, a replacement for our application's model layer. It is much more than just storage; it also manages the life cycles of our data objects, tracks and validates any changes to our data, provides effortless undo support, and, yes, saves our data to disk. The UIManagedDocument class only further improves on Core Data, automatically setting up our Core Data stack, managing file input and output on background threads, and adding simple iCloud integration. In this chapter, we will look at the technologies underlying both Core Data and UIManagedDocument. Then we will replace Health Beat's entire model layer with a UIManagedDocument-based model. As you will see, this provides a much simpler, much more robust system than our previous custom-built approach.

INTRODUCING **CORE DATA**

The Core Data framework provides support for automatically managing many common model layer tasks. We have already seen how Xcode simplifies our application's view layer. With Interface Builder, we can draw our application's scenes. The built-in guidelines ensure that our application follows Apple's Human Interface Guidelines, but it goes beyond that. We can draw connections between our view and controllers, linking objects to outlets and events to actions. With storyboards, we can link scenes with segues, letting us rapidly sketch out the entire application's workflow. With a few clicks of the mouse, Xcode helps us build complex structures that would normally require a considerable amount of boilerplate code.

Core Data brings a similar magic to our model. For most applications, the models share a number of features. This includes one or more object graphs. These graphs define both the content and the relationships in our application's data. Applications need to manage the life cycles of these object graphs, adding, modifying, and deleting objects in the graphs. They also need to validate the graphs, and save and load them to disk. Undo and redo support would also be nice. Furthermore, if the format of our data changes, we need to migrate our saved data from one schema to the next.

Core Data provides all of these features and more. In many cases, it can perform these tasks automatically. In others, it presents a rich API for expanding and customizing its behavior. It is also tightly integrated with Xcode's tool chain. Core Data is mature, well tested, and highly optimized. It is used by millions of customers across thousands of applications. While we could try to build a custom solution to better fit our specific needs, it would require a considerable amount of effort to match the performance and stability already provided by Core Data. In most cases, it's more cost effective to just use Core Data and to focus the developer effort on other areas.

And, yes, we can even graphically lay out our object graphs.

This chapter will start with a quick overview of Core Data's architecture, to give you an idea of how it works and how you might use it for other projects. Then we will convert our Health Beat application over from a custom model to Core Data. Along the way, we will look at many of the tricks and tips (and possible traps) involved in using Core Data.

CORE DATA IS NOT A DATABASE

Always remember that Core Data is not a relational database. Yes, we can save and load our data. We can search through our data using SQL-like fetch requests. We can even use SQLite to persist this data. However, Core Data isn't simply a front end to SQLite. We cannot open arbitrary SQLite databases using Core Data—it only works with its own files.

More importantly, Core Data represents a much broader set of technologies. It really is a replacement for much (if not all) of our model layer. After all, Core Data has a number of features that have nothing to do with persisting data to disk. For example, we can create an in-memory store and simply use Core Data to manage the life cycles of our objects, including tracking, managing, and validating any changes to those objects at runtime.

ARCHITECTURE OVERVIEW

Our Core Data model can be divided into two parts. The managed object model defines our data's schema, describing how our data is organized. We also have the Core Data stack. This combines both the managed object context (our application's live data) and the persistence stack (for saving and loading our entities to disk).

MANAGED OBJECT MODEL

The NSManagedObjectModel object defines the structure of our data. It describes what type of data we can store, and how the individual pieces of data relate. We do this by creating one or more entity descriptions. The managed object model then maintains the mapping between these descriptions and the corresponding NSManagedObject objects in our Core Data stack.

You can create managed object models programmatically at runtime, but we generally use Xcode's Data Model Design tool to graphically lay out our schema.

USING MULTIPLE MODELS

Each persistent store coordinator must have one and only one data model. For this reason, it's generally best to create a single model for each Core Data stack.

Of course, there are valid reasons to split up our model. We might want to divide a large, complex model across several sub-models to make them easier to work with. We may want to combine our application's model with one defined by a third-party library. Or, we may want to create multiple versions of some subsection of our model and dynamically load the correct version at runtime. Fortunately, NSManagedObjectModel has a number of methods for merging models, allowing us to unify our models before passing the combined version to the persistent store.

ENTITY DESCRIPTIONS

Core Data uses the NSEntityDescription class to define our model's entities. At a minimum, this description includes a unique name for the entity and the name of the managed object class that will be instantiated in the Core Data stack (either NSManaged Object or a custom subclass). Most entities also have one or more properties.

Properties represent the type of data stored in our entity. They become our instance variables when we instantiate objects for our entities. All Core Data properties are completely key-value compliant; Core Data automatically defines equivalent Objective-C properties for us. Finally, Core Data supports three types of properties: attributes, relationships, and fetched properties. Each specifies a different relationship between the entity and its data.

Attributes are the simplest Core Data property type. They represent values stored within the entity itself. Unfortunately, we are somewhat limited in the type of attributes that we can use. **Table 7.1** shows the complete list of Core Data attribute types and their corresponding Objective-C data types.

TABLE 7.1 Core Data Attribute Types

ATTRIBUTE TYPE	OBJECTIVE-C TYPE
Undefined	id
Integer 16	NSNumber
Integer 32	NSNumber
Integer 64	NSNumber
Decimal	NSDecimalNumber
Double	NSNumber
Float	NSNumber
String	NSString
Boolean	NSNumber
Date	NSDate
Binary Data	NSData
Transformable	Special

Some of these deserve a little special attention. Let's take the easiest one first. Internally, Core Data saves date attributes as the number of seconds since the reference date (January 1, 2001 GMT). It doesn't store the time zone. Internally, NSDate operates the same way—however, NSDate will implicitly use the device's default time zone. This means your date values will appear in PST when saved in Los Angeles, and in EST when read in New York. If you need to save the time zone information, you must explicitly create a separate attribute to store it.

Next, let's look at the undefined attribute type. This type can only be used with transient attributes (attributes that are not saved to the persistent store but whose changes are monitored, allowing undo/redo support). Any Objective-C object can be assigned to an undefined attribute. As we will see in the "Managed Objects" section, undefined attributes are often used to provide a friendly Objective-C wrapper around more primitive Core Data types.

Finally, we have the transformable data type. This type uses an NSValueTransformer object to convert the attribute to and from an instance of NSData. By default, Core Data will use NSKeyedUnarchiveFromDataTransformerName. In practice, this means we can assign any Objective-C object that adopts the NSCoding protocol to a transformable attribute, without requiring any additional work on our part. Of course, if we're feeling ambitious, we could always select a different NSValueTransformer or even write our own custom transformer to handle various special cases.

Attributes also have a number of settings. They can be optional, transient, or indexed.

- **Optional:** The attribute can have a nil value. More specifically, if the optional setting is turned off, we must assign a non-nil value before we can save the entity.

- **Transient:** Core Data does not save or load the attribute's value from the persistent store. It will still track the value, however, for undo, redo, and validation.

- **Indexed:** This attribute is important when searching through a list of entities. Persistent stores may use indexed attributes to improve search performance on fetch requests. This is particularly true of SQLite-backed stores.

Additionally, each attribute type has a number of validation settings. For numeric attributes, we can assign a minimum, maximum, and default value. For strings, we can set the minimum length, maximum length, default value, and regular expression that the string must match.

Relationships represent the second property type. Core Data uses relationships to define connections between entities. We will typically define both sides of a relationship. For example, if our Department entity has a Manager relationship, then the Manager entity should have a matching Department relationship. Furthermore, the Manager's relationship should be assigned as the Department's inverse relationship.

NOTE: While inverse relationships are not required, they are highly recommended. Core Data uses this information to ensure that the object graph remains consistent as the application makes changes. If you do not use inverse relationships, then you are responsible for ensuring the consistency, tracking changes, and managing the undo support. See the "Unidirectional Relationships" section of the Core Data Programming Guide for more information.

Relationships can be either to-one or to-many. To-one references are modeled using a pointer to the target object. Before iOS 5, all to-many relationships were modeled using NSSets. The relationship did not have any inherent order; it could be sorted based on any of the values from the entities. With iOS 5, we can also create ordered relationships, which use an NSOrderedSet. This allows us to place our entities into any arbitrary order we wish, without regard to the entities' values.

Like attributes, relationships support optional and transient settings. For to-many relationships, we can also set the minimum and maximum number of entities in the relationship. Finally, we can specify a delete rule. Delete rules describe what happens to the relationship when we delete our entity. The different options are listed here:

- **Cascade:** Deleting the source object also deletes all the objects at the relationship's destination. For example, deleting a Course object also deletes all its Students.

- **Deny:** If there is at least one object at the relationship's destination, then the source object cannot be deleted. If you want to delete a Course entity, you first need to remove all its Students.

- **Nullify:** Sets the inverse relationship for any entities at the destination to nil. Deleting the Course entity sets all the Students' Course relationship to nil.

- **No Action:** The entity at the other end remains unchanged. In general, this should only be used for unidirectional relationships. If it has an inverse relationship, that relationship now points to an entity that no longer exists. For example, our Students will still think they're registered for the now-nonexistent Course.

MANY-TO-MANY RELATIONSHIPS

Relationships are implicitly either one-to-one or one-to-many. It's possible to create a many-to-many relationship—but this requires a bit more work.

There are two recommended approaches. You can just make sure both ends are set as to-many relationships and set them as the inverse of each other. If you save these objects to an SQLite-based store, Core Data will automatically build the join table for you. Alternatively, you can explicitly build a join entity that represents these relationships. See the "Many-to-Many Relationships" section of the Core Data Programming Guide for more information.

Fetched properties are similar to relationships, but they are used to model weak one-way connections between entities. As the name suggests, the fetched property's value is calculated using a fetch request. We will discuss fetch requests in more detail later this chapter, but basically fetch requests let us look up entities that match a given entity description. We can also apply a predicate to filter our results and then sort them according to a set of sort descriptors. For example, we could create a fetch request that returns all students (entity description) who are taking more than 18 credit hours (predicate), and then we could sort them by descending GPA (sort description).

Fetched properties use lazy initialization. The actual fetch is not performed until the property's value is accessed. However, once the value is calculated, it is cached for future use. Our system models fetch properties using arrays, not sets, since fetched properties have a defined sort order. Additionally, fetched properties are the only way to model cross-store relationships. Normal relationship properties can only refer to objects saved in the same persistent store.

In many ways, an entity description is similar to a class. It is a blueprint used to instantiate managed objects—and, like classes, entity descriptions support inheritance. If you have a number of similar entities, you can factor out the common properties into a super-entity. You can even explicitly declare abstract entities (something not supported by the Objective-C object model).

However, there are a few important differences between entity inheritance and object inheritance. Remember, the entities describe how our data is organized. We use the entities to create objects—but the resulting object inheritance tree is separate from our entity inheritance tree. For example, we will often use NSManaged Objects for all of our entities—superclasses and subclasses alike. If we are creating custom classes for our entities, we probably want the model's inheritance tree to match our entities—but that's not required, and it's something we will have to manage by hand.

Most importantly, however, entity inheritance can have unexpected performance implications. If you save your entities in an SQLite-based store, then the database will place your entire hierarchy in a single table. It will create a column for each property, requiring a table large enough to contain all the properties from all the different sub-entities.

If you have a large number of sub-entities, and your sub-entities each add a significant number of unique properties, you may end up with large, sparsely populated tables. This can affect both the amount of disk space you need to store your entities, and the performance of fetch requests.

MIGRATING DATA

Changes to the schema may make the model incompatible with previously created data stores. When this happens, you will need to migrate the old stores before you can open them. By default, Core Data manages this with a three-step process:

1. Model versioning

2. Mapping model

3. Data migration

Core data lets us create multiple versions of our managed object model. We can add a new version by selecting our managed object model and then selecting Editor > Add Model Version.

The mapping model describes how to transform the data from one version to the next. Typically, we add a new mapping model to our project by selecting File > New File and then selecting iOS > Core Data > Mapping Model (**Figure 7.1**). Xcode's mapping model editor allows us to graphically set the transformations between the source and destination models.

Finally, you must migrate the existing data from your old model to your new one. Most of the time, you will perform automatic migration by calling addPersistent StoreWithType:configuration:URL:options:error: to open your persistent store. For the options: parameter, pass in an NSDictionary containing the NSMigrate PersistentStoresAutomaticallyOption key with an NSNumber object set to YES.

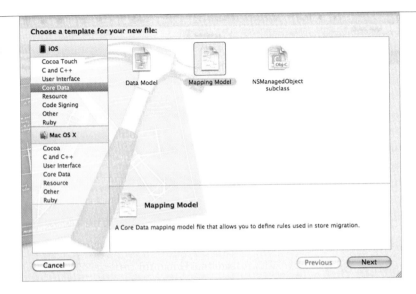

FIGURE 7.1 Adding a mapping model

```
NSDictionary *optionsDictionary =
[NSDictionary
 dictionaryWithObject:[NSNumber numberWithBool:YES]
 forKey:NSMigratePersistentStoresAutomatically];
if (![self.persistentStoreCoordinator
     addPersistentStoreWithType:NSSQLiteStoreType
     configuration:nil URL:storeURL
     options:optionsDictionary
     error:&error]) {
   NSLog(@"Unable to open persistent store at %@, %@: %@",
   storeURL, error, [error userInfo]);
   abort();
}
```

Not surprisingly, data migration gets quite complex. To help manage this, Core Data provides additional support for injecting custom code when detecting version skew and while performing the actual data migration. See Apple's Core Data Model Versioning and Data Migration Programming Guide for more information.

LIGHTWEIGHT MIGRATION

In the simplest cases, you may not need a mapping model. Core Data can often infer the differences between the source and destination models and automatically migrate your data. In particular, you can perform lightweight migration if you are only adding attributes to an existing entity or changing a non-optional attribute to an optional attribute. You can also change an optional attribute to a non-optional attribute as long as you provide a default value.

In this case, open your persistent store by calling `addPersistentStoreWith Type:configuration:URL:options:error:` and setting both the `NSMigrate PersistentStoresAutomaticallyOption` and the `NSInferMappingModel AutomaticallyOption` keys to YES.

Remember, not all changes require migration. You can change an attribute's default value or validation constraints without altering the existing stores. Additionally, you will want to test your data migration very carefully. You don't want to corrupt or lose your user's data. If you've ever updated an app only to have it erase all your data, you know exactly what I mean.

SUPPORT DATA

The model may also contain fetch requests and configurations. As noted, fetch requests let us request all the entities that match a given specification. While we often create our fetch requests at runtime, we may want to build complex or commonly used fetch requests directly into our model.

Xcode's predicate builder can be helpful when creating complex fetch requests—though the version included with Xcode 4 lacks many of the features found in previous versions. We can only select attributes in the left-hand side and constants in the right—no variables, keys, or nested compound predicates. Hopefully Apple will restore the full set of features in later releases.

Additionally, we cannot add a sort description using the graphic interface. This isn't a huge problem, though, since we can use the predicate builder to build the basic fetch request, and then we can add the sort descriptors at runtime, if necessary.

Configurations, on the other hand, represent the second type of support data. Technically, they are just arrays of entity descriptions. We access our configurations using `NSManagedObjectModel`'s `entitiesForConfiguration:` and setEntities:forConfiguration: methods. We can use these to define different subsets of our model. For example, a user logged in as an administrator may have access to a broader set of entities than someone logged in as a user.

Mostly, however, we use configurations when we want to split our model across several persistent data stores. In this case, we need to partition our model using configurations. Then we specify the correct configuration for each store as we add them to our persistent store coordinator. Core Data handles the rest.

MANAGED OBJECT CONTEXT

We now move from defining our data to actually managing it. The managed object context acts as a temporary scratch space. When you fetch objects from a persistent store, they are placed in the context. We can then manipulate them, change their properties, or even add or remove objects from the context. The managed object context monitors these changes, recording them and enabling undo/redo support. In addition, when we save these changes back to our persistent store, the context validates our objects, ensuring that everything remains in a valid state before committing the changes.

We can open more than one managed object context at a time. In fact, an object in our persistent store may be modified by multiple contexts simultaneously. By default, the context will attempt to merge these changes, causing an error if there are conflicts. We can further control the merge process by changing the merge policy or by observing NSManagedObjectContextObjectsDidChangeNotification notifications. Note that the system may use its own managed object contexts internally, so we want to make sure we specify known contexts when we register as an observer. Otherwise, we may receive notifications from these system-level sources.

Starting with iOS 5, we can create nested contexts, where each parent context may contain one or more child contexts. When connected this way, saving a child context merely pushes the changes up to the parent context. Data is not saved to the persistent store until the top-level context is saved. Fetch requests will pull data down through every context level, while objectWithID: will pull through the fewest number of contexts possible.

Nested contexts can greatly simplify a number of difficult problems, including performing asynchronous saves on a background thread, sharing unsaved changes between different contexts, and even simplifying background fetching.

For example, to implement asynchronous saves, we simply need to create two managed object contexts with a simple parent-child relationship. Our application makes all its changes to the child context. When it wants to save, we start by saving the child context on the main thread. This creates a snapshot of our data—pushing our changes up to the parent context. Then we save the parent context on a background thread. As we will see, UIManagedDocument uses this technique when auto-saving document data.

> **NOTE:** In previous Core Date project templates, Xcode's auto-generated code accessed the managed object context directly from the app delegate. With iOS 5, Apple highly recommends switching to a "pass the baton" approach, where the correct context is handed from object to object along the view controller hierarchy. This is especially true in any applications using multi-layer contexts.

MANAGED OBJECTS

All Core Data entities are instantiated as an NSManagedObject or one of its subclasses. Each managed object is associated with an entity description. This includes both the object's metadata and information about the managed object context where our object resides.

In many cases, we can simply use raw managed objects in our project. Each managed object will automatically generate both public and primitive accessors for all the modeled properties. For attributes and other to-one relationships, these follow the standard <key> and set<Key> naming conventions.

For to-many relationships, these accessors can be used to get and set the entire collection (as an NSSet or NSOrderedSet, depending on the type of to-many relationship). However, if we want to simply add or remove individual members, we can request a mutable set using the mutableSetValueForKey: or mutableOrdered SetValueForKey: method. We can then add or remove entities from this set—all changes will be made to the managed object context's object graph. We can also use the dynamic relationship accessors add<Key>Object: and remove<Key>Object: (insertObject:in<Key>AtIndex: and removeObjectFrom<Key>atIndex: for ordered to-many relationships).

`NSManagedObject` also creates primitive accessors. These take the form `primitive<Key>` and `setPrimitive<Key>:`. Unlike the public accessors, these do not trigger KVO notifications. We will typically use these primitive accessors when writing our own custom accessors. We will see some examples later.

While these auto-generated accessors are cool, they have a downside. Unfortunately, the compiler does not know about these methods, so they may generate warnings (and if you're following my advice, these warnings will be treated like errors, preventing your app from building successfully). There are a couple of ways around this. First, we can always use key-value coding to access data from raw managed objects. Alternatively, we could create a category on `NSManagedObject` that declares the properties. Finally, we could create a custom subclass for our entity.

Xcode 4 makes creating custom subclasses easy. Just select File > New > New File and select the iOS > Core Data > NSManagedObject subclass template. Xcode will automatically generate the properties for you and link your subclass to its entity in the managed object model.

Custom subclasses are particularly important when you need to implement custom accessors or validation methods, implement non-standard attributes, specify dependent keys, calculate derived values, or implement other custom logic. However, there are a few points you should keep in mind when subclassing `NSManagedObject`:

- Core Data relies on `NSManagedObject`'s implementation of these methods to function properly: `primitiveValueForKey:`, `setPrimitiveValue:forKey:`, `isEqual:`, `hash`, `superclass`, `class`, `self`, `zone`, `isProxy`, `isKindOfClass:`, `isMemberOfClass:`, `conformsToProtocol:`, `respondsToSelector:`, `managedObjectContext`, `entity`, `objectID`, `isInserted`, `isUpdated`, `isDeleted`, and `isFault`. You should never override any of these methods.

- You are discouraged from overriding the following methods: `description`, `initWithEntity:insertIntoManagedObjectContext:`, `valueForKey:`, and `setValue:forKeyPath:`. If they are not handled properly, they can cause unexpected results.

- You should invoke the superclass's implementation before executing your own code for the following methods: `awakeFromInsert`, `awakeFromFetch`, and validation methods like `validateForUpdate:`.

- You can override the `awakeFromInsert` and `awakeFromFetch` methods to perform any custom initialization when a new object is created or when an object is loaded from the persistent store, respectively.

- You should not provide instance variables for any properties in the model. Core Data will automatically manage the life cycles of these objects.

- The declaration for any object properties should use (`nonatomic, retain`). In iOS 5, we can declare scalar properties for any of our scalar values; these properties should be declared using (`nonatomic`). In both cases, we should use the `@dynamic` property implementation directive for all of these. `NSManaged Object` will create the correct accessors based on our declaration.

- If you create custom accessors for any modeled properties, be sure to manually trigger KVO access and change notifications by calling `willAccess ValueForKey:`, `didAccessValueForKey:`, `willChangeValueForKey:`, `did ChangeValueForKey:`, `willChangeValueForKey:withSetMutation:using Objects:`, and `didChangeValueForKey:withSetMutation:usingObjects:`, as appropriate. Core Data disables automatic KVO notification for any modeled properties.

> **NOTE:** Even though we're using ARC, we can use (`nonatomic, retain`) to declare the properties generated by our managed object context. Actually, (`strong, nonatomic`) also works, but Xcode will use (`nonatomic, retain`) in its auto-generated code. Remember, Core Data manages the object's life cycle. We don't need to think too hard about what it's doing behind the scenes.

We often create custom subclasses when we want to implement non-standard attributes. There are two ways of doing this. The first is to set the attribute's type to transformable and then assign an `NSValueTransformer` that can convert the class to and from an `NSData` object. The vast majority of the time, we can simply use the default transformer—just make sure the properties adopt the `NSCoding` protocol. Everything will just work.

If we need more control, we can create custom accessors. Typically, we declare two attributes. One is the non-standard attribute. We declare this as transient with an undefined type. The other attribute must be a standard, concrete type—this will hold the actual data that is saved to our persistent store. Then we write our accessor methods to convert our data back and forth between the two attributes.

Let's say we want to add a non-standard NSTimeZone attribute to our entity. NSTimeZone adopts the NSCoding protocol, so the simplest approach is to just declare it as a transformable attribute. We can then declare the property in our custom subclass, as shown here:

```
@property (nonatomic, retain) NSTimeZone* timeZone;
```

Then, in the @implementation block, declare the property as dynamic. This tells the compiler that the accessors' implementations will be provided at runtime (if not earlier). Remember, NSManagedObject automatically creates these accessors for us.

```
@dynamic timeZone;
```

That's it. Core Data will automatically handle the conversion to and from an NSData object.

Next, let's look at implementing the same non-standard attribute using custom accessors. This time add both a transient, undefined timeZone attribute and a string timeZoneName attribute. In our NSManagedObject subclass's @interface, declare the timeZone property as shown in the previous example. However, in the implementation file, start by declaring two private properties:

```
@interface MyManagedObject()
@property (nonatomic, retain) NSString * timeZoneName;
@property (nonatomic, retain) NSTimeZone* primitiveTimeZone;
@end
```

Then, in the implementation block, declare the two private properties as dynamic:

```
@dynamic timeZoneName;
@dynamic primitiveTimeZone;
```

Since we will be implementing our own custom accessors for the timeZone property, we don't need to call either the @dynamic directive or the @synthesize directive. Instead, just implement the methods as shown here:

```objc
- (NSTimeZone*)timeZone {
    // Get transient value.
    [self willAccessValueForKey:@"timeZone"];
    NSTimeZone* timeZone = self.primitiveTimeZone;
    // If we have no transient value,
    // try to generate it from the persistent value.
    if (timeZone == nil) {
        // Get the persistent value.
        NSString* name = self.timeZoneName;
        if (name != nil) {
            timeZone = [NSTimeZone timeZoneWithName:name];
            // Set the transient value.
            self.primitiveTimeZone = timeZone;
        }
    }
    [self didAccessValueForKey:@"timeZone"];
    return timeZone;
}
- (void)setTimeZone:(NSTimeZone *)timeZone {
    // Set transient value.
    [self willChangeValueForKey:@"timeZone"];
    self.primitiveTimeZone = timeZone;
    // Set persistent value.
    self.timeZoneName = [timeZone name];
    [self didChangeValueForKey:@"timeZone"];
}
```

The getter simply calls the auto-generated `primitiveTimeZone` method to access our transient attribute's current value. Remember, unlike the other attributes, `timeZone` is transient. Its value is not loaded from the persistent store. If we haven't programmatically set it, its value defaults to `nil`. In this case, we try to create a new `NSTimeZone` object using the value stored in our private `timeZoneName` attribute. We then set the `timeZone`'s value and return that value. The next time we call `timeZone`, we will be able to pull the value directly from the `timeZone` attribute.

The setter is even simpler. Here, we first set our `timeZone` attribute, and then we set the underlying `timeZoneName` attribute. Remember, in both accessors we need to send out the proper KVO notifications.

These are probably the simplest implementations, but there are other possibilities. You could pre-calculate the `timeZone` attribute during the `awakeFromFetch` method, or you could delay setting the `timeZoneName` attribute until the `willSave` method is called. Both of these approaches are shown in the "Non-Standard Persistent Attributes" section of Apple's Core Data Programming Guide.

NOTE: Although we declared the `timeZoneName` attribute as private in our sample `NSManagedObject` subclass, this is not necessarily required. We could declare a public read-only property for `timeZoneName`. We could even declare it as publicly read/writeable—however, this complicates things. We would need to make sure our `timeZone` value is updated whenever the `timeZoneName` value is changed. We would also need to make sure our implementation is KVO compliant by declaring `timeZone` as a dependent key.

A hybrid approach is sometimes useful when trying to save non-object values. This is especially true for structures that are supported by the `NSValue` class (e.g., `CGPoint`, `CGRect`, and `CGSize`). Here, you simply define the attribute as a transformable type and then write custom accessors to convert the structs to and from an `NSValue` object.

Before iOS 5, we had to use a similar approach to simplify access to scalar values (`floats`, `ints`, and `BOOLs`). This is even easier: You set the attribute to the correct numeric type and then write custom accessors to convert your values to and from `NSNumber`.

However, while these approaches can simplify the interface, they are not generally recommended. Core Data tries to optimize its auto-generated accessors. The performance advantages gained by letting Core Data manage its own data usually outweigh any ease of use that is granted by dealing directly with the structs and scalar values. This is especially true in data-intensive applications.

FETCH REQUESTS

We access our managed objects using `NSFetchRequest`. At a minimum, our fetch request needs an entity description. Traditionally, this involved accessing the entity descriptions from our modeled object contexts using the `entityForName:inManaged ObjectContext:` and then instantiating our `NSFetchRequest` object. With iOS 5, we can use the `fetchRequestWithEntityName:` convenience method to create a new fetch request with a single method call. Once we have our fetch request, we call the `executeFetchRequest:error:`, which returns an array containing all instances of the named entity, including any sub-entities.

The fetch will return objects based on their state in the managed object context—even if these changes have not yet been saved. This means a fetch will return new objects added to the context and will not return any objects deleted from the context. Likewise, the system will evaluate predicates based on the object's in-memory state—not its saved state. Of course, if we haven't yet loaded the objects into managed object context, then the fetch request loads them from their persistent store (or from the parent context, if it has one).

We have a lot of control over which objects are returned and how they are organized. By adding an `NSPredicate` to our fetch request, we can set constraints on our request. Our fetch request will return only those entities that match our predicate. An array of `NSSortDescriptors` defines the order in which our objects are returned.

Predicates are a rich and complex topic. Previous versions of Xcode included a robust predicate editor to help visually design complex predicates. Unfortunately, the predicate builder in Xcode 4 is severely limited by comparison. We can only use it for fetch requests, not fetched properties, and we can only use it to create a small subset of relatively simple predicates. This means that (at least for the time being) if you want to make any moderately complex fetch requests, you need to learn how to write your own predicate expressions.

Basically, a predicate is a logical operator. When the predicate is evaluated on an object, it performs the specified comparison and then returns YES or NO.

We can build our `NSPredicate` object using a combination of `NSComparison Predicate`, `NSCompoundPredicate`, and `NSExpression` objects; however, it's usually easier to create our predicate using a formatting string. The NSPredicate class then parses this string and builds a predicate to match.

The predicate parser is whitespace insensitive. It is also case insensitive when it comes to keywords, and it supports nested parenthetical expressions. The simplest predicates have three parts: the left expression, a comparison, and the right expression.

These expressions can be constants, key paths, or variables. Most of the time, we will compare one of the object's key paths against a constant. String constants can be typed directly into the formatting string, but they must be surrounded by double quotes. Most of the other values (e.g., NSDate or NSNumber) are passed in using the %@ formatting argument. We can even pass in string constants using %@, and the parser will automatically quote them for us.

The comparison includes most of what we expect: ==, <, >, <=, >=, and !=. The parser often understands common variations for these. For example, the following comparisons are also valid: =, =<, =>, and <>. The parser also adds the BETWEEN comparison—whose right-hand side must be a two-value array.

For strings, we have the BEGINSWITH, CONTAINS, ENDSWITH, LIKE, and MATCHES comparisons. Most of these should be relatively straightforward. LIKE simply checks to see if the left-hand string is equal to the right-hand string. However, it supports the ? and * wildcards for matching a single character or zero or more characters. MATCHES, on the other hand, treats the right-hand value as a regular expression. Appending [cd] to the end of the comparison makes it case and diacritic insensitive.

A few sample predicates are shown below:

```
// Determines if the object's lastName attribute equals @"Jones".
[NSPredicate predicateWithFormat:@"lastName LIKE 'Jones'"];
// Determines if the object's pubDate occurred before
// the given targetDate.
[NSPredicate predicateWithFormat:@"pubDate < %@", targetDate];
// Determines if the person is in our target demographics.
[NSPredicate predicateWithFormat:@"age BETWEEN %@",
    [NSArray arrayWithObjects: [NSNumber numberWithInt:18],
                               [NSNumber numberWithInt:34], nil]];
```

Note that we can also include literal array constants by placing a comma-separated list of values inside curly braces. This means that the target demographics example could be simplified as shown:

```
// Determines if the person is in our target demographics.
[NSPredicate predicateWithFormat:@"age BETWEEN {%@, %@}",
    [NSNumber numberWithInt:18], [NSNumber numberWithInt:34]];
```

The key paths can even include to-many relationships. Often we will prefix these expressions with one of the aggregate operators: ANY, ALL, or NONE, as shown:

```
// The target has at least one child under 18.
[NSPredicate predicateWithFormat:@"ANY children.age < %@",
    [NSNumber numberWithInt:18]];
// All the target's children are under 18.
[NSPredicate predicateWithFormat:@"ALL children.age < %@",
    [NSNumber numberWithInt:18]];
// None of the target's children are under 18.
[NSPredicate predicateWithFormat:@"NONE children.age < %@",
    [NSNumber numberWithInt:18]];
```

We can also check the size of the to-many relationship by appending [size] to the key path.

```
// Determines if the target has at least 3 children.
[NSPredicate predicateWithFormat:@"children[size] < 3"];
```

Finally, we can combine simple comparisons using AND, OR, or NOT.

```
// Determines if the target has at least 3 adult children.
[NSPredicate predicateWithFormat:
    @"(children[size] < 3) AND (NONE children.age < %@)",
    [NSNumber numberWithInt:18]];
```

These formatting strings allow us to specify a wide range of predicates in a relatively compact format. Unfortunately, it's very easy to accidentally misspell a key path or inadvertently pass in the wrong type of object. These mistakes will only show up as runtime errors. It is, therefore, very important to test all your predicates.

Additionally, not all data sources support all of NSPredicate's features. This is particularly important for Core Data, since the predicate's behavior can change when we switch from one type of persistent store to another. The behavior can also vary depending on whether we use it in a fetch request or to filter the returned NSArray. We'll talk about these differences more in the "Persistent Stores" section, later in this chapter.

OK, this should be enough to get you started. For more information, check out Apple's Predicate Programming Guide. It covers a number of advanced topics, like programmatically creating predicates, creating predicate templates with variables, and dynamically setting key paths. It also includes a full description of the syntax for predicate format strings.

NOTE: Each fetch request requires a round trip to the persistent store. Therefore, if you need to get a subset of objects, it is faster to filter an existing array than to perform a new fetch request. Additionally, you cannot perform fetch requests using predicates based on transient attributes, since these attributes are ignored by the persistent store. You can, however, use these attributes when filtering arrays of objects in memory.

Finally, iOS provides additional support for Core Data-driven table views using the NSFetchedResultsController class. This class analyzes the results of a fetch request (including any predicate or sorting descriptors) and automatically maps the returned objects to their corresponding index paths. You can even specify a key path that will be used to partition the results into sections.

In addition, the NSFetchedResultsController monitors changes to the objects in its managed object context and reports these changes to its delegate. The controller also caches its results, improving performance if the table is re-displayed.

We will get a chance to use an NSFetchedResultsController when we revise Health Beat's history view (see "Updating the View Controllers," later in this chapter).

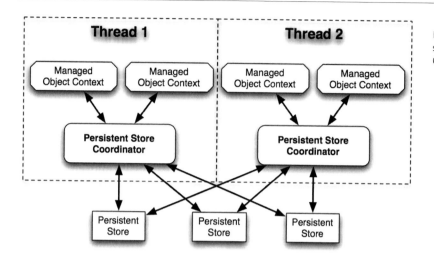

FIGURE 7.2 The persistent store coordinator's role in the Core Data stack

PERSISTENT STORE COORDINATOR

Each managed object context has a single persistent store coordinator. This coordinator sits between the context and the stores. Each managed object context can have one and only one persistent store coordinator. The coordinator, however, can support more than one context. It can also connect to any number of persistent stores (**Figure 7.2**).

The persistent store coordinator primarily acts as a façade for a number of stores. We could have just a single persistent store, or we could have a hundred. As far as the managed object context is concerned, it doesn't matter. The persistent store coordinator provides a single, unified interface, presenting the union of all the data in all the provided stores.

The persistent store coordinator also plays an important role in concurrent application, by serializing access to the underlying data. By default, if you want to access data in multiple threads, then each thread should have its own persistent store coordinator (and by extension, its own managed object context).

This is also referred to as thread confinement concurrency. With iOS 5, we have two additional concurrency options: private queue concurrency and main queue concurrency. These options often remove the need to create multiple managed object contexts—greatly simplifying our code.

Private queue concurrency uses a private queue to manage access to the managed object context. Whenever we want to use our context, we call `performBlock:` or `performBlockAndWait:`. We can then access the managed object context normally within the provided block.

Main queue concurrency works similarly to private queue concurrency, except the managed object context is created on the main thread. All our code on the main thread can access the context normally. Any code on any other thread must use `performBlock:` or `performBlockAndWait:` to access the context. This concurrency model is highly recommended when interacting with the user interface, since most UI work must be done on the main thread.

When creating hierarchies of managed object contexts, all parent contexts must use either private queue or main queue concurrency. The final child contexts can use any concurrency model.

PERSISTENT STORES

Persistent stores act as a wrapper for a data source (usually a file saved to disk). The store is responsible for mapping objects in the managed object context to the data in the data source—both saving objects to disk and instantiating objects from disk. iOS supports three types of persistent stores: binary, in-memory, and SQLite.

All three stores are fast, especially when compared to plists or other XML-based storage. The binary format stores the object graph in a single binary file. As a result, the persistent store must load the whole object graph into memory at once. In most cases, however, this produces the smallest file size of any data store. Binary stores also write out their data as an atomic action—either the entire file will be written or nothing will be written. You will never have corrupted data from a half-written file.

The in-memory store acts more like a virtual scratch space. It does not store the objects to disk; rather it keeps them in active memory. Objects placed into an in-memory store benefit from Core Data features like validation, change tracking, and undo support; however, you would have to write additional code to load and save these objects outside Core Data.

Most of the time we will use the SQLite persistent stores. This has a significant advantage over the other stores: We do not need to load the entire object graph into memory. We only load the objects we actually intend to use.

By default, a fetch request to an SQLite-based store only instantiates the objects it returns. All the relationships for those objects are represented by faults. Basically, a fault is a placeholder for an object or array. If you access the fault, it fires, and Core Data uses lazy initialization to instantiate an actual copy of the object. Most of the time this occurs transparently behind the scenes. The NSFetchRequest class includes a number of methods to manage whether the request returns faults or objects, how many objects it returns, and whether any of the objects' relationships are also pre-fetched.

While faults help us save memory by letting us limit the number of objects we need to load, firing faults can be inefficient, particularly if you fire a number of faults in series. If you know you're going to need a large number of faulted objects, it may be better to batch fire all the faults or pre-fetch all the objects.

To batch fire a number of faults, you just need to create a fetch request to load those objects. Of course, this means that all your faults must be of the same entity type. Simply build an array containing the faulted relationships, and then build a predicate using the IN operator as shown here:

```
NSArray* faults =
    [NSArray arrayWithObjects: fault1, fault2, fault3, … , nil];
NSPredicate* predicate =
    [NSPredicate predicateWithFormat:@"self IN %@", faults];
```

Alternatively, you can use NSFetchRequest's setRelationshipKeyPathsFor Prefetching: method. This lets you set an array of key paths. All the relationships represented by those key paths are also instantiated as full objects when the fetch is executed. This lets us pre-fetch objects that we know we are going to need.

We have to be careful with this, however. It is easy to accidentally grab more memory than we originally intended. As always, it's a good idea to profile our code. Looking at actual performance numbers will help us find the right balance between runtime performance and memory usage.

We can also reduce memory overhead by re-faulting individual objects. To do this, call the managed object context's refreshObject:mergeChanges: method. If the mergeChanges: flag is set to NO, then the object is converted back into a fault and all pending changes are lost. In addition, all of the object's relationships are released—possibly trimming them from the in-memory object graph as well.

Faulting is just one of many differences between SQLite and other stores. With non-SQLite stores (and when working with NSArrays or other collections), the system executes both predicates and search descriptors in Objective-C. This means we have full access to NSStrings comparison methods. We can even incorporate our own Objective-C code (by providing a custom selector or NSComparator block for our sort descriptor, or by creating a predicate using the predicateWithBlock: method).

When using SQLite stores, however, the predicates and sort descriptors are translated into SQL and executed in the database. We cannot use predicates or sort descriptors that incorporate custom Objective-C code. SQLite only supports the following NSString sort selectors: compare:, caseInsensitiveCompare:, localized Compare:, localizedCaseInsensitiveCompare:, and localizedStandardCompare:. Finally, key paths in predicates can only include a single to-many relationship. But you can string together any number of to-one relationships and attributes with the to-many relationship (**Table 7.2**).

TABLE 7.2 Sample Key Path Patterns

VALID	INVALID
<to_one>.<to_one>.<to_many>	<to_many>.<to_one>.<to_many>
<to_one>.<to_many>.<to_one>	<to_many>.<to_many>.<to_one>
<to_many>.<to_one>.<to_one>	<to_one>.<to_many>.<to_many>
<to_one>.<to_one>.<to_one>	<to_many>.<to_many>.<to_many>

Remember that if you need additional features, you can always perform a more general fetch request and then execute the custom sorting and filtering on the resulting array. This wastes memory, but sometimes you just gotta do what you gotta do.

NOTE: iOS 5 also allows the creation of custom incremental stores, letting us connect Core Data to any arbitrary data storage. This involves creating a subclass of the NSIncrementalStore abstract class, overriding a number of methods to support data access. This lets us connect Core Data to the data storage technology of our choice. It is also the preferred way to connect Core Data to a Web service.

USING **SQLite STORES** TO **REDUCE MEMORY USAGE**

Remember that for SQLite stores, predicates and sort descriptors are translated into SQL and executed in the database. While this can be a bit of a pain, it also means we can filter and sort based on relationships, but those relationships are still returned as faults. We never have to instantiate the corresponding managed objects into memory.

If we wanted to perform the same sorting or filtering in Objective-C, we would need to instantiate all those relationships as well—and then execute the sort descriptors and predicates. This is just one of the ways an SQLite-based store helps improve performance and reduce your application's memory footprint.

DATA PROTECTION

For iOS 5 applications, the persistent stores now encrypt the data on disk. The persistent stores support a range of encryption options:

- NSFileProtectionNone turns off encryption.

- NSFileProtectionComplete provides the tightest security. The files can only be accessed after the device is authenticated and as long as the device is unlocked. Unfortunately, this can prevent your app from accessing the data while operating in the background.

- NSFileProtectionCompleteUnlessOpen prevents access to files unless the device is authenticated and unlocked. Your application can continue to access any open files while locked; however, you cannot open new files.

- NSFileProtectionCompleteUntilFirstUserAuthentication prevents access to files while the device is booting and until the user authenticates with their password. However, once the user authenticates, the files remain accessible, even if the device is later locked.

Core Data will use NSFileProtectionCompleteUntilFirstUserAuthentication by default. We can change the protection level by assigning a value to the NSPersistent StoreFileProtectionKey when configuring our persistent store.

iCLOUD SUPPORT

Core Data provides easy integration with iCloud. The iCloud support focuses on managing many of the details that were dealt with in Chapter 6. If you're using a single centralized Core Data store, then setup is simple: Set a couple of preferences when setting up the persistent store, then listen for updates. Everything else is handled automatically. There's no need to use NSMetadataQuery to search for the file. We no longer need to worry about merging conflicts. We don't even need to tell the application how to save and load our data. All of that is handled for us automatically.

When using Core Data with SQLite stores, each application manages its own local database, and the database is never actually uploaded into iCloud storage. Instead, each database saves transaction log files and uploads the log files to iCloud. Other copies of the application can then identify and download these log files, using them to update the local database. This also means the file is only uploading deltas—the differences between the files on a per-entry basis. This greatly minimizes the amount of data that Core Data transmits between the app and iCloud.

iCloud also uses three-way merges to automatically resolve conflicts on a per-entry basis. Here, the system compares both of the conflicting copies with the original. This allows for a much more accurate and autonomous merging.

For example, look at the two-way merge we implemented in Chapter 6. Imagine a case where a WeightEntry instance is present in version A, but missing from version B. Our two-way merge had no way of telling whether this entry had been added to A or deleted from B. So, we erred on the side of caution, always choosing to keep the mismatched entry.

A three-way merge, on the other hand, would be able to positively identify whether the entry had been added or deleted and would be able to take the appropriate action when merging. If it had been added to A, it should be included in the merged version. If it had been deleted from B, it should be removed.

To set up a centralized Core Data store, we simply set the NSPersistentStore UbiquitousContentNameKey and NSPersistentStoreUbiquitousContentURLKey keys in the options dictionary that we pass to addPersistentStoreWithType: configuration:URL:options:error: when creating our persistent store. We then register for the NSPersistentStoreDidImportUbiquitousContent ChangesNotification (probably the longest constant name in Objective-C history), and in the notification block, we call the managed object context's `mergeChanges FromContextDidSaveNotification:`. That's it. Core Data handles the rest.

Of course, if we want to have a separate Core Data store for each document, things get a little more complicated—especially when opening a saved document. We will need to use `NSMetadataQuery` to search for the `DocumentMetadata.plist` file inside our Core Data package. Then, we'll need to open this and extract the `NSPersistentStoreUbiquitousContentURLKey` for that store. With this in hand, we can instantiate our local copy of the store. See the "iCloud Storage" section of the iOS App Programming Guide for all the details.

The transaction logs are stored in a directory named `<NSPersistentStore UbiquitousContentNameKey>/<NSPersistentStoreUbiquitousContentKeyName>`. If we delete our data file or remove it from iCloud, we must also make sure we delete the transaction logs by using a coordinated write block.

UIMANAGEDDOCUMENT

`UIManagedDocument` is a concrete subclass of `UIDocument` that is specifically designed for managing Core Data. `UIManagedDocument` greatly simplifies the setup of a Core Data model. It will automatically merge all model objects in the application bundle and then use the combined model to create an SQLite-based persistent store attached to a two-layer managed object context. The two-level context helps support asynchronous background saves.

The child layer uses main queue concurrency, letting us interact with this context directly on the main thread. `UIManagedDocument` monitors changes made to this context and automatically saves the changes at a convenient point during the application's run cycle.

When it decides to save changes, it starts by making a snapshot of the changes. This is easily accomplished by saving the child context. This will push the current batch of changes up to the parent context. Then, it saves the parent context on a private background queue. This actually saves the changes to disk. During this step, it also logs the changes to the iCloud storage container, letting them sync up with the cloud.

Much of the time, we can use `UIManagedDocument` without further subclassing. We simply instantiate a new `UIManagedDocument` object, then set the options for the persistent store. Finally, we call `openWithCompletionHandler:` to open an existing document, or we call `saveToURL:forSaveOperation:completionHandler:` to create a new document.

We can subclass UIManagedDocument to modify its default behaviors. For example, we can change the name of the persistent store in our document package. We can change the type of persistent store or modify how the document models or stores are created. We can even enable support for saving and loading data from outside Core Data. For more information, check out the UIManagedDocument Class Reference.

iCLOUD LIMITATIONS

Now for the bad news. Currently, using Core Data on iCloud imposes the following restrictions:

- No support for ordered relationships.

- We cannot use mapping models to migrate our schema. Lightweight migration is still OK.

- When creating a new store, we should not populate it with a pre-existing database file. If we need to set up some initial data, we should either programmatically create the data in code or use NSPersistentStoreCoordinator's migratePersistentStore:toURL:options:withType:error: to load the data from an existing file.

For more information, be sure to look over the latest release notes.

CORE DATA PERFORMANCE

Core Data is a mature, efficient object graph management framework. Its classes have been highly optimized. For example, NSManagedObject instances use reflection to examine their internal data. The managed object then leverages this information to optimize access to this data. Therefore, accessing values from an NSManaged Object is often faster than comparable accessors on generic Objective-C objects.

SQLite-based persistent stores help us minimize the number of objects held in active memory, letting us fetch and hold only the objects we need. This is especially important for iOS applications, since memory management remains one of our key concerns.

Still, there are some key points to remember to avoid poor performance.

FETCH REQUESTS

Fetch requests are expensive. They start by accessing the data from the persistent store. Then they merge this data with the existing data in the managed object context. Most of the time, we want to reduce the total number of fetches. In general, this means combining groups of smaller fetches into a single larger fetch.

However, there are times when we want to quickly return a small subset of the data and then fill in the rest while the system is idle. We might do this, for example, when filling in a table view.

We can restrict the number of objects loaded into memory by setting either `setFetchLimit:` or `setFetchBatchSize:`. In both cases, the full fetch is calculated, and all the other objects are returned as faults. When calling `setFetchLimit:`, we can manually load in the remaining objects by calling `setFetchOffset:` and then setting the fetch limit to 0. A second fetch will then grab the remaining objects.

Setting the batch size, on the other hand, returns a proxy array that automatically faults new batches when needed.

FAULTING

When a fault fires, it acts like a fetch request, except only a single object is returned. This becomes very expensive if we accidentally iterate over an array of faults, firing each one individually. Instead, we need to batch fault or pre-fetch our data to reduce the total number of trips to the persistent store (see "Persistent Stores" for more information).

Note that we can safely call the following methods on a fault without causing it to fire: `isEqual:`, `hash`, `superclass`, `class`, `self`, `zone`, `isProxy`, `isKindOfClass:`, `isMember OfClass:`, `conformsToProtocol:`, `respondsToSelector:`, `description`, `managed ObjectContext`, `entity`, `objectID`, `isInserted`, `isUpdated`, `isDeleted`, and `isFault`.

Among other things, this means we can freely store faults into collections. However, we must treat these collections carefully. It is easy to accidentally trigger faults when calling the collection's methods. Anything that calls `valueForKey:` on the collection's objects will trigger faults—most likely triggering all the faults in the entire array.

REDUCING MEMORY OVERHEAD

In general, unless you have a very good reason to do otherwise, you should always use an SQLite-based store. You should also avoid loading more objects into memory than is absolutely necessary. I also recommend saving changes as you go—rather than letting unsaved changes accumulate in the managed object context. This also helps free up memory and can help you avoid problems with overly long save times.

By default, Core Data only retains objects that have unsaved changes. However, managed objects do retain each other through relationships. This can easily create retain cycles, which will prevent objects from being released. If you find that you are accumulating large numbers of objects in memory, you can break these cycles by re-faulting the objects.

We can manually refault objects by calling the context's `refreshObject: mergeChanges:` method. We can also clear the entire managed object context by calling its `reset` method.

NOTE: Calling `reset` on the managed object context will invalidate any objects currently in the context. Be sure to dispose of all references you have to these objects before resetting. Accidentally holding onto these references will produce dangling pointers, leading to errors that are bizarre, intermittent, and otherwise difficult to debug.

LARGE DATA OBJECTS

Adding large binary objects (i.e., images, sounds, videos, etc.) to a persistent store can severely affect performance. Here we get into an area that's more art than science. How large is large? Well, the answer really depends on how your application uses the data. If you're only loading one or two objects into memory at a time, then large attributes may not be a problem. If you're loading hundreds or thousands— you really need to think things through.

In general there are three approaches. You can store the object directly in the data as an attribute. This is usually only recommended for small binary objects.

Next, you can create a separate entity for the data and refer to it using a to-one relationship. This can be particularly helpful if the binary data isn't always used. When your object is fetched, the to-one relationship will be a fault. You won't load the binary data unless you actually need it. This is recommended for modestly sized data objects.

Finally, you can store the data object directly in the device's file system and save the path in the database. You then manually load the data when necessary. This is recommended for the largest objects.

As a rule of thumb, if your object is measured in kilobytes, it's probably modest; if it's measured in megabytes, it's large. However, this is an area where you definitely want performance testing. Just remember, the end users often use applications in unexpected ways. Don't be surprised when they add 100,000 entities to the persistent store or try to load a 10 MB text file. Try to test these extremes, if possible.

Fortunately, iOS 5 simplifies all this. Binary data attributes now have an Allows External Storage checkbox. Simply select this when configuring the attribute. The system will heuristically decide whether to store your binary data directly in the database or to simply store a URL and load the file as needed. All of this is transparently handled behind the scenes. There is, however, one small restriction: Once external storage is enabled, we cannot use the binary data in our fetch request's predicate.

TOOLS

Performance testing is covered in more detail in Bonus Chapter B, which can be found at the book's website: http://www.freelancemadscience.com/book. However, it's worth noting that Instruments has a number of tools to help troubleshoot Core Data performance issues. These include instruments to track Core Data fetches, saves, faults, and cache misses. You will want to use these in conjunction with the regular allocations, leaks, and time profile when testing your application.

As always, you should focus on getting the application working properly first and then try to optimize the code based on actual performance data. Premature optimization often wastes your time without producing any tangible results.

CONVERTING **HEALTH BEAT**

Throughout the rest of this chapter, we will modify our Health Beat application so that it uses Core Data. Let's start by gutting our old model. Open up Health Beat and delete both WeightHistory.h and WeightHistory.m. We can also delete NSMutableArray+Union.h and NSMutableArray+Union.m.

Next, rename our WeightEntry class. Open WeightEntry.m, right-click the class name, and select Refactor > Rename. Set the new name to OldWeightEntry, and follow the prompts to accept the changes. Note that you'll still have to change the WeightEntry.m filename to OldWeightEntry.m once we are done. The header file, however, is modified automatically.

Finally, add the Core Data framework to our project. Click the project icon, and make sure the Health Beat target is selected. In the Build Phases tab, add the CoreData.framework in the Link Binary with Libraries listing.

We still need to remove the references to WeightHistory and WeightEntry in our view controllers; however, much of the time we'll simply be replacing the old references with new ones. So let's start by setting up Core Data. Then we can fix everything else in a single step.

CREATING UIMANAGEDDOCUMENT

First, open TabBarController.h and delete both the WeightHistory forward declaration and the property. In the implementation file, delete the line to import WeightHistory and the line to @synthesize our property. Then delete everything in viewDidLoad except the call to super. That gives us a fresh palette to work on.

Now, create a property to hold our document. In TabBarController.h, start by importing the Core Data framework.

```
#import <CoreData/CoreData.h>
```

Next, add the following declaration.

```
@property (strong, nonatomic) UIManagedDocument* document;
```

And, in the implementation file, synthesize it.

```
@synthesize document = _document;
```

Now, scroll back down to the `viewDidLoad` method. We will create our document here. Let's take it in steps.

```
- (void)viewDidLoad {
    [super viewDidLoad];
    // Override point for customization after application launch.
    NSFileManager* fileManager = [NSFileManager defaultManager];
    NSURL* ubiquitousURL =
    [fileManager URLForUbiquityContainerIdentifier:nil];
```

The first few lines simply get a reference to the default file manager and then look up the URL for our iCloud storage container. Remember, this will return nil if iCloud is unavailable. Additionally, this method also extends our sandbox to include the iCloud container—letting us call other iCloud methods.

```
    NSDictionary *options;
    if (ubiquitousURL != nil) {
        options = [NSDictionary dictionaryWithObjectsAndKeys:
            [NSNumber numberWithBool:YES],
            NSMigratePersistentStoresAutomaticallyOption,
            [NSNumber numberWithBool:YES],
            NSInferMappingModelAutomaticallyOption,
            @"com.freelancemadscience.Health_Beat.history",
            NSPersistentStoreUbiquitousContentNameKey,
            ubiquitousURL,
            NSPersistentStoreUbiquitousContentURLKey, nil];
    } else {
        // Create options for local sandbox storage only.
        options = [NSDictionary dictionaryWithObjectsAndKeys:
            [NSNumber numberWithBool:YES],
            Converting Health Beat 401
```

```
        NSMigratePersistentStoresAutomaticallyOption,
        [NSNumber numberWithBool:YES],
        NSInferMappingModelAutomaticallyOption, nil];
    }
```

Here, we create an option dictionary. These are the options that UIManaged
Document will pass to addPersistentStoreWithType:configuration:URL:options:
error: when it adds the SQLite persistent store to its persistent store coordinator.

In both cases, we enable both automatic and lightweight migration. If iCloud
is available, we also set the options needed to enable automatic iCloud support.
NSPersistentStoreUbiquitousContentNameKey sets the content's name. This
name is used to uniquely identify our store across all of the user's different devices,
ensuring the application can find and sync its updates. Not surprisingly, all our
stores must have unique names. Here we use an inverted domain name, followed
by the app-specific label Health_Beat.history.

We also set the NSPersistentStoreUbiquitousContentURLKey. This key should
contain the URL to a directory inside one of our iCloud storage containers. We
could place this inside the Documents directory—but then each individual transaction log would show up in our documents list. We really don't want to let the
user delete just one or two of these—that could leave our database in a bad state.
Instead, we are just using the URL for our iCloud container. Our transaction logs
will be saved in the com.freelancemadscience.Health_Beat.history directory
inside the container.

According to the documentation, Core Data should automatically set the
NSPersistentStoreUbiquitousContentURLKey key for us. However, I've had trouble
with it generating URLs into a different container than the one defined in my
entitlements. It's probably easiest to just set it with a known good value.

```
    NSURL* localURL = [fileManager URLForDirectory:
                NSDocumentDirectory
                inDomain:NSUserDomainMask
                appropriateForURL:nil
                create:NO
```

```
                    error:nil];
    NSURL* localCoreDataURL =
    [localURL URLByAppendingPathComponent:@"MyData"];
    // Now Create our document.
    self.document =
    [[UIManagedDocument alloc] initWithFileURL:localCoreDataURL];
    self.document.persistentStoreOptions = options;
```

Next, we create a URL for our SQLite database inside the local sandbox. We instantiate our document using that URL and then set the persistent store options. Again, the only differences between a local document and an iCloud-synced document are the persistent store options.

```
    if ([fileManager fileExistsAtPath:[localCoreDataURL path]]) {
        [self.document openWithCompletionHandler: ^(BOOL success) {
            [self passDocumentToSubViewControllers];
        }];
    } else {
        // Clean up the container.
        NSFileCoordinator* coordinator =
        [[NSFileCoordinator alloc] initWithFilePresenter:nil];
        [coordinator
         coordinateWritingItemAtURL:ubiquitousURL
         options:NSFileCoordinatorWritingForDeleting
         error:nil
         byAccessor:^(NSURL *newURL) {
            [[NSFileManager defaultManager]
             removeItemAtURL:newURL error:nil];
        }];
```

```
[self.document
  saveToURL:localCoreDataURL
  forSaveOperation:UIDocumentSaveForCreating
  completionHandler:^(BOOL success) {
      [self passDocumentToSubViewControllers];
  }];
  }
}
```

Finally, if the file exists, we open it. Otherwise, we create a new file by calling `save`
`ToURL:forSaveOperation:completionHandler:`. In both cases, we call `passDocument`
`ToSubViewControllers` in the completion handler to pass our document along to
our other view controllers.

Note that, before creating a new document, we clear out the container. We need
this code to work around a fairly serious problem.

Turns out, if the user goes into their iCloud settings and deletes this document, it will automatically revert to a local document. The devices won't sync their
updates to iCloud ever again. However, we still have our transaction logs in the
iCloud container. If the user removes the app from the device, then reinstalls it, it
will go into an invalid state. The app will try to load the transaction data but won't
be able to, and the document will fail to open. By clearing the container before we
create a new document, we prevent this problem.

NOTE: Alternatively, we can use `NSMetadataQuery` to confirm the document's
presence in the cloud. If the document isn't found, we clear the iCloud
storage and ask the user if they want upload it again. Additionally, the
`UIManagedDocument` creates a directory for our logs. `NSMetadataQuery`
cannot search for directories. Instead, we search for the package's
`DocumentMetadata.plist` file.

We still need to create passDocumentToSubViewController. Declare this method in a class extension, and then implement it as shown.

```objc
- (void)passDocumentToSubViewControllers {
    // Create a stack, and load it with the view
    // controllers from our tabs.
    NSMutableArray* stack =
    [NSMutableArray arrayWithArray:self.viewControllers];
    // While we still have items on our stack.
    while ([stack count] > 0) {
        // Pop the last item off the stack.
        id controller = [stack lastObject];
        [stack removeLastObject];
        // If it is a container object, add its view
        // controllers to the stack.
        if ([controller
            respondsToSelector:@selector(viewControllers)]) {
            [stack addObjectsFromArray:
                [controller viewControllers]];
        }
        // If it responds to setDocument, pass our document.
        if ([controller
            respondsToSelector:@selector(setDocument:)]) {
            [controller setDocument:self.document];
        }
    }
}
```

The first half of this method should look familiar. It's the same code we used to forward the WeightHistory objects in Chapter 6. The only real difference is that this time we extracted it into its own method.

```
[[NSNotificationCenter defaultCenter]
    addObserverForName:
NSPersistentStoreDidImportUbiquitousContentChangesNotification
    object:[self.document.managedObjectContext
            persistentStoreCoordinator]
    queue:nil
    usingBlock:^(NSNotification *note) {
        [self.document.managedObjectContext performBlock:^{
            NSLog(@"Merging Changes");
            [self.document.managedObjectContext
             mergeChangesFromContextDidSaveNotification:note];
        }];
    }];
}
```

In the last half, we register for change notifications. Whenever we receive updates from iCloud, we need to refresh our managed object context. However, remember that the context may contain its own unsaved changes. mergeChanges FromContextDidSaveNotification: lets us automatically merge these changes with the incoming data.

That's it. It's still long. We have to take into account both whether the file exists and whether the device supports iCloud storage. Still, it's clearly an order of magnitude simpler than what we wrote in Chapter 6.

DOCUMENT HANDLING AND ERROR CHECKING

Both in this chapter and in Chapter 6, I have been a bit cavalier about checking for errors. This isn't inherently a problem—however, it does assume that we will never try to load corrupted documents.

In general, this is a safe assumption, since both UIDocument and UIManaged Document use atomic saves. However, if we update our application and change the document's format, we may run into problems. After all, the users may not update all their devices at the same time.

Let's say I update my iPhone but not my iPad. Then I open a document in my iPhone. The application migrates my data to the new format and saves it again. Then I open it on my iPad. Now, the iPad tries to open a file format that it doesn't understand. This can lead to a number of problems, possibly crashing the application or even uploading the corrupted data back to the cloud.

Robust error checking can help prevent problems, but it isn't sufficient. Be sure to test your project thoroughly before submitting an update. This includes testing the interactions between the old version and new version. Try opening both new and old documents in both versions. Try triggering conflicts, and have each version merge the documents. Make sure nothing bad is going to happen.

This may require building metadata into the file format from the beginning. For example, adding a version number to our document's data. We can then check the version number each time we load the file. If the version number is greater than what our current application supports, we fail gracefully. Unfortunately, we need to build this support into our original application—which means we need to anticipate possible future changes and plan for them.

Alternatively, we could change the document's UTI. This acts as a one-way gate. The old application won't even see the new file, preventing any possible problems.

FIGURE 7.3 Adding a new entity

FIGURE 7.4 Setting the attribute's type

CREATING THE MANAGED OBJECT MODEL

Next, we need to build the managed object model for our project. In Xcode, right-click the Model group and select New File > iOS > Core Data > Data Model. Then click Next. Name the file WeightHistory and click Create.

Xcode will add an empty WeightHistory.xcdatamodeld file to your project. Make sure this is selected. You should see the data model editor in the Editor area. For this project, our model is about as simple as it gets. We just need a single Weight Entry entity. Click the Add Entity button to add this to your model (**Figure 7.3**).

A new entity is added to the Entities list. Xcode should automatically highlight its name. If not, click the entity to select it, and change its name to WeightEntry.

Now we need to add our date and weightInLbs attributes. With WeightEntry still selected, click the Add Attribute button. This adds an undefined attribute to the list of attributes. Again, Xcode should automatically select the name. Type in the new name: date. Under the Type setting, click Undefined and then select Date (**Figure 7.4**).

FIGURE 7.5 The date attribute's settings

FIGURE 7.6 The weightInLbs attribute's settings

FIGURE 7.7 The completed managed object model

Make sure the Utilities panel is visible, and select the Data Model inspector. We want to index our date attribute, but it should not be optional or transient. Also, it does not need Min, Max, or Default values (**Figure 7.5**).

Repeat these steps, but this time name the attribute weightInLbs and set the type to Float. This attribute should not be indexed, transient, or optional; however, it should have a 0.00 Minimum value and a 0.00 Default value (**Figure 7.6**).

The data model should now match **Figure 7.7**.

FIGURE 7.8 The entity's Class setting

GENERATING A CUSTOM WEIGHTENTRY CLASS

We could use the model exactly as it is, but I like creating custom NSManagedObject Model subclasses for my entities. Fortunately, Xcode 4 makes this as simple as possible. Right-click the Model group, select New File > iOS > Core Data > NSManaged Object subclass, and click Next.

When generating multiple NSManagedObject subclasses, Xcode may try to infer the model and entity we wish to implement. Other times it will ask us to specify one or both—especially the first time we generate a subclass. In our case, we only have one model, so just select WeightEntry. We also only have one entity—but Xcode should automatically detect that. In the next page, it will ask us where we want to save our files. We aren't given the chance to name our class, but that's OK. Xcode will use our entity's name.

We can just accept the default location; however, let's select the "Use scalar properties for primitive data types" checkbox. This will force Xcode to generate scalar properties for our attributes. Click the Create button to continue.

Xcode now adds a new WeightEntry object to our project. If you select WeightEntry.h, you will see that it automatically created properties for all our attributes. Now select the Core Data model again. Make sure the WeightEntry entity is selected, and open the Data Model inspector (**Figure 7.8**). Xcode has automatically set our entity's class to our new WeightEntry class.

Unfortunately, there are two problems with the auto-generated properties. First, our original WeightEntry class was immutable; the new version is not. Second, Xcode generated a scalar property for our date attribute—we really want it to return NSDate. Fortunately, both of these are easy to fix. Open WeightEntry.h, and modify the property declarations as shown:

```
@property (nonatomic, readonly, retain) NSDate* date;
@property (nonatomic, readonly) float weightInLbs;
```

Now open the implementation file, and add the following extension:

```
@interface WeightEntry()
@property (nonatomic, readwrite, retain) NSDate* date;
@property (nonatomic, readwrite) float weightInLbs;
@end
```

We've seen this pattern before, when declaring public getters and private setters for our properties.

We also need to copy all the class methods from OldWeightEntry to our new WeightEntry class. Open OldWeightEntry.h, and copy all the method declarations that start with a +. There should be two conversion methods and three string generation methods. Paste these into WeightHistory.h as shown:

```
@interface WeightEntry : NSManagedObject {

@private

}

@property (nonatomic, retain) NSDate * date;

@property (nonatomic, retain) NSNumber * weightInLbs;

+ (CGFloat)convertLbsToKg:(CGFloat)lbs;

+ (CGFloat)convertKgToLbs:(CGFloat)kg;

+ (NSString*)stringForUnit:(WeightUnit)unit;

+ (NSString*)stringForWeight:(CGFloat)weight
                      ofUnit:(WeightUnit)unit;

+ (NSString*)stringForWeightInLbs:(CGFloat)weight
                           inUnit:(WeightUnit)unit;

@end
```

Now open the implementation files. First, let's copy our static LBS_PER_KG and formatter variables (we won't need the WeightInLbsKey or DateKey variables). Place these before the WeightEntry() extension.

```
#import "WeightEntry.h"

static const CGFloat LBS_PER_KG = 2.20462262f;

static NSNumberFormatter* formatter;

@interface WeightEntry()
```

Next, copy the implementations for the following methods: convertLbsToKg:, convertKgToLbs:, initialize, stringForUnit:, stringForWeight:, and stringFor WeightInLbs:inUnit:. Note that in stringForWeight: and stringForWeight InLbs:inUnit:, you need to change all the references to OldWeightEntry back to WeightEntry as shown:

```
+ (NSString*)stringForWeight:(CGFloat)weight
                  ofUnit:(WeightUnit)unit {
    NSString* weightString =
    [formatter stringFromNumber:
        [NSNumber numberWithFloat:weight]];
    NSString* unitString = [WeightEntry stringForUnit:unit];
    return [NSString stringWithFormat:@"%@ %@", weightString,
            unitString];
}
+ (NSString*)stringForWeightInLbs:(CGFloat)weight
                     inUnit:(WeightUnit)unit {
    CGFloat convertedWeight;
    switch (unit) {
        case LBS:
            convertedWeight = weight;
            break;
        case KG:
            convertedWeight = [WeightEntry convertLbsToKg:weight];
            break;
        default:
            [NSException raise:NSInvalidArgumentException
                format:@"%d is not a valid WeightUnit", unit];
    }
```

```
    return [WeightEntry stringForWeight:convertedWeight
                             ofUnit:unit];
}
```

Finally, let's copy the weightInUnit: and stringForWeightInUnit: methods over from our OldWeightEntry class. In both cases, we need to make sure we change OldWeightEntry back to WeightEntry.

```
#pragma mark - Public Methods
- (CGFloat)weightInUnit:(WeightUnit)unit {
    switch (unit) {
        case LBS:
            return self.weightInLbs;
        case KG:
            return [WeightEntry convertLbsToKg:self.weightInLbs];
        default:
            [NSException
             raise:NSInvalidArgumentException
             format:@"The value %d is not a valid WeightUnit", unit];
    }
    // This will never be executed.
    return 0.0f;
}
- (NSString*)stringForWeightInUnit:(WeightUnit)unit {
    return [WeightEntry stringForWeight:[self weightInUnit:unit]
                               ofUnit:unit];
}
```

Finally, instantiating new managed objects takes a bit of boilerplate. Let's wrap that in a convenience method. While we're at it, let's add a second convenience method that returns our entity's name—we will use this when looking up the entity description in our managed object context.

Declare the following methods in the header file:

```objc
+ (NSString*)entityName;
+ (WeightEntry*)addEntryToDocument:(UIManagedDocument*)document
                usingWeightInLbs:(CGFloat)weight
                            date:(NSDate*)date;
```

Our entityName implementation is, not surprisingly, very simple.

```objc
+ (NSString*)entityName {
    return @"WeightEntry";
}
```

Unfortunately, addEntryToDocument:usingWeightInLbs:date: requires a bit more work. Let's go over this implementation a step at a time.

```objc
#pragma mark - Convenience Methods
+ (WeightEntry*)addEntryToDocument:(UIManagedDocument*)document
                usingWeightInLbs:(CGFloat)weight
                            date:(NSDate*)date
{
    NSManagedObjectContext* context = document.managedObjectContext;
    NSAssert(context != nil,
            @"The managed object context is nil");
```

This is just a bit of sanity checking. We're getting a local reference to the managed object context, and we check to make sure it isn't set to nil. We cannot create new managed objects without the context.

```objc
    NSEntityDescription* entity =
    [NSEntityDescription entityForName:[WeightEntry entityName]
                inManagedObjectContext:context];
    NSAssert1(entity != nil,
            @"The entity description for WeightEntry in %@ is nil",
```

```
            context);
    WeightEntry* entry =
    [[WeightEntry alloc] initWithEntity:entity
        insertIntoManagedObjectContext:context];
```

Next, we grab our entity description from the context, and then we use that description to instantiate a new WeightEntry object. WeightEntry is automatically inserted into our context as part of its initialization.

```
    entry.weightInLbs = weight;
    entry.date = date;
    // Save a snapshot to the parent context.
    NSError *error = nil;
    if (![context save:&error]) {
        // Ideally, we should replace this
        // with more-robust error handling.
        // However, we're not saving to disk,
        // we're just pushing the change
        // up to the parent context--so most errors should be
        // caused by mistakes in our code.
        [NSException
         raise:NSInternalInconsistencyException
         format:@"An error occurred when saving the context: %@",
         [error localizedDescription]];
    }
    return entry;
}
```

Finally, we push the change up to the parent context and then return our new entry. Remember, we're working with a child managed object context, so we aren't actually saving anything. We're just updating the document's snapshot.

Actually, this save isn't strictly necessary. UIManagedDocument will handle all the saves automatically. However, this helps make our intentions clear and will assist the undo manager. Without the explicit saves, the undo manager will register all changes as undo actions—including the undo actions themselves. This means that our shake will undo and then redo the same action repeatedly. By explicitly adding these saves, the undo actions are not recorded, letting us undo multiple changes.

That's it. Our WeightEntry is complete, and we're done with the OldWeightEntry class. Delete OldWeightEntry.h and OldWeightEntry.m from the project. Now we just need to update our view controllers.

UPDATING THE VIEW CONTROLLERS

Let's start with EnterWeightViewController. Open the header file, and delete the forward declaration and the property. In the implementation file, start by deleting the import and synthesize lines. Repeat this procedure for the GraphViewController and HistoryViewController classes. If we try to build the application now, we will see a number of orphaned weightHistory references in our implementation file. That's OK. We will use these as guideposts, helping us find all the methods that need to be modified.

Next, we need to add the following document property to our enter weight, graph, and history view controllers:

```
@property (strong, nonatomic) UIManagedDocument* document;
```

Be sure to synthesize it in all three implementation files. With that out of the way, the real work can begin.

ENTERWEIGHTVIEWCONTROLLER

Now, open EnterWeightViewController.m. Start by importing WeightEntry.h. Next, we want to clear out all our error messages. Navigate down to the saveWeight: method. Replace the existing implementation with the following:

```
- (IBAction)saveWeight:(id)sender {
    CGFloat weight =
    [[self.numberFormatter
        numberFromString:self.weightTextField.text]
```

```
    floatValue];
    if (getDefaultUnits() != LBS) {
        weight = [WeightEntry convertKgToLbs:weight];
    }
    // This creates a new weight entry and adds
    // it to our document's managed object context.
    [WeightEntry addEntryToDocument:self.document
                   usingWeightInLbs:weight
                               date:self.currentDate];
    // Automatically move to the second tab.
    // Should be the graph view.
    self.tabBarController.selectedIndex = 1;
}
```

Here, we call the convenience method we just wrote, adding a new WeightEntry to our document. Once that's done, we tell the tab bar controller to shift to the graph view.

Next, scroll down to the setWeightHistory: method. We just need to convert this to use UIManagedDocument instead. That essentially means replacing all the weight history references with document references.

```
#pragma mark - Custom Accessor
- (void)setDocument:(UIManagedDocument *)document {
    NSNotificationCenter* notificationCenter =
    [NSNotificationCenter defaultCenter];
    // If we're assigning the same document, don't do anything.
    if ([_document isEqual:document]) {
        return;
    }
    // Clear any notifications for the old document, if any.
    if (_document != nil) {
```

```
            [notificationCenter
             removeObserver:self
             forKeyPath:UIDocumentStateChangedNotification];
        }
        _document = document;
        // Add new notifications for the new document, if any,
        // and set the view's values.
        if (_document != nil) {
            // Register for notifications.
            [notificationCenter
             addObserver:self
             selector:@selector(updateSaveAndEditStatus)
             name:UIDocumentStateChangedNotification
             object:_document];
            // Update our save and edit status.
            [self updateSaveAndEditStatus];
        }
    }
```

Both UIManagedDocument and our old WeightHistory class are subclasses of UIDocument—so everything should still work fine. Specifically, we still want to watch the document's state, and disable editing or display save warnings when necessary.

Finally, look at the updateSaveAndEditStatus method. We need to change self.weightHistory to self.document in the first few lines.

```
- (void)updateSaveAndEditStatus {
    if (self.document == nil) {
        // Disable editing.
        [self.weightTextField resignFirstResponder];
```

```
        self.weightTextField.enabled = NO;          return;
    }
    UIDocumentState state =
    self.document.documentState;
```

Our EnterWeightViewController class is now finished and ready to go. Next, let's look at the history view.

HISTORYVIEWCONTROLLER

We need to modify the history view controller so that it uses an NSFetchedResults Controller. As we will see, the NSFetchedResultsController manages data from Core Data, letting us easily display the data in a UITableView. We can also assign a delegate to the fetched request controller, letting us respond to any changes in the underlying data.

To begin, open HistoryViewController.h. Import the Core Data framework, and have HistoryViewController adopt the NSFetchedResultsControllerDelegate protocol.

```
#import <UIKit/UIKit.h>

#import <CoreData/CoreData.h>

@interface HistoryViewController : UITableViewController

    <NSFetchedResultsControllerDelegate> {

}
@end
```

Switch to the implementation file. We start by updating our #import directives. Make sure we are importing WeightEntry.h.

```
#import "HistoryViewController.h"

#import "DetailViewController.h"

#import "HistoryCell.h"

#import "WeightEntry.h"
```

Next, we need to update the class extension. Delete the `weightHistoryChanged:` declaration and add a new property and the `instantiateFetchedResults Controller` method.

```
@interface HistoryViewController()
@property (nonatomic, retain) NSFetchedResultsController*
fetchedResultsController;
- (void)instantiateFetchedResultsController;
- (void)reloadTableData;
@end
```

Basically, the `fetchedResultsController` manages our table's data, and `instantiateFetchedResultsController` sets up and configures that data. Since we've added a new property, we need to synthesize it.

```
@synthesize fetchedResultsController = _fetchedResultsController;
```

Next, delete both `ObserveValueForKeyPath:ofObject:change:context:` and `weightHistoryChanged:`. We no longer need them.

With these preliminaries out of the way, we finally reach the table view methods. Here we get to see our fetched results controller in action. Let's begin by modifying `numberOfSectionsInTableview:` as shown:

```
- (NSInteger)numberOfSectionsInTableView:(UITableView *)tableView
{
    return [[self.fetchedResultsController sections] count];
}
```

In our old implementation, we hard-coded the number of sections. Here, we can pull this data from our fetched results controller. This lets us easily change the number of sections without modifying this code.

Similarly, `tableView:numberOfRowsInSection:` should extract the row count from our fetched results controller.

```
- (NSInteger)tableView:(UITableView *)tableView
 numberOfRowsInSection:(NSInteger)section
{
    id <NSFetchedResultsSectionInfo> sectionInfo =
        [[self.fetchedResultsController sections]
          objectAtIndex:section];
    return [sectionInfo numberOfObjects];
}
```

Here, we get the section information for the given section index. This gives us direct access to the array of objects, as well as to the section's name and index title. In this case, we are only interested in the number of objects.

Then we change the way we access our WeightEntry objects in tableView:cellForRowAtIndexPath:. Here, we access them directly from our fetched request controller.

```
- (UITableViewCell *)tableView:(UITableView *)tableView
        cellForRowAtIndexPath:(NSIndexPath *)indexPath
{
    static NSString *CellIdentifier = @"History Cell";
    HistoryCell *cell =
    [tableView dequeueReusableCellWithIdentifier:CellIdentifier];
    WeightEntry* entry =
    [self.fetchedResultsController objectAtIndexPath:indexPath];
    [cell configureWithWeightEntry:entry
                    defaultUnits:getDefaultUnits()];
    return cell;
}
```

Ironically, our code for tableView:commitEditingStyle:forRowAtIndexPath: actually gets more complex. However, it's doing a bit more work, so that's only fair.

```objc
- (void)tableView:(UITableView *)tableView
commitEditingStyle:(UITableViewCellEditingStyle)editingStyle
forRowAtIndexPath:(NSIndexPath *)indexPath
{
    if (editingStyle == UITableViewCellEditingStyleDelete)
    {
        WeightEntry* entry =
        [self.fetchedResultsController objectAtIndexPath:indexPath];
        // Delete the managed object for the given index path.
        NSManagedObjectContext *context =
        [self.fetchedResultsController managedObjectContext];
        [context deleteObject:entry];
        NSError* error;
        if (![context save:&error]) {
            // Again, we should replace this with
            // more-robust error handling.
            [NSException
             raise:NSInternalInconsistencyException
             format:@"An error occurred when saving the context: %@",
             [error localizedDescription]];
        }
    }
}
```

If the user deletes a row, we need to get the weight entry for the provided index path. Fortunately, NSFetchedResultsController understands index paths; in fact, it is the direct support for sections and index paths that makes NSFetchedResults Controller such a good fit for UITableViews. With the weight entry in hand, we request a reference to our managed object context from the fetched request controller, and we delete the entry from the context. Finally, we save our changes.

We still need to modify the behavior when the user selects a row. As before, prepareForSegue:sender: does all the real work.

```
- (void)prepareForSegue:(UIStoryboardSegue *)segue
                 sender:(id)sender {
    if ([segue.identifier
        isEqualToString:DetailViewSegueIdentifier]) {
        NSIndexPath* path =
        [self.tableView indexPathForSelectedRow];
        DetailViewController* controller =
        segue.destinationViewController;
        controller.weightHistory =
        self.fetchedResultsController.fetchedObjects;
        controller.selectedIndex = path.row;
    }
}
```

Here, instead of passing our model object, we return the array of fetched objects from our fetchedResultsController. We will need to update our WeightView Controller, but other than that, everything remains unchanged.

Next, we need to set up our fetched results controller. This is a big method, so we'll take it in steps.

```
- (void)instantiateFetchedResultsController {
    // Create the fetch request.
    NSFetchRequest *fetchRequest =
```

```
[NSFetchRequest fetchRequestWithEntityName:
    [WeightEntry entityName]];
// Set the batch size.
[fetchRequest setFetchBatchSize:20];
```

Here, we create a fetch request for our weight entry. By default, this fetch request will return all the weight entries in our Core Data store. Unfortunately, this could cause performance issues—especially when our application attempts to load a large number of entries all at once.

To solve this, we set the batch size. The batch size determines the number of objects that the fetch request will return in each batch. In our case, it will return the first 20 entries as objects and will return the rest as faults. If we try to access one of the faulted entries, the fetch request will fill in a new batch of 20 objects, including the fault. This provides a nice compromise between performance and memory usage. We don't need to load unnecessary objects into memory, but we also minimize the number of faults triggered while scrolling through the history.

```
// Set up sort descriptor.
NSSortDescriptor *sortDescriptor =
    [[NSSortDescriptor alloc] initWithKey:@"date" ascending:NO];
NSArray *sortDescriptors =
    [[NSArray alloc] initWithObjects:sortDescriptor, nil];
[fetchRequest setSortDescriptors:sortDescriptors];
```

This section adds a sort descriptor to the fetch request. First, we create our sort descriptor. This will sort our weight entry objects in descending order based on their date property. We then place this descriptor in an array of sort descriptors and assign it to our fetch request.

Our code only uses a single sort descriptor, but we could assign more than one. Their order of precedence is determined by their order in the array. The first descriptor will perform the initial sort. Any objects that are still equal are then sorted by the second descriptor. Objects that are still tied are passed to the third descriptor, and so forth.

```
// Nil for section name key path means "no sections."
self.fetchedResultsController =
    [[NSFetchedResultsController alloc]
        initWithFetchRequest:fetchRequest
        managedObjectContext:self.document.managedObjectContext
        sectionNameKeyPath:nil
                    cacheName:@"History View"];
self.fetchedResultsController.delegate = self;
```

Here, we create our NSFetchedResultsController using our fetch request and our managed object context. The sectionNameKeyPath: argument can be used to partition the entities into sections. The system will look at the values associated with the given key path and create a section for each unique value. In our case, we simply pass nil, indicating that we want all the data in a single section.

The cacheName: argument is used to specify a cache for the fetched results controller. The controller will try to use the cache to avoid duplicating the effort that goes into splitting the data into different sections and sorting it. The cache persists across application launches. If two fetch request controllers are requesting the same data (same entity, predicate, and sort descriptors), then they can share a cache. Otherwise, each controller needs a unique cache. Alternatively, you can pass in nil, but then the system won't perform any caching.

Once we have instantiated the fetched request controller, we assign our view controller as its delegate.

```
NSError *error = nil;
if (![self.fetchedResultsController performFetch:&error])
{
    // We may want more-thorough error checking; however,
    // at this point, the main cause for errors tends to be
    // invalid keys in the sort descriptor. Let's fail fast
    // so we're sure to catch that during development.
    [NSException
```

```
           raise:NSInternalInconsistencyException
           format:@"An error occurred when performing our fetch %@",
           [error localizedDescription]];
    }
}
```

Finally, we call performFetch: to gather the requested data. As with other Core Data methods, this can produce errors. However, errors at this point are typically caused by sort descriptors with invalid key paths. These errors should be caught and fixed during development.

If you're just accessing data from a locally created store, then the call should be reasonably safe. If there is an I/O problem, we should have detected it when instantiating the persistent store. However, you may want to add better error checking if you are doing things that reduce the reliability (e.g., modifying the entity in two or more managed object contexts, using user input in the sort descriptors, downloading Core Data files from a remote server, or using Core Data to access a remote store).

We're almost done. We still need to add the NSFetchedResultsController Delegate methods. First, let's implement controllerWillChangeContent: and controllerDidChangeContent:.

```
#pragma mark - Fetched results controller delegate
- (void)controllerWillChangeContent:
    (NSFetchedResultsController *) controller
{

    [self.tableView beginUpdates];

}
- (void)controllerDidChangeContent:
    (NSFetchedResultsController *) controller
{

    [self.tableView endUpdates];

}
```

Here, we're just bracketing our changes with calls to `beginUpdates` and `endUp dates`. If we make multiple changes to our table, all the changes will be animated at once. For example, if a row is moved, we first delete it from its old location in the table and then insert it into its new location. This ensures that the deletion and insertion are animated simultaneously.

Next, we need to implement `controller:didChangeObject:atIndexPath: forChangeType:newIndexPath:`. This method is called whenever the underlying data changes.

```
- (void)controller:(NSFetchedResultsController *)controller
    didChangeObject:(id)anObject
        atIndexPath:(NSIndexPath *)indexPath
     forChangeType:(NSFetchedResultsChangeType)type
      newIndexPath:(NSIndexPath *)newIndexPath
{
    UITableView *tableView = self.tableView;
    WeightEntry* entry;
    HistoryCell* cell;
    switch(type)
    {
        case NSFetchedResultsChangeInsert:
            [tableView
             insertRowsAtIndexPaths:
             [NSArray arrayWithObject:newIndexPath]
             withRowAnimation:UITableViewRowAnimationAutomatic];
            break;
        case NSFetchedResultsChangeDelete:
            [tableView
             deleteRowsAtIndexPaths:
             [NSArray arrayWithObject:indexPath]
```

```
            withRowAnimation:UITableViewRowAnimationAutomatic];
        break;
    case NSFetchedResultsChangeUpdate:
        entry =
        [self.fetchedResultsController
         objectAtIndexPath:indexPath];
        cell = (HistoryCell*)
        [self.tableView
         cellForRowAtIndexPath:indexPath];
        [cell configureWithWeightEntry:entry
                         defaultUnits:getDefaultUnits()];
        break;
    case NSFetchedResultsChangeMove:
        [tableView
         deleteRowsAtIndexPaths:
         [NSArray arrayWithObject:indexPath]
         withRowAnimation:UITableViewRowAnimationAutomatic];
        [tableView
         insertRowsAtIndexPaths:
         [NSArray arrayWithObject:newIndexPath]
         withRowAnimation:UITableViewRowAnimationAutomatic];
        break;
    }
}
```

As you can see, we receive notifications when an entity has been added or deleted, when its attributes change, or when it moves (i.e., when its indexPath changes). In every case, we simply modify the table to match.

The system sends these notifications whenever the model changes—even when our code has programmatically triggered the change. It's a good idea to trace through your code and make sure you're not accidentally creating any change loops or other unnecessary work. For example, what happens when the user edits the table and deletes a row? In our case, the system first calls `tableView:commit EditingStyle:forRowAtIndexPath:`. Here, we delete the specified object from the model; however, we don't change the table. Instead, changing the model triggers a call to `controllerWillChangeContent:` and then a call to `controller:didChange Object:atIndexPath:forChangeType:newIndexPath:`. This is where we actually modify the table. Finally, the system calls `controllerDidChangeContent:` and our animation begins.

While this is the typical use case, there may be times when you want to respond to a bulk set of changes, rather than monitoring and animating each and every change (e.g., when loading new data on a background thread). In these cases, you may just choose to wait and reload the entire table in the `controllerDidChange Content:` method.

We still need to update our undo code. In `motionEnded:withEvent:`, change `self.weightHistory` to `self.Document`.

```
- (void)motionEnded:(UIEventSubtype)motion
          withEvent:(UIEvent *)event {
    // Only respond to shake events.
    if (event.type == UIEventSubtypeMotionShake) {
        [self.document.undoManager undo];
    }
}
```

Finally, we need to update our `setWeightHistory:` accessor to use our new document property. In this case, it may be easiest to just delete the old method and write an entirely new one.

```
- (void)setDocument:(UIManagedDocument *)document {
    // If we're assigning the same history, don't do anything.
    if ([_document isEqual:document]) {
        return;
    }
```

```
// Remove any old fetched results controller.
if (_document != nil) {
    self.fetchedResultsController = nil;
}
_document = document;
// Add new notifications for the new history, if any.
if (_document != nil) {
    [self instantiateFetchedResultsController];
    // If the view is loaded, we need to update it.
    if (self.isViewLoaded) {
        [self.tableView reloadData];
    }
}
}
```

We no longer need to set up or tear down our notifications, since we'll get all our updates directly from the fetched results controller. Instead, if we have a fetched results controller, we clear it. If we're adding a new document, we call instantiateFetchedResultsController to create a new controller, and then we update our table.

That's it. Our HistoryViewController is now completely converted to Core Data. However, we still need to modify our DetailViewController class. Let's tackle that next.

NOTE: Most of the changes we made in this section are boilerplate code. You can use exactly the same pattern for any navigation controller/ fetched results controller pair. In fact, if you're using a lot of Core Data-backed navigation controllers, it would be worth creating a UINavigationController subclass to encapsulate much of this. I'll leave that as homework.

Open DetailViewController.h. Change the weightHistory's type to NSArray.

```
@property (nonatomic, strong) NSArray* weightHistory;
```

Now switch to the implementation file. Start by deleting the import declaration for WeightHistory.h. Next, there are two references to self.weightHistory.weights in the viewWillAppear: method. We need to change them to self.weightHistory.

```
- (void)viewWillAppear:(BOOL)animated
{
    [super viewDidAppear:animated];
    WeightUnit unit = getDefaultUnits();
    WeightEntry* currentEntry =
    [self.weightHistory objectAtIndex:self.selectedIndex];
    CGFloat weight = [currentEntry weightInUnit:unit];
    // If the entry is within the same month.
    NSDate* startOfMonth;
    NSTimeInterval monthLength;
    [[NSCalendar currentCalendar] rangeOfUnit:NSMonthCalendarUnit
                                    startDate:&startOfMonth
                                     interval:&monthLength
                                      forDate:currentEntry.date];
    CGFloat minWeight = CGFLOAT_MAX;
    CGFloat maxWeight = CGFLOAT_MIN;
    int monthlyCount = 0;
    CGFloat monthlyTotal = 0.0f;
    for (OldWeightEntry* entry in self.weightHistory) {
        CGFloat sampleWeight = [entry weightInUnit:unit];
        ...
```

FIGURE 7.9 Replacing all instances of `OldWeightEntry`

We also need to replace all occurrences of `OldWeightEntry` with `Weight Entry`. Enough with the scrolling and fixing. This time, let's use a simple replace all. Press Command-F to bring up the find bar at the top of the Editor area. On the left side, switch from Find to Replace. Type OldWeightEntry in the search field. Type WeightEntry in the bottom text field, and then click Replace All (**Figure 7.9**).

There's only one view controller left. Let's update the graph view.

GRAPHVIEWCONTROLLER

`GraphViewController` needs to populate the graph with data from Core Data, but unlike what we did with `HistoryViewController`, we won't be using an `NSFetchedResultsController`. Instead, we will be using a raw `NSFetchRequest`. This means we must manage any changes ourselves. Of course, for the graph view, it's easy to handle these changes; we simply redraw the entire graph.

Let's start by opening `GraphViewController.m`. and importing `WeightEntry.h`. Next, delete the `WeightKey` string constant. Then, create a class extension and declare a `weightHistory` property. Don't forget to synthesize the property.

```objc
#import "GraphViewController.h"

#import "GraphView.h"

#import "WeightEntry.h"

@interface GraphViewController()

@property (strong, nonatomic) NSArray* weightHistory;

@end

@implementation GraphViewController

@synthesize document = _document;

@synthesize weightHistory = _weightHistory;
```

Now, navigate to `viewDidLoad`. We use `self.weightHistory.weights` twice in this method. Change them both to `self.weightHistory`.

```objc
- (void)viewDidLoad

{
```

```
[super viewDidLoad];
id graphView = self.view;
[graphView setWeightEntries:self.weightHistory
               andUnits:getDefaultUnits()];
// Register to receive notifications when the default unit changes.
[[NSNotificationCenter defaultCenter]
 addObserverForName:NSUserDefaultsDidChangeNotification
 object:[NSUserDefaults standardUserDefaults]
 queue:nil
 usingBlock:^(NSNotification *note) {
     [graphView setWeightEntries:self.weightHistory
                    andUnits:getDefaultUnits()];
 }];
}
```

Next, find the observeValueForKeyPath:ofObject:change:context: method. Delete it. We won't be using KVO in this implementation.

Finally, just as with the other view controllers, we need to convert our setWeightHistory: custom accessor into setDocuments:. This is long, but we've seen most of it before.

```
#pragma mark - Custom Accessor
- (void)setDocument:(UIManagedDocument*)document {
    NSNotificationCenter* center =
    [NSNotificationCenter defaultCenter];
    // If we're assigning the same history, don't do anything.
    if ([_document isEqual:document]) {
        return;
    }
    // Clear any notifications for the old history, if any.
    if (_document != nil) {
```

```
    [center
      removeObserver:self
      name:NSManagedObjectContextObjectsDidChangeNotification
      object:self.document.managedObjectContext];
}
_document = document;
// Add new notifications for the new history, if any,
// and set the view's values.
if (_document != nil) {
    // Create the fetch request.
    NSFetchRequest *fetchRequest = [NSFetchRequest
      fetchRequestWithEntityName:[WeightEntry entityName]];
    // Set up sort descriptor.
    NSSortDescriptor *sortDescriptor =
    [[NSSortDescriptor alloc] initWithKey:@"date" ascending:NO];
    NSArray *sortDescriptors =
    [[NSArray alloc] initWithObjects:sortDescriptor, nil];
    [fetchRequest setSortDescriptors:sortDescriptors];
    NSError* error;
    self.weightHistory =
    [self.document.managedObjectContext
      executeFetchRequest:fetchRequest
      error:&error];
    if (self.weightHistory == nil) {
        // We may want more-thorough error checking; however,
        // at this point, the main cause for errors tends to be
        // invalid keys in the sort descriptor. Let's fail fast
        // so we're sure to catch that during development.
```

```
      [NSException
       raise:NSInternalInconsistencyException
       format:@"An error occurred when performing our fetch %@",
       [error localizedDescription]];
    }
  [center
   addObserverForName:
   NSManagedObjectContextObjectsDidChangeNotification
   object:self.document.managedObjectContext
   queue:nil
   usingBlock:^(NSNotification* notification) {
       NSError* fetchError;
       self.weightHistory =
       [self.document.managedObjectContext
        executeFetchRequest:fetchRequest
        error:&fetchError];
       if (self.weightHistory == nil) {
// We may want more-thorough error checking; however,
// at this point, the main cause for errors tends
// to be invalid keys in the sort descriptor. Let's
// fail fast so we're sure to catch that during development.
[NSException
 raise:NSInternalInconsistencyException
 format:@"An error occurred when performing "
       @"our fetch %@",
       [fetchError localizedDescription]];
       }
       // If the view is loaded, we need to update it.
```

```
            if (self.isViewLoaded) {
                id graphView = self.view;
                [graphView setWeightEntries:self.weightHistory
                                    andUnits:getDefaultUnits()];
            }
    }];
    // If the view is loaded, we need to update it.
    if (self.isViewLoaded) {
        id graphView = self.view;
        [graphView setWeightEntries:self.weightHistory
                            andUnits:getDefaultUnits()];
    }
  }
}
```

By now, there shouldn't be any surprises. Obviously, we change many references from weightHistory to document. We also switch from using KVO to using notifications. Here, we observe the managed object context directly, watching for changes.

The only really interesting part is the fetch request, and even this is largely identical to what we saw in HistoryViewController's instantiateFetched ResultsController method. The main difference is that instead of wrapping our fetch request in a fetch results controller, we execute it directly. Additionally, since we're going to use all the objects immediately, we don't set a fetch batch size.

NOTE: Our implementation has some duplicate code. Specifically, we execute the fetch request and handle errors both in our method and in the notification block. My first instinct was to refactor these into a separate method—however, doing it this way has an advantage: We use the same NSFetchRequest object for both. Fetch requests can be somewhat costly to create, so it's always good to reuse them whenever possible.

Of course, there's a lot of room for improvements. We could share a single fetch request between both the `HistoryViewController` and the `GraphViewController`. Better yet, we could use an `NSFetchedResultsController` here as well, sharing the same cache as the `HistoryViewController`. Having the caching and the built-in support for change detection would be nice. We don't need the section or index path support, and it would be a little harder to get our array of `WeightEvents`, but it might be worth the effort.

Still, users often only enter a single weight per use. This means we only call the fetch request once. So, go easy with the changes. Unless we find a compelling reason to make changes (after profiling and stress testing, that is), it's probably best to just leave things alone.

WRAPPING **UP**

That's it. Run the application. Try adding and deleting weights. Navigate to the history view, and shake to undo. Everything should work as expected. Launch it on a second device; all the weights should transfer over. Put the first device on the graph view. Then enter a new weight on the second device, and put that app into the background. Within a minute or so, the first device's screen should change. If everything looks good, commit your changes.

Of course, there is one big difference between this version and the last. Shake to undo no longer asks for permission before making a change. It immediately undoes the last action. It turns out that we threw out most of our undo support code when we deleted the old `WeightHistory` class. That means we didn't even register any actions for undo, or create the inverse undo methods. Core Data handled everything for us automatically.

I'll leave the alerts as homework. It shouldn't be hard to move the relevant `WeightHistory` code over to the `HistoryViewController`. Just be sure to set the undo action name every time you save the context. Then add the alert methods.

Next chapter, we will take a break from the Health Beat application to look at custom controls. In particular, we will focus on using Core Motion and custom gestures. Finally, in Chapter 9, we will look at all the little details that need to be completed before submitting your app to the App Store.

8

DESIGNING CUSTOM CONTROLS

This chapter covers a broad range of advanced topics that focus on creating an immersive custom user interface. We start by building a view hierarchy that divides our dynamic and static elements into separate layers, allowing us to rapidly redraw the interface as changes occur. We also create a custom UIView Controller container to manage our subviews, while using Core Animation to control the transition between these views. Next, we respond to user input using gesture recognizers to track different touch-based commands and Core Motion to monitor the device's rotation. Finally, we will use Core Location to geotag images, then export those images by saving them to the photo library, attaching them to email, or tweeting them using the new integrated Twitter API.

INTRODUCING
GRAVITYSCRIBBLER

FIGURE 8.1 GravityScribbler
in action

This chapter is going to be somewhat different from the rest of the book. We're going to take a break from our Health Beat application to examine a number of advanced topics: from custom view hierarchies and animation to motion detection and geotagging. Since most of these topics cannot be easily shoehorned into our existing application, we will look at a new, immersive application: GravityScribbler.

GravityScribbler is a simple drawing application (**Figure 8.1**). It begins with a cursor in the center of the screen, and the user can direct the cursor by tipping and tilting their phone. The cursor will roll downhill, drawing a line behind it. The user can also utilize an assortment of gestures to control the application. A single-finger horizontal pan will control the cursor's speed. A two-finger touch will pause and restart the application, while a three-finger swipe will drag out the export menu. Finally, shaking the phone clears the current drawing, letting the user start over.

Unlike what we've done thus far, we won't go through a step-by-step walk-through and build the entire application from scratch. There is just too much ground to cover. Instead, we will focus more tightly on the individual topics. If you want to see how these topics integrate into a completed application, check out the complete source code from http://freelancemadscience.com/source.

Additionally, since GravityScribbler depends so strongly on touch gestures and device motion, we cannot effectively test it in the simulator. You must run it on the device itself. This means you must have a valid iOS Developer Program membership, as well as the proper provisioning profiles for your device. We examined this in detail in the section "Running and Testing on iOS Devices" in Chapter 3.

Let's start by looking at techniques for creating a truly custom dynamic user interface.

CUSTOMIZING THE INTERFACE'S APPEARANCE

Often the standard user interface elements work just fine. They're reasonably attractive. Users recognize them and understand them. They know exactly what they do and how to use them. But let's face it: If you just use Apple's default controls, your application may begin to look somewhat bland. Sometimes it's important to color outside the lines.

How radical should your interface be? The answer depends on a number of things. What kind of application are you building? How comfortable are your users with new interfaces? How clearly can you communicate its intended use? While I can't answer these questions for you, I can show you some techniques to help you when you start striking out on your own.

Right off the bat, our GravityScribbler app needs to make two important changes to the default application behavior. As an immersive app, we want to seize control of the entire screen, hiding the device's status bar. This isn't something we should do lightly. The status bar contains vital information, including the time and the battery status. Hiding the status bar means your users won't have access to that information while using your app. Still, in many cases it's necessary to hide the status bar. If you're trying to build an immersive application, it can be a real distraction. Nobody wants to see the status bar while watching movies. Similarly, we don't want it to appear in GravityScribbler.

We also want to disable the system's idle timer. Again, the idle timer usually performs a vital role. If the application doesn't detect any user touches for a short period, it will dim the screen and then put the device to sleep. This helps save battery power when the device is not in use. Unfortunately, in our case, the user may use the device for long periods without ever touching the screen. Instead, they control the cursor using the accelerometer, and we don't want our application to go to sleep while someone is using it.

Both of these changes are incredibly easy to make. Add the following lines of code to the application delegate's `application:didFinishLaunchingWith Options:` method.

```
UIApplication* app = [UIApplication sharedApplication];
[app setStatusBarHidden:YES];
[app setIdleTimerDisabled:YES];
```

SEPARATING DYNAMIC AND STATIC VIEWS

We looked at drawing custom views in Chapter 5. However, that chapter focused on drawing a single, static view. Now we need to create a dynamic view. Our view needs to change over time—ideally, we would like to update it at 60 frames per second. That means we need to update it frequently, and each time we update it, we need to redraw it quickly.

Fortunately, not everything changes. At any given time, most of our view remains static, and only a small section changes. We need to update our cursor's position, and we need to draw a line from our old position to our new one. Other than that, everything else remains untouched.

We will create a new UIView subclass, Canvas, to handle our custom drawing. However, we will actually split the drawing into three sections: the background, the line, and the cursor. The background will remain static. It won't change at all. Our line will change. We continue to add new segments to it, but the existing portions remain untouched. We simply accumulate new line segments as time passes. Finally, the cursor will change its location but not its appearance as it moves about the screen.

Let's start by looking at the Canvas class and its companion CanvasView Controller. View and view controller pairs are typically created in one of two ways. They are either loaded from a nib (possibly as part of a storyboard) or created in code. In this case, we will do everything in code.

We instantiate our view controller by calling its designated initializer, initWithNibName:bundle:. Now, when we pass a nil-valued nib name, the system expects that we will either provide a nib file whose name matches our view controller (in this case, CanvasViewController.nib) or override the controller's loadView method. In our case, we simply use loadView to instantiate our Canvas view and set its background color.

```
// Implement loadView to create a view hierarchy programmatically,
// without using a nib.
- (void)loadView
{
    self.view = [[Canvas alloc] init];
    self.view.backgroundColor = [UIColor lightGrayColor];
}
```

Here, the background color acts as our static background. As we saw in the "Performing Custom Drawing" section of Chapter 5, the system automatically draws the background color before calling drawRect:.

> **NOTE:** You must either provide a nib file or override loadView, but not both. If you provide a nib, you cannot override loadView.

DRAWING THE LINE SEGMENTS

For our Canvas class, we have a slight problem. We want to incrementally draw our line over time. Every frame, we will add a new line segment to our image. Drawing the new segment is easy enough. We just calculate the bounds around the line segment, and call setNeedsDisplayInRect: to redraw those bounds. The problem is, any old line segments that also intersect any part of our bounding box also need to be redrawn or they will be erased.

Now, we could simply keep a list of all our line segments, then iterate over our list and redraw any that might be affected by the bounds. This works well enough at first but quickly bogs down as our drawing gets more and more complex. After a minute or so, the application becomes noticeably sluggish. Instead, we need a way to save and access subsections of our entire line in constant time.

We'll do this by creating an offscreen context and then drawing our new line to this context. We can then convert the context to an image and use the image to update only the region of the screen that has changed.

Our offscreen context needs to be the same size as our screen—so let's set it whenever our Canvas view's frame size changes. Override its setFrame: accessor as shown:

```
- (void)setFrame:(CGRect)frame {
    // If the frame is the same, do nothing.
    if (CGRectEqualToRect(self.frame, frame)) return;
    // If the frame size has changed, generate a new image context.
    if (!CGSizeEqualToSize(self.frame.size, frame.size)) {
        UIGraphicsBeginImageContextWithOptions (
            frame.size, NO, 0.0f);
```

```
        [[UIColor blackColor] setStroke];
        CGContextRef context = UIGraphicsGetCurrentContext();
        NSAssert(context != nil, @"Created a nil context");
        CGContextSetLineWidth(context, 1.0f);
        dispatch_sync(self.serialQueue, ^{
            self.imageContext = context;
        });
        UIGraphicsEndImageContext();
    }
    [super setFrame:frame];
}
```

We could use the Core Graphics function `CGBitmapContextCreate()` to create our offscreen context; however, setting up a correctly formatted bitmap context is not trivial. We also want to make sure our context's coordinates and scale match our main screen. The easiest way to do this is to call UIKit's `UIGraphics BeginImageContextWithOptions()` function.

`UIGraphicsBeginImageContextWithOptions()` takes just three parameters. The first is the desired size—we pass in our view's frame size. The second determines whether the context is opaque. By passing in `NO`, we create a transparent context. Finally, the third parameter determines the context's scale. By passing in `0.0f`, we set the scale equal to our device's main view (2.0 for a Retina display, 1.0 for older iPhones).

This function will create a correctly formatted context and set it as our current context. We can then set the stroke color, grab a reference to the context, and set the line width. Finally, we use a property to store this context, and we clean up after ourselves by calling `UIGraphicsEndImageContext()`.

OK, if you were paying attention, you may have noticed that I just skimmed over something sort of important. What the heck is the whole `dispatch_sync()` function doing in there?

Here's the problem. We will add new line segments to our image context on a background thread. However, we will update our view using the image context in the main thread. As a result, we need to synchronize these reads and writes.

Traditionally, we would do this using a mutex to block access to critical sections. In Objective-C, we could do this by adding the @synchronized directive. However, starting with iOS 4.0, we have a better way.

iOS 4.0 brought Grand Central Dispatch (GCD) to iOS. GCD is a block-based technology that lets us manage concurrency without explicitly using threads. It is highly optimized, and it can automatically balance access to system resources based on your system's capabilities. For example, it will automatically split a concurrent task among more threads when running on a 12-core Mac Pro than it does when running on an iPhone 4.

For more information, check out the Grand Central Dispatch Reference and the Concurrency Programming Guide in Apple's documentation. In this chapter, we simply use GCD to place tasks on a background queue or to move tasks back to the main thread. We will also use it here, to protect critical sections.

We start by creating a dispatch queue in Canvas's initWithFrame: method.

```
_serialQueue = dispatch_queue_create(
    "com.freelancemadscience.GravityScribbler.canvas",
    DISPATCH_QUEUE_SERIAL);
```

The dispatch_queue_create() function takes two arguments. The label can be used to identify our queue in the debugger and in crash reports. We use reverse DNS-style naming to guarantee that we have a unique label for our queue. Next, the DISPATCH_QUEUE_SERIAL attribute defines our queue as a serial queue.

> **NOTE:** While GCD greatly simplifies concurrent programming, it doesn't protect us from all the ugly, underlying details. For example, we can still create deadlocks by nesting dispatch_sync() calls (e.g., dispatch_sync(queue, ^{dispatch_sync(queue ^{[self myMethod]})});). The primary advantage of using dispatch_sync() over block-based threading is simply performance. GCD code will run significantly faster than its block-based equivalent.

All GCD queues operate in strict FIFO order—the first block in is the first block out. Serial queues also guarantee that only one block will run at a time. Concurrent queues may process multiple blocks at once, splitting them across two or more threads, depending on system resources.

Now back to our previous code, dispatch_sync() simply dispatches a block to the specified queue and then waits until the block is finished. Since our serial queue will only process one block at a time, we can wrap our critical sections in dispatch_sync() blocks, serializing access to our image context.

Now let's look at the actual drawing. When our cursor moves, the view controller will call Canvas's addLineToPoint: method.

```
// Returns the bounds of the line.

- (CGRect)addLineToPoint:(CGPoint)endPoint {

    CGFloat xdist = endPoint.x - self.currentDrawPoint.x;

    CGFloat ydist = endPoint.y - self.currentDrawPoint.y;

    // Just ignore any tiny movements.

    if (((xdist * xdist) + (ydist * ydist)) < self.minDistance)

        return CGRectZero;

    __block CGRect bounds;

    dispatch_sync(self.serialQueue, ^{

        CGContextBeginPath(self.imageContext);

        CGContextMoveToPoint(self.imageContext,

                            self.currentDrawPoint.x,

                            self.currentDrawPoint.y);

        CGContextAddLineToPoint(self.imageContext,

                            endPoint.x,

                            endPoint.y);

        bounds = CGContextGetPathBoundingBox(self.imageContext);

        CGContextStrokePath(self.imageContext);

    });
```

```
    bounds = CGRectInset(bounds, -1.0f, -1.0f);
    NSAssert2(CGRectContainsPoint(bounds, self.currentDrawPoint),
        @"%@ does not contain starting point %@",
        NSStringFromCGRect(bounds),
        NSStringFromCGPoint(self.currentDrawPoint));
    NSAssert2(CGRectContainsPoint(bounds, endPoint),
        @"%@ does not contain ending point %@",
        NSStringFromCGRect(bounds),
        NSStringFromCGPoint(endPoint));
    // Update the invalid rectangle.
    if (CGRectEqualToRect(self.invalidRect, CGRectZero)) {
        self.invalidRect = bounds;
    } else {
        self.invalidRect = CGRectUnion(self.invalidRect, bounds);
    }
    // Update the current drawing point.
    self.currentDrawPoint = endPoint;
    return self.invalidRect;
}
```

We start by calculating the distance between our current cursor position, self.current
DrawPoint, and our new end point. If this distance is below our preset minimum,
we just skip the update.

Next, we use dispatch_sync() to wrap our drawing code—again, protecting
access to our image context. The drawing code simply creates a path from our old
draw point to our new end point. We store a copy of the path's bounds (the __block
storage type modifier lets us access the value of bounds outside the dispatch_sync()
block). Then we draw the actual path.

We then expand the size of the bounding box by 1 pixel on all sides, just to
make sure the entire line segment gets updated, including any joins and line caps.
Then we update our invalidRect property. If we don't have an invalid rectangle,

we just assign our current bounds. Otherwise, we combine the bounds by storing the union of the two rectangles.

This is important because our line-segment drawing and our view-updating code run on two different threads. If our updates from the accelerometer get ahead of the screen updates, we could add two or more new line segments between each screen update. We want to make sure all of them are drawn correctly.

Once we've added the line segment, our view controller will call updateCanvasUI on the main thread.

```
// Should be called on the main thread.
-(void)updateCanvasUI {
    self.cursor.center = self.currentDrawPoint;
    // As long as we have a non-zero bounds, redraw the screen.
    if (!CGRectEqualToRect(self.invalidRect,CGRectZero)) {
        [self setNeedsDisplayInRect:self.invalidRect];
        self.invalidRect = CGRectZero;
    }
}
```

This simply updates our cursor's position, then calls setNeedsDisplayInRect: and clears our invalid rectangle. Next time through the run loop, the system will call drawRect:.

```
- (void)drawRect:(CGRect)rect
{
    CGContextRef context = UIGraphicsGetCurrentContext();
    [self drawSketchToContext:context];
}
- (void)drawSketchToContext:(CGContextRef)context {
    // Draw the changed region of the image context.
    __block CGImageRef fullImage;
    dispatch_sync(self.serialQueue, ^{
```

```
        fullImage = CGBitmapContextCreateImage(self.imageContext);
    });
    // Need to adjust the coordinates to draw the image.
    CGContextSaveGState(context);
    CGContextTranslateCTM(context, 0.0f, self.bounds.size.height);
    CGContextScaleCTM(context, 1.0f, -1.0f);
    CGContextDrawImage(context, self.bounds, fullImage);
    CGContextRestoreGState(context);
    CGImageRelease(fullImage);
}
```

Our drawRect: method is fairly simple. We just grab a reference to the current context, then call drawSketchToContext:. We're breaking out the actual drawing code so that we can reuse it later when we export our images.

In drawSketchToContext: we create an image from our image context (again, protected by a dispatch_sync block). Then we just want to draw our image to our context. The context will already have a clipping path set to the rect argument— so we don't need to do any additional clipping. CGContextDrawImage() is smart enough to only copy the data inside the clipping path.

However, we have a problem. If we just call CGContextDrawImage(), our image will appear upside down (flipped vertically, not just rotated 180 degrees). The problem comes from the difference in coordinate systems. By default, iOS uses a coordinate system with the origin at the upper-left corner, with positive numbers going down and to the right. Mac OS X has the coordinate system in the lower-left corner, with the coordinates going up and to the right. Core Graphics (and some other technologies, like Core Text) are based on the original OS X coordinate system.

Usually this isn't a problem, since the graphics contexts are typically inverted and offset before we perform any drawing. For example, in Chapter 5 we freely mixed UIKit and Core Graphics methods with no coordinate problems. However, we will occasionally find some rough patches in odd corners of the framework. CGContextDrawImage() is a prime example. This method places the image in the correct position for our graphics context, but internally it flips the image contents.

In our case, this can be particularly confusing, since the drawing rectangle will be on the opposite side of the screen from the new line segment. So, unless this rectangle happens to lie over a previously drawn section of line, we will simply be copying a transparent rectangle to the screen—making it appear that our app is not drawing at all.

To compensate for this, we temporarily flip the coordinate system and then offset it by the image's height (which also happens to be our screen height). This will then draw the image correctly.

NOTE: Flipping and translating the coordinate system is not the only solution to the flipped image problem. We could simply convert the CGImageRef to a UIImage using [UIImage imageWithCGImage:fullImage] and then draw the image using UIImage's drawInRect: method. When profiled, the UIImage approach actually appears to be slightly (though largely insignificantly) faster than using Core Graphics directly. However, if I had used that approach here, I wouldn't have had an excuse for talking about the flipped-coordinate problem.

DRAWING THE CURSOR

That's two of our three layers. All that's left is our cursor. Here, we will create a subview to hold our cursor, and then move the subview around the screen.

We start by creating a separate UIView subclass named Cursor. This is a very simple class. We don't even create a view controller for it. Rather, it will be managed by our CanvasViewController as part of its view hierarchy. Cursor only has two methods, one of which is its designated initializer. The other is drawRect:.

```
- (id)initWithFrame:(CGRect)frame
{
    self = [super initWithFrame:frame];
    if (self) {
        self.opaque = NO;
    }
    return self;
}
```

```
- (void)drawRect:(CGRect)rect {
    // Draw the dot.
    [[UIColor redColor] setFill];
    UIBezierPath* dot =
        [UIBezierPath bezierPathWithOvalInRect:self.bounds];
    [dot fill];
}
```

The designated initializer simply sets our Cursor view's opaque property to NO, while drawRect: simply draws a round circle to fill the provided frame.

> **NOTE:** Our Cursor class will call drawRect: once, when the view is first created. The result is then cached and reused. This means we can move our cursor without triggering any additional drawing calls.
>
> Additionally, having our cursor separated from the lines and background means we don't need to delete the old position from the image context. We simply change the cursor's center property, and UIKit handles the rest.

Then, we instantiate our Cursor object during our Canvas class's designated initializer.

```
CGRect dotFrame = CGRectMake(0.0f, 0.0f, 8.0f, 8.0f);
_cursor = [[Cursor alloc] initWithFrame:dotFrame];
[self addSubview:_cursor];
```

We also add a method to center the cursor in the screen. We then call this whenever the view is reset (e.g., in the CanvasViewController's viewDidAppear: method).

```
-(void)centerCursor {
    self.cursor.center = self.center;
    self.currentDrawPoint = self.center;
}
```

We've already seen how the cursor's position is updated to the current draw point in Canvas's updateCanvasUI method. That's all we need to support our cursor layer.

NOTE: We explicitly do not use Core Animation to animate the cursor's motion. The cursor's position is already updated every frame. The motion should therefore appear smooth without needing Core Animation support. In fact, the time period between frames is too short to effectively use Core Animation. Core Animation is intended for animating changes over longer intervals (usually a quarter second or longer).

CREATING A UIVIEWCONTROLLER CONTAINER

There are two basic types of view controllers: content view controllers and container view controllers. A content view is a view controller created to present some sort of data. Most of the view controllers we've created so far have been content view controllers. However, iOS also uses container view controllers. These controllers manage one or more other view controllers.

UINavigationController, UITabBarController, and UIPageViewController are all examples of container view controllers. In addition, any view controller can act as a temporary container by calling presentViewController:animated: completion: to present a modal view.

On the iPhone, each content view controller typically fills most, if not all, of the screen. We call methods on the container to swap one controller view for another, animating the transition between them. The iPad, however, gives us a little more flexibility. The UISplitViewController lets us display two content views simultaneously, while the UIPopoverController lets us layer a view controller over part of the current user interface without taking over the entire screen. Even modal views don't necessarily take over the entire screen—instead, the iPad's UIViewController supports several different modal presentation styles.

Before iOS 5, there was no good way to create custom container classes. Developers were strongly encouraged to use only the containers provided by Apple—but often, they didn't quite fit the application's needs. To get around this, developers often faked a container view controller by grabbing a child view controller's view property and shoving it directly to an existing view hierarchy.

While this more or less works, it creates a few problems. First and foremost, iOS expects both the views and the view controllers to be in well-formed hierarchies. The system uses the view controller hierarchy to pass along a number of appearance and rotation messages, including `viewWillAppear:`, `viewDidAppear:`, `viewWill disappear:`, `viewDidDisappear:`, `willRotateToInterfaceOrientation:duration:`, `willAnimateRotationToInterfaceOrientation:duration:`, and `didRotateFrom InterfaceOrientation:`.

Having an invalid controller hierarchy usually doesn't create an immediately obvious problem. Rather, issues begin to crop up much later in the development cycle. At that point, the bugs can be very difficult to resolve.

In iOS 5, Apple deals with this issue by providing an enhanced `UIViewController` class, letting us subclass it to make our own view controller containers. They have also formalized the timing of method calls when views appear and disappear, as well as explicitly defining their expectations for view and view controller hierarchies.

When creating a view controller container, we must perform all of the following steps to add a new child view controller.

1. Add the subview controller to the container by calling `addChildView Controller:`. This will automatically trigger a call to the child view controller's `willMoveToParentController:` method.

2. In general, the container view should set the subview's frame to define where it should appear, how large it should be, and so on.

3. Add the subview to the container's view by calling `addSubview:`. This will automatically trigger the calls to `viewWillAppear:` (before adding the view) and `viewDidAppear:` (after adding).

4. Perform any animation accompanying the view's appearance.

5. When done, call the subview controller's `didMoveToParentViewController:` method. The subview controller is now properly attached to the container.

Removing the child controller follows a similar series of steps:

1. Call the subview controller's `willMoveToParentViewController:` method, passing in `nil` as an argument.

2. Perform any animation accompanying the view's disappearance.

3. Remove the subview from the container's view by calling the subview's removeFromSuperview method. This will trigger viewWillDisappear: and viewDidDisappear: before and after the view is actually removed from the view hierarchy.

4. Remove the subview controller from the container by calling the subview controller's removeFromParentViewController: method. This will automatically call the subview controller's didMoveToParentViewController: method, passing in nil as an argument.

As we will see, UIView's transition... methods can be used to combine some of these steps (particularly adding a new view, removing an old view, and any state change animations). However, in general, you must follow all of the above steps to create a valid view controller hierarchy.

NOTE: Some of these methods should only be called within our container controller subclass. In particular, addChildViewController: and removeFrom Superview should only be called internally within our container. We must provide our own wrapper methods to add and remove the subview controller as necessary. As a corollary, we should never call addChild ViewController: on another view controller—as it is undoubtedly not prepared to handle the new view controller appropriately.

Apple still recommends using their pre-built container view controllers whenever possible. However, custom containers provide an excellent method for customizing an application's flow. In GravityScribbler, we will use a custom container to display pop-up messages in response to different gestures from the user.

We will start by creating a UIViewController subclass, GSRootViewController. As the name suggests, this will act as the root view for our application. It will contain both our canvas and our pop-ups as child view controllers.

MANAGING THE CANVASVIEWCONTROLLER

Let's start by creating a property to hold our CanvasViewController. We'll then write a custom setter to properly set up our canvas.

```
#pragma mark - Background View Controller

- (void)setCanvasViewController:(CanvasViewController *)
canvasViewController {
    // If we are passing in the same background view, do nothing.
    if ([canvasViewController isEqual:_canvasViewController])
        return;
    // Make it the same size as our current view.
    canvasViewController.view.frame = self.view.bounds;
    // Then swap views.
    [self addChildViewController:canvasViewController];
    [self.canvasViewController willMoveToParentViewController:nil];
    [self
     transitionFromViewController:_canvasViewController
     toViewController:canvasViewController
     duration:1.0f
     options:UIViewAnimationOptionTransitionCurlUp
     animations:^() {/* Do nothing */ }
     completion:^(BOOL finished)
     {
         [canvasViewController didMoveToParentViewController:self];
         [_canvasViewController removeFromParentViewController];
         _canvasViewController = canvasViewController;
     }];
}
```

Here, we start with a quick sanity check. If the new canvas controller is the same as our current canvas controller, we don't have to do anything. We just return. Next, we make sure the new controller's view fills our root view's bounds completely. Then we swap in our new controller.

We start by adding the new controller as a child controller and letting the current canvas view know that it's about to be removed. Then we call `transitionFromView Controller:toViewController:duration:options:animations:completion:` to animate the swap. This automatically adds our new controller's view to our view hierarchy, removes the old controller's view, and animates the transition between views.

We have a number of pre-bottled transition animations we could choose from: cross fade, flips for different orientations, and a page curl. Alternatively, we could use the animation block to change any of our view's animatable properties. Here, we simply use the page curl animation. Whenever we add a new canvas view controller, our old view will peel off, revealing the new view underneath. Then, in the completion block, we finish adding our new controller, remove the old controller, and assign our new canvas view controller to our instance variable.

NOTE: To call `transitionFromViewController:toViewController: duration:options:animations:completion:`, **both controllers must be children of the same container controller. This means we must add the new controller using** `addChildViewController:` **before we initiate the transition, but we cannot call** `removeFromParentViewController` **on the old controller until after the transition has started. It doesn't have to be called in the transition's completion block, as long as it occurs after the call to** `transitionFromViewController:...`.

We'll use this method to reset our canvas, as shown:

```
- (void)reset {
    self.canvasViewController = [[CanvasViewController alloc] init];
}
```

We'll then attach this method to a shake gesture. Whenever the user shakes their phone, we'll swap in a new canvas controller, peeling away their old drawing and giving them a fresh new canvas to draw on (**Figure 8.2**).

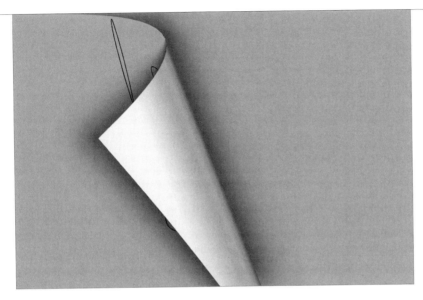

FIGURE 8.2 Resetting the
canvas

Our reset method looks deceptively simple, but this hides a subtle feature. When we instantiate our new CanvasViewController, we are not calling the designated initializer. Instead, we're calling the generic init method. This will then call [self initWithNibName:nil bundle:nil]. When the system goes to create our view hierarchy, it will call our controller's loadView method. Since we passed in a nil value for the nib name, the default implementation would normally look for a nib file named CanvasViewController.xib. However, as we saw earlier, we've overridden loadView to programmatically create our view hierarchy instead.

CREATING POP-UP VIEWS

GSRootViewController will also be able to display pop-up views over the top of our canvas. We will use this to display a number of support views, including custom alert messages, a pause indicator, our acceleration control, and an export menu. GSRootViewController will also provide different animation options for when the view appears. It could slide in from the sides (with an animated bounce at the end), drop down from the top (also with a bounce), or simply fade in and out.

The pop-ups themselves consist of view and controller combinations. All of them use the same UIView subclass, PopupView. This is a simple, non-opaque view that draws a semi-transparent, rounded-rectangle backdrop, on which we will place our labels and other controls.

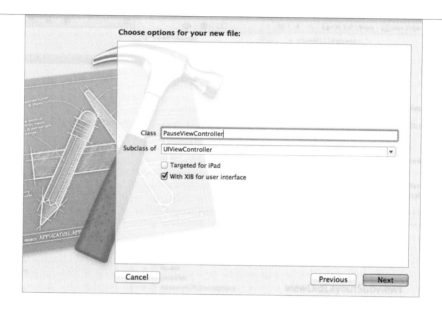

FIGURE 8.3 Creating a nib-based view controller

To create a pop-up view, add a new UIViewController subclass to the project. In the options panel, make sure the "With XIB for user interface" check box is selected (**Figure 8.3**). This will create our class header, an implementation file, and an initial nib file.

Then open PauseViewController.xib. Working with a nib is almost the same as working with a storyboard. However, we will find a few differences. The scene list is gone, as is the scene dock. Instead, we have a single dock that holds the top-level objects for the entire nib. Meanwhile, the Interface Builder area simply displays our top-level views.

Our nib starts with three top-level objects: the File's Owner, the first responder, and our view (**Figure 8.4**). Of the three, only the File's Owner is new. Like the first responder, it is a placeholder (also sometimes called a proxy object). The system does not instantiate the placeholders when we load the nib. Instead, we instantiate an instance of the File's Owner in our code and then pass it to the nib-loading method. This is implicitly handled for us when we call UIViewController's initWithNibName:bundle: method. Our newly instantiated controller will be passed to the nib-loading code, which will in turn set up and configure our controller. The File's Owner represents the main link between the nib and the rest of your application. In our case, the File's Owner is our PauseViewController instance.

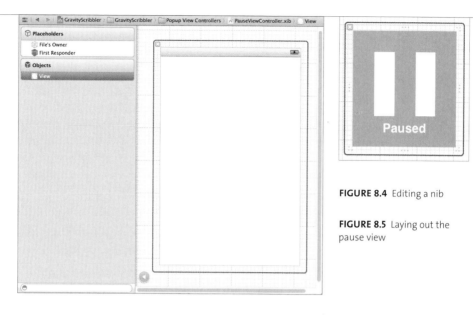

FIGURE 8.4 Editing a nib

FIGURE 8.5 Laying out the pause view

Within the nib file, I typically set the view's Status Bar attribute to None. This is one of the simulated metrics attributes; that means it doesn't actually affect the nib at runtime—it just modifies how the nib appears within Interface Builder. Specifically, it removes the status bar from our view, just leaving us a blank white rectangle. Since our pop-up view won't fill the entire screen, we don't need to worry about leaving space for any of the system elements.

We also need to change the view's class to PopupView and set its size (200 x 216 points for the PauseViewController). GSRootViewController will set the view's position, centering it in the screen. However, it will respect the size that we set in the nib.

Eventually, we will also want to set the view's background color to clear—but since we will be placing white controls on the view, they can be somewhat hard to see. Therefore, I use a gray background color while designing the interface, and I change it back when I'm done. We can then drag out whatever controls we need, drawing connections back to the File's Owner as necessary. Our pause view is relatively simple. We just add an image view to hold the pause.png image and a label saying "Paused" (**Figure 8.5**).

NOTE: Most of our views are relatively simple, especially our pause indicator and our acceleration control. In many ways, they could be more easily managed by the `CanvasViewController` directly, without requiring either a container or their own view controllers. Creating child view controllers really starts to make sense when we begin adding more complex views. For example, the export menu controller not only dynamically sets the content for its views based on your device's capabilities, it also coordinates the actual creation and export of our images. We really don't want to add these features directly to our `CanvasViewController` class.

MANAGING POP-UP VIEWS

We need to build support for adding our pop-up views to our container class. To start with, lets create an enum for our different animation sequences.

```
typedef enum {

    GSPopupFade,

    GSPopupDropDown,

    GSPopupSlideFromHomeButton,

    GSPopupSlideTowardsHomeButton,

} GSPopupAnimationType;
```

Now we can define a method to show a pop-up. This is a bit long, so let's look at it in chunks.

```
#pragma mark - Popup View Animation Methods
- (void)showPopupController:(UIViewController*)controller
            animationType:(GSPopupAnimationType)type
    withCompletionHandler:(void (^)(BOOL finished))completion {
    NSAssert(controller != nil, @"Trying to show a nil controller");
    // Add to the controller hierarchy.
    [self addChildViewController:controller];
```

This starts simply enough. We perform a quick sanity check, just to make sure we're not trying to add a `nil` pop-up view controller. Then we add the controller to our container class.

```
switch (type) {
    case GSPopupDropDown:
        [self initialPositionForDropDown:controller.view];
        break;
    case GSPopupSlideTowardsHomeButton:
        [self initialPositionForSlideTowardsHome:
            controller.view];
        break;
    case GSPopupSlideFromHomeButton:
        [self initialPositionForSlideFromHome:controller.view];
        break;
    case GSPopupFade:
        [self initialPositionForFade:controller.view];
        break;
    default:
        [NSException
         raise:@"Invalid value"
         format:@"%d is not a recognized GSPopupAnimationType",
         type];
        break;
}
```

Next, we call a method that sets the pop-up view's initial state. Each of our animation variations has its own initialPosition... method.

```
// Rotate the view.
CGFloat rotation = 0.0f;
switch (self.bestSubviewOrientation) {
    case UIDeviceOrientationLandscapeLeft:
        rotation = M_PI_2;
```

```
            break;
        case UIDeviceOrientationLandscapeRight:
            rotation = -M_PI_2;
            break;
    default:
        [NSException
         raise:@"Illegal Orientation"
         format:@"Invalid best subview orientation: %d",
         self.bestSubviewOrientation];
        break;
};
controller.view.transform =
CGAffineTransformMakeRotation(rotation);
[self.view addSubview:controller.view];
```

Here, we determine the correct orientation for our pop-up view and rotate it as needed. We'll talk more about view rotations in a bit. For now, just be aware that we're not using UIKit's autorotations. Our root view and canvas are always kept in portrait orientation—this simplifies the motion detection and drawing code. However, users will typically hold the device in one of the two landscape orientations. If we want our pop-up views to appear properly, we have to monitor the device's position and set the pop-up rotations by hand.

Here, we simply calculate the correct rotation angle. Then we create an affine transform to rotate our pop-up view, and assign it to the pop-up view's transform property. We then add the pop-up to our view hierarchy.

```
    // Now animate its appearance.
    switch (type) {
        case GSPopupDropDown:
            [self animateAppearDropDown:controller
                    withCompletionHandler:completion];
            break;
```

```
        case GSPopupSlideTowardsHomeButton:
            [self animateAppearSlideTowardsHome:controller
                        withCompletionHandler:completion];
            break;
        case GSPopupSlideFromHomeButton:
            [self animateAppearSlideFromHome:controller
                        withCompletionHandler:completion];
            break;
        case GSPopupFade:
            [self animateAppearFade:controller
              withCompletionHandler:completion];
            break;
        default:
            [NSException
             raise:@"Invalid value"
             format:@"%d is not a recognized GSPopupAnimationType",
             type];
            break;
    }
}
```

Finally, we start the animation. Again, each of our animation sequences has its own animateAppear... method.

Let's look at the initialPosition... methods. We'll start with initialPositionForDropDown:.

```
- (void)initialPositionForDropDown:(UIView*)view {
    view.center = self.view.center;
    CGRect frame = view.frame;
    switch (self.bestSubviewOrientation) {
        case UIDeviceOrientationLandscapeRight:
```

```
            frame.origin.x = -frame.size.width;
            break;
        case UIDeviceOrientationLandscapeLeft:
            frame.origin.x = self.view.frame.size.width;
            break;
        default:
            [NSException
             raise:@"Illegal Orientation"
             format:@"Invalid best subview orientation: %d",
             self.bestSubviewOrientation];
            break;
    };
    view.frame = frame;
    view.alpha = 1.0f;
}
```

This is conceptually straightforward. We want the pop-up view to be centered horizontally, but positioned off the top of our screen. Again, the definition of "top of the screen" will change depending on whether the device is held landscape left or landscape right.

Here, we center the pop-up view in our root view. Then we offset its x-coordinates based on the best device orientation. Finally, we set the frame and set our alpha value.

The ...SlideTowardsHome: and ...SlideFromHome: methods use a very similar logic— they're even simpler since they don't need to check the device orientation and can just offset the y-coordinate. So, let's skip them and look at initialPositionForFade:.

```
- (void)initialPositionForFade:(UIView*)view {
    // Center the view.
    view.center = self.view.center;
    // And make it invisible.
    view.alpha = 0.0f;
}
```

This is even simpler. We just center our pop-up view and then set its `alpha` property to `0.0f`. This will make the view completely transparent.

Now we just need to animate our views' appearance. We'll use Core Animation to do this. I won't lie to you: Core Animation is a rich, complex framework. Entire books have been written on this topic. There are lots of little knobs to tweak. However, for most common use cases it is easy to use.

To give you the most basic explanation, all `UIView`s have a number of animatable properties. These include `frame`, `bounds`, `center`, `transform`, `alpha`, `backgroundColor`, and `contentStretch`. To animate our view, we create an animation block. Inside the block, we change one of these properties. Core Animation will then calculate the interpolated values for that property for each frame over the block's duration—and will smoothly animate the view's transition.

If I want to move the view, I just change the `frame`. If I want to scale or rotate the view, I change the `transform`. If I want it to fade in or fade out, I change the `alpha`. Everything else is just bells and whistles.

Let's look at our fade animation, since it is the simplest.

```
- (void)animateAppearFade:(UIViewController*)controller
    withCompletionHandler:(void (^)(BOOL finished))completion {
    [UIView animateWithDuration:0.25f
                     animations:^()
     {
         controller.view.alpha = 1.0f;
     } completion:^(BOOL finished)
     {
         [controller didMoveToParentViewController:self];
         if (completion != nil) {
             completion(finished);
         }
     }];
}
```

Here, we just call `animateWithDuration:animations:completion:`. We set the duration argument to a quarter second. Inside the animation block, we simply set our `alpha` property to `1.0f`. Core Animation will therefore animate the transition from `0.0f` alpha (completely transparent) to `1.0f` alpha (completely opaque), causing our view to fade in.

The completion block runs once the animation is done. Its `finished` argument is set to `YES` if the animation ran to completion and to `NO` if it stopped prematurely. In this block, we simply call `didMoveToParentViewController` to completely add our subview controller. Then we call our provided completion handler, if any.

For the drop down and slide animations, we want to add a little bounce at the end. To do this, we'll chain together several animation sequences. `animateAppearDropDown:withCompletionHandler:`, `animateAppearSlideTowardsHome:withCompletionHandler:`, and `animateAppearSlideFromHome:withCompletionHandler:` all calculate the horizontal or vertical bounce offset and then call `animateWithBounce:verticalBounce:horizontalBounce:withCompletionHandler:`.

This is where the real work is done. Basically, `animateWithBounce:...` defines three separate animation blocks. The first block's completion handler will call the second block, and the second block's completion handler will then call the third block. However, it's easiest to define these blocks in reverse order. Let's look at the method, one block at a time.

```
- (void)animateWithBounce:(UIViewController*)controller
           verticalBounce:(CGFloat)vBounce
         horizontalBounce:(CGFloat)hBounce
    withCompletionHandler:(void (^)(BOOL finished))completion {
    CGPoint center = self.view.center;
    // Chaining together animation blocks,
    // declare the bounce down animation block.
    void (^bounceDown)(BOOL) = ^(BOOL notUsed) {
    [UIView
     animateWithDuration:0.15f
     delay:0.0f
     options:UIViewAnimationCurveEaseIn
```

```
    animations:^{
        controller.view.center = center;
    }
    completion:^(BOOL finished) {
        [controller
         didMoveToParentViewController:self];
        if (completion != nil) {
            completion(finished);
        }
    }];
};
```

We start by creating a local variable, center, that contains the coordinate of our root view's center. Next, we define our bounceDown block. This is the final animation sequence in our chain.

Much like animationAppearFade:..., this method simply sets the final position for our view (centered in the root view) and then calls didMoveToParentView Controller: and any provided completion handler when the animation finishes. There are two important changes. First, we're only using a 0.15-second duration. Second, we added the UIViewAnimationCurveEaseIn option.

By default, Core Animation will interpolate the animations evenly over the duration. This makes the animation appear at a constant duration. UIViewAnimation CurveEaseIn causes the animation to begin slowly, then speed up over the animation's duration.

```
    // Declare the bounce up animation block.
    // This will call bounce down when completed.
    void (^bounceUp)(BOOL) = ^(BOOL notUsed) {
        [UIView animateWithDuration:0.15f
                              delay:0.0f
                            options:UIViewAnimationCurveEaseOut
                         animations:^{
```

```
                              controller.view.center =
                              CGPointMake(center.x + vBounce,
                                            center.y + hBounce)
                  }
                  completion:bounceDown];
      };
```

Here, we define our bounceUp block. Again, we're using a 0.15-second duration; however, this time we use UIViewAnimationCurveEaseOut. The animation will start quickly and slow down over the duration. In the animation block, we simply move the view to the top of its bounce position (defined by the vertical and horizontal bounce offsets). When this animation is finished, we call our bounceDown block.

```
      // Initial movement onto the screen.
      // This will call bounce up when completed.
      [UIView animateWithDuration:0.5f
                      delay:0.0f
                    options:UIViewAnimationCurveEaseIn
                  animations:^{
                      controller.view.center = center;
                      controller.view.alpha = 1.0f;
                  }
                  completion:bounceUp];
  }
```

Finally, we have the initial animation block. This takes a half second, with a UIViewAnimationCurveEaseIn animation curve. Again, this will cause the view to start moving slowly, but it will accelerate over the duration of the sequence.

This simply centers our pop-up view. We also set the alpha value to 1.0f, just in case. After all, it is possible to both move and fade-in our view at the same time. When the animation sequence is done, we call our bounceUp method.

To hide our pop-up views, we create a similar set of methods, starting with the hidePopupController:animationType: method and then delegating out to the various animateDisappear… methods for the actual changes.

```
- (void)hidePopupController:(UIViewController*)controller
            animationType:(GSPopupAnimationType)type {
    [controller willMoveToParentViewController:nil];
    [UIView animateWithDuration:0.25f
     animations:^()
     {
         switch (type) {
             case GSPopupDropDown:
                 [self animateDisappearDropDown:controller.view];
                 break;
             case GSPopupSlideTowardsHomeButton:
                 [self animateDisappearSlideTowardsHome:
                     controller.view];
                 break;
             case GSPopupSlideFromHomeButton:
                 [self animateDisappearSlideFromHome:
                     controller.view];
                 break;
             case GSPopupFade:
```

```
                    [self animateDisappearFade:controller.view];
                    break;
            default:
                [NSException
                  raise:@"Invalid value"
                  format:@"%d is not a recognized "
                            @"GSPopupAnimationType", type];
                break;
        }
    } completion:^(BOOL finished)
    {
        [controller.view removeFromSuperview];
        [controller removeFromParentViewController];
    }];
}
```

Here, we call `willMoveToParentViewController:` before we start the animations. This lets our controller know that it's about to be removed. Inside the animation block, we call the appropriate `animateDisappear`... method to change our animatable properties. `animateDisappearFade:` just sets the view's alpha to `0.0f`, while the others change the frame, moving the view off the screen. Finally, when the animation is complete, we remove the view from its superview and call `removeFromParentViewController` to complete our child view controller's removal.

CUSTOMIZING UIKIT CONTROLS

The default appearance for iOS's controls looks pretty sharp, but sometimes we need something a little different. Maybe we want to use a default color scheme for our app. We don't need to go full bore and build our own custom controls—we just want to tweak the appearance a bit.

Fortunately, with iOS 5, UIKit lets us easily customize the appearance of many of the built-in controls. In this section, we'll look at using the new UIAppearance protocol, as well as using resizable and tiled images for buttons and view backgrounds.

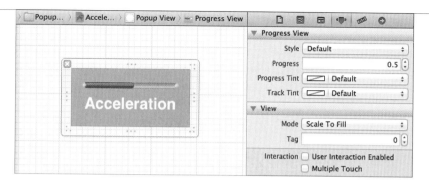

FIGURE 8.6 Our accelera-
tion pop-up with the default
UIProgressView

INTRODUCING THE UIAPPEARANCE PROXY

iOS 5 added a number of methods to its views and controls that let us modify
their appearance. In this app, we will be modifying the color scheme used by the
UIProgressView in our acceleration pop-up.

By default, the UIProgressView shows a white track with a blue progress bar
(**Figure 8.6**). However, the class has four new properties that can modify this appearance: progressTintColor, progressImage, trackTintColor, and trackTintImage.
The tint color methods will allow you to set a base color for the specified part of
the interface. The system won't necessarily use this color directly. Instead, it will
take this color and modify it (e.g., adding highlights or shadows) before displaying
the view. The image methods let us assign a resizable image which will be used to
draw the track and progress bar—giving us even more control over our interface's
appearance.

There are several different ways in which we can use these methods. Most
obviously, we can call them directly in our code to modify our view's appearance.
For example, to change the acceleration pop-up, we could add the following to our
AccelerationViewController's viewDidLoad method:

```
self.progressBar.progressTintColor = [UIColor colorWithRed:0.5
                                                      green:0.0
                                                       blue:0.0
                                                      alpha:1.0];
self.progressBar.trackTintColor = [UIColor colorWithRed:0.5
                                                  green:0.3
                                                   blue:0.3
                                                  alpha:1.0];
```

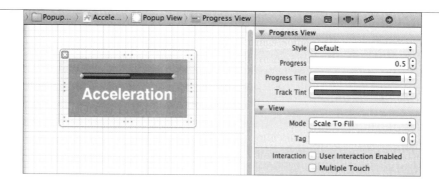

FIGURE 8.7 Our custom
UIProgressView

Alternatively, we can set the tint values (but not the images) directly in Interface Builder (**Figure 8.7**).

Unfortunately, both of these approaches only let us modify one particular instance of UIProgressView. What if we wanted to change the appearance of all the UIProgressViews throughout our entire application?

Ah, this is where things get interesting. iOS 5 also adds a UIAppearance protocol. This allows us to modify the adopting class's appearance proxy—modifying all instances of that class.

To set the appearance for all our progress views, just call the following code:

```
UIProgressView* proxy = [UIProgressView appearance];
proxy.progressTintColor = [UIColor colorWithRed:0.5
                                          green:0.0
                                           blue:0.0
                                          alpha:1.0];
proxy.trackTintColor = [UIColor colorWithRed:0.5
                                       green:0.3
                                        blue:0.3
                                       alpha:1.0];
```

Or, if we want to be more selective, we can use appearanceWhenContainedIn: to limit our modifications to those instances contained in the specified class. For example, this will modify the appearance of all UIProgressView instances in any PopupView classes.

CLASSES SUPPORTING THE APPLICATION PROXY

Two things must happen before a class can support setting its appearance through an application proxy. First, the class must adopt the UIAppearanceContainer protocol. Next, it must flag the relevant accessors with the UI_APPEARANCE_SELECTOR tag.

A quick search shows that only the following classes currently support the appearance proxy:

- UIActivityIndicatorView
- UIBarButtonItem
- UIBarItem
- UINavigationBar
- UIProgressView
- UISearchBar

- UISlider
- UISwitch
- UISegmentedControl
- UITabBar
- UITabBarItem
- UIToolbar

Unfortunately, the documentation does not clearly label the flagged accessors. However, if you have any questions, you can always open the class's header file. For example, opening UIActivityIndicatorView.h shows that only the color property is properly flagged (OK, you probably could have guessed that from the docs, but still...).

Most notably, UIButton is missing from this list. So, even though iOS 5.0 adds a tintColor property, this property may not do what you want. It won't actually change the color of a rounded rectangle (though, see our custom buttons in the "Rounding Corners with Core Animation" section of Chapter 4). And we cannot simply modify the proxy; we must modify the appearance of each button individually. We'll see this when we create custom buttons using resizable images, coming up next.

```
UIProgressView* proxy =
[UIProgressView appearanceWhenContainedIn:[PopupView class], nil];
proxy.progressTintColor = [UIColor colorWithRed:0.5
                                          green:0.0
                                           blue:0.0
                                          alpha:1.0];
proxy.trackTintColor = [UIColor colorWithRed:0.5
                                       green:0.3
                                        blue:0.3
                                       alpha:1.0];
```

FIGURE 8.8 Low- and high-resolution background images

However, since we only have a single `UIProgressView` instance in this application, setting the tint colors in the nib is probably the path of least resistance.

RESIZABLE AND TILED IMAGES

Often, we want to modify a view or control by adding a custom background image. The naive approach is to simply create an image that is the exact size needed by our interface. This, however, has two problems. First, it wastes a lot of memory, since we need to load all these full-size images into memory. Second, it limits our flexibility. If we want to resize the control, we need to redesign our background image as well.

Fortunately, iOS offers a solution: We can use resizable or tiled images. Admittedly, iOS has supported stretchable and tiled images since iOS 2.0; however, the old `stretchableImageWithLeftCapWidth:topCapHeight:` method has been deprecated and replaced with the new `resizableImageWithCapInsets:` method. Resizable images give us a greater range of options than their older, stretchable cousins.

Let's start with tiled images. We'll create two different versions of our background image. The first will be a 24 x 24 pixel image named `tile.png`. The system will use this for lower-resolution screens. The second will be a 48 x 48 pixel version named `tile@2x.png` for devices with Retina displays (**Figure 8.8**).

Now we load the tile image using `UIImage`'s `imageNamed:` convenience method. This will automatically load the correct tile image, based on the current device's screen scale.

```
self.tileImage = [UIImage imageNamed:TileImageName];
```

To draw our tiled background, we simply create a `UIColor` using the image as a pattern. We can then set this as our fill color, and fill in any closed path. In this application, we use it in `PopupView`'s `drawRect:` method to draw the view's background.

```
- (void)drawRect:(CGRect)rect
{
    // Draw the background with rounded corners and a tiled body.
    UIColor* border = [[UIColor blackColor]
                        colorWithAlphaComponent:0.75f];
    [border setStroke];
```

```
UIColor* fill = [UIColor colorWithPatternImage:self.tileImage];
[fill setFill];
UIBezierPath* path =
[UIBezierPath
 bezierPathWithRoundedRect:
 CGRectInset(self.bounds, 1.0f, 1.0f)
 byRoundingCorners:UIRectCornerAllCorners
 cornerRadii:CGSizeMake(20.0f, 20.0f)];
path.lineWidth = 2.0f;
[path fill];
[path stroke];
// Not strictly necessary since we're subclassing
// UIView directly
[super drawRect:rect];
}
```

UIKit will draw repeated copies of our image pattern both vertically and horizontally to fill the entire path. In this case, we're filling in the rounded rectangle and then drawing a 2-point-wide border around it. Notice that we inset our rounded rectangle by half our line width. This gives us enough space to draw our entire line, while still filling the view. This is then used as the background for our pop-ups, like our acceleration control, giving us a nice tessellated background (**Figure 8.9**).

Next, let's look at creating resizable images. We will use these for the buttons in our export menu. Just like the tile image, we need to create two versions, one for low-resolution screens, the other for Retina displays (**Figure 8.10**). This time they will be 20 x 20 pixels and 40 x 40 pixels.

To make a resizable image, we take a normal UIImage and call its resizableImage WithCapInsets: method. This takes a single argument, a UIEdgeInsets structure holding the value of the cap insets on the top, left, bottom, and right.

When this image is resized, the areas covered by the cap insets are drawn normally. Areas between the cap insets are tiled to fill in the remaining space both horizontally and vertically. In our application, we create resizable images for our buttons during the ExportViewController's tableView:cellForRowAtIndexPath: method.

FIGURE 8.9 Our tiled background in action

FIGURE 8.10 Low- and high-resolution resizable images

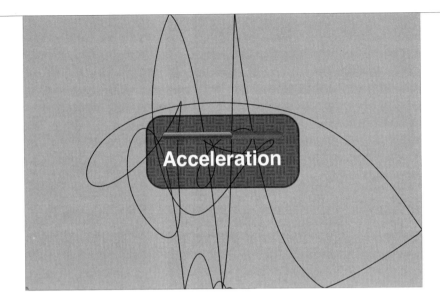

```
UIImage* button = [UIImage imageNamed:@"Button"];
UIEdgeInsets insets =
UIEdgeInsetsMake(10.0f, 10.0f, 9.0f, 9.0f);
UIImage* resizableButton =
[button resizableImageWithCapInsets:insets];
[cell.button setBackgroundImage:resizableButton
            forState:UIControlStateNormal];
```

Again, we load the correct image by calling imageNamed:. We then define our insets. In our case, we are leaving only a single point both vertically and horizontally. When the image is stretched horizontally, the column of pixels at x = 10 will be used to fill in the extra width. Similarly, when stretched vertically, the row at y = 10 will be used. On a regular display, both of these are a single pixel wide, so that pixel will be used for the entire width (or height). On a Retina display, these regions are actually two pixels wide, so the rows (or columns) will be tiled to fill the extra space. We can see the resizable images in action by opening our application's export menu using a horizontal three-finger swipe (**Figure 8.11**).

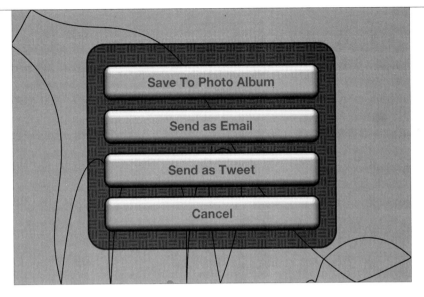

FIGURE 8.11 Resizable images in action

Both tiled images and resizable images allow us to create visually interesting backgrounds while minimizing the memory requirements and size of our final application. Of course, you have to design your images carefully so they will work well as either tiled or stretched images. You cannot simply stretch any image and expect it to look good.

NOTE: In this example, the interiors of our resizable images are filled with a solid color, since we are tiling a single pixel (or, in the case of a Retina display, two pixels with identical colors). However, by increasing the size of the area between the inset regions, we can create patterns that will then be tiled to fill the entire area covered by the image. It takes additional effort to make sure the tiled areas match well with the inset designs, but when done properly it can produce resizable images based on tessellated patterns.

RESPONDING TO USER INPUT

Customizing the appearance is nice, but it's not much of a control if we cannot respond to user input. Again, UIKit's controls cover most of the common interactions, but sometimes we need to respond to taps, swipes, pinches, tilts, or shakes in ways that the built-in controls simply don't allow.

Please note that when I'm talking about controls, I don't necessarily mean literal subclasses of `UIControl`. Rather, I am referring to any objects that respond to user input. Many of these will be simple subclasses of `UIView`, or, in the more complex situations, `UIView` and delegate pairs.

This often becomes a real stumbling block for many new iOS developers. When we start thinking about creating custom controls, we often assume that we must shoehorn our idea into the target/action pattern used by the more common UIKit controls. Unfortunately, when we try to subclass `UIControl` ourselves, we quickly find a lack of guidance in the documentation. It's easy to feel overwhelmed and frustrated. Fortunately, it is also unnecessary.

The harsh truth is that the narrow range of `UIControlEvents` heavily constrains the target/action pattern's usefulness. `UIControl` subclasses work well when they closely match these events—largely limiting us to monitoring touches and drags. Some of the more general events (e.g., the value changed and editing events) can be used to model a broader range of interactions, but they give us a relatively weak interface between the control and its view controller. For more complex controls, we typically need to create a delegate. This delegate may work in tandem with `UIControlEvents` (e.g., `UITextField`), or it may stand on its own (e.g., `UITextView`).

Bottom line, we should not feel like we need to use `UIControls`. Even in UIKit itself, most of the more complex controls don't bother subclassing `UIControl`. Instead, classes like `UITextView`, `UITableView`, and `UIPickerView` prefer to use delegates and data sources over target/action pairs. This allows them to define a much richer interface between the control and its view controller.

For this reason, we won't spend much time on the relatively narrow topic of subclassing `UIControl`. Instead, we're going to focus on the broader task of responding to user input. In particular, we will look at using gesture recognizers to easily detect a wide range of multi-touch commands. We will also look at using the Core Motion framework to monitor changes to the device's orientation—in our case, letting the user control the cursor by tilting their phone.

SUBCLASSING UIControl

In my opinion, there are two key questions that we must answer when we're considering subclassing UIControl. First, do we plan to reuse this control, either in this project or in other projects? If this is strictly a one-off custom control, then it's probably not worth the effort. Simply create a solid delegate protocol for your control and use that instead.

Second, do we want to wire the control's events to actions in Interface Builder? Again, if the answer is no, there's really no reason to consider UIControl. A delegate will still be simpler both to implement and to use.

However, if we've thought through our design and answered yes to both questions, how do we go about building a UIControl subclass? Well, all controls have two parts. The first is their appearance. Just like any custom view, we will have to provide custom drawing code. However, unlike static images, we probably want our control to visually respond to user input. The Core Animation techniques we used earlier in this chapter are often key to making that happen. Additionally, just like any custom view, our control does not need to be drawn as a single view. We can decompose the view into a multi-layer view hierarchy. This is particularly useful when using images. The UIImageView class is highly optimized, and we should generally try to add it to our view hierarchy, instead of using UIKit to draw the images ourselves.

The second part is the actual user interaction. UIControl already responds to a number of touch-based commands, and it will automatically trigger any assigned actions for the touch events (any event starting with UIControlEventTouch...).

We can modify this behavior in two ways. First, we can override sendAction:to:forEvent: to monitor and change how events are dispatched. Note that sendAction:to:forEvent: is only called if there is a target and action assigned to the given event. So we must first assign a default target/action pair. Then we can use this method to cancel or change the target or action based on the control's state. Next, we can track touch events by overriding beginTrackingWithTouch:withEvent:, continueTrackingWithTouch:withEvent:, and endTrackingWithTouch:withEvent:, though—as we will soon see—it's often a lot easier to manage complex touch events using gesture recognizers. In fact, there's no reason we can't add gesture recognizers directly to our UIControl subclass.

continues on next page

Finally, we can call sendActionsForControlEvents: to programmatically trigger our own events. Typically, we would use this to trigger UIControlEventValueChanged or one of the UIControlEventEditing... events. Simply call sendActionsForControlEvents: and pass in a bitmask with a flag set for each of the events we wish to trigger. Our UIControl subclass will then automatically call sendAction:to:forEvent: once for each target/ action pair assigned to those events.

As a quick example, let's say we wanted to create a 2D slider. We basically want a simple grid with a cursor that can be moved both horizontally and vertically. Our design might look something like the following:

First, we decompose our view into two layers: the grid and the cursor. This allows us to move the cursor without affecting the underlying grid.

Second, we add three state variables. One contains the relative x-coordinate of the cursor (from 0.0 on the left edge to 1.0 on the right). The other contains the relative y-coordinate (again, ranging from 0.0 at the top to 1.0 at the bottom). Finally, the third variable contains a BOOL to monitor our editing state (YES if we are currently modifying the control's values, NO otherwise).

Next, we're not doing anything terribly complex here, so the existing touch methods are probably sufficient. Simply override beginTrackingWithTouch:withEvent:, continueTrackingWithTouch:withEvent:, and endTrackingWithtouch:withEvent:.

In beginTracking..., we check to see if our touch is close enough to our cursor. If it is, we start editing our control. At a minimum, this involves setting self.editing = YES and calling [self sendActionsForControl Events:UIControlEventEditingDidBegin] to trigger the editing did begin event. We may also want to change the cursor's appearance (e.g., by highlighting it).

In continueTracking..., if self.editing == YES, we update our x- and y-coordinates based on the touch's location in the view. We then update the cursor's position. Finally, we call [self sendActionsForControlEvents: UIControlEventEditingChanged | UIControlEventValueChanged] to trigger actions for both the editing changed and value changed events.

Then, in endTracking..., if self.editing == YES, we set self.editing = NO and call [sendActionsForControl Events:UIControlEventEditingDidEnd].

That's it. We can probably enhance and improve it, but that's all our control really needs. Next time we're in Interface Builder, we can drag a UIView out from the library, position it wherever we would like, and change its class to our custom UIControl subclass. Now we'll be able to draw connections to its events, just like any of UIKit's controls.

GESTURE RECOGNIZERS

Gesture recognizers were added with iOS 3.2. They greatly simplify the detection of common touch-based commands, like taps, swipes, drags, pinches, rotations, and long presses. In many ways, the gesture recognizers allow us to abstract away the ugly details involved in tracking and analyzing individual touches, letting us define our interactions at a high level. Say we want to detect a two-finger triple tap. No problem. We simply create an instance of UITapGestureRecognizer and set the desired number of taps and touches. That's it. We don't need to worry about monitoring the individual touch locations, the number of touches detected, how long each one lasted, or even the duration between the different sets of touches. The gesture recognizer handles all of those details for us, and it handles them in a way that will be consistent across all applications.

> **NOTE:** While the existing UIGestureRecognizer subclasses cover all the common multi-touch gestures, we can create our own subclass to recognize custom gestures. For more information, check out "Creating Custom Gesture Recognizers" in Apple's Event Handling Guide for iOS.

Gesture recognizers come in two basic flavors: discrete and continuous. This determines the type of action messages that the recognizer sends. A discrete gesture recognizer will send a single action message once the gesture is complete. These are used for quick gestures that mark a single point in time: taps and swipes.

Continuous gesture recognizers, on the other hand, track the gesture over time. They will continue to send multiple action messages until the gesture ends. Pinches, pans, rotations, and long presses are all modeled using continuous gesture recognizers.

In particular, look at the difference between a swipe and a pan gesture. Superficially, they appear quite similar. Both involve dragging a finger across the screen. However, for a swipe, we're just interested in triggering a single action. Once the swipe is detected, we call our action and we're done. It's a discrete, single event. For the pan, we actually want to track the user's finger as it moves. The location of the finger, how far it has moved, which direction it has moved—all of these details may be important. As a result, we might use a swipe gesture to trigger a move from one page to another, while we'd use a pan gesture to fast forward through a video or change the app's volume.

We use a number of different gestures in GravityScribbler. A single-finger pan adjusts the app's acceleration rate (basically, the responsiveness of the gravity cursor). A two-finger tap pauses the app. Finally, a three-finger horizontal swipe will bring up our export menu.

NOTE: Instead of attaching the gesture recognizers to individual control elements (e.g., a pause button), we're attaching them directly to the root view. This means we can perform the gestures anywhere on the screen. In effect, the entire view is our control, and the pop-up views are simply our way of visualizing the user interaction.

CREATING GESTURE RECOGNIZERS

Let's start with the simplest, our pause gesture. We'll begin by creating our gesture recognizer in GSRootViewController's viewDidLoad method.

```
// Add 2-finger tap to pause.
UITapGestureRecognizer* pauseGesture =
[[UITapGestureRecognizer alloc]
    initWithTarget:self
    action:@selector(pauseGesture:)];
pauseGesture.numberOfTapsRequired = 1;
pauseGesture.numberOfTouchesRequired = 2;
[self.view addGestureRecognizer:pauseGesture];
```

Here, we instantiate a UITapGestureRecognizer object, setting its target and selector. Every time this gesture recognizer identifies a tap gesture, it will call our view controller's pauseGesture: method. Next, we set the number of taps and the number of touches. In our case, we must tap with two fingers at the same time—but we only require a single tap (not a double or triple tap). Finally, we add our gesture recognizer to our root view. It is now active.

Next, we define the pauseGesture: method.

```
- (void)pauseGesture:(UIGestureRecognizer*)gestureRecognizer {
    if (self.canvasViewController.running) {
        [self showPopupController:self.pauseController
```

```
                animationType:GSPopupDropDown
        withCompletionHandler:nil];
    } else {
        [self hidePopupController:self.pauseController
                    animationType:GSPopupDropDown];
    }
    self.canvasViewController.running =
    !self.canvasViewController.running;
}
```

UITapGestureRecognizer is a discrete gesture recognizer. This means our pauseGesture: method will only be called once for each tap gesture that it detects. If our canvas view is currently running, we display our pause pop-up; otherwise, we hide it. Then we toggle the canvas view's running property. Note that we also receive a UIGestureRecognizer argument. While we're not using it in this method, we could use it to monitor the gesture recognizer's state or determine the location of our tap gesture. We'll see examples of this in later gesture recognizers.

Next, let's do the three-finger swipe. Like our tap gesture, this is a discrete gesture. The action method will be called once the entire gesture has been recognized.

```
// Add 3-finger swipe to export--we will add twice
// because we want to distinguish the different directions.
UISwipeGestureRecognizer* swipeToExportDown =
[[UISwipeGestureRecognizer alloc]
    initWithTarget:self
    action:@selector(exportGesture:)];
swipeToExportDown.numberOfTouchesRequired = 3;
swipeToExportDown.direction =
UISwipeGestureRecognizerDirectionDown;
[self.view addGestureRecognizer:swipeToExportDown];
UISwipeGestureRecognizer* swipeToExportUp =
```

```
[[UISwipeGestureRecognizer alloc]
    initWithTarget:self
    action:@selector(exportGesture:)]];
swipeToExportUp.numberOfTouchesRequired = 3;
swipeToExportUp.direction = UISwipeGestureRecognizerDirectionUp;
[self.view addGestureRecognizer:swipeToExportUp];
```

This is superficially similar to our tap gesture recognizer. We instantiate a UISwipeGestureRecognizer, giving it a target/action pair. Next, we set the number of required touches to three, and we set the required swipe direction. Finally, we add the swipe to our view. However, there are a couple of key points worth mentioning.

First, we want to detect horizontal swipes. Now remember, we are keeping our view locked in portrait orientation; however, we assume users will hold it in either landscape left or landscape right. This means the horizontal swipes will actually be detected using UISwipeGestureRecognizerDirectionUp and UISwipeGestureRecognizerDirectionDown.

Second, we're actually creating two swipe recognizers—one for each direction. We could have easily combined the two directions into a single bitmask and used it to detect either horizontal swipe, but then we'd have no way to determine which direction the user had swiped. In the animation sequence, we want our view's motions to match the direction of our swipe. By using two separate gesture recognizers, we can easily identify the swipe direction.

```
- (void)exportGesture:(UIGestureRecognizer*)gestureRecognizer {
    self.exportSwipeDirection =
    [(UISwipeGestureRecognizer*)gestureRecognizer direction];
    GSPopupAnimationType animation;
    switch (self.exportSwipeDirection) {
        case UISwipeGestureRecognizerDirectionDown:
            animation = GSPopupSlideTowardsHomeButton;
            break;
        case UISwipeGestureRecognizerDirectionUp:
```

```
          animation = GSPopupSlideFromHomeButton;
      break;
   default:
    [NSException
     raise:@"Invalid Swipe Direction"
     format:@"Should only recognize swipes up or "
            @"down, however this swipe was %d",
            self.exportSwipeDirection];
      break;
}
// Don't process export gestures if paused.
if (!self.canvasViewController.running) return;
// Pause the view.
self.canvasViewController.running = NO;
// Pass the image snapshot to the export controller.
self.exportController.imageToExport =
[self.canvasViewController snapshotOfCanvas];
self.exportController.deviceOrientation =
self.bestSubviewOrientation;
// And show the export options.
[self showPopupController:self.exportController
          animationType:animation
    withCompletionHandler:nil];
}
```

This method starts by accessing the gesture recognizer's direction property. Note that this is not the direction of the swipe. It is a bitmask indicating the directions permitted by the recognizer. However, since we created two recognizers, each with their own direction value, we can use this property to distinguish between them.

Once we determine the direction of the swipe, we use that information to set the animation type. Specifically, we select an animation sequence that will slide our view in from the side, making sure its motion follows the direction of our swipe.

Next, we check to see if our canvas view is currently paused. If it is, we simply return. We don't want to display any other pop-up views while our application is paused. Once this check is passed, we pause our canvas, grab a snapshot of our current drawing, and pass both the snapshot and our current best orientation to the export view. Finally, we display the pop-up view, using the showPopupController: animationType:withCompletionHandler: method we developed in the first part of this chapter.

Unlike what we did with the pause menu, we do not provide any code for dismissing the pop-up view and restarting the canvas here. Our export menu must handle those tasks when an export item is selected.

Now let's add the one-finger pan gesture for our acceleration control. Add the following code to our viewDidLoad method, after the code that creates our swipe gestures.

```
// Add 1-finger pan for acceleration.
UIPanGestureRecognizer* accelerationGesture =
[[UIPanGestureRecognizer alloc]
    initWithTarget:self
    action:@selector(accelerationGesture:)];
accelerationGesture.maximumNumberOfTouches = 1;
// This can only succeed if we definitely don't have a swipe.
[accelerationGesture requireGestureRecognizerToFail:
    swipeToExportDown];
[accelerationGesture requireGestureRecognizerToFail:
    swipeToExportUp];
[self.view addGestureRecognizer:accelerationGesture];
```

Here, we create a pan gesture recognizer and then set it for a singe touch. Next, we create a dependency between our pan recognizer and our swipe recognizers. Both swipe recognizers must fail before a pan gesture can be recognized.

Unlike the others, pans are continuous gestures. There is no difference when the recognizer is created, but we have to design our accelerationGesture: method to handle multiple calls. Not surprisingly, the method is more complicated than our previous examples. Let's step through it.

```
- (void)accelerationGesture:(UIGestureRecognizer *)gestureRecognizer {
    // Don't process acceleration gestures if paused.
    if (!self.canvasViewController.running) return;
    CGPoint motion =
        [(UIPanGestureRecognizer*)gestureRecognizer
        translationInView:self.view];
    [(UIPanGestureRecognizer*)gestureRecognizer
        setTranslation:CGPointZero inView:self.view];
```

Just like before, we check to see if the canvas view is running before we proceed. We don't show the acceleration control if the canvas is paused.

Then we calculate the distance that the user's finger has moved since the last update. UIPanGestureRecognizer has three methods to help track the pan gesture: translationInView:, velocityInView:, and setTranslation:inView:. translation InView: tracks the touch's change in position in the given view's coordinates. This is the cumulative distance moved—by default, it gives the offset from the gesture's starting position. Similarly, velocityInView: gives the gesture's current velocity using the given view's coordinate system. The velocity is broken into both vertical and horizontal components. Finally, setTranslation:inView: lets us reset the reference point for translationInView: and resets the velocity.

Since we're only concerned with the position, not the velocity, we only need to use translationInView:. However, we want the change in position for each update. To calculate this, we simply reset the translation by calling setTranslation:inView: and passing in CGPointZero—effectively assigning a new starting point for the next iteration.

```
    // Update the value in the gesture recognizer screen.
    CGFloat min = logf(0.05f);
    CGFloat max = logf(10.0f);
```

```
CGFloat range = max - min;
CGFloat current =
logf(self.canvasViewController.accelerationRate);
CGFloat change = motion.y;
// If we're landscape left, reverse the acceleration changes.
if (self.bestSubviewOrientation ==
    UIDeviceOrientationLandscapeRight) {
    change *= -1;
}
current += range / self.view.bounds.size.height * 4.0f / 3.0f *
        change;
if (current < min) current = min;
if (current > max) current = max;
self.canvasViewController.accelerationRate = expf(current);
[self.accelerationController.progressBar
 setProgress:(current - min) / range
 animated:YES];
```

Next, we calculate the acceleration value. We will use this value to scale the results from Core Motion in the next section. The larger the value, the more quickly the cursor responds when tilting the phone. Here, we're going to scale the value from 0.05 to 10.0. The exact math isn't too important. However, there are two points worth noting. First, a linear change in the gesture's location results in an exponential change in the cursor's responsiveness. Second, we've set the scale so that you only need to pan three-quarters of the way across the screen to go from the lowest setting to the highest.

Once the acceleration value is calculated, we assign it. We set the canvas's accelerationRate property to the exponential value. However, we use the linear value to set our acceleration control's progress bar. This means that the minimum value will correspond to 0.0f on the progress bar (a completely empty bar), while the maximum value will correspond to 1.0f (a completely filled bar).

```
    switch (gestureRecognizer.state) {
        case UIGestureRecognizerStateBegan:
            [self showPopupController:self.accelerationController
                        animationType:GSPopupFade
                withCompletionHandler:nil];
            break;
        case UIGestureRecognizerStateChanged:
            // Do nothing.
            break;
        case UIGestureRecognizerStateEnded:
            [self hidePopupController:self.accelerationController
                        animationType:GSPopupFade];
            break;
        case UIGestureRecognizerStateCancelled:
            NSLog(@"Acceleration Gesture Canceled");
            break;
        case UIGestureRecognizerStateFailed:
            NSLog(@"Acceleration Gesture Failed");
            break;
        case UIGestureRecognizerStatePossible:
            NSLog(@"Acceleration Gesture Possible");
            break;
    }
}
```

Finally, we check and respond to the gesture recognizer's state. Since this is a continuous recognizer, we're really only worried about the ...Began, ...Changed, and ...Ended states. We're already recalculating the acceleration values for each update. So, all we really need to do here is display our acceleration view in the ...Began state, and hide it in the ...Ended state. We don't pause the canvas, since the user might want to see how the cursor's behavior changes as they adjust the cursor acceleration.

CORE MOTION

The gestures give us access to all our ancillary controls, but we still haven't dealt with our device's main control; we want the user to steer the cursor by tipping and tilting their device. To do this, we must dig into the Core Motion framework.

Core Motion lets us access data from a variety of sensors on the device. The CMMotionManager class acts as the gateway to all our motion data. It provides access to our device's accelerometer, gyroscopes, and magnetometer, as well as the processed device motion data.

Device motion combines data from all the sensors using a sensor fusion algorithm. This produces more accurate motion estimates but comes at a somewhat higher computational cost. Device motion also provides some features that individual sensors cannot perform on their own. For example, it automatically separates acceleration from the device's motion, and acceleration from gravity.

Unfortunately, not all devices have the same set of sensors. In particular, iPhone 4 and iPad 2 both have access to all the sensors. iPhone 3GS and the original iPad only have the accelerometer and the magnetometer. The 4th generation iPod touch has both the accelerometer and gyroscopes, but no magnetometer. The 3rd generation iPod touch only has the accelerometer. And the simulator doesn't support any of these sensors. Fortunately, Core Motion provides methods to check and make sure a feature is supported before you attempt to use it.

NOTE: Device motion is only available on devices that have both the accelerometer and the gyroscopes. If you have a magnetometer, that will be used to improve accuracy, but it is not necessary. Unfortunately, this means the iPhone 3GS, the original iPad, and the 3rd generation iPod touch do not support device motion.

Core Motion also provides both push and pull approaches to accessing the data. In the push approach, Core Motion runs on its own operation queue. We set the interval, and we provide a block of code to execute. Core Motion will then sample the sensors and call this block at every interval.

In the pull approach, Core Motion updates the motion data in the background, and we sample it whenever we need to. In general, the pull approach is recommended for most applications. It is more efficient and typically requires less code. The push data should only be used for applications that focus on data collection, where we want to make sure we don't accidentally miss any samples.

Games are an interesting case. We want accurate motion results, which implies that we might want to use push data—but most of the time, games already have a run loop running at the game's frame rate (usually around 60 frames per second). Since we are already updating the game state in each frame, it makes sense to use the pull approach and access the sensors at that time as well. This way, the motion updates are synced with the frame rate.

While we could do this for GravityScribbler, it would require creating a separate timer to run our game loop. Instead, we will use the push approach and let Core Motion's updates drive the game loop for us.

We will use Core Motion directly in our CanvasViewController class. Let's start with our init method. Here, we set up the needed infrastructure.

```
- (id)init {
    self = [super initWithNibName:nil bundle:nil];
    if (self) {
        _motionManager = [[CMMotionManager alloc] init];
        _updateQueue = [[NSOperationQueue alloc] init];
        // Set the rate to 60 frames per second.
        if (_motionManager.deviceMotionAvailable) {
            _motionManager.deviceMotionUpdateInterval = 1.0 / 60.0;
        } else {
            _motionManager.accelerometerUpdateInterval = 1.0 / 60.0;
        }
        // Set the queue to only 1 concurrent thread.
        [_updateQueue setMaxConcurrentOperationCount:1];
    }
    return self;
}
```

We start by instantiating both our Core Motion manager and an operation queue. Our motion manager will use the operation queue to run the push updates.

Once this is in place, we check to see if our device supports device motion. If it does, we set the device motion update interval to 60 updates per second. If not, we will just have to use the accelerometer alone, so we set its update interval instead.

Finally, we ensure that our operation queue will only execute one operation at a time—essentially making it a serial operation queue.

Next, let's add a method to start motion updates. We'll take this method in steps.

```
#pragma mark - Gravity Updates
- (void) startGravityUpdates {
    if (self.motionManager.deviceMotionAvailable) {
        [self.motionManager
        startDeviceMotionUpdatesToQueue:self.updateQueue
        withHandler:^(CMDeviceMotion *motion, NSError *error) {
            CGPoint location =
            [self addAcceleration:motion.gravity];
            [self.canvas addLineToPoint:location];
            dispatch_async(dispatch_get_main_queue(), ^{
                [self.canvas updateCanvasUI];
            });
        }];
    }
```

Here we check to see if the device supports device motion. If it does, we start the motion updates.

Here we're primarily interested in the acceleration data. Typically, accelerometers register both the pull of gravity as well as the actual acceleration of the device. Often, we need to separate these two signals, using a low-pass filter to focus on the pull of gravity, and a high-pass filter for device motion. Fortunately, the device motion sensor fusion algorithm uses additional information from the gyros and (if present) the magnetometer to automatically separate the device's total acceleration into its gravity and user acceleration components.

Here, we simply grab the gravity vector (the direction of gravity given the phone's reference frame) and pass it to our addAcceleration: method. Then we update the canvas UI. Note that the motion update block runs in our operation queue's thread. Therefore, we need to dispatch the UI updates back to the main thread.

As you can see, using device motion is simple, short, and sweet. Unfortunately, if we're running the app on an iPhone 3GS, an original iPad, or a 3rd generation iPod touch, we only have access to the raw accelerometer data. This means we have to pull out the gravity signal ourselves.

```
    } else {
        CGFloat filterFactor = 0.1f;
        __block CGFloat xAccel = 0.0f;
        __block CGFloat yAccel = 0.0f;
        [self.motionManager
         startAccelerometerUpdatesToQueue:self.updateQueue
         withHandler:^(CMAccelerometerData* motion, NSError *error) {
             xAccel = (xAccel * (1.0f - filterFactor)) +
             ((CGFloat)motion.acceleration.x * filterFactor);
             yAccel = (yAccel * (1.0f - filterFactor)) +
             ((CGFloat)motion.acceleration.y * filterFactor);
             CMAcceleration gravity;
             gravity.x = xAccel;
             gravity.y = yAccel;
             gravity.z = 0.0f;
             CGPoint location = [self addAcceleration:gravity];
             [self.canvas addLineToPoint:location];
             dispatch_async(dispatch_get_main_queue(), ^{
                 [self.canvas updateCanvasUI];
             });
         }];
    }
}
```

This code uses a simple low-pass filter to pull out the gravity signal. Each update step, we nudge the current gravity value slightly based on our current acceleration information. High-frequency changes (like shaking the phone) tend to cancel themselves out before they can accumulate enough to have much of an effect. Gravity, on the other hand, provides a constant pull that changes relatively slowly compared to user-imparted motion. This lets the pull of gravity accumulate rapidly, producing a relatively accurate gravity vector.

Note that we only need the x- and y-components of our gravity vector. Therefore, we don't even bother to calculate the z-component. Instead, we simply set it to 0.0f. This saves us a little computation time on each update.

Once we have calculated our gravity vector, the steps are the same as before. We pass it to addAcceleration: and update our UI.

Next, let's look at the addAcceleration: method.

```
- (CGPoint)addAcceleration:(CMAcceleration)acceleration {
    // Update velocity.
    CGPoint velocity = self.velocity;
    velocity.x += (CGFloat)acceleration.x * self.accelerationRate;
    velocity.y -= (CGFloat)acceleration.y * self.accelerationRate;
    // Update location.
    CGPoint location = self.canvas.currentDrawPoint;
    location.x += velocity.x;
    location.y += velocity.y;
    self.velocity = velocity;
```

We start by updating our cursor's velocity based on the x- and y-components of the gravity vector. We multiply this by our accelerationRate parameter, letting us scale the device's responsiveness.

It's worth noting that Core Motion can use a number of different reference frames. Here, our gravity vector is given in the device's reference frame. If you're holding the phone in front of you in portrait orientation, x points to the right, y points up, and z points straight ahead through the phone's screen.

The CMDeviceMotion's attitude works somewhat differently. It gives the device's orientation in a fixed reference frame. We can select the desired reference frame when starting motion updates. This is particularly useful for augmented reality applications. For example, CMAttitudeReferenceFrameXMagneticNorthZVertical defines a reference frame where the z-axis is vertical and the x-axis points toward magnetic north. This lets you determine the device's orientation in the real world (assuming, of course, your device has a magnetometer).

However, for our motion updates, we just need to realize that our gravity's reference frame is different from our view coordinates. In our view, the y-axis points down the screen. In gravity, it points up. We therefore reverse the gravity's y-component when calculating our velocity.

Once we have the current velocity, we simply calculate our cursor's next location.

```
// Get the max bounds.
CGRect bounds = self.view.bounds;
// Make sure the cursor cannot leave the screen.
if (location.x < 0) {
    location.x = 0;
    velocity.x *= -0.5f;
}
if (location.y < 0) {
    location.y = 0;
    velocity.y *= -0.5f;
}
if (location.x >= bounds.size.width) {
    location.x = bounds.size.width;
    velocity.x *= -0.5f;    }
if (location.y >= bounds.size.height) {
    location.y = bounds.size.height;
    velocity.y *= -0.5f;
}
self.velocity = velocity;
return location;
}
```

In the second part of the addAcceleration: method, we check to make sure our cursor remains within the screen's bounds. If either the x- or y-component is out of bounds, we set it to the screen's edge and reverse the velocity along that axis. We also reduce the velocity by half. This gives our cursor a nice little bounce when it hits the edge of the screen.

Finally, we assign our new velocity and return the updated cursor location. Now we just need a method to turn off motion updates.

```
- (void)stopGravityUpdates {
    // Turn off gravity updates.
    if (self.motionManager.deviceMotionAvailable) {
        [self.motionManager stopDeviceMotionUpdates];
    }
    else {
        [self.motionManager stopAccelerometerUpdates];
    }
}
```

Here, we just check to see which type of motion updates we're using and then stop the appropriate one.

DEVICE ORIENTATION

As mentioned earlier, we keep our canvas view locked in portrait orientation. There are a couple of reasons for this. First, it's easier. As we just saw, our gravity vector comes in the device's reference frame. Keeping the view orientation constant makes it easy to translate our gravity coordinates to the view coordinates; we just need to invert our y-coordinate. However, if we allowed the view to rotate to different orientations, we would have to convert the gravity coordinates separately for each orientation.

The biggest problem, however, is simply usability. The user will be tilting and tipping their phone as they steer the cursor about the screen. We don't want to accidentally rotate the view just because they tilted the phone too far in one direction or another.

However, this gives us a problem. How do we orient our pop-up views when we display them? There are two main approaches. The easiest is to simply pick an orientation and stick with it. We could, for example, decide that the interface will always be used in landscape mode with the home button to the right, and display all our pop-ups appropriately.

This has a few advantages. It's easy. It's consistent. And it works particularly well when the UI gives the user some indication of the correct orientation from the beginning, so they aren't surprised when a pop-up view appears. However, it can cause problems. It's always a little annoying to launch an app and find out that it thinks you're holding your phone wrong. I don't mind changing from portrait to landscape or from landscape to portrait—but having to change from landscape right to landscape left always bothers me.

This is even worse with the iPad. I find that many iPad cases make it easier to hold the device in one particular orientation. What's worse, the natural orientation can vary from case to case (or even from person to person). Running an app that forces the user to hold their device in an uncomfortable position won't win you any friends.

If you're developing an app that is likely to run while the phone is mounted—for example, running music or GPS apps while the phone is placed in a car mount—then we probably need to let our app support all possible orientations. After all, some mounts may hold the phone in landscape mode. Some will hold it in portrait mode. We can't expect the user to pop the phone out of its mount and rotate it around just to use our app.

So, we probably want to support both landscape orientations. This means that we need to try to predict the device's correct orientation and then use that. In our case, we will track orientation changes and record the last landscape orientation. This will be our best guess for the current user orientation. We won't get it right 100 percent of the time, but since users typically tilt the phone more vertically before using the gesture controls, it works most of the time.

Now, we could use our current motion updates and the gravity vector to determine our interface's current orientation—but there's a better way. Let's step out of Core Motion and use a higher-level interface. The UIDevice class can generate orientation notifications for us. Here, UIDevice will monitor the device's motion and determine the most likely orientation. These calculations already filter the motion data and apply a hysteresis to avoid unexpected changes and rapid flip-flopping between orientations. We simply need to register to receive the notifications and then turn the notifications on. This is done in GSRootViewController's viewDidLoad method.

```
// Catch device orientation changes.
[[NSNotificationCenter defaultCenter]
addObserverForName:UIDeviceOrientationDidChangeNotification
object:[UIDevice currentDevice]
queue:nil
usingBlock:^(NSNotification *note) {
    UIDeviceOrientation orientation =
    [[UIDevice currentDevice] orientation];
    switch (orientation) {
        case UIDeviceOrientationLandscapeLeft:
        case UIDeviceOrientationLandscapeRight:
            self.bestSubviewOrientation = orientation;
            break;
        default:
            // Ignore anything else.
            break;
    }
}];
[[UIDevice currentDevice]
    beginGeneratingDeviceOrientationNotifications];
```

Here, when we receive the orientation did change notification, we simply check to see if the current orientation is one of the two landscape modes. If it is, we assign it to our bestSubviewOrientation property. Otherwise, we ignore it. We can then use the bestSubviewOrientation to manually rotate our pop-up views as needed.

EXPORTING IMAGES

There's one last set of features we should explore before leaving GravityScribbler. We want to let the user export and share their drawings. Now, we've already seen the first half of this. We know how to create an image from a graphics context. So how do we get that image off our device?

We'll look at four different options. These are hardly exclusive. There are dozens of online photo sharing services, and many of them already produce Objective-C frameworks that can be easily added to your applications. However, our list of export options will focus on methods that are included in the iOS SDK. These include saving the image to your phone's photo library, sending it as an MMS message, attaching it to an email message, or sending it in a tweet.

SAVING TO THE PHOTO LIBRARY

There's an easy way to save images to the photo library. Simply call `UIImageWriteToSavedPhotosAlbum()`. That's it. We're done here. Move along.

OK, so there's a bit more to it than that. `UIImageWriteToSavedPhotosAlbum()` is fine, but it doesn't give us a lot of control. In our case, it has two problems. First, we cannot set the image's orientation. If we just create an image from our graphics context, the resulting `UIImage` will be a portrait snapshot of the screen. We want it to be landscape.

While we're at it, it would be nice if we could geotag the image. The phone has a GPS unit, after all. Why not add a rough location to the image while saving it?

Fortunately, the Assets Library framework gives us low-level access to all the videos and photos managed by our photo library. In our case, it lets us add metadata to an image, letting us both change its orientation and add geotagging.

However, before we can do this, we need to learn how to use Core Location.

USING CORE LOCATION

Core Location lets us determine the location and heading of the iOS device. In some ways, it is the complement to Core Motion. Core Location tells us about large motions—the location of the phone on a map. Core Motion tells us about the phone's orientation and the small-scale motions.

At its base, Core Location provides us with the latitude, longitude, altitude, and heading of our iOS device, along with the accuracy estimates. However, it has a number of helper functions that can provide a range of additional information. We can calculate the distance between two locations. We can use geocoding to look up the latitude and longitude of an address, or use reverse geocoding to get the address from the location data. We can even calculate our device's current speed.

Core Location also supports two specialized tracking techniques. The first, significant location change monitoring, is an ultra low power tracking method. It is not as accurate as standard tracking, and it only returns updates when the device has moved a significant distance. Next, region monitoring lets us define geographic regions and receive notifications when our iOS device enters or leaves those regions. You can find more information in Apple's Core Location Framework Reference.

Core Location uses four techniques when determining an iOS device's location. First, it can triangulate its location using cell towers. This provides a very fast rough estimate. It is the quickest approach and uses the least amount of battery power, but it has the lowest accuracy.

Next, the device scans for wireless hotspots and uses them to calculate a more accurate location estimate. This requires a bit more time and—since it requires turning on extra radios—a bit more energy, but it can drastically improve our location estimates.

For the greatest accuracy, the device can use GPS. Of course, this approach is the most expensive, both in terms of time and battery power.

Finally, Core Location can access the magnetometer to determine the device's heading.

Unfortunately, as with Core Motion, not all iOS devices have all the required sensors. For the more specialized tracking techniques (heading, region monitoring, and significant change monitoring), we need to check the feature's availability before we try to use it. Fortunately, for standard location tracking the difference between devices is largely abstracted away. We simply set the desired accuracy, and Core Location will do what it can to meet our expectations. It may provide an initial rough estimate and then improve it as additional data comes in.

Of course, Core Location creates a number of privacy concerns. To help avoid problems, the system will ask the user for permission the first time an application attempts to use Core Location. No matter what the application is, some users will undoubtedly say no. Our application needs to check and see if it's authorized to use location services, and react reasonably if authorization is denied.

Conceptually, Core Location is simple. We create an instance of `CLLocation Manager`. We provide a `CLLocationManagerDelegate` that will respond to our location events. We set the desired properties—in particular, we should always set the desiredAccuracy and distanceFilter based on our application's needs, since these can have a significant impact on our application's performance. Then we call startUpdatingLocation to begin generating location updates. When we're done, we call stopUpdatingLocation.

In GravityScribbler, we don't need super accuracy, and we're not going to be tracking the user as they move. Instead, we really want a quick snapshot of their general location. To simplify this, we'll create a wrapper class, CurrentLocationManager. This will also act as our CCLocationManagerDelegate. This class will provide three methods: startNewSearch, cancelSearch, and getLocationWithCompletionHandler:.

We'll call startNewSearch as soon as our export menu is displayed. This will let us begin generating location updates in the background. Likewise, we'll call cancelSearch when the pop-up is dismissed. If the user exports an image, we can get our best location estimate by calling getLocationWithCompletionHandler:.

```
- (void)startNewSearch {
    self.location = nil;
    self.callbackBlock = nil;
    self.done = NO;
    // Check on our location authorization status.
    switch ([CLLocationManager authorizationStatus]) {
        case kCLAuthorizationStatusNotDetermined:
        case kCLAuthorizationStatusAuthorized:
            // If we have permission, or if we haven't yet asked,
            // start checking for location (will ask if necessary).
            self.manager = [[CLLocationManager alloc] init];
            self.manager.delegate = self;
            self.manager.distanceFilter = 10.0f;
            self.manager.desiredAccuracy =
                kCLLocationAccuracyNearestTenMeters;
            self.manager.purpose =
            @"Location data is used to geotag"
```

```
                @" images when they are exported.";
            [self.manager startUpdatingLocation];
        default:
            // If permission has been denied, we're done.
            // We will return a nil location. No need to do
            // anything more.
            self.done = YES;
            break;
    }
}
```

We start by clearing a few properties, and then we check to see if our application is authorized to use location services. If we're authorized, authorizationStatus will return kCLAuthorizationStatusAuthorized. If our application has not yet asked for permission, it will return kCLAuthorizationStatusNotDetermined. Otherwise, it will return one of the failure constants, depending on whether permission was denied, or whether permission cannot be granted (e.g., due to parental controls).

If we explicitly don't have permission, we don't bother setting up our location manager. We just set the done property to YES and leave our location property as nil. Otherwise, we go ahead and try to set up our location manager. The system will automatically ask the user for permission to use location services, if it hasn't done so already.

We still need to set three properties. First is the distance filter. This is the distance (in meters) that the device must move before generating a new location update. Setting this to kCLDistanceFilterNone will produce update notifications for any motion at all. In our case, we only want updates if the user moves a significant distance, so we set this value to 10 meters.

Next, we set the desired accuracy. Core Location sets a number of constants that we can use here. In our case, speed is more important than accuracy, so we set it to the nearest 10 meters. That should be good enough. In fact, if it's not fast enough, you may want to lower the accuracy even more. Be sure to test your application in a variety of environments, including indoors and in areas with little or no GPS reception (basement parking garages are good for this).

Finally, we need to set the location manager's purpose property. This is our chance to explain to the user why our application needs access to location services. It will be displayed when the system asks the user for permission to use location services.

> **NOTE:** When using location services, the initial update may not have the desired accuracy. This is particularly true when requesting high-accuracy data. Core Location will calculate an initial estimate as quickly as possible and then refine the estimate as additional information comes in.

Once everything is configured properly, we start generating location updates.

```
- (void)cancelSearch {
    [self.manager stopUpdatingLocation];
    self.done = YES;
}
```

By comparison, our cancel method is dead simple. We turn off location updates, and then we set our done property to YES.

```
- (void)getLocationWithCompletionHandler:
    (void (^)(CLLocation* location))completionHandler {
    self.callbackBlock = completionHandler;
    // If we've already found a location (or an error).
    if (self.done) {
        [self dispatchCallbackAndStopSearching];
    }
}
```

This should also be relatively straightforward. If we already have a location update, we'll call our callback immediately. To do this, we start by saving a reference to our callback block. If we're done, we go ahead and call dispatchCallbackAnd StopSearching. If not, we keep waiting.

```
- (void)dispatchCallbackAndStopSearching {
    [self.manager stopUpdatingLocation];
    // Make local copies that will be captured by the block.
    void (^callback)(CLLocation* location) = self.callbackBlock;
    CLLocation* location = self.location;
    // This will be added to the end of the main queue.
    dispatch_async(dispatch_get_main_queue(), ^{
            callback(location);
    });
    // Clear the originals.
    self.callbackBlock = nil;
    self.location = nil;
    self.done = NO;
}
```

This method stops our updates and then calls our callback block. However, our location updates may arrive on a background thread, and we want to make sure our completion handler is always run on the main thread. Therefore, this method dispatches our callback back to the main thread, passing in our most recent location estimate.

Of course, there's a bit of subtlety here. We start by making local copies of both our location data and our callback block. Then we dispatch the callback block to the main queue, and clear our properties. If we didn't make local copies, our dispatch block would capture the properties, but they would be set to nil before the dispatch block executed. By saving the properties as local variables, we ensure that the current values are captured by the local block and that they're not affected when we clear the properties.

Now we simply need to implement the delegate methods.

```
- (void)locationManager:(CLLocationManager *)manager
    didUpdateToLocation:(CLLocation *)newLocation
           fromLocation:(CLLocation *)oldLocation {
```

```
NSDate* timestamp = newLocation.timestamp;
NSTimeInterval age =
[timestamp timeIntervalSinceNow];
// If our location is more than
// 10 minutes old, ignore it.
if (age < - 600.0) return;
self.location = newLocation;
self.done = YES;
// If we have a callback waiting, call it.
if (self.callbackBlock != nil) {
    [self dispatchCallbackAndStopSearching];
}
}
```

This method is called whenever we receive a location update. We start by checking to see if our location data is old. If it's more than 10 minutes old, we ignore it and wait for the next update. Otherwise, we simply save a reference to the new location and set the done property to YES. If we already have a callback block, we dispatch it immediately. If not, we wait, allowing us to receive any additional updates that may come in, and then as soon as getLocationWithCompletionHandler: is called, the completion handler will be dispatched immediately.

```
- (void)locationManager:(CLLocationManager *)manager
        didFailWithError:(NSError *)error {
    self.done = YES;
    // If we have a callback waiting, call it.
    if (self.callbackBlock != nil) {
        [self dispatchCallbackAndStopSearching];
    }
}
```

Finally, we have to respond to any errors. There are two basic types of errors. First, we have transient errors. These occur when Core Location cannot correctly determine your location. For example, you might be trying to use location services from the basement of a parking garage. In that case, the system will continue to work, and you may start receiving updates once you have a clear signal. The second type of error is terminal errors—these won't go away. Most commonly, terminal errors come from having the user decline when prompted for permission to use location services.

This implementation will work for either case. Just like a successful update, set the done property to YES. Then we check to see if we have a callback block yet. If we do, we dispatch it immediately. If we don't, we wait for a call to getLocationWithCompletionHandler:.

If we haven't already received a successful update, the location property will be set to nil. The dispatch method will then pass that value back to the completion block. However, we can still receive additional updates, so if we get a clear signal we may still get a valid location before the callback is dispatched.

USING THE ASSETS LIBRARY FRAMEWORK

The ExportViewController receives a snapshot of the screen when the pop-up is displayed. We simply need to create an instance of the assets library and save it.

```
- (void)saveToPhotoAlbum {
    [self.currentLocationManager
     getLocationWithCompletionHandler:^(CLLocation *location) {
        ALAssetsLibrary* library = [[ALAssetsLibrary alloc] init];
        NSDictionary* metadata =
        [self generateMetadataForLocation:location];
        [library
         writeImageToSavedPhotosAlbum:[self.imageToExport CGImage]
         metadata:metadata
         completionBlock:
         ^(NSURL *assetURL, NSError *error) {
```

```
            [self.delegate exportController:self
                              sendMessage:@"Image Saved"];
      }]; // write image block ends
  }]; // location completion handler ends
  [self.delegate exportControllerFinished:self];
}
```

The first thing we do is call getLocationWithCompletionHandler:. Then, inside the completion handler block, we instantiate our assets library and call the generate MetadataForLocation: helper function to generate the required metadata. Then we write the image to the photo library.

writeImageToSavedPhotosAlbum:metadata:completionBlock: takes a CGImage, not a UIImage, but other than that, we simply pass in our image and metadata. In the completion block, we display a quick pop-up message to let the user know that the file has saved successfully.

The message pop-ups are just like the pop-ups we've seen previously. The only difference is that they fade in and then automatically fade out again after a few seconds. Still, I'll leave exploring their implementation as an optional homework assignment.

Finally, the last line of code dismisses our export menu. Even though this is the last line in the method, it will be called before any of the blocks. This means that the export menu will disappear immediately once the button is pressed. Then, after the image saves (which could take a while, depending on Core Location), a brief notification is flashed on the screen.

This has two key effects. First, the app seems very responsive, since something happens the second they tap the button. Next, the user is informed when the image saves, so they aren't left worried and unsure.

There's also another key design point at play here. We use a temporary pop-up to alert the user—not an alert view. Alert views are great if you have a question that needs to be answered. The problem is they bring the app to a complete halt. If you're displaying an alert view with a single OK button, then you're probably using it wrong. Instead, try to find another way to alert the user without interrupting the application's flow.

That seems simple enough. Of course, the real work is done in generateMetadata ForLocation:. Our image property metadata is represented by an NSDictionary. This dictionary may also contain sub-dictionaries. In our case, we will set the orientation property in the main dictionary and then add a location dictionary, which will hold the latitude, longitude, altitude, accuracy, and time stamp. Additional information on the available keys can be found in the CGImageProperties Reference.

This is a long method, so let's look at it in chunks.

```
- (NSDictionary*)generateMetadataForLocation:
(CLLocation*)location {
    NSMutableDictionary* metadata =
    [[NSMutableDictionary alloc] initWithCapacity:1];
    // Set Orientation.
    NSNumber* orientation;
    switch (self.deviceOrientation) {
        case UIDeviceOrientationLandscapeLeft:
            orientation = [NSNumber numberWithInt:8];
            break;
        case UIDeviceOrientationLandscapeRight:
            orientation = [NSNumber numberWithInt:6];
            break;
        default:
            [NSException raise:@"Illegal Orientation"
                        format:@"Invalid best subview"
                              @" orientation: %d",
                              self.deviceOrientation];
            break;
    }
    [metadata setObject:orientation
                forKey:(NSString*)kCGImagePropertyOrientation];
```

In this section of code, we instantiate an `NSMutableDictionary`. We then check the `deviceOrientation` property. This value was passed to our export pop-up when it was displayed. We then set the orientation value in our dictionary.

```
// Set Location -- if we have a valid location.
if (location) {
    CLLocationDegrees lat  = location.coordinate.latitude;
    CLLocationDegrees lon = location.coordinate.longitude;
    NSString *latRef = @"N";
    NSString *lngRef = @"E";
    if (lat < 0.0) {
        lat *= -1.0f;
        latRef = @"S";
    }
    if (lon < 0.0) {
        lon *= -1.0f;
        lngRef = @"W";
    }
```

Here we check to make sure we have valid location data. Remember, our location completion handler may have a nil-valued location if Core Location is not available or if it experiences errors. If we have a valid location, we add it to the image.

We also need to massage our latitude and longitude values. Core Location returns a latitude value from −90.0 to 90.0. The image preferences expect a value from 0.0 to 90, with either an "N" or "S" reference. Similarly, our longitude value starts from −180.0 to 180.0. It should be from 0.0 to 180.0 with a "W" or "E" reference.

```
    // Create location sub-dictionary and add it to our
    // metadata dictionary.
    NSMutableDictionary *locationMetadata =
    [[NSMutableDictionary alloc] init];
    [metadata setObject:locationMetadata
```

```
        forKey:(NSString*)kCGImagePropertyGPSDictionary];
    // Fill the sub-dictionary.
    [locationMetadata setObject:[NSNumber numberWithFloat:lat]
        forKey:(NSString*)kCGImagePropertyGPSLatitude];
    [locationMetadata setObject:latRef
        forKey:(NSString*)kCGImagePropertyGPSLatitudeRef];
    [locationMetadata setObject:[NSNumber numberWithFloat:lon]
        forKey:(NSString*)kCGImagePropertyGPSLongitude];
    [locationMetadata setObject:lngRef
        forKey:(NSString*)kCGImagePropertyGPSLongitudeRef];
    [locationMetadata
     setObject:[NSNumber numberWithFloat:
        location.horizontalAccuracy]
     forKey:(NSString*)kCGImagePropertyGPSDOP];
    [locationMetadata
     setObject:[NSNumber numberWithFloat:location.altitude]
     forKey:(NSString*)kCGImagePropertyGPSAltitude];
    [locationMetadata
     setObject:location.timestamp
     forKey:(NSString*)kCGImagePropertyGPSTimeStamp];
    }
    return metadata;
}
```

Here, we instantiate a sub-dictionary and fill it with our location information. We then add it to our main dictionary. That's it. We return the main dictionary and we're done.

There are many, many other image properties that you might want to add to your application. I'll also leave that as an optional homework assignment.

SENDING MMS MESSAGES

OK, I have some good news and some bad news. First the good news: The MessageUI framework has excellent support for sending SMS messages. You can use the MFMessageComposeViewController class to display the standard interface for creating SMS messages. We can even set the initial recipients and message text. With iOS 5, this support has been expanded to automatically use iMessage instead of SMS whenever possible.

Unfortunately, the MessageUI only supports text messages. We cannot use the framework to programmatically attach images or video.

However, this doesn't mean the user cannot send their image as an MMS. It just means that they have to do it on their own. If they save the image to their photo library, they can then attach it to their own MMS messages. It's not ideal, but right now it's one of the few options available.

Alternatively, we could programmatically copy the image to the pasteboard. This would let the user paste it into an SMS message. This will be difficult to clearly communicate to the user, however.

SENDING EMAIL ATTACHMENTS

Email attachments also use the MessageUI framework. However, unlike SMS messages, the email composer lets us set the sender, the subject, and the message body, and (most importantly) it lets us add attachments.

In theory, to send an email message we just need to instantiate our message composition view, set a few parameters, and display it for the user. We cannot send the message ourselves. We can prepare the message for the user, but they have to press the send button.

Unfortunately, we cannot attach a UIImage directly. Rather, we must attach an NSData object holding the contents of the file we wish to attach. Also, we would typically want to check and make sure the device supported email before creating the compose view. In this case, however, we performed that check when the export menu was created. If the device does not support email, then the email button will not appear in our menu.

Again, this is a long method, so let's break it into several sections.

```objc
- (void)sendAsEmail {
    [self.delegate exportControllerFinished:self];
    [self.delegate exportControllerWaitingForModalView:self];
    [self.currentLocationManager
     getLocationWithCompletionHandler:
     ^(CLLocation *location) {
```

So far, this is just setup. We call a few of the ExportViewControllerDelegate methods. The delegate will use these calls to dismiss our export menu and display a "loading…" message pop-up, letting the user know we are loading another view. Then we get the current location—the rest of the view setup takes place in the completion handler.

```objc
        // Create our email composer view on a background thread.
        dispatch_queue_t queue =
        dispatch_get_global_queue(DISPATCH_QUEUE_PRIORITY_DEFAULT, 0);
        dispatch_async(queue, ^(void) {
```

The completion handler runs on the main thread, but saving our image to a temporary file might take a bit of time. We're going to be writing it to memory, not to disk, so it should be fast. Still, it's not a bad idea to do this on a background thread, freeing up our main thread.

```objc
            // Create Image Data.
            NSMutableData* imageData = [[NSMutableData alloc] init];
            CGImageDestinationRef destination =
            CGImageDestinationCreateWithData(
                (__bridge CFMutableDataRef)imageData,
                (CFStringRef)@"public.jpeg", 1, nil);
            NSDictionary* metadata =
            [self generateMetadataForLocation:location];
```

```
CGImageDestinationAddImage(
    destination,
    self.imageToExport.CGImage,
    (__bridge CFDictionaryRef)metadata);
CGImageDestinationFinalize(destination);
CFRelease(destination);
```

Here, we're going to use a CGImageDestination to write out our image data as a JPEG file in memory. Image destinations abstract the task of writing images in various formats. A single image destination can save one or more images, including thumbnails.

There are simpler ways to generate image file data. UIImageJPEGRepresentation() and UIImagePNGRepresentation() both return an NSData containing the raw data for their respective image file formats. However, these methods don't let us add our image metadata.

Using an image destination takes three steps. First, we create our CGImage DestinationRef, passing in the NSMutableData to hold our file contents, a uniform type identifier for the image type, and the number of images. The final argument, options, doesn't yet do anything, but it is reserved for future use. Next, we add the images—including our metadata—to the destination. Finally, we finalize the destination. This will write the image files to our NSData.

```
// Open email compose window & set initial values.
MFMailComposeViewController* composer =
[[MFMailComposeViewController alloc] init];
[composer setSubject:@"My GravityScribbler drawing"];
[composer setMessageBody:@"Here's a drawing I created"
 @" using GravityScribbler." isHTML:NO];
[composer addAttachmentData:imageData
                mimeType:@"image/jpeg"
                fileName:@"GravityScribbler.jpg"];
composer.mailComposeDelegate = self;
```

FIGURE 8.12 Exporting our image using email

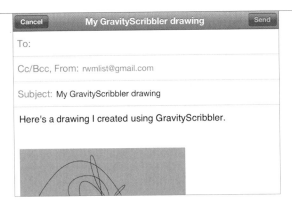

Here we instantiate our `MFMailComposeViewController`. We set the subject and message body and then add our attachment. Finally, we set our `ExportView Controller` as the mail composer's delegate. As the delegate, we will be informed if the message is sent, saved, or canceled or if it fails.

```
    // Present the view on the main thread.
    dispatch_async(dispatch_get_main_queue(), ^(void) {
        [self.delegate exportControllerWillShowModalView:
            self];
        [self.rootViewController presentViewController:
            composer
                                             animated:YES
                                           completion:nil];
    });
   });
 }];
}
```

Last but not least, we want to display our mail composer as a modal view (**Figure 8.12**). There are two key points here. First, we dispatch this back to the main thread. Second, we need to create a `rootViewController` property to hold a reference to our export menu's parent view controller—we assign this property each time our export view is displayed. This allows us to use that controller to display our modal view.

```
// Save the parent view controller.
self.rootViewController = self.parentViewController;
```

This is a bit unusual. Typically with iOS 5, you can simply use any child view to present a modal view. The system will work its way back up the view controller hierarchy and find the root view controller (or the first controller whose defines PresentationContext property is set to YES). That view then presents our modal view. This is important, since the child controller's view may not fill the entire screen. We want to make sure we move back through our hierarchy until we find a controller whose view does.

However, this won't work in our case. We dismiss our child view as soon as the user presses any of the menu buttons. This makes our app feel very responsive, but it also removes our controller from the view controller hierarchy. Therefore, we have to store and use our own reference back to the root view controller.

Now we just need to dismiss the modal view when we're done. We can do this by implementing the `mailComposeController:didFinishWithResult:error:` delegate method.

```
- (void)mailComposeController:
    (MFMailComposeViewController*)controller
    didFinishWithResult:(MFMailComposeResult)result
    error:(NSError*)error {
    [self.rootViewController.modalViewController
     dismissViewControllerAnimated:YES
     completion:^{
        switch (result) {
            case MFMailComposeResultFailed:
                [self.delegate
                 exportController:self
                 sendMessage:@"Send Mail Failed!"];
                break;
            default:
```

```
                    // Do nothing
                    break;
              }
         }];
    }
```

Here, we dismiss the view, and then in the completion block we check to see if we had an error. If we did, we display a quick warning to the user. Otherwise, we don't do anything. Sent mail messages already have a distinct audio cue, and we really don't need to alert the user when they save or cancel the message .

NOTE: UIKit provides a number of views that follow the same general pattern. We instantiate the controller and display it as a modal view. The view communicates back to the main application either through a delegate or by using a block-based API. Most are also designed for single use. We create the view, use it, and dispose of it. If we need it again, we just create a new instance. Obviously, the `MessageUI` compose views follow this pattern, as does the Twitter view. But there are other examples. `UIImagePicker` `Controller` (which lets us select pictures from the photo library or take pictures with the camera) follows the same general pattern.

SENDING MESSAGES USING THE TWITTER API

iOS 5 includes integrated Twitter support. This comes at two different levels. If we just want to let the user send a quick tweet using the system's Twitter account, then we just need to create, configure, and display a `TWTweetComposeViewController`. However, there is additional support for sending HTTP requests, directly accessing the Twitter API. The `TWRequest` class assists in properly formatting `GET`, `POST`, and `DELETE` requests, and it can even manage authorization using any of the accounts from the account framework. You can learn more about the Twitter API at http://dev.twitter.com/docs.

For our purposes, the default Twitter compose view is sufficient. Of course, there are a couple of catches. Unlike our other export features, the Twitter controller allows us to add `UIImages` directly. Unfortunately, this means we cannot add our metadata to the image. This means we must use Core Image to rotate the image to its proper orientation.

Additionally, we cannot programmatically add location data to the tweet. However, the compose window does include a check box to let the user manually set the location.

Much like the mail composer view, we merely set up the initial values. The user then decides if they want to modify it, cancel it, or send it as is. They are, ultimately, in complete control.

OK, let's step through the sendAsTweet message.

```
- (void)sendAsTweet {
    // We cannot add location directly;
    // user must do that from the tweet sheet.
    // Start by canceling the location lookup
    // and dismissing the controller.
    [self.currentLocationManager cancelSearch];
    [self.delegate exportControllerFinished:self];
    [self.delegate exportControllerWaitingForModalView:self];
    // Now do the rest on a background thread.
    dispatch_queue_t queue =
    dispatch_get_global_queue(DISPATCH_QUEUE_PRIORITY_DEFAULT, 0);
    dispatch_async(queue, ^(void) {
```

The initial code simply cancels our Core Location updates, and it then removes the menu view and has the delegate display a "loading..." message while we instantiate and configure the compose view. The rest of the method is then dispatched onto a background thread to avoid blocking the main thread.

```
        TWTweetComposeViewController* controller =
        [[TWTweetComposeViewController alloc] init];
        [controller setInitialText:
            @"Check out my latest masterpiece."
         @" #GravityScribbler"];
```

Here, we create our tweet composer and set the initial text. Note that the TWTweet ComposeViewController methods to modify the tweet's contents all return BOOL values. Typically we would want to check these values to make sure our message will fit within the allotted 140 characters; however, with only a 32-character message and a single image, we're at no risk of running over.

```
// We cannot set the image's orientation.
// Instead, use Core Image to rotate the image.
CIImage* image =
[CIImage imageWithCGImage:self.imageToExport.CGImage];
```

This code creates a CIImage from our imageToExport property. A CIImage object represents an image in the Core Image framework.

Core Image is an image manipulation framework. It lets us change an image's appearance by scaling, cropping, rotating, or adding filters to the image. The CIImage object is really more of an image recipe. It contains a set of instructions, but the framework does not actually create the final image until the CIImage is rendered onto a context. In our case, the CIImage's instructions will include our input image and our rotation matrix.

This is a rather simplistic example of Core Image's capabilities. The Core Image framework comes with a rich set of filters that can be combined in an almost unlimited number of ways to produce a wide range of visual effects. You can find a lot more information in the Core Image Programming Guide.

```
CGFloat rotation;
switch (self.deviceOrientation) {
    case UIDeviceOrientationLandscapeLeft:
        rotation = M_PI_2;
        break;
    case UIDeviceOrientationLandscapeRight:
        rotation = -M_PI_2;
        break;
    default:
        [NSException
```

```
        raise:@"Illegal Orientation"
        format:@"Invalid best subview orientation: %d",
        self.deviceOrientation];
      break;
  }
  CGAffineTransform transform =
  CGAffineTransformMakeRotation(rotation);
```

Here, we simply create our rotation matrix, based on the device's orientation. Remember, our image will appear in a portrait orientation by default. We want to rotate it into one of the two landscape orientations.

```
image = [image imageByApplyingTransform:transform];
    CIContext* context = [CIContext contextWithOptions:nil];
  UIImage* rotatedImage =
  [UIImage imageWithCGImage:
   [context createCGImage:image
                 fromRect:image.extent]];
  // Add the rotated image to our tweet sheet.
  [controller addImage:rotatedImage];
```

Next, we apply the rotation to our image, and then we create a Core Image context. We can then render a `CGImageRef` using the context. The `CGImageRef` is in turn used to instantiate our new `UIImage`.

```
  controller.completionHandler =
  ^(TWTweetComposeViewControllerResult result) {
      [self.rootViewController.modalViewController
      dismissViewControllerAnimated:YES
      completion:nil];
  };
  // Now present it on the main thread.
```

FIGURE 8.13 Exporting our image using Twitter

```
dispatch_async(dispatch_get_main_queue(), ^(void) {
        [self.delegate exportControllerWillShowModalView:self];
        [self.rootViewController presentViewController:controller
                                             animated:YES
                                           completion:nil];
    });
  });
}
```

Now we create a completion handler that dismisses our tweet composer. This block will be executed once the tweet is either canceled or sent. Unlike the mail message, there's no failure result here. The system handles that for us.

Finally, we display the tweet composer on the main thread, and we're done (**Figure 8.13**).

WRAPPING **UP**

This chapter has covered a grab bag of topics. The first two-thirds largely focused on creating custom controls. In this context, a control is any UI element that responds to user input. This task can be split into two parts: displaying the control and capturing the user's input.

We handled the first part by creating a custom `UIViewController` container and a series of pop-up views and then using Core Animation to animate our pop-ups' appearances and disappearances. We also looked at techniques for customizing UIKit controls. For user input, we explored techniques for detecting touches using gesture recognizers, as well as techniques for tracking the device's motion using Core Motion.

The last third of the chapter rounded out our discussion, as we exported the drawings we created with our custom controls. This let us explore some advanced image handling techniques, including the Asset Library framework, image destinations, and Core Image. We also got a chance to get our hands dirty with Core Location and iOS's built-in support for both email and Twitter.

Most of these topics are quite deep, and we've barely scratched their surfaces. Please use this chapter as a starting point for exploring these topics in more detail. All of these topics are covered extensively in Apple's documentation.

Our last chapter will discuss the last mile. Here we will polish our app before submitting it to the App Store. This includes everything from setting the startup image and icons, to localization and accessibility.

9

THE **LAST MILE**

This chapter covers all the tasks needed to polish our application and get it ready for sale in the App Store. We'll look at the details that go into a finished app, from icons and startup screens to localization and build settings. Finally, we'll examine the process of building the app for distribution—both for ad hoc distribution and for sale in the iTunes App Store.

This is a grab bag of additional features and settings. Some are required before we can submit our application, others are strongly recommended, and a few merely add a touch of convenience to our apps.

APPLICATION ARTWORK

Our application expects a number of icons and other images. These are not functional parts of the application itself. Rather, they are used by the system to represent our application in a variety of circumstances.

ICONS

The system will use both application icons and search icons to represent our application. The application icon appears on the phone's home screen. The search icon appears in search results. Different devices require images of different sizes. We can use whatever names we wish, but the images must be PNG files. See **Table 9.1** for the details.

TABLE 9.1 Icon Sizes

DEVICE	ICON	SIZE
iPhone (regular)	Application	57 x 57
iPhone (Retina)	Application	114 x 114
iPad	Application	72 x 72
iPhone (regular)	Search	29 x 29
iPhone (Retina)	Search	58 x 58
iPad	Search	50 x 50

There's an easy way and a hard way to add these icons. The easy way is to simply open the target's summary settings. Scroll down until you find the icon settings, and drag the icons into place. Unfortunately, this only lets us set the application icons.

The search icons are optional. They will be generated automatically using our application icon. However, for the best appearance, we really should create custom icons at the correct resolution. To add these, we need to modify the `Info.plist` file directly.

▼ Icon files (iOS 5)		Diction...	(2 items)
▼ Primary Icon	‡ ⊖ ⊕	Diction... ‡	(2 items)
▼ Icon files		Array	(4 items)
Item 0		String	HBAppIcon
Item 1		String	HBiPadAppIcon
Item 2		String	HBSearchIcon
Item 3		String	HBiPadSearchIcon
Icon already includes gloss effect		Boolean	NO
▶ Newsstand Icon		Diction..	(3 items)

FIGURE 9.1 Icon settings

Let's add icons to Health Beat. You can create your own icons or copy them from the source code at www.freelancemadscience.com/source. Start by adding all the icons to our project. Then, open Health Beat-Info.plist and add a new key. Select Icon files (iOS 5) from the drop-down list. This will automatically generate a dictionary with Primary Icon and Newsstand Icon entries.

The Primary Icon entry is also a dictionary. Expand it. It should contain two elements: an "Icon files" array and an "Icon already includes gloss effect" Boolean value. Expand the array and add new items to it. We will need four items.

Set the string values of these items to the names of our icon files without the extensions. If our Retina display icons follow the @2x naming convention, we don't need to add them to this list. Simply add the name of the lower-resolution file, and the system will choose the Retina display version when appropriate.

If you're using the Health Beat icons, the final settings should match **Figure 9.1**.

LAUNCH IMAGES

The system displays our application's launch image as the application is initialized. Many developers use this as an opportunity to display a splash screen or advertisement, but this is actually discouraged.

Apple strongly recommends that we use a streamlined version of the application's main interface as the launch image. We want to strip out anything that might change. Obviously, this includes date fields and table view contents, but it also includes button titles and other labels that need to be localized.

Displaying only a partial user interface has a psychological advantage. The user won't accidentally try to use it until all the details are filled in. Furthermore, displaying a partial user interface creates the illusion that our application is launching faster. Our app seems snappier, and the users appreciate being able to get to work immediately.

iOS uses filename conventions to distinguish the different launch screens. However, we usually don't need to worry about these details, unlike with the icons. Most of the time, we can simply drag our launch screens into the proper locations on the target summary settings screen.

The iPhone only supports portrait launch screens. We must include a 320 x 480 PNG file for normal display, and a 640 x 960 PNG for Retina display.

The iPad supports both portrait and landscape. These must be a 768 x 1004 PNG file and a 1024 x 748 PNG file, respectively.

NOTE: The iPad also allows us to specify different images for landscape left, landscape right, and portrait upside down. We can also specify a separate launch image for all devices if the app is launched using a custom URL scheme. For more information on these cases, check out the "App-Related Resources" section of the iOS App Programming Guide.

iTUNES ARTWORK

We also need an image to represent the app in iTunes. Create a 512 x 512 PNG file, and name it iTunesArtwork. Notice that the name does not have an extension. We need to include this file in our application's main bundle for ad hoc distributions. Simply add it to the project. We will also use the file when we submit the application to iTunes Connect.

REQUIRED CAPABILITIES

We must declare any special capabilities that our application requires (or explicitly prohibits). Most of the defined capabilities are hardware-based, but some (like Game Center or Location Services) have a software component.

The iOS system will not launch the application if the device does not meet its required capabilities. Furthermore, the iTunes App Store will use this information to generate its device requirements—preventing users from downloading applications that they cannot run.

To set the required capabilities, add a UIRequiredDeviceCapabilities key to the application's Info.plist file. Set this key to either an array or a dictionary. If we use an array, then simply adding a feature's key to the array means that the feature is required. If it's not listed, the app can manage without it.

> **NOTE:** Your app may be rejected from the App Store if it needs a capability but does not properly declare that requirement in the Info.plist.

If you use a dictionary, you should give each feature in the dictionary a true or false Boolean value. If it's true, the app requires the capability. If it's false, the app explicitly prohibits the capability. If the feature is not included in the dictionary, it's optional.

All the capability keys are listed here. For more information about these keys, refer to the "App-Related Resources" section of the iOS App Programming Guide.

- accelerometer
- armv6
- armv7
- auto-focus-camera
- bluetooth-le
- camera-flash

- front-facing-camera
- gamekit
- gps
- gyroscope
- location-services
- magnetometer
- microphone
- opengles-1
- opengles-2
- peer-peer
- sms
- still-camera
- telephony
- video-camera
- wifi

DEPLOYMENT TARGET

There are two build settings that determine which SDK our application uses to compile, and which version of the OS it supports: the base SDK and the iOS deployment target.

The base SDK should always be set to the latest version of iOS. In fact, the default setting is Latest iOS—which will automatically select the latest version available. We should never need to touch this setting.

The deployment target, on the other hand, lets us specify the earliest version of the OS that can still run our app. We can set the deployment target either directly in the target's build settings or at the top of the target's summary page. Xcode 4.2 lets us select any major and minor build number, starting with iOS 3.0.

Just to be clear, the application is compiled using the latest SDK, but it may still run on earlier devices. This works through the magic of weak linking.

The compiler will compare the symbols in the frameworks of the base SDK and the deployment target SDK. Anything that's available in the base SDK but not available in the deployment target will be weak linked. This means that when the process is running, the symbol does not need to be present. As long as a missing symbol isn't actually called, the application will continue to run normally. Of course, calling a missing symbol will cause a crash.

This means we can include iOS 5-only features in an app targeting iOS 3 and above. We just need to perform runtime checks before calling any iOS 5-only code, and degrade gracefully if those features are not available.

To check if a class is available, we simply call [<class name> class]. If this returns nil, the class is not available. To see if a method is available, we simply call the object's respondsToSelector: method. To see if a function is available, check to see if the function's name evaluates to NULL.

```
if ([UIDocument class]) {

    // We can use UIDocument.

} else {

    // We must use old-school file I/O.

}

if ([self respondsToSelector:

    @selector(childViewControllers)]) {

    // We can create a custom UIViewController container.

}

if (UIAccessibilityIsClosedCaptioningEnabled != NULL) {

    // The function is safe to use.

}
```

Unfortunately, the [<class name> class] test is only available if the base SDK is 4.2 or greater, and if the deployment target is 3.1 or greater. So if you're supporting iOS 3.0, you need to use a more verbose test.

```
Class cls = NSClassFromString(@"UIDocument");

If (cls) {

    // We can use the document.

} else {

    // We still have to use old-school file I/O.

}
```

Additionally, if you're going to be developing for earlier devices, you will need to download the debugging support. Select Xcode > Preferences from the main menu. Switch to the Downloads tab and download the required components.

On the surface, this is amazing. It means we can have our cake and eat it too. We can support old iOS 3.0 phones while also on newer devices enabling the newest iOS 5 features, like iCloud storage and Core Location regions. However, there is one huge problem here. There is no way to check the code at compile time and verify that we aren't accidentally calling something above the deployment target in a generally reachable branch.

Things aren't so bad when you're just adding a new feature to an existing app. You know that the code you're adding is above the deployment target, and you can take care to isolate it properly. The real problem comes in when you're doing general coding or debugging. It's so easy to unknowingly use parts of the SDK that are above the deployment target—especially when using autocomplete.

Unfortunately, there's only one way to catch these errors: testing. Sure, I like testing. I'm a huge fan of testing, but testing alone is not a sufficient solution for this problem. Here's the hard, cold truth: It's very hard (I would say impractical if not impossible) to make sure that we actually execute every possible branch of our code during our test cycles. And if we don't test every branch, we don't really know if we're safe. Above-deployment API calls may be scattered throughout any part of our code, lying in wait like little land mines, just waiting to kill our apps.

So, if you go down this route, test your code. Test it hard and test it often. If possible, find a bunch of beta testers who still run older versions of iOS. Otherwise, you're just asking for a bunch of bad reviews when your app starts crashing on older devices.

Finally, there are also some important limitations that weak linking just cannot work around. Storyboards, for example, are only available on iOS 5 and later. ARC is available for iOS 4.0 and above, but weak references are not supported before iOS 5. Therefore, if you want to support earlier devices, you must use nibs and manual memory management.

LOCALIZATION

Localization involves adapting our application to two or more culturally distinct markets. People often think about localization in terms of translating written text—and it can involve a lot of translation. However, it also involves a wide range of other cultural aspects that have nothing to do with language. For example, we've already used NSNumberFormatter to create locally formatted numbers. There, it's not about language—we're not translating the number; we're simply choosing the best representation based on our user's locale. Similarly, a stop sign icon should look very different in Japan than it does in the US. Both of these are prime examples of localization.

Localization affects a wide range of application features, including:

- Storyboards and nibs
- Static text
- Icons and graphics
- Sounds and spoken words
- Dynamically generated text
- Text editing
- Sorting orders

Xcode supports localization by creating localized bundles. These bundles are represented by directories ending in .lproj. The localized bundles can be used to distinguish between different languages or, in some cases, even different regional dialects. iOS will try to select the best match, based on the device's settings; however, it's generally best to use the most general location specifiers possible.

When we load a resource from our application bundle, the system starts searching in the general bundle. If it cannot find a match, it begins searching through the localized bundles. The actual search order is based on the user's preferences. By placing localized resources in the correct bundles, we ensure that our application loads the correct versions at runtime.

We have a number of tools to help ease the internationalization effort, especially when it comes to finding and translating string values.

- ibtool

  This command-line utility can be used to extract strings from a nib file. The resulting string file can then be translated into another language. Once that is done, ibtool can merge the translated strings back with the original nib to create a translated nib file.

- NSLocalizedString()

  This method and its siblings will return a localized string value for a given key. NSLocalizedString() is the simplest. It takes two parameters: the key and a comment. It then searches the bundle for the Localizable.strings file, and then it searches that file for the key. If a match is found, it returns the string associated with the key; otherwise, it returns the key itself. The other variants let us search different files, return different default values, or otherwise modify the search. Also note that the comment argument is not used at runtime. Instead, it is used by genstrings when creating our .strings files.

- `genstrings`

  This command-line utility can parse C and Objective-C files and can find all the keys declared using one of the `NSLocalizedString()` methods. It will then build the `.strings` files containing all the unique values it found. This file can then be sent to translators, and the translated versions can be placed in the appropriate language bundles.

Additionally, we don't need to translate every single string in our application. We only need to localize the strings that the user actually sees. Strings used as internal keys or as the names of notifications should be left alone.

For more information, see the Internationalization Programming Topics.

ACCESSIBILITY

Recently, iOS has received a lot of praise and press for its excellent accessibility features. Out of the box, iOS provides a wide range of alternate input and output settings to assist people with low vision or blindness, hearing disabilities, and motor or physical disabilities. For the most part, these features are available to our application for free. We may need to be a little careful when creating custom gestures, since assistive touch won't support them, but other than that, we can focus all our attention on supporting VoiceOver.

For most standard controls, we just need to set the Accessibility settings in Interface Builder. These can be found in the Identity inspector. The label is a string that succinctly identifies the control. For example, "Units" or "Enter Weight."

The hint is a brief string that describes the effect of performing an action on the control. This should avoid mentioning either the control or the action. For example, "enter a new weight" not "select this text field to enter a new weight."

This, however, is just the beginning. iOS accessibility support provides a number of methods to help truly customize and refine the interface. I highly recommend reading through the Accessibility Programming Guide for iOS for more information.

FILE SHARING

As we have seen, iOS 5 added document sharing using iCloud. However there are some older file sharing techniques we can still use. Even in the age of iCloud, these techniques have important roles to play.

For example, adding the `UIFileSharingEnabled` key to our application's `Info.plist` and setting its value to YES shares our application's Document directory with iTunes. From within iTunes, the user can see all the files in the Document directory. They can add new files and delete existing files.

This is still particularly useful if your users are likely to load a number of large files. Over-the-wire transfers from iTunes are still the fastest way to get large amounts of data onto our device. Furthermore, documents shared this way do not take up space in iCloud storage (though they may take up space in iCloud backup, depending on how the device is configured).

Applications can also transfer documents among themselves. To transfer a document to other applications, simply create an instance of `UIDocumentInteraction Controller`. Then call either `presentOpenInMenuFromBarButtonItem:animated:` or `presentOpenInMenuFromRect:inView:animated:`, depending on whether you want to anchor the menu to an arbitrary rectangle or to a bar button.

```
- (IBAction) exportButtonPressed:(id)sender {
    // Open file in other apps.
    UIDocumentInteractionController* controller =
    [UIDocumentInteractionController interactionControllerWithURL:
        fileURL];
    [controller presentOpenInMenuFromBarButtonItem:sender
                                          animated:YES];
}
```

The system will dynamically create a menu, listing all the applications that have registered support for the given document type.

The complement to this is, of course, that our applications can also register all the documents that they support. This requires two steps. First, add an appropriate document type to the target's Document Types list. We already did this in the "Preparing the Application" section of Chapter 6, when we registered our Health

Beat History document type. But when you're using pre-existing document types, it's even easier.

Click the project icon, and make sure the correct target is selected. Then select the Info tab and expand the Document Types list. Click the add button and select Add Document Type.

Expand the type, and give it a name. In the Types field, enter its UTI. You can find a complete list of system-supported UTIs in the "System-Declared Uniform Type Identifiers" section of the Uniform Type Identifiers Reference. For example, to register to open text files, set the document Types field to **public.text**.

Next, in `application:didFinishLaunchingWithOptions:`, we need to check the options argument for the `UIApplicationLaunchOptionsURLKey`. If this key is present, we need to try to open the file at the corresponding URL.

```
NSURL* url =
[launchOptions objectForKey:UIApplicationLaunchOptionsURLKey];
if (url != nil) {
    // Open the file from the URL.
}
```

BUILDING FOR DISTRIBUTION

Once everything's ready, it's time to build our application for distribution. There are two ways to do this. First, we can build an ad hoc distribution. This allows us to distribute our application to up to 100 devices. We often do this as part of our application's testing, letting us send the application out to a select group of beta testers.

To create an ad hoc build, we need to first create a distribution provisioning profile. Log into your account at Apple's Developer site (http://developer.apple.com/iphone), and click the link for the iOS Provisioning Portal (it should be in the upper-right corner).

Before creating a new profile, be sure to add all of your test devices. We can have up to 100 test devices at any one time. You will need the unique device identifier (UDID) from each device. Your testers can get the ID by viewing the device's summary in iTunes. Click the serial number to view the UDID.

With all the UDIDs in place, select Provisioning from the left-hand column and select the Distribution tab. Then click the New Profile button.

Select Ad Hoc distribution. Enter a profile name, and select the App ID. Then select the devices you are going to authorize. When that's done, press Submit. If the provisioning portal seems to be taking a while, you may want to refresh the page. Once the distribution profile is created, download it, and then double-click it to automatically import it into Xcode.

Now we need to create an ad hoc build configuration. Select the project icon in the navigator, but this time select the Health Beat project—not the target. Make sure the Info tab is selected. In the Configurations settings, click the + icon and select Duplicate "Release" Configuration. Name this configuration **Ad Hoc**.

Switch to the Build Settings tab and scroll down until you find the Code Signing settings. Switch the code signing identity for the Ad Hoc build configuration to our new Ad Hoc distribution profile (**Figure 9.2**).

Next, we have to edit our scheme. In the Archive action settings, change the Build Configuration setting to Ad Hoc. That's it. Click OK. We can now build and distribute our application. Make sure you have a connected device or the generic iOS Device selected in the scheme. Then select Product > Archive from the main menu.

To access this archive, open the Organizer and select the Archives tab. Highlight the version you wish to share, and click the Share button. In the pop-up screen, leave the Contents option set to the iOS App Store Package (.ipa), but change the Identity setting to the Ad Hoc distribution profile. Then click Next, and select a location to save it.

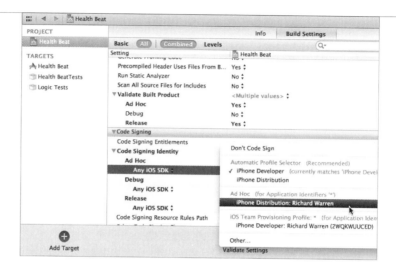

FIGURE 9.2 Setting the code signing identity

You can then distribute this file to your beta testers. Users can use either iTunes or Xcode to load the ad hoc application onto their device. For example, on a Mac you would simply drag the application down to the iTunes icon and then sync your device.

SUBMITTING TO THE APP STORE

Next, we can submit our application to the App Store for distribution. The procedure is similar. We need to create a distribution profile for the App Store. We'll also need to make another build configuration to use the distribution profile. This is essentially the same as what we did for the ad hoc distribution.

Next, we need to sign up for an iTunes Connect account. We also need to gather all the required information for our app:

- Description
- Categories
- Parental control rating
- Keywords
- SKU number
- Application URL
- Support URL

- Screen shots
- Support email address
- End user license agreement
- 512 x 512 application icon
- Price
- Availability date
- Available territories

Finally, we modify the scheme to use the correct build configuration. In most cases, I actually prefer to create a new scheme specifically for distribution builds. Archive the app. Then from the Organizer's Archives tab, we can validate and submit our app.

Remember that all applications submitted to the iTunes App Store must follow both the App Store Review Guidelines and the Human Interface Guidelines. Reviews are typically performed within seven days, and you can monitor the status from iTunes Connect. Good luck.

WRAPPING **UP**

This chapter covered a broad range of topics. If it didn't answer all your questions, I hope it at least pointed you in the right direction and helped you find the solutions you need.

And that's all for the book. I hope the information has proven useful. However, the fun doesn't end here. Check out the book's website at freelancemadscience.com/book/ for two bonus chapters—additional material that we just couldn't squeeze in between this book's covers.

Bonus Chapter A, "From iPhone to iPad," covers the differences in developing for the iPad. We also convert Health Beat into a Universal application, capable of running on both platforms. Bonus Chapter B, "Other Tools of the Trade," discusses the tools, tips, and techniques behind source control, unit testing, performance testing, and debugging.

The website also hosts the book's FAQs and errata, as well as a forum for discussion. Please stop by and leave your questions or comments. I look forward to continuing the conversation with you online.

INDEX

A

abstract classes
  about, 67
  NSNumber, 182
  UIDocument, 287–288, 294–297, 299, 300–305, 310, 342
acceleration pop-up view, 471–474, 486–489
accelerometer, 490, 492–496
accessibility support, 532
accessor methods
  custom Core Data, 381–383
  managed object, 379–380
  properties creating, 79, 81
  setting WeightHistory defaults with, 155
accuracy of location data, 502–503
actions
  adding method stub for, 176
  connecting events and, 38–39
  implementing, 177
  saveWeight, 185
addChildViewController: subclass, 453, 454
alert views, 507
animation
  adding, 460–462
  calculating rotations of, 462–463
  fade and bounce, 465–469
  starting, 463–464
anti-aliasing graphics, 250
application sandbox
  about, 272
  exploring contents of, 282
  including containers in, 324
  SQLite database URL for local, 403–404
apps. See also converting app to Core Data; polishing apps; and specific apps
  adding Settings to, 284, 355–359
  application proxy, 473
  application sandbox, 272, 282, 324, 403–404
  data conflicts when saving, 311–314, 319
  designing gestures on, 185
  developing with iOS, 4–5
  document type setup for, 292–294
  entitlements for, 291–292
  file handling by iOS, 272
  iCloud support in, 291–297, 299–305

including and reading resource files in, 278
launch images for, 525–526
managing user preferences, 283–284
opening and closing, 130–131
productivity, 120–122
saving data to iCloud, 285–289
saving state of, 290–291
selecting location for, 9
sending to background and saving, 352
single tab bar in, 122
state flag disabling user from editing, 342, 346–347
syncing defaults in iCloud, 352–355
utility, 120
when to load and save, 306–307
ARC (Automatic Reference Counting), 91–98
  about, 91
  documentation for, 117
  finding and preventing memory cycles, 92–95
  garbage collection vs., 92
  guidelines for, 95–96
  managing Objective-C objects with classes, 53
  memory management for Core Foundation data types, 96–98
  retain attributes inoperable with, 80
  selecting, 9
  toll-free bridging with, 96–97
  using blocks with, 116
architecture
  building Health Beat model classes, 141–157
  Core Data managed object model, 370–378
  created by Tabbed Application template, 123, 124
  linking model to controller, 158–163
arguments
  about function, 59
  hidden method, 74
  passing values in functions, 61–63
  separating, 73
arrays
  about, 50–51
  collection classes vs., 51
  immutable, 152
  loading and saving with keyed archiver, 295–299
  mutable, 159–160

NSMutableArray and NSArray collection classes, 151
asserts, 253–255
Assets Library framework, 506–510
@dynamic directive, 82
@interface block, 73, 86
@optional keyword, 85
@property declaration, 81
@required keyword, 85
@synthesize directive, 81, 82
@implementation block, 73, 87
attributes
  changing readwrite/readonly, 88
  common property, 80
  Core Data, 371
  indexed, transient , and optional Core Data, 372
  setting graph view, 238–239
  setting managed object model date, 408–409
Automatic Reference Counting. See ARC
autorelease block, 13
autorotating views, 170–172
autosizing views, 170–172
awakeFromNib method, 241

B

background
  remaining static in dynamic view, 442–443
  resolving conflicts with URL in, 311–312
  saving apps after sending to, 352
  transitioning apps into, 306
Background attribute, 30
backing up files, 274–275
binary operators, 57
blocks, 112–116
  about, 112–113
  Apple's documentation for, 117
  declaring block variables, 113
  passing index to, 215–216
bounce animation, 466–469
buttons
  background colors for, 190
  control states for, 178–179
  creating custom, 176
  modifying Core Animation layer for, 198–202

C

C language
  abstract classes, 67
  allocating memory for data structure
    in, 96
  Carbon written in, 51
  class inheritance in, 65–67
  data structures, 49–53
  data types, 46–48
  enumerations in, 54–56
  functions in, 58–63
  Objective-C as superset of, 44
  objects, 64–70
  operators in, 56–58
  order of operator precedence, 57–58
CAGradientLayer, 200–201
CALayer, 200–202, 205
callback blocks, 503–506
canvas
  adding line segments on, 443–450
  modifying with gesture recognizers,
    481–489
  resetting with shake, 456–457
  view controller setting up, 455–457
Canvas class, 442–450
canvasViewController class, 455–457
categories, 86–87, 88
cells
  about, 210
  connecting table to/from prototype,
    136–137
  customizing table view history,
    206–210
  designing for static displays, 221–227
  reusing, 139, 210
CGContextRestoreGState(), 248
CGContextStateGState(), 248
child view controllers, 453, 454,
  456, 460
classes. *See also* abstract classes;
  and specific classes
  calling methods for, 74
  categories for adding methods to,
    86–87
  collection, 51, 151
  convenience methods for, 78–79
  defining object, 69–70
  hierarchy of UIView, 66–67
  iCloud-compatible protocols for, 287
  inheritance of, 65–67
  managing Objective-C objects with, 53
  objects vs., 64

prefixes for, 8
  using delegate with, 101
closing apps, 130–131
_cmd argument, 74
Cocoa framework, 44, 51
Cocoa Touch framework
  Objective-C language in, 44
  use of enumerations in, 56
  using with Carbon and Cocoa, 51
  view object inheritance in, 66
collection classes, 51, 151
color
  assigning for progress bar, 471–473
  button's background, 190
  pause view background, 459
comments, 59
comparisons in predicates, 386
conflicts
  merging, 305, 308–320
  resolving when saving data,
    311–314, 319
connections
  adding relationship to view
    controller, 135
  configuring outlet, 32–33
  deleting to HWMainViewController
    delegate outlet, 28
  drawing between actions and events,
    38–39
  making gesture recognizer, 184
constants, 55
containers
  accessing files in iCloud, 287
  sharing among apps, 285
  syncing data in local and iCloud, 289
  view controllers for, 452, 453–455
controls. *See* designing controls
convenience methods, 78–79
converting app to Core Data, 400–437
  adding Core Data to app, 400
  building managed object model,
    408–416
  creating UIManagedDocument,
    395–396, 400–406, 418
  duplicate handle errors and fetch
    requests, 436
  generating custom WeightEntry
    object, 410–416
  modifying HistoryViewController,
    419–432
  populating graph with data from
    Core Data, 432–437

registering explicit saves for undo
    actions, 416
  replacing weight history with
    document references, 417–418
  setting managed object model
    attributes, 408–409
  updating
    EnterWeightViewController,
    416–419
coordinate systems
  about, 252
  calculating weight trend lines with,
    255–256
  changing cursor velocity using,
    494–496
  flipping and translating, 449–450
  setting data coordinates, 260–263
  using for gravity signals, 493–494, 495
Core Animation, 465–468
  about, 198
  controlling view transitions with,
    465–469
  modifying button layer using,
    198–202
  performance issues with, 204–205
  supporting drawing for Retina
    display, 252, 253
  unneeded to support
    GravityScribbler cursor, 452
Core Data, 368–399. *See also* converting
    app to Core Data
  about, 282, 368
  adding to Health Beat, 400
  attributes, 371
  custom accessors for, 381–383
  features of, 369
  fetch requests, 385–388
  handing contexts to object, 379
  instantiating managed objects,
    379–385
  limitations of iCloud on, 396
  managed object context, 378–389
  managed object model of, 370–378
  migrating data to, 375–377
  optimizing performance for, 396–400
  persistent store coordinator, 389–392
  properties, 370–375
  replacing model layer with, 367
  using UIManagedDocument subclass
    with, 395–396, 418
Core Foundation, 96–98
Core Graphics, 449–450
Core Image, 516–520

.nib files
  encapsulating in storyboards, −15
  function of, 164–165
  incompatible with loadView
      override, 443
  methods calling, 241
  storyboards vs., 14
nil values
  accessing outlets without, 38
  freeing up memory for property
      using, 34
notifications, 104–106
  defined, 104
  enabling and disabling KVO, 339
  for fetched results controller
      changes, 428–429, 430
  implementing, 104–105
  posting manual, 155–157, 212–215
  receiving from iCloud key-value
      store, 354
  sending, 105
  synchronous and asynchronous,
      105–106
  unregistering methods from, 350–352
NSArray collection class, 151
NSAssert, 253–255
NSFetchedResultsController, 419
NSFFileCoordinator, 287
NSKeyedArchiver objects, 298, 299
NSKeyedUnarchiver objects, 298, 299
NSLocalizedString( ) method, 531
NSManagedObject object, 380–381
NSManagedObjectModel object, 370
NSMetadataQuery, 404
NSMutableArray collection class, 151
NSNumberDate, 182
NSNumberFormatter, 147, 180, 182
NSUbiquitousKeyValueStore:, 289
NSURL objects, 279
numbers
  current date formatting, 177, 180
  formatting decimals, 147
  restricting input of invalid, 169

O

Object library, 30
Objective-C language, 43–117
  about, 5, 43–45
  abstract classes, 67
  attributes in Core Data and, 371
  blocks, 112–116
  C data structures used in, 49–53
  C data types used in, 46–48

case sensitivity of, 51
categories and extensions in, 86–88
declaring class interfaces, 69–70
delegates, 101–104
enumerations, 54–56
exceptions used in, 147
functions, 58–63
key elements of, 46
key-value coding, 106–107
key-value observing, 107–108
memory management in, 89–98
methods, 68, 71–79
MVC framework and, 44, 100–101
.nib file technology in, 164–165
notifications, 104–106
objects, 64–70
operators, 56–58
order of operator precedence, 57–58
properties, 79–83
protocols, 83–85
recommended documentation for,
    45, 117
refactoring code in, 149
required knowledge of, 45
single and double quotes in, 51
singletons, 109–112
objects, 64–70
  adding and removing from
      weightHistory array, 157
  adding user interface, 30
  asynchronous accessing of, 335–341
  calling methods on class, not, 74
  classes vs., 64
  defining class for, 69–70
  delegate, 21
  duplicating bouncing, 469
  dynamically adding methods to, 75
  encapsulating, 64–65
  graph of Hello World, 29
  handing context to, 379
  implementing class definitions,
      69, 70
  inheritance for, 65–67
  instantiating, 68–69
  loading custom, 164
  managed, 379–385
  memory cycles for, 92–95
  multiple initialization methods for, 69
  NSURL, 279
  optimizing large data, 398–399
  receiving notifications, 104
  removing from tables, 218–220
  retain counts for, 90–91
  saving object hierarchies, 296

one-to-one relationships, 373
opaque property, 244, 245
OpenGL ES, 253
opening
  and closing apps, 130–131
  iCloud documents, 321
operands, 56, 57
operators, 56–58
order of precedence, 57–58, 59
orientation
  autorotating to interface, 25, 26
  calculating animation rotations,
      462–463
  changing GravityScribbler, 496–498
  launch screen, 526
  positioning pop-up views, 464–465
  rotating graph views, 267–268
  rotating Twitter image, 516–520
  selecting supported device, 125
  setting view's autorotating and
      autosizing methods, 170–172
outlets
  accessing safely, 38
  creating and configuring Hello
      World, 32–34
  deleting connection to delegate, 28
  EnterWeightViewController,
      173–174
  format for naming auto-generated, 174
  providing gesture recognizer, 184
  setting with nibs, 165

P

pan gestures, 481, 486–489
paths
  creating to resource files, 278
  generating directory, 272–273,
      276–277
  key, 106, 107–108, 154
  manipulating, 279–282
  NSURL objects vs. string-based, 279
pause gesture, 482–483
pause view controller, 458
performance
  alert view effect on, 507
  minimizing objects saved and
      loaded, 298
  NSAssert effect on, 254
  optimizing Core Data, 396–400
  speed of GCD's dispatch_sync,
      445–446
  when to load and save apps, 306–307